JOHN GARDNER

GARLAND REFERENCE LIBRARY
OF THE HUMANITIES
(VOL. 434)

JOHN GARDNER
An Annotated Secondary Bibliography

Robert A. Morace

GARLAND PUBLISHING, INC. • NEW YORK & LONDON
1984

Library of Congress Cataloging in Publication Data

Morace, Robert A.
John Gardner : an annotated secondary bibliography.

(Garland reference library of the humanities ;
v. 434)
Includes index.
1. Gardner, John, 1933–1982—Bibliography.   I. Title.
II. Series.
Z8234.17.M67 1984 [PS3557.A712] 016.813'54   83-48266
ISBN 0-8240-9081-0 (alk. paper)

Printed on acid-free, 250-year-life paper
Manufactured in the United States of America

To my parents,
Anthony R. and Josephine G. Morace

CONTENTS

PREFACE

John Gardner is a rewarding but elusive subject for bibliographical study. First, there is the question of which of the many John Gardners we are talking about: not the founder of the political action group Common Cause, whose book *Morale* appeared in the same year as *On Moral Fiction*; not the San Francisco poet; not the British mystery writer who has recently revived Ian Fleming's James Bond series; not the British composer who has written a number of operas; and not the editor of the newspaper the *Southern Illinoisan* which is published in the same city (Carbondale) where this bibliography's John Gardner lived, taught, and wrote for several years. The John Gardner of this bibliographical study is, of course, the author of *Grendel*—"the *Beowulf* story told from the monster's point of view"—as he is best known to most readers and, more particularly, high school and college students. (A step up, one assumes, from being known, as Herman Melville was, as "the man who lived among the cannibals.") Yet even this John Gardner is a difficult figure to pin down, somewhat like the questing beast of his beloved medieval literature: scholar, teacher, translator, editor, reviewer, poet, critic, popular biographer, realist, fabulist, best-selling novelist, academic new fictionist, librettist, author of radio plays and of books for children, and, following the publication of *On Moral Fiction* in 1978, one of the most outspoken and controversial literary figures of the past decade.

Simply stated, the career of this "Lon Chaney of contemporary fiction," as one reviewer dubbed him, has been remarkably varied and, in some ways, unpredictable. And critical opinion—both popular and academic—has been nearly as varied. *Grendel* and *The Sunlight Dialogues*, for example, received the acclaim of reviewers and critics. The response to *The King's Indian: Stories and Tales*, however, was mixed and uncertain, and Gardner's literary sports (if that is what they are), the epic poem *Jason and Medeia* and the deliberately boring novel *Freddy's Book*, met with widespread disapproval. On the other hand, *Mickelsson's Ghosts*, Gardner's last novel, which was savaged in such national publications as *Esquire, New York Magazine*, and *Saturday Review*, was generally well received in local newspapers around the country. Concerning the elusive John Gardner, this much, at least, can be said with certainty: he was, until his sudden death on 14 September 1982, an energetic, prolific, and committed writer who made a significant—though much debated—contribution to contemporary American literature.

The debate over the nature and quality of that contribution is recorded in the more than fifteen hundred annotations that follow. Part I provides a chronological listing of Gardner's interviews and speeches; because so many of these items appear in sources not readily (or inexpensively) available, the annotations have been made as detailed and thorough as possible. Part II lists all known reviews of Gardner's books; the reviews (1) are grouped according to the work reviewed and (2) are alphabetically arranged by author's last name (or, in the case of anonymous items, by title) within each group. Part III, "Reviews of Books to Which Gardner Contributed," cites only those reviews that specifically discuss or mention Gardner or Gardner's contribution. Part IV records all essays, articles, books, and notices (other than reviews) that deal with Gardner and/or his work either in their entirety or in part; the entries are arranged (1) by year and (2) alphabetically by author's last name (or, in the case of anonymous items, by title) within each year. Part V includes items either not cited or, in a very few cases, incorrectly cited in John Howell's *John Gardner: A Bibliographical Profile* (1980). *John Gardner: An Annotated Secondary Bibliography* is intended to complement Howell's work, not to replace it. Except for some necessary overlapping in the annotations of interviews and speeches, each of the two bibliographies has its own distinctive emphasis and use.

In compiling this work, I have attempted to be as accurate, thorough, and useful as possible to both scholars and students of Gardner and his writings. The only items that have been deliberately excluded are (1) perfunctory contributor's notes, (2) objective summaries and reprinted excerpts in such common reference sources as *Abstracts of English Studies, Book Review Digest*, and *Contemporary Criticism*, and (3) simple, nonevaluative citations of Gardner's published works (usually *On Moral Fiction* and the scholarly criticism) in footnotes to articles and books. There are a number of items that I was not able to examine; these are designated by an asterisk (*) following the citation. For some items culled from newspaper and publisher's files, full bibliographical information was not available, and as a result my citations are unfortunately incomplete. And finally, the user of this bibliography should be aware of the following: item 1096, although correctly cited, is incorrectly listed in section IV under the year 1970 (instead of 1975); item 1515 was located too late to be included in the interviews section where it belongs; the same problem occurred with items 1243a, 1440a, 1518a, 1529, and 1530, which are reviews (of *The Life & Times of Chaucer, Freddy's Book,* and *Mickelsson's Ghosts*) and so belong in Part II rather than Part IV.

My thanks to all the reviewers, librarians, editors, scholars, and friends too numerous to name who have assisted me in so many ways. I especially wish to thank Joseph Baber; William Luckey, Richard Tanner and the staff of the Publicity Department at Alfred A. Knopf, Publisher; Brian Mulally; Karen Markott, former inter-library loan librarian at Daemen College; Carrie Berthon and Jorette Martin of the *Binghamton Press*; Sallie Bingham of the *Louisville Courier-Journal*; the Faculty Research Allocations Committee at Daemen College and Patricia Curtis, Dean of the College; my brother Eugene; my wife Barbara; and my son Jason who believes that John Gardner's monsters, motorcyclists, devils, giants, and as-sorted other grotesques are well worth his father's time. And I particularly wish to thank Marilyn Sherman, for her marathon typing, patience, and consistent good humor; and John Howell of Southern Illinois University–Carbondale for his generosity and encouragement.

LIST OF ABBREVIATIONS

AL	*The Art of Living and Other Stories*
AMA	*The Alliterative Morte Arthure . . .*
CB	*A Child's Bestiary*
CCP	*The Construction of Christian Poetry in Old English*
Dragon	*Dragon, Dragon and Other Tales*
FB	*Freddy's Book*
G	*Grendel*
Gudgekin	*Gudgekin the Thistle Girl and Other Stories*
Howell	*John Gardner: A Bibliographical Profile* by John Howell
ISM	*In the Suicide Mountains*
JM	*Jason and Medeia*
KH	*The King of the Hummingbirds and Other Stories*
"KI"	"The King's Indian"
KI	*The King's Indian: Stories and Tales*
LTC	*The Life & Times of Chaucer*
MG	*Mickelsson's Ghosts*
NM	*Nickel Mountain: A Pastoral Novel*
OBN	*On Becoming a Novelist*
OL	*October Light*
OMF	*On Moral Fiction*
PC	*The Poetry of Chaucer*

Res	*The Resurrection*
SD	*The Sunlight Dialogues*
Vlemk	*Vlemk the Box-Painter*
SUNY	State University of New York
WA	*The Wreckage of Agathon*
Wakefield	*The Construction of the Wakefield Cycle*

Part I
Interviews and Speeches

1 Harris, Bruce. "Let No Man Write My Epitaph; None Did."
  Chico State Wildcat, 5 October 1961.
     The college literary magazine, Selection, will no
  longer be published, Gardner explained, because "Chico
  State College does not at this time have the caliber
  of student to put out and to appreciate such a publication." (See Gardner's 12 October 1961 letter in
  response to this article.)

2 Harris, Bruce. "Faculty Resignations Rise." Chico State
  Wildcat, 5 April 1962, pp. 1, 9.
     Quotes from the Faculty Council minutes of 23 May
  1961 concerning the college president's denying
  Gardner promotion on the basis of Gardner's youth and
  the president's opposition to making any accelerated
  appointments. The president also questioned Gardner's
  teaching of his creative writing class, the faddishness
  of material published in the student literary magazine,
  Selection, edited by Gardner, his failure to wear a
  coat and tie during his television program on creative
  writing, and his failure to meet deadlines for Selection
  and a history of the college.

3 Gelman, Ben. "Five Seek Posts on CCHS Board." Southern
  Illinoisan (Carbondale), 7 April 1968, p. 2.
     Gardner is one of five candidates for the three open-
  ings on the Carbondale Community High School Board of
  Education. Having served as a consultant to high
  schools in the area of reading and having worked with
  various youth programs such as Head Start, he
  emphasizes the need for a strong and expanded reading
  program for disadvantaged students. He also favors
  allowing superior students to participate in university
  programs at Southern Illinois, merit pay for teachers
  to encourage good teaching, sex education that stresses
  responsibility rather than specific definitions, and,
  in general, open board meetings.

4 Ryzak, Joan. "U-D's Rebel with a Pen--Compleat Wrangler."
  Detroit Sunday News, 20 December 1970, p. B16.
     Among the influences on his writing, Gardner cites his
  father's poetry, his large Welsh family, and the
  letters he used to write to keep the bill-collectors
  at bay. Today, with two novels published and two
  others sold, Gardner is "making it." He was not
  always so financially stable: MSS, his literary
  magazine (800 subscribers), went bankrupt after three

issues and the novel he bought back from Random House
cost him his $2000 advance. Gardner sees himself as a
"polite anarchist" and as a writer of "experimental
fiction" aimed at the same kind of audience--now
greatly enlarged--for which Joyce wrote.

5 Diehl, Digby. "Medievalist in Illinois Ozarks." Los
   Angeles Times, 5 September 1971, "Calendar" sec., p. 43.
     The same "mixture of primitive and Christian symbolism"
   found in Beowulf and the same sense of despair and collapse that characterizes the late medieval period can
   also be found in southern Illinois. Chaucer, Malory,
   and the Wakefield poet responded to their times with a
   form of black humor; Morte D'Arthur is, in fact, a
   typically "20th-century book." Gardner does not approve
   of Anglo-Saxon values, including "the concept of heroism."
   He views Beowulf as part of an epic dialogue which
   extends from Homer to Dante; Grendel is a Sartrean
   monster. Barth, Barthelme, Elkin, Ellison, Gass, and
   Gardner are stylists who have "nothing to say" other
   than that language is beautiful. G for example, "is
   pure style." Its philosophy is not disturbing because
   "there are no disturbing philosophies left any more.
   We've hit bottom and we're just bouncing." Forthcoming are SD, drawn from the author's memories of his
   grandfather, and "Jason," an epic poem for which
   Gardner will re-trace Jason's travels.

6 "Backstage with Esquire." Esquire, 76 (October 1971), 56.
     "What G does is take, one by one, the great heroic
   ideals of mankind since the beginning and make a case
   for these values by setting up alternatives in an
   ironic set of monster values. I hate existentialism."
   Gardner is currently writing a long poem in twenty-four
   books called Jason and for three years has, "with two
   poets," edited MSS in order to publish generally hard
   to publish works, such as short novels and long poems.
   ("The Song of Grendel" appears in this issue of
   Esquire.)

7 Lair, Bill. "Visiting Authors Say Novels Are Merely
   Rearranged Facts." Argus (Rock Island, Illinois), 27
   November 1972, p. 17.
     Fiction influences society. It is better than the
   news, which is boring, or television, which is
   simplistic. Good fiction requires revision and a love

of literature and language; it must be "as real as any
experience." The prospects for literature and writers
are good. Both Gardner and fellow writer Fletcher
Knebel speak approvingly of the grant from the Illinois
Arts Council which has enabled them to visit Rock Island
and nearby colleges.

8 Natale, Richard. "John Gardner: 'Great Age of the Novel
   Is Returning'" Women's Wear Daily, 8 December 1972,
   p. 16.
   SD is written in epic form and parodies the Nineteenth-Century novel; it is told from the point of view
of Warburton Hodge who, like Tolstoi, believes in
writing "as an imitation of God." The Sunlight Man
advocates absolute freedom but ends up in a cage;
Clumly begins in a cage but ends up free. These two
positions--radical and conservative--are parts of
Gardner's own character; his novel implies that neither
creation nor decay are absolute states but, instead,
alternate phases in a single rhythm. Gardner criticizes
contemporary fiction as overly concerned with "surface"
but foresees the return of the novel's greatness, as
exemplified by Fielding, in such works as Roth's
"cartoon autobiography" Portnoy's Complaint. Unlike
novelist Fletcher Knebel, who writes in the unironic
manner of Hemingway and Faulkner, Gardner prefers to
undercut his characters and their positions with humor.
He admires Capote's In Cold Blood as a novel and the
"richly expressed alternate world" of Gass's fiction.
Barth, however, is too much a cold-hearted
"technician."

9 Johnson, Chuck. "John Gardner: Author: 'That rare
   creature, a Philosophical Novelist'" Southern
   Illinoisan (Carbondale), 21 January 1973, p. A3.
   The end of a civilization is, as the careers of
Tolstoi and Dickens attest, a "great moment for fiction,"
for only in such moments of crisis do men discover
their affinity with nature. Agreeing with Whitehead
concerning the sentience of all matter, Gardner takes
as his major theme the idea of connectedness, the
absence of which is tragic. Gardner sketches his
philosophical position in Res, dramatizing "the
terrifying feeling of aloneness when you can no
longer make connections with the world"; the book

James Chandler writes is "a well-executed but insane
reply" to Kant. G concerns an intellectual monster, a
Sartrean existentialist, whom Beowulf finally recon-
nects with the world. WA is a muddled and unsuccessful
book. Seven years in the making, SD was inspired by
Gardner's study of the Gilgamesh epic and "snapped ...
together" around the idea of "a cops and robbers story."
Gardner began his "addiction" to writing at age eight
and wrote perhaps seven "wrong" novels before Res.
Forthcoming are "Jason and Medeia" (currently in
galley proof), "The King's Injun and Other Fireside
Tales," one study of Chaucer (already fifteen years in
the making) and another of Old English poetry, and a
novel. Highly critical of most contemporary fiction,
he defines "an ideal novel" as one "seriously concerned with people and places," having "a perfectly
Aristotelian action," and causing the reader to "know
something," though that knowledge need be nothing more
than a vague feeling.

10 Davis, Tony. "John Gardner Heroes Include Achilles,
Aeneas, Beowulf, Hector. . . ." Daily Northwestern, 31
January 1973, p. 3.
    Gardner, currently a visiting professor at North-
western University, views the Iliad and the Odyssey as
important philosophical works and admits that the epic
is his "first love." Barth, Barthelme, and Vonnegut
are "cynical bastards," though "technically very good."
Today's best writers are Bellow, Purdy, and "Eliza
Thrush." Turning to SD, Gardner says Clumly is in an
impossible situation, caught between responsibility to
his job and his desire to be "just and fair"; his
wanting to be a hero makes him an admirable character.
"It's as if God put me on the ground to write,"
Gardner claims, adding that he spends long hours on his
writing, usually working on several books concurrently.
Teaching interferes with his writing but is necessary
because it is his "only contact with the outside world."
Moreover, in his opinion the only people who care deeply
about culture are the ones engaged in making it. In
passing, he also mentions his love for southern Illinois
and the need for college composition courses.

11 Van Slyke, Judy. "The Scholar Who Wrote a Best Seller."
Chicago Daily News Panorama, 7-8 April 1973, p. 4.
    SD, begun in 1962 and developed from "a stupid novel"

in which Clumly was a minor character, was intended as
a collection of closely related stories emanating from a
central point. The situation between its characters is
more important than the novel's "philosophical idea."
Philosophical systems, Gardner adds, are never entirely
"adequate"; only human relationships are satisfying.
Gardner feels little sympathy for the modern nihilistic
view expressed by the Sunlight Man but acknowledges that
his handling of this character "lacks ironic distance
and detachment." The author predicts that the praise
accorded SD will result in a generally unfavorable
response to his forthcoming epic poem.

12 Pratt, Kathie. "Gardner May Use Grant for Year in France."
Daily Egyptian (Southern Illinois University-Carbondale),
24 April 1973, p. 15.
The success of SD, Gardner believes, led to his being
awarded a $10,000 Guggenheim grant. Gardner, who had
applied for the grant unsuccessfully in the past,
ironically adds that although Guggenheim is intended to
encourage artists who need support, it most often goes to
those who have already begun to sell their work.

13 Brown, Bill. Focus, WBTA (Batavia, N.Y.). Radio tape.
Recorded 28 April 1973 for future airing.
Commenting on his generally unadventuresome youth,
Gardner recalls his having been around people who liked to
read, his father's "poetic" sermons, his earliest writings,
his Aunt Mildred (whom he distorted into Millie Hodge in
SD), his athletic cousin Duncan, and his attendance at
DePauw, Washington University, and the University of Iowa.
He also summarizes at length the plot of SD. Begun in
1964, the novel was offered for publication, rejected,
and a second, not "very different" draft written. The
critical response has generally been favorable, although
Gardner points to a negative review in the New Yorker, a
magazine he considers snobbish. All of the characters in
SD are "likeable," and many are based on real people, including his parents (Ben and Vanessa Hodge), T. Murray
Steele, and Mae Brumstead. Gardner also briefly discusses
his addiction to writing ("I live to write"), his good
fortune in having had as his editor the late David Segal,
the planned movie version of SD, the negative effects of
urban renewal on Batavia, the need for young writers to
trust themselves, on novels as "big beautiful toys"--
"sand castles" rather than intellectual tomes--and on
forthcoming works: JM, "The King's Indian and Other Fireside Tales," and NM, which can be classified as a novel,
an episodic novel, or a collection of related stories.

14 Pfalzer, Marilyn. "'The Sunlight Dialogues': Will Soon Be
Made Into a Movie." Batavia (N.Y.) Daily News, 30 April
1973, p. 1.
    Returning to Batavia as guest speaker at the Knights of
Columbus-Masonic dinner, Gardner mentions that his profit-
able but oft-rejected novel, SD, would be soon made into a
film. Commenting on his writing habits, Gardner says he writes
slowly (Res was begun "at least 10 years before it was published"), is highly conscious of technique, and works for
long continuous periods. He advises would-be writers to
forego famous writers' schools and to be "ordinary....
Fancy stuff makes people nervous and they won't enjoy your
work." His forthcoming works are NM and "The King's Indian
and Other Fireside Tales."

15 Pfalzer, Marilyn. "Writing 'Celebrates,' Top Author Asserts."
Batavia (N.Y.) Daily News, 30 April 1973, pp. 1, 4.
    Speaking at the Knights of Columbus-Masonic dinner-dance,
Gardner acknowledges that, except for Clumly and the Sunlight Man, all the characters in SD are based on real people
(e.g. his uncle, Harris Day Gardner, as Will Hodge; his Aunt
Mildred). Writing is Gardner's way of celebrating the things
and people he loves. Only by making sympathetic connections
can people today hope to counter the prevailing "anarchy."

16 "Writers on Writing." [Rochester: The University of Rochester
Writers Workshop, 1973].
    (This sixteen-page pamphlet is a transcription of a panel
discussion held at the University of Rochester Writers Workshop, 9 July 1973, and televised on WXXI-TV, Rochester. The
participants included Gardner, George P. Elliott, Judith
Rascoe, and moderator L.J. Davis.) Writers of Gardner's
generation have been influenced chiefly by films and by
writers of the grotesque such as Dickens and the Russians.
From films, writers have learned to narrow their focus, to
create the "hard-edged image," and to avoid flashbacks and
cliches. Movies, which involve subtle variations on a very
few basic conventions, do not serve as an American mythology.
Gardner likens his own novels to Disney cartoons. Contemporary fiction should be, like cartoons, thrilling and also
intricately textured; it should no longer concern itself
with ideas and thought (as in Jean Stafford's stories).
It should not deal with immaturity (as in Henry James);
instead it should deal with adult problems (as in Cheever's
The World of Apples). Whereas Gardner's earliest writings
are sociological in nature, his later work concerns more
universal, and mature, matters. G is an exception in that
its title character is "an arrested child." In Gardner's
view, "the age of Emerson's philosopher child is over."
Although goodness and happiness are appropriate subjects
for fiction, today's writers do not know how to handle them
properly. The humor in Gardner's works derives from his

stance as a critical observer. His humor is comic, not
bitter; it is akin to the comedy of Laurel and Hardy or
Buster Keaton in its honest depiction of child-like helplessness. The comedy of Chaplin, on the other hand, is
sentimental and even harmful. Unlike Hemingway or Fitz-
gerald, Gardner is not a distinctly American writer;
rather, like Nabokov, he and other contemporary writers
can use America as a subject (as Gardner did in WA) without feeling obliged to adopt an American point of view.
What is most important in writing comes about through
"accident," as in the emergence of Clumly as a minor
character in the novel Gardner scrapped in order to write
SD. Critics and reviewers are not particularly helpful to
the writer. The French critics are "cold-blooded"; the
English are personal in their attacks and dislike those
writers (e.g., Updike, Sillitoe, and Margaret Drywell)
who do not follow the prescribed "casual" style. American
reviewers though not always intelligent, are at least "generous." (Gardner calls himself "a gentle critic.") One of
his great pleasures as a writer is to work out a specific
technique and then to teach that technique to a good student
writer.

17 Mikkanen, Mildred. "Word Addict." Rochester-Times-Union,
   10 July 1973, pp. C1-C2.
   Gardner loves to write: he is dedicated, even addicted
but not at all disciplined. By writing in various styles
and forms, he comes to understand the world more fully and
makes life "richer." He also says that long, pleasurable
novels are replacing those "spare and scholarly" ones which
are really "exercises in thought."

18 Flickner, Sandy. "Author John Gardner: A Serious Clown."
   Rochester Democrat & Chronicle, 12 July 1973, pp. C1-C2.
   While conducting a class at the University of Rochester
writers workshop, Gardner explains that "It's not an age
for grandiose posturing unless you're a clown." He mentions his adaptation of real people as characters in his
fiction and his "brilliant" book on the forms of fiction.
Sentences are "the biggest problem in all of writing," he
says. "What makes the whole story go wrong is the same
thing that makes a sentence go wrong." The interviewer
cites Gardner's appearances on one radio program and two
television shows [one not located] in connection with his
appearance at the writers workshop. That filming of SD
should begin in the fall is also mentioned.

19 Janus, Pat. "Interview: Pat Janus and John Gardner."
   Valley Magazine (Rochester, N.Y.), 1 (September 1973),
   21-24.
      Gardner does not see himself as a regional writer; nor
   does he find it more difficult to write about the past than
   the present (as a scholar he has, in a sense, already lived
   in the past). He is not interested in constructing plots,
   only in the play of words. Because he thinks out his
   stories in detail before actually writing them down, his
   characters rarely surprise him. Clumly, however, began
   as a minor character in a novel about a monk. The pref-
   atory cast of characters in SD is a "joke"--a game he
   plays with reality and with the reader (some of the characters that are listed do not appear in the novel; others
   appear but are not listed). Critics who mistakenly believe that fiction imitates reality in a meaningful way
   fail to see that a story is not imitation but character,
   action, moral and philosophical implication, and fun (a
   point the New Critics forgot). Gardner's Forms of
   Fiction and George P. Elliott's Types of Fictions attempted to break down the New Critics' intellectual approach. Illustrated books are another means for making
   reading more pleasurable and less cerebral. Although the
   illustrations for JM were to suggest the universality of
   the myth (which Gardner believes is the most powerful myth
   of all), the effect was unintentionally "campy." Gardner
   attributes some of his success to the Beatles, who pop-
   ularized non-realistic art. He denies that G and WA are
   spin-offs of SD, though all three novels deal with the
   same ideas, or that the relationship between Grendel and
   his mother has any special meaning. Gardner says that a
   writer's sense of structure is a "gift" and that writing
   and teaching are complementary activities. Currently he
   is writing a homiletic poem about the temptations of St.
   Guthlac.

20 McCullough, David. "Eye on Books." Book-of-the-Month Club
   News, November 1973, pp. 8-9.
      Interviewed at the University of Rochester writers work-
   shop, Gardner establishes the order his novels were composed: NM (written nearly twenty years ago and subsequently
   much revised), SD (first completed in 1965 and then oft-
   refused), Res (written as the "all-time pop novel"),
   WA, G, JM (which was written concurrently with the revision of SD; the two are "companion volumes" dealing with
   "the uneasy relationship between freedom and law"), and
   the forthcoming KI, which imitates "bad 19th-century tales

and ghost stories." All his work is parodic, even NM, which he says is "not an innocent novel but an imitation of an innocent novel." Gardner thinks of himself as a "serious clown...a storyteller...not a philosopher."

21 Hansen, Linda. "Fiction and 'So-Called Reality.'" Rochester Times-Union, 1 November 1973, p. Cl.
Quotes from Gardner's talk, "Fiction and So-Called Reality," delivered at the University of Rochester. "Popular lore," Gardner says, accepts the "pseudo-scientific" view that man is depraved. The antidote, Gardner explains in an interview, is optimistic novels which "present a different perspective on human behavior." The writer of fiction must be concerned with human emotion. Filming of SD has been postponed due to difficulty in finding a producer.

22 "Life Follows Fiction--Never Doubt It." University of Rochester Currents, 9 November 1973, pp. 1, 3 Photograph, p. 4.
(Prints Gardner's speech at the University of Rochester Wilson Day Celebration, 1 November 1973.) Gardner rejects the view that reality is "mere dead mechanics," separateness; instead, citing Whitehead's theory of the sentience of all matter, he believes in the world imagined in art and religion, the world of connections. Unfortunately, it is the former view which is pervasive today because it seems to explain events such as Vietnam and Watergate. American intellectuals have been "lobotomized" by their easy lives and the capitalistic "trash" culture which leads to a "naive complacency" on the one hand and a cynical belief in chance on the other. Because art does affect life, there is virtually no market for "honest" literature (e.g., the film version of SD by Gardner and Jules Dassin). Gardner approves of those modern writers who, like himself, speak against the evils contemporary man no longer even perceives or who, like poets Van Duyn, Nemerov, Hecht, Ted Weiss, and fiction writers Elkin, Gass, Oates, Welty, search for ideals.

23 Boyd, Robert. "A Writer's Offhanded Dazzle." St. Louis Post-Dispatch, 28 November 1973, p. F2.
Gardner has a "multiple personality": there is "the literary celebrity," "the scholar," the family man, and "the elusive artist" ready to "agree with most any observation the interviewer makes." On the strength of his "tour de force" G, Gardner was able to negotiate the

publication of his oft-refused SD (for which Gardner has
recently been writing the screenplay with filmaker Jules
Dassin). Of his works his favorite is JM, "a daring
attempt to use the most restrictive of forms to cope with
the problems of our anarchistic age." His forthcoming
NM was begun fifteen years ago as a series of stories;
the version published in Redbook is distorted, he feels,
by editorial cuts. Gardner, who enjoys his teaching and
scholarly work, is currently working on a biography of
Chaucer and a study of Beowulf. (All quotations are
Boyd's.)

24 "Telling a Story." Newsweek, 82 (24 December 1973), 84.
Despite the "despair on both coasts," all the New York
talk about the death of the novel, and the "rarefied"
state of fiction, "people are again realizing it is telling a story that really is important." Gardner prefers
the simple rural values and finds the Midwest "tempera-
mentally" well-suited to his needs as a writer.

25 Mattos, Edward. Writer in Society: John Gardner. Color
videotape: 28 min. Washington, D.C.: United States
Information Agency, 1974.
The purpose of good art is to help people stay human;
it leaves the reader "totally confused," teaching him
that life is complicated and throwing him back on his
"own emotional and moral nature." Tolstoi, for example,
did this in Anna Karenina but not in later, propagandistic
works such as Resurrection. Novelists should never take
social stands in their fiction. American writers today--
including Barth, Barthelme ("a very great writer"), and
Updike--escape to "fable," "non-reality," and "non-
responsibility" rather than tell lies about life. They
escape into technique, but for Gardner the important
question is not can a story be written but is it worth
writing. Truly important issues require a non-realistic
treatment, thus JM (which Gardner implies is his best
work) and the pastoral novel NM. Finally, Gardner says
it is too easy to write about hate; some of the best
contemporary fiction is being written by young blacks
who are not interested in racial welfare. (Taped for
Gardner's United States Information Service tour of
Japan, 8 September-5 October 1974.)

26 "John Gardner." East West Journal, 4 (February 1974), 34-35.
The contemporary artist should not strive to be
original but, instead, should imitate existing forms in
order to strike a balance between the individual and the

universal. Today there is an unhealthy emphasis on
individualism and psychological anarchy. The arts can
remedy this "sickness"; a good poem, for example, causes
the reader to share the poet's feeling. In a traditional
culture, people feel assured because their roles are
"genetically and socially" determined. Research in
brain wave patterns proves that individual abilities
are predetermined.

27 Ensworth, Pat, and Joe David Bellamy. "John Gardner: An
Interview." fiction international, 2-3 (Spring-Fall
1974), 32-49. Rpt. in The New Fiction: Interviews with
Innovative American Writers, ed. Joe David Bellamy
(Urbana: University of Illinois Press, 1974), pp. 169-
93.
   Contemporary fiction is characterized by a "tale-and-
yarn" style involving unreliable narrators and, as in
the Middle Ages, a breakdown of traditional genres. The
concerns of the novelist are plot, characters, emotion,
drama, celebration, and affirmation, not sociological
motivation or philosophizing. True imagination is the
kind Clumly develops in SD; it involves patience,
tolerance, understanding, and empathy. Today's writers
are becoming more affirmative, largely as a result of
their ties to the universities, and more concerned with
form. They comprise no single literary movement for
ours is a literary period of "individual genius and
freakiness" when "every writer now is lost in the fun-
house--and pretty happy with it." Of his own work,
Gardner notes that all his writings are collaborations
in the sense that he uses his wife's sociological-
psychological imagination to complement his own, which
is poetic and philosophical. Chaucer, Melville, Gass,
and Disney have been major influences. In G, for
example, a work which is based upon "the main ideas of
Western civilization" and astrological signs, the
Anglo-Saxon subject is given a cartoonish treatment.
Having at first found it difficult to get published,
Gardner has a backlog he has been publishing alternately
with his newly written work; his most recent is "The
King's Indian and Other Fireside Tales," which he
describes as "a very jazzy thing."

28 Miyamoto, Yokichi. ["The Star of the 1970's in American
Literature: An Interview with John Gardner"]. Yomiuri
Shimbun (Japan), 17 September 1974, p. 7.
   G, which was written in reaction to the mainstream of
realism in the 1960's, was not published until more than

ten years later, by which time American readers were more
willing to accept non-realistic works. (Annotation is
based on a translation--of excerpts--provided by John
Howell.)

29 ["Mr. John Gardner: Visiting American Writer Here to Lecture
on Contemporary American Literature"] . Mainichi Shimbun
(Japan), 21 September 1974, p. 3.
    Gardner praises the Japanese people's aesthetic sense
and says that although Japanese literature is of high
quality, it is too rarely translated to be widely known
internationally. Gardner attributes Mishima's popularity
to his offering the past as an alternative to modern
cultural change. Unlike American writers (except for
Mailer), Akiyuki Nosaka tried to combine literary and
political careers and had his opponents use his novel
The Pornographers against him. (Annotation is based on
a translation--of excerpts--provided by John Howell.)

30 Kitazawa, Masakuni. ["Downfall and Restoration of American
Society: A Dialogue with John Gardner']. Asahi Journal
(Japan), 27 September 1974, pp. 80-85.
    Gardner comments briefly on the Vietnam war (including
one of its results: the end of realism and the rise of
fabulation), Watergate, American Indian culture as an
alternative to capitalism, constructive changes occurring
in America, JM as a fable about various forms of oppres-
sion, Bellow, Welty, and Oates as his favorite authors,
and the demise of progressivism, as well as the rock
music it spawned, and the popularity of country music
and Negro spirituals. (Annotation is based on a trans-
lation--of excerpts--provided by John Howell.)

31 "Powerful Firms Will Destroy Us." Mainichi Daily News
(Japan), 2 October 1974, p. 4.
    Speaking as a participant in a panel discussion,
Gardner said that the Korean War spelled the beginning
of the end for realism and with the Vietnam War came a
non-realistic fiction that enabled American writers to
"get to the heart of the matter." It is not the
American people but American government and corpora-
tions that are to blame for the wrongs committed by
America today. Gardner calls on artists and intellectuals to remake the world (a view dismissed as
"American optimism" by Japanese poet Ryuichi Tamura).
(Annotation is based on a translation--of excerpts--
provided by John Howell.)

32 Iwamoto, Iwao. "John Gardner no Sekai: Taiden to Sakuhin wo Toshite" ["John Gardner's World Through His Works and an Interview"]. Eigo Seinen (Tokyo), 120 (1974-75), 397, 454-55.

Gardner sees himself as perhaps "the most optimistic" of today's American writers and suggests that his optimism may derive from his rural upbringing. In writing NM, he wanted to write about characters who embodied "the true experience of the countryside." (Annotation is based on a translation--of excerpts-- provided by John Howell.)

33 Parker, Gail Thain. "An Interview with John Gardner." Quadrille (Bennington College), 9 (Spring 1975), 3-6.

Gardner briefly comments on his dislike of farming, his having felt socially more at ease at the state-run Washington University than at DePauw, and his housekeeping chores earlier in his marriage. College, he says, should be an enjoyable experience. Truly dedicated teachers who are interested in their students' well-being are essential at schools such as Southern Illinois University, but the kind of student who attends Bennington can benefit greatly from its high-caliber faculty, "if they both survive." In either case, the student develops best when he is encouraged. Gardner thinks of himself as a tolerant person, the trait partly deriving from his having to understand his fictional characters so thoroughly, but tolerance should never lead to mindless approval nor to the idea, recently advanced by John Leonard in the New York Times Book Review, that parents cannot help guide their children. (Gardner briefly alludes to fellow Bennington faculty members, Bernard Malamud and Nicholas Delbanco.)

34 Askins, John. "Conversations with John Gardner on Writers and Writing." Detroit Magazine (Detroit Free Press), 23 March 1975, pp. 19-21. Rpt. in Authors in the News, ed. Barbara Nykoruk, vol. 1 (Detroit: Gale Research, 1976), pp. 168-69.

As a child Gardner wrote stories he would then read to his cousins. He still writes with an audience in mind (only Res did he write solely for himself) and largely for "oral effect," making up words and reciting his work to his two children before revising it. That "things are very good for serious writers right now" is indicated by his own popularity and that of Joyce Carol Oates, "a wonderful writer" who shares Gardner's

16

interest in "the novel form" but not his belief in a
human "'core of being.'" Each of his novels treats "one
aspect" of a "single philosophical question": the loss
of idealism in the Twentieth Century. Simply stated,
man is happiest "when he knows he has certain duties
and he performs them. When he has boundaries." As a
writer Gardner thinks of himself as a workman making
"really nice houses" and as "a playful person" engaged in "very serious playing." (The interview also
briefly treats Gardner's married life.)

35 Darbenne, Bob. "The Gardner's Dialogues." Rochester
    Times-Union, 25 March 1975, pp. C1-C2.
       Unlike the fiction of Kurt Vonnegut, much of which "is
    written to self-destruct," Gardner wrote SD to endure.
    He doesn't mind the speculation about real-life paral-
    lels to the novel's characters and events, adding that
    "I never set out to make a character bad." He also
    notes his being a very careful observer. (The article
    quotes from Anthony Hecht's citation designating Gardner
    winner of the Friends of the Rochester Public Library
    annual literary award: as a medievalist and novelist
    Gardner is deeply concerned with "history and civiliza-
    tion" and "cumulative human endeavor.")

36 Prichard, Peter. "Gardner--A Writer at 8?" Rochester
    Democrat & Chronicle, 25 March 1975, pp. C1-C2.
       Accepting the Friends of the Rochester Public Library
    annual literary award, Gardner spoke of the unity--
    "cousinhood"--of all people. The characters in SD, he
    told one interviewer, "are not so much like real people
    in the factual sense but in the sense that people are
    like other people because they feel the same emotions."
    All art does the same thing: it reminds "people that
    they're people." Gardner says he began writing when he
    was eight, composing chapters of stories he would then
    read to his family each night.

37 Meagher, Tom, and Josh Hanft. "John Gardner Presents
    'Shadows.'" Middlebury Campus, 24 April 1975, p. 4.
       Although Gardner describes "Shadows" as "just a
    story," it involves a good deal of "cosmological jazz,"
    including black and white holes and the Norse world
    wolf myth. Robert Pack's introductory comments
    (Gardner is a prolific "story teller") and a detailed
    summary of the excerpt read by Gardner are included.

38 Teicholz, Thomas. "Conversation with John Gardner."
Middlebury Campus, 24 April 1975, p. 4.
   Gardner is optimistic about the future of the novel
though he admits the visual media may be affecting the
novel's form. Much of contemporary fiction he finds
boring because, as Gore Vidal noted, too many writers
today are trying to write the great novel. Gardner,
who does not believe writing can actually be taught,
believes the student writer should devote himself to
his writing, especially to developing his own style.
Gardner's ideal reader is someone who enjoys his
fiction, not someone who can identify all the allusions
and certainly not reviewers, who are chiefly concerned
with author-ratings.

39 Blades, Nancy. "A New Novelist in Old Bennington."
Bennington Banner, 26 April 1975, pp. 1, 2.
   Gardner comments candidly on life in Bennington,
Vermont, where he plans to reside for at least the next
six years. He notes its honest workers and the high
school's excellent music department, but, too, the
townspeople's provincialism. His outward appearance
belies a conservative streak; Gardner favors sterner
punishment for repeat offenders and laments the migration
of farmers to the cities. He mentions his earliest
writings, "about gangsters, most likely," which he
read aloud to his family, and later the musical plays
he wrote with his future wife while at Washington
University. He is currently writing a novel, "Stillness,"
set in southern Illinois, and believes he is still too
unfamiliar with the Bennington area to use it in his
fiction.

40 Cross, Leslie. "No Rest for John Gardner." Milwaukee
Journal, 11 May 1975, sec. 5, p. 4.
   Great literature celebrates, but modern literature is
trivial and, in so far as it is judged important, phony
as well. For the next six years Gardner plans to reside
in Bennington and devote himself more fully to his
writing. Concerning his in-progress biography of Chaucer,
Gardner notes that his extensive "sleuthing" led him to
realize how incorrect our understanding of this poet
actually is.

41 Johnson, Ken. "Best-Selling Novelist Talks about Work,
SIU." Daily Egyptian (Southern Illinois University-
Carbondale), 25 August 1975, p. B18.
   Although he has recently purchased a home in Benning-
ton, Vermont, and has been offered a number of lucrative
writer-in-residence positions, Gardner feels a strong

commitment to Southern Illinois University. Next year
he will make a month-long tour of Russia and western
Europe for the United States Information Service. There
he will meet writers who, like himself and unlike
Solzhenitsyn, write about non-political matters.
Gardner's fiction deals with the "enduring values,"
specifically "brotherhood, compassion and security."
Currently he is working on seven novels, including one
that is autobiographical and set in southern Illinois,
and several radio plays, one dealing with the Loch Ness
monster ("The Water Horse") and a series of six plays
about the Revolutionary War in which the major historical
figures are de-mythologized.

42 White, Jean M. "The Modern Novel Is an Awful Thing."
   Washington Post, 3 December 1975, pp. C1, C6.
      Contemporary fiction--from trash to New Yorker--is
   "awful" and "boring" because it buries the reader in a
   character's subconscious. The critic's function should
   be to aid the reader; in short, criticism is subservient
   to art. Gardner's fiction is "very heavily textured";
   his new novel [OL] concerns a "bicentennial theme on
   popular democracy which gives freedom but also brings
   trash." Also mentioned are Gardner's Folger Library
   readings, his proposed tour of Russia, and his planned
   resignation from Southern Illinois University.

43 Quackenbush, Rick. "Dialogue with Gardner in a Sunlit Hotel
   Room." Ann Arbor News, 14 December 1975, p. 30.
      Gardner, a guest speaker at the University of
   Michigan's annual Hopwood Award presentations, comments on
   various aspects of his work: its metaphysical dimension,
   the "fun" he has writing, his not having any one favorite
   among his books, and his not being satisfied with what
   he has written. He is pleased with the current state
   of serious fiction. Novels such as Ragtime and Beyond
   the Bedroom Wall are not only fun to read; they are also
   less self-conscious and less self-important [than
   fiction written the generation before]. Moreover, due
   to the deplorable state of film and television, fiction
   is attracting a large audience. Gardner reads chiefly
   for pleasure--"animal stories, myths, philosophy and
   anthropology," and currently a book about the evolution
   of apes from men. In his writing, he works from "a
   complete outline" and repeats the story to himself
   numerous times before actually starting to write. His
   current work in-progress, "Lost Souls Rock," concerns

but "of course...won't change the American character. "

44 Banker, Stephen. <u>John Gardner</u>. Tapes for Readers. LIT-
   025, [1976]. 16 min.
   Gardner laments the rise of middle-class literature
(parodied by Fielding and Defoe in <u>Tom Jones</u> and
<u>Robinson Crusoe</u>, an intentionally boring novel) as well
as the contemporary ignorance of the literary tradition
and the loss of those values that would enable readers
to distinguish aesthetic greatness. Whereas today's
fiction (in the <u>New Yorker</u>, for example) is journalistic
and self-indulgent, classical literature is a way of
testing ideas and values. Apollonius Rhodius, for
example, was a Donald Barthelme-like parodist who
imitated the epic form in order to criticize his decadent
age. In parodying these intellectual classical genres,
Gardner writes an exceptionally clear prose because he
is trying to think out a problem step by step. In
Gardner's view, the writer must both reflect his times
and perpetuate the literary tradition; only by knowing
the great works of the past can he hope to measure his
achievement. Moreover, the writer must attempt to
understand not only his age but, more importantly,
human nature as well, as Gardner attempted in writing
<u>JM</u>. The characters in his fiction for children tend
to be more uncertain than those in traditional fairy
tales. In stories such as "The Miller's Mule" and
<u>ISM</u>, Gardner freely mixes past and present time in order
to create a convincing and completely imagined world.
(According to Howell, this interview was conducted on
2 December 1975.)

45 Brousseau, Elaine. "Talk with an Author Whose Fiction
   Tries to Celebrate Goodness." <u>Providence Sunday Journal</u>,
   4 January 1976, p. H19.
   While making preparations for his United States Information Service tour of Russia and Eastern Europe in
February, Gardner is also writing a new novel set in
Vermont which includes an inside novel. He notes his
preference for classical music to modern, which he finds
too subjective and intimate, and for the long poem, which
requires that the poet "put on a voice," to "the
sensitive little lyric" currently in vogue, which lacks
authority. He recognizes only two basic kinds of art--
"that which sets up transcendent ideals and that which
bitterly criticizes an age" and sees the fiction of the

seventies as more heroic and less cynical than the fiction of the previous decade. Gardner, who began writing when he was eight or ten, writes slowly and for long stretches; parts of JM were dreamed into being. He thinks of his works as "word-objects" designed to invite the reader's involvement. Gardner does not socialize regularly with other writers; in his view, good writing requires isolation, "not the agonizing isolation" of the Romantics but the comfortable exile of Joyce.

46 Cackley, Phil. "Gardner Recites From Newest Novel." Observer (University of Notre Dame--St. Mary's College), 17 February 1976, p. 1.

    During a reading from OL (the manuscript of which had recently been sent to Knopf), Gardner mentioned that the novel's subject is the problem of communication and its effect on democracy. The novel juxtaposes old and new, conservative and liberal; it is not a distinctly contemporary work--Gardner continues to use older works and ideas to enrich his own fiction. (Gardner and Borges were featured speakers at the Sophomore Literary Festival and as panelists discussed Anglo-Saxon poetry.)

47 Bonham, Eupha. "John Gardner Wins Over an Audience." Bennington Banner, 20 March 1976, p. 8.

    Gardner, the guest speaker at the Bennington, Vermont, chapter of the American Association of University Women, read three poems from his forthcoming CB--"The Possum," which the Saturday Evening Post had at one time rejected; "The Cat and Dog"; and "The Mosquito," Gardner's response to a film about kamikaze pilots he had seen while in Japan--and one story, "The Miller's Mule," from Dragon. His stories for children combine traditional characters and a modern style; they evidence his interest in "non-real" literature which Gardner says derives from his father. Gardner sees himself as a gentle person whose fiction is free of the sex and violence which preoccupies many contemporary writers.

48 "Distinguished Alumni Citees." Washington University Alumni News, 28 (Spring 1976), 4-5.

    Quotes from Gardner's reading of OL. Includes a brief biographical sketch (which mentions the "numerous radio plays" Gardner has written) and quotes from the introductory remarks of Gardner's former teacher, Jarvis Thurston, who recognized Gardner's talent upon reading the story "Nickel Mountain."

49 Icen, Richard H. "Carbondale Author John Gardner Advises: Remain Insulated." Southern Illinoisan (Carbondale), 28 March 1976, p. 27.
    Writers should avoid the literary "centers of style and taste," explains Gardner concerning his tenure at Southern Illinois University. He has temporarily moved to Bennington, Vermont in order that his children can be near the area's numerous music camps. Although now a well-known author, he had been greatly discouraged by the poor reception of Res, a "very intellectual" novel. For his best-selling SD, he chose the Batavia setting because of the general decline the area represents. Unlike Faulkner, he was never inclined to create a mythic land. As poet Dan Guillory notes, Gardner's strength and popularity as a novelist derive from his ability to create "believable" ordinary characters and "to express through them the concerns of many."

50 Marcus, Noreen. "Dragon Eyes Crowd at Novelist's Yard Sale." Southern Illinoisan (Carbondale), 10 May 1976, p. 3.
    Marcus provides some biographical background (e.g. Gardner's three-year leave of absence from Southern Illinois University and the sale of his farm) and quotes Gardner's banter with a customer and his favorable comments on his different but equally pleasurable homes in Carbondale and Bennington. The comments of friends saddened by the Gardners' departure are also recorded.

51 Ephron, Nora. "The Bennington Affair." Esquire, 86 (September 1976), 148.
    Quotes Gardner's comments in support of Gail Parker, the deposed president of Bennington College.

52 Modert, Jo. "John Gardner on Chaucer, Medieval Women, Fairy Tales: An Interview with John Gardner." St. Louis Post-Dispatch, 26 December 1976, p. 4E.
    The inspiration of his teacher, John McGalliard, at the University of Iowa and "the extraordinary beauty of the literature itself" attracted Gardner to medieval studies. Written in a popular style and gathering together material that will be new to most scholars, LTC should appeal to a wide and varied audience; PC is a bit more specialized. Gardner describes Chaucer as "a social, gentle, wise man, generally a man of integrity," though not above some financial chicanery. Not at all an alienated artist, Chaucer was a keen observer of humanity. On stories for children, Gardner says they should, like adult fiction,

entertain and lead to "insights and discoveries." His
own stories for children were written for his son and
daughter and without any "moral purpose." Of OL he notes
that James and Sally "come off as interesting, even
beautiful people, and the war proves one more typical
human war, its cruelty is really nothing compared to the
age-old cruelty of just plain existence. It's one of
those sad, sad books that's eventually liberating (or so
I hope) because the pain is finally over."

53 Frazer Clark, Jr., C.E. "John Gardner." Conversations
with Writers. Detroit: Gale Research/A Bruccoli
Clark Book, 1977, pp. 83-103.
    Scholars no longer seem concerned with scholarship as a
mode of understanding, only with tailoring a literary work
to their own preconceived pattern. In two books, "Thor's
Hammer: A Literary Manifesto" [OMF] and an in-progress
"description of what all the major writers today are doing,"
Gardner takes a broader approach. Based on his own teaching experience and the success of John Jakes's novels
(which are not art but instead "a wonderful, loving sashay
through soap opera history"), Gardner believes that a
large American reading public does exist. His enthusiasm
for American democracy and distaste for the image of the
writer as "romantic hero" may be one reason he experiments
with a variety of literary forms. Despite this enthusiasm,
Gardner delimits democratic pluralism and claims that the
function of literature is not to "apply new values" but to
"assert traditional values which have worked and question
values when they seem to be risky." The dramatization of
this process of reassessment is what makes fiction entertaining. Today's writers, however, are chiefly concerned
with "performance," with propounding a view, or with an
art "absolutely divorced from reality." True art is
further threatened by commercialization and the unwillingness of publishers and reviewers to recognize new talent
(e.g., Mark Helprin and Charles Johnson). As counter-
measures Gardner is planning a radio talk show on the
arts and advises readers to convey their dissatisfaction
directly to the publishers. Gardner also mentions major
influences on his writing--his parents, Shakespeare,
Scott, Dickens, Disney, and music, especially opera.
Asked how he would like to be remembered, Gardner replies,
"as the greatest living librettist of the twentieth
century."

54 The Sally Jesse Raphael Show, WMCA Radio (New York),
   c. 13 January 1977.*
   Cited in "Extensive Publicity Follows on Awards,"
   National Book Critics Circle Journal, Spring 1977, p. 6
   Gardner and NBCC judges Richard Locke and Digby Diehl
   were interviewed on the subject of the 1976 awards. Tape
   no longer available.

55 Straight Talk. WOR-TV (New York), c. 13 January 1977.*
   Cited in "Extensive Publicity Follows on Awards,"
   National Book Critics Circle Awards, Spring 1977, p. 6.
   Gardner and NBCC judge Timothy Foote were interviewed on
   the subject of the 1976 awards. Tape no longer available.

56 Alexander, John. "Premiere of 'Rumpelstiltskin' Brings
   John Gardner to Town." Lexington (Kentucky) Herald-
   Leader, 16 January 1977.
      Preferring to be known as a librettist rather than a
   novelist, Gardner observes that opera "combines all the
   arts into one package": story, music, visuals. Unfortunately this "potential" is usually wasted. Thanks to
   the financial power exerted by women today, opera
   companies are flourishing and the opportunities for the
   staging of new works are many. Gardner's work in-progress
   includes two more operas, the novel "Rage" (still five
   years away from publication), a book on aesthetics, and
   a radio show for the airing of new work "coming from
   middle America" (i.e., from outside New York and Los
   Angeles).

57 Swindell, Larry. "Our Best Novelist: He Thinks So Too."
   Philadelphia Inquirer, 16 January 1977, pp. F1, F13.
      In this interview, given prior to the naming of OL as
   the outstanding work of fiction in 1976 by the National
   Book Critics Circle, Gardner expresses his desire that he
   receive the award. Gardner sees himself as an industrious,
   rather than a prolific, writer whose fiction and philosophy
   continually change and whose "time has come." Of his own
   works, he says he is fond of JM, G, and NM (his "simplest
   novel"), but calls WA "a mess" and SD more a "performance
   than a novel." He notes the closeness of his fiction to
   that of Isak Dinesen, as well as Faulkner and Thomas Wolfe,
   cites the genius of Dinesen, Gass, Andre Biely, and Hermann
   Broch, and calls Robbe-Grillet the best living writer.
   That Gardner has been ranked as a major contemporary writer
   is, he says, "a sad commentary on things." His current
   interests include writing operas with Louis Callabro [sic]

(William Wilson) and Jimmy Vannatos (an adaptation of
Tolstoi's "Ivan the Terrible"), his Chaucer work (Knopf
will be publishing his Chaucer biography and his selection
of the poetry), and literary criticism. Gardner also
speaks candidly of his separaticn from his wife and the
adverse effect of his "incest[uous]" marriage on his two
children.

58 Williams, Edgar. "Authors See an Angry Light." Philadelphia Inquirer, 20 January 1977, p. B3.

Speaking at the Inquirer's Book and Author Luncheon,
Gardner read from the first chapter of OL and described
James Page as "a sort of contemporary Everyman" who is
"thoroughly angry" about today's society. Other speakers
were Pat Watters, Gloria Emerson, and George Eells.

59 Mootz, William. "Collaborators Prepare Opera, 'Rumpel-
stiltskin,' for World Premiere in Lexington Opera House:
First It Was Boito, Verdi--Now It's Gardner, Baber."
Louisville Courier-Journal, 21 January 1977, p. E5.

Gardner, who idolizes Mozart and Wagner, says opera can
be "more fun than Broadway and a lot more profound." The
best American opera thus far, Porgy and Bess, fails because the characters remain unrealized and the philosophy
is unsound. Rumpelstiltskin concerns the themes of forgiveness and, Baber adds, the importance of childhood.
(The interview-essay also includes background on the
Baber-Gardner relationship, Baber's career, and the staging of Rumpelstiltskin at the Lexington Opera House.)

60 Quindlen, Anna. "Why He Writes." New York Post, 24
January 1977, p. 25.

During a suicidal period in his life, Gardner listened
to Tchaikovsky's "Pathetique" and was led beyond self-pity
to a "tragic vision." He considers himself one of today's
best writers but does not believe ours is a period of
literary quality. Presently living apart from his family,
he devotes his time to writing, not for his ego but from
"grief." He defends the inside novel in OL, saying that
only by showing what a character is reading can the writer
point to the effects of fiction. Gardner finds Updike an
honest man but a "dishonest writer"; Gass is a brilliant
writer who "got hung up in his own idiosyncrasies."
Gardner admires the work of Hilma Wolitzer and enjoys
reading "lightweights," such as Frederick Forsyth, who
"deliver what they say they're going to deliver."

61 White, Jean M. "Books and Authors: Three Speak Out."
   Washington Post, 17 February 1977, p. D9.
   Gardner, James Dickey, and Joseph P. Lash were the
   speakers at the _Post's_ Book and Author Luncheon, 16
   February 1977. In his talk, Gardner criticized contemporary writers for failing to use fiction as "a
   technique of discovery"; instead they serve up per-
   formances, sermons, or "linguistic sculpture."

62 Cuomo, Joseph, and Marie Ponsot. "An Interview with John
   Gardner." _A Shout in the Street_, 1, ii (1977), 45-63.
   Gardner's criticism of certain writers led a number of
   New York publishers to reject "Thor's Hammer " [OMF], which
   criticizes performance fiction (Sukenick), linguistic
   sculpture (Gass), essay-novels (Bellow), and cold-hearted
   writing. In Gardner's view, fiction must "actually [do]
   something for society." In teaching writing, he advises
   students to write from the heart, not from theory, and to
   write the kind of "charged description" found in Gass,
   Barth, and Davenport. Noting the wrongheadedness of one
   review of OL [the one by Josephine Hendin in the New
   Republic], Gardner says that the "deep evil" in Western
   civilization can be metaphorically summed up as the conflict between male and female. Righting a wrong and
   exploring an idea discovered in his study of literature
   are the "two basic impulses" behind his fiction-writing.
   In JM, for example, he wanted to understand the ancients
   from a modern point of view. When his writing bogs down,
   as it did while writing "Rage," a novel about a woman who
   is a teacher of philosophy and an artist, he puts it away
   and works on something else; the danger is that he may
   temporarily lose the particular voice central to each of
   his books. His method of composition involves voluminous
   notes, a "pour it out" rough draft which includes plot
   and "lots of detail about the characters," and endless
   revisions during which he makes connections and often
   changes the story completely. The revision of OL, for
   example, entailed setting up parallels between the stories
   that would lead to greater emotional effect--as opposed to
   intellectual effort--on the reader's part; the parallels
   are not meant to distract the reader from the narrative.
   Gardner uses fiction "to discover," not, as Flannery
   O'Connor and Barth (in _Chimera_) do, "to instruct." Like
   O'Connor, Disney (whose flaw was sentimentality), and
   opera, Gardner uses caricature. He and Oates, along with
   other contemporary writers, are concerned with the theme
   of isolation and "what monsters the isolated become."
   (Howell dates this interview 12 March 1977.)

63 Mable, Sheila. "Gardner Fans Grow. . . ." Vermont Cynic
   (University of Vermont at Burlington), 17 March 1977,
   p. 23.
      Quotes from Gardner's lecture, "Death by Art" (drawn
   from "Thor's Hammer").

64 Mable, Sheila. "Behind the Author's Life." Vermont Cynic
   (University of Vermont at Burlington), 17 March 1977,
   p. 23.
      The contemporary reader's fear of long poems accounts
   for the neglect of JM. Gardner calls NM his "neatest and
   smoothest" work and KI his "masterpiece." He also defends
   the inside novel in OL, the theme of which is the need for
   "models of just behavior," and notes the humor in his
   essentially serious novels. He advises his writing
   students to write and revise continually ("the whole art
   of writing is revision"), to transcend experience by means
   of intelligence and imagination, and to "be honest with
   themselves." Good fiction encourages people to read; the
   fiction he attacks in "Thor's Hammer" does not. Gardner
   also notes his interest in Disney, non-realistic tales,
   mysteries, books on philosophy and archaeology, music of
   various kinds (he is involved in a Bennington orchestra),
   horses and dogs.

65 "Transcript of Award Ceremony." National Book Critics
   Circle Journal, 3 (Spring 1977), p. 3. Photograph on
   p. 1.
      In accepting the National Book Critics Circle Award
   for OL, Gardner tells a tall-tale about a novelist and a
   poet who win a free trip to the Bahamas but find they have
   to row there and back, whipped all the way; upon returning
   to New York, the novelist asks the poet if they have to
   tip the whipper. (The citation read by Digby Diehl
   appears on pp. 2-3.)

66 Sachs, Sylvia. "Heritage, God, Schools, Comedy--Authors
   Cover It All." Pittsburgh Press, 14 April 1977, p. A23.
      At the Book and Author Dinner for the Children's
   Hospital, Gardner read from CB. The other speakers were
   John Jakes, Nat Hentoff, Richard Reeves, and Jack Douglas.

67 Jennes, Gail. "John Gardner Buys Solitude to Unleash
   the 'Monsters' in His Mind." People, 7 (18 April 1977),
   60-61.
      To talk about his work-in-progress--his "monster"--
   would bring bad luck and be a betrayal. Gardner does

discuss his need for solitude in order to write, his love
of music ("the one thing I'd die without"), and the value
his parents placed on writing. Gardner's publication history,
current teaching (at Williams and Skidmore Colleges), and
his recent separation from his wife are briefly considered.

68 Reddin, Debbie. "John Gardner Speaks on the Moral Aspects
   of Fiction." Alabamian (University of Montevallo), 20
   April 1977, p. 4.
   Briefly quotes from two lectures from OMF given 12 April;
   Gardner is described as "a true believer in happy endings."

69 Barbato, Joseph. "Novelist and Medievalist: John Gardner
   on Geoffrey Chaucer." Chronicle of Higher Education, 14
   (25 April 1977), 17.
   As a medievalist Gardner has been "interested in making
   major discoveries," not in presenting scholarly treatises.
   His "scofflaw indifference" to the scholar's rules has resulted in highly critical academic reviews of his work,
   but it is not the scholars (much of whose work he calls
   "junk") for whom Gardner writes, but the lovers of literature. He hopes scholars will feel challenged by his two
   Chaucer books, and not react simply to defend their own
   views. It was his editor at Knopf who suggested that PC
   was not suitable for a general audience. The biography,
   Gardner says, is "not original, except as an assimilation."
   Unlike most contemporary American writers, who "don't know
   any literature except contemporary American writing"--
   much of it distinctly "minor"-- Gardner knows the classics
   and uses medieval forms to "analyz[e] contemporary problems."
   Though he would like to devote all of his time to his
   fiction-writing, Gardner does not intend to leave teaching
   or the universities, which he considers "the strongholds
   of our culture." Except for a study of Dante, which he
   does not intend to publish, and his editing the [Literary
   Structures] series for Southern Illinois University Press,
   in which he encourages young scholars to develop his ideas,
   Gardner is finished with scholarship.

70 Oliven, Cathy. "Interview: Gardner." Loyola Phoenix
   (University of Loyola, Chicago), 29 April 1977, pp. 6, 11.
   The writer's chief obligation is to himself, says
   Gardner, a participant in Loyola's Symposium on Human
   Responsibility, adding that the end result benefits the
   entire society because art is, as Plato said, truth,
   goodness, and beauty. One enemy of true art is
   capitalism, which fosters "lovable art." Of his own

writing, Gardner claims he has no difficulty making up
plots, never has a writer's block, and believes "revision
is absolutely necessary." He is currently writing a play
for his daughter and, when asked to name the greatest novel,
responds (apparently tongue in cheek), "Finnegan's [sic]
Wake, but I still want to write a better one."

71 Mooney, Karen. "Imagination Sole Authority, Novelist Tells
   Group Here." Emporia (Kansas) Gazette, 30 April 1977, p. 2.
   Speaking at a workshop held during Emporia State
   University's Literary Week, Gardner warned writers against
   using any symbolism that was not inherent in their stories,
   advised careful and extensive revision, and defined the
   novel as the "reassessment of values." At a lecture,
   Gardner read from JM and "Thor's Hammer," emphasizing
   fiction as a mode of thought and the need for literature
   to provide socially useful myths.

72 Edwards, Don, and Carol Polsgrove. "A Conversation with
   John Gardner." Atlantic, 239 (May 1977), 43-47.
   Gardner, a self-styled half-upstate New York conservative and half-Bohemian, outlines the "three main positions
   in modern fiction": fiction as object (Gass), as performance
   (Elkin), as exploration (Gardner). Bellow, too, uses fiction as a means of exploration, but he is more an essayist
   than a novelist, a distinction Gardner feels is evident in
   Res. Gardner finds much of modern literature "boring" and
   usually turns to "archaic forms" in order "to think out
   so-called modern questions." The philosophical question
   dealt with in OL concerns the ways in which art and life
   affect each other and is carefully worked out in terms of
   the two "parallel" stories (The Smugglers being a parody
   of a "popular form of serious contemporary fiction"). As
   the novel makes clear, the self-righteous laws a man like
   James Page lives by are very different from the "difficult,
   complicated suggestions" made by art.

73 Newall, Robert H. "Author of Grendel UMO Guest." Bangor
   Daily News, 7-8 May 1977, p. 6.
   Begun in 1964, G concerns an entirely rationalistic "mind
   that refuses to have faith in anything." Grendel and the
   dragon, "the ultimate evil," represent the realistic and
   romantic points of view. Gardner has faith in the public
   audience but not in commercial publishing or certain
   popular authors (e.g., Taylor Caldwell and Joseph Heller),
   or popular theories such as Freudian psychology. In discussing opera, Gardner mentions, in passing, a wide

variety of librettists and composers, notes the similar
effects of animated cartoons (America's "only powerful
original art") and his work with composers Joseph Baber
and Domenic Argento. Although he at first intended the
Rumpelstiltskin libretto for children, he discovered
"children cannot be talked down to or patronized."
(Gardner's claiming a prepublication sale of 20,000
copies of JM is grossly exaggerated.)

74 Chargot, Patricia. "Blasting Away at Today's Top Writers."
    Detroit Free Press, 12 June 1977, p. C5.
       Gardner, who is in Detroit to address the Friends of the
    Detroit Public Library, is planning a radio show to pro-
    mote "good art." Today such art is not what is published
    by corporately-owned houses like Knopf but the generally
    unknown work of such unrecognized writers as Hilma
    Wolitzer, Rosellen Brown, and Charles Johnson. Gardner
    praises Oates and Cheever (citing the ending of Falconer)
    but criticizes Bellow (a preacher), Didion (a fine
    journalist but a terrible novelist), Barth (more concerned
    with technique than belief), Judith Guest, Thomas Williams,
    and Walker Percy (for Lancelot). True fiction has plot
    and characters, promotes civilization, and "makes every-
    thing so difficult that all you can do in the end is
    forgive everybody."

75 Hoover, Barbara. "Gardner: Words Don't Come Effortlessly."
    Detroit News, 19 June 1977, p. L2.
       In Detroit to talk to the Friends of the Detroit Public
    Library on "the desperate state of fiction in America,"
    Gardner briefly discusses the faults of Updike, Nabokov,
    Mailer, Bellow and Heller and notes his preference for
    the fiction of Kobo Abe and Italo Calvino. At some length
    he describes his own slow process of composition, which
    includes an "elaborate" planning stage. Calling the
    writer of the review of OL in the New York Times Book
    Review "not very bright," Gardner claims, "I don't really
    pay attention to reviews."

76 Dixon, Philip H. "John Gardner: Hard Work, Diversity Mark
    His Writing." St. Louis Post-Dispatch: Pictures, 22
    August 1977, p. 11.
       Gardner finds writing easy but has to discipline himself
    "to do the ordinary things of life." He claims his fiction
    for children differs from his work for adults only as to
    subjects; in both, characters and emotions must be
    "honestly" presented. Although he prefers non-realistic

forms, such as medieval literature and Disney cartoons,
he admires John Jakes's fiction and points out the "more
or less realistic" Vermont setting of OL. (The article
includes a biographical sketch and comments by Professor
Jarvis Thurston, Gardner's writing teacher at Washington
University, who recalls Gardner's talent and his helpfulness in criticizing the work of his fellow students.)

77 Lague, Louis. "John Gardner & Literature: Just a Loyal
Serf in the Kingdom of Words." Washington Star, 19
September 1977, pp. D1-D2.
    Gardner, who is teaching at George Mason University in
order to be near the Washington, D.C.-based National
Public Radio, hopes NPR will produce his children's opera,
Rumpelstiltskin, and his proposed talk show on the arts.
Financial reasons and a strong commitment to literature
are the reasons he continues to teach. He prefers the
kind of hardworking students he has had at Southern
Illinois and George Mason to the smarter but lazier
students at elite schools like Bennington. Gardner is
himself a most industrious person. He sees the novel,
which he compares to a cathedral, as the highest achievement of the human mind. He approves of Fowles and
Nabokov but objects to writers who fail to explore
character or who talk "to one group and think that's the
answer." Believing that art should not be pretentious,
he would like to stage a three-hour version of the Wakefield cycle with comedians Woody Allen, Marty Feldman,
and Mel Brooks.

78 Rutrell, Martin. "Writing of the 70's Is Here but We're
Not Seeing It." College Voice (Connecticut College), no.
3 (7 October 1977), p. 5.
    Artists believe in art, not in politics or religion.
Art is the perfect combination of texture, style, and
structure; it involves following an emotion wherever that
emotion leads. "Life is raw material and art is what you
make out of the raw material." Because art does affect
life, the artist must be socially responsible. Although
there are many fine writers today, they are all either
"underground" or, like Charles Johnson and Tim O'Brien,
only slightly known.

79 Kreitler, Ellen. "Gardner: Grendel Arrives at GMU." Broadside (George Mason University), 20 (31 October 1977), 4.
    Gardner is teaching at George Mason University in order
to be near Washington, D.C.-based National Public Radio

which he hopes will air his planned show for introducing
new talent in the arts and criticizing "establishment"
figures. George Mason is "sort of average" in the es-
sentials of college education: faculty, library, and
students. For Gardner, teaching is both financially and
personally necessary. Everyone should "fool around with
writing." The artist, however, must be deeply committed
to his craft and unconcerned about his ego. "First rate
writing" must be philosophical, concerned with character,
and involve "totally meaningful" events. Gardner believes
he is "a very good serious writer," though not as good as
John Fowles. Today's readers are not ignorant, he main-
tains--merely different, in terms of what they know, from
readers in the past.

80 Allen, Henry. "John Gardner:'I'm One of the Really Great
   Writers.'" Washington Post Magazine, 6 November 1977,
   pp. 23, 28, 33, 37.
   The shortcomings of Mailer, Pynchon, Updike, Donleavy,
Salinger, Barthelme, Barth, Nabokov, Tolstoy, New York
City, existentialism, and professors who write fiction are
all briefly noted, as is Gardner's praise of Melville,
James, Chaucer, Dante, Homer, and Shakespeare. Gardner
hopes that his own fiction, reviews, and the forthcoming
"Moral Fiction" [sic] serve to clarify what good art really
is. Having perfected the biggest bag of tricks of any
writer, he now wants to write the most important novel of
our time. "I spent a lot of time evading the dark center
of things by, usually, technical tricks." Signalling this
change is Gardner's shifting to the subdued style of his
recent stories, "Redemption" and "Stillness." The former
is based on an actual event--the accidental death of
Gardner's younger brother, Gilbert. Writing the story has
freed him of his sense of guilt.

81 Abernathy, Russell. "Religion and Art: 'About the Same
   Business.'" Macon News, 18 November 1977, p. B1.
   American artists, writers and musicians have no sense of
cultural tradition; this situation can result in the genius
of a Stevie Wonder, but more often it leads to merely innovative trash. Life imitates popular art, which is itself
an imitation of serious art. Religion and art are both
concerned with behavior--religion with the general rule,
art with the particular case. The theologian turns a
religious ideal into a narrow, easy to follow rule; the
literary critic works in a similar fashion, turning the
writer's intuitions into the critic's precepts. In teach-

ing people to read more carefully, the critic performs a useful service. Every reader knows Macbeth is wrong, but, unless he has the critic's help, he probably does not recognize the play's imagery or that Macbeth's mistake is his atheism.

82 Trotter, Herman. "Novelist John Gardner: Life is Tragic and Joyful." Buffalo Evening News, 25 December 1977, pp. G2-G3. Gardner does not believe he has evaded "the dark center of things" (see interview with Henry Allen, 6 November 1977) nor that the center is dark; rather it is a mysterious combination of "tragic and joyful possibilities." The "resurrection of people who have lost touch with their feelings and the realities of life" and "the difficulty of holding onto [sic] one's youthful idealism" are the major concerns in his fiction. As he demonstrates in "John Napper Sailing Through the Universe," a "true story," the artist must create visions which affirm and even improve life. The signs of the true artist are compassion, interest in discovery, mastery of technique, and dedication to his art. Not yet a great writer, Gardner says he has the potential to be one. (He cites Charles Johnson as another writer of great promise.) His aim in each of his novels is to bring people to a greater understanding of each other. NM, for example, begun when he was nineteen, was an attempt to make the "apple-knockers" of upstate New York understandable and likable to a young Jewish girl from New York City whom he knew. Clumly, in SD, is at first a bigot who by the end of the novel becomes "a real fictional hero" comparable to Achilles or Hamlet.

83 Sklar, Dusty. "Money--Or Your Life?" Bookviews, 1 (March 1978), 22-25. Gardner, who believes there is no idea so difficult it cannot be explained to a child, sees himself as a middlebrow writer. His editor at Knopf suggests only those changes involving the aesthetic integrity of his work, never the commercial possibilities. Res and the first edition of Barth's The End of the Road were both heavily edited but only in ways their editors thought would improve them as art. Gardner likes teaching--the students, the careful study of literature, and the break from writing--and strenuously objects to the "arrogance" of academic fiction: "I would never be consciously difficult. I hate Ezra Pound. I'm bored to tears by 'Finnegan's [sic] Wake.'"

84 Biederman, Patricia Ward. "Nostalgia is Factor As UB Woos Gardner for Famous Writer Slot." Buffalo Courier-Express, 10 March 1978, p. 9.

In Buffalo, in connection with a possible faculty appointment at the University of Buffalo, Gardner fondly recalls the Buffalo of his youth but finds the new university campus "an ugly place." Turning to his own work, he says his novels are not without their faults, but as a writer "You keep waiting for the book that's coming." Currently he has in-progress four novels and a "how-to-write-fiction" book in which he argues that existentialism has had a negative effect on literature. Gardner used to think out his novels during late-night walks; lately he has given up the walks in favor of oil-painting. About his frenetic pace, the interviewer speculates that Gardner's recent illness or his approaching middle-age may be the cause.

85 Sternésky, Gerard. "John Gardner: 'Fiction Needs Characterization.'" Spectrum (SUNY-Buffalo), 28 (17 March 1978), 11, 16.

Gardner, who is currently being considered for an endowed chair at SUNY-Buffalo, read from his novel-in-progress (originally called "Shadows" and tentatively changed to "Crane") at the Albright-Knox Art Gallery on 9 March 1978. According to Gardner, "The book asks what do you do when you can't protect your loved ones?" A "slow" writer but an energetic reader, he noted that "Part of everything I do is parody," and in "Crane" he is parodying Ross MacDonald. The following day he read from "The Art of Fiction," also in-progress, at the University of Buffalo. Referring both to bulk and traditional approach, he mentioned his interest "in a kind of dinosaur fiction." The "dream" good fiction should create can be vitiated in three ways: by "sentimentality," which asks for effect without giving due cause," by "frigidity" which "happens when a reader takes a scene more seriously than the writer does," and by "manneristic writing" in which the writer's cleverness is more important than the story.

86 Harvey, Marshall L. "Where Philosophy and Fiction Meet: An Interview with John Gardner." Chicago Review, 29, iv (1978), 73-87.

Writing is "basically" philosophical in that it is a way of testing ideas, of seeing the world in new ways (thus, Gardner's "genre-jumping"); chiefly, fiction is concerned with intuition rather than reason. Gardner agrees for the most part with the philosophy of Whitehead and has a "love-hate" attitude towards Sartre. At length, he comments on NM (it is a pastoral novel only in a limited

sense; the Goat Lady serves as a symbolic contrast with
Henry), KI (Gardner's "study in aesthetics," it is "about
literary form as a vehicle of vision"), OL (which concerns
the use of models by people), WA ("a mean novel in some ways")
and ISM (it does what Bettelheim says all fairy tales do).
Gardner's current intrests include writing radio plays
and "breaking up the art establishment." Only recently
has he discovered (in reading a thesis by Byron Hoot
[unlocated]) that he tends to repeat specific ideas from
novel to novel, sometimes in exactly the same words. He
would not, however, consider revising already published work.

87   Natov, Roni, and Geraldine DeLuca. "An Interview with John
     Gardner." The Lion and the Unicorn, 2 (Spring 1978),
     114-36.
     Gardner started writing children's stories as Christmas
presents for his own children. After reading Bruno
Bettelheim he began "writing to issues," though never in a
way which would lead to "simplistic" truths. In general
his stories are aimed at "older kids" already familiar with
fairy tales. "The Griffin and the Wise Old Philosopher,"
for example, is "basically a joke" involving Heisenberg's
uncertainty principle. The simplicity of the fairy tale
form appeals to Gardner; his own tales are modernized,
heavily detailed, and peopled with "cunning" middle-
class characters who learn to abandon their "nice clear
codes." Speaking of his other works, he points out that
G grew out of his interpretation of the Beowulf-monster
as "a cosmic principle of intellectual disorder," a view
he then developed partly in terms of Sartre's Being and
Nothingness. "Among other things," he adds, G is about
heroism. In OL, Sally is "the most interesting character and James merely "a stereotype"; his use of an inside
novel in OL (and in ISM) is not successful. More broadly,
Gardner notes that ninety percent of each of his novels
is comprised of supportive material, which often develops
in surprising ways. After he became bored with The Smugglers, the invention of Pearl renewed his interest and
gave him a reason to continue writing. In the first version
of SD (about a murder in a monastery), Clumly is a minor
character. And in his novel-in-progress about an alcoholic
detective, the focus has shifted to a young girl. What
he stresses in his fiction is the need for a balanced view
of human dignity. The stories argue against existentialism
and imply that "we have a history and history moves us,"
that "most human life is not a crisis," and that true
virtues are those which "work socially." Critical of the
plotlessness, coldheartedness, and frequent use of unreliable

narrators (as opposed to those who are merely befuddled)
in contemporary fiction, Gardner does speak approvingly
of Fowles, Toni Morrison, and the recent work of Donald
Barthelme.

88 Spilka, Mark, ed. "Character as a Lost Cause." Novel, 11
(Spring 1978), 212-13.
Commenting from the floor during a panel discussion on
character in fiction held at Brown University, April 1977,
Gardner explains the contemporary preference for dropping
character as a reaction against that realism which formed
the mainstream of American literature when Gass, Gardner,
Hawkes, Elkin, and Sukenick were beginning to write fiction.
Others, such as Bellow and Gaddis, use characters as "platforms of reformation." (Gardner's remarks are briefly re-
ferred to on pp. 214, 216.)

89 Dell, Twyla. "Dickey, Gardner; 'Impromptu Trialogue.'"
Broadside (George Mason University), 21 (27 March 1978),
15-16.
Speaking to James Dickey's writing class at George Mason
University, Gardner cites his "deep down inferiority" as
his imaginative wellspring. He objects to three kinds of
writing: "sentimental" (striving for effect without showing
sufficient cause), "frigid" (lack of concern for characters),
and "mannered" (attention is diverted from subject to style,
as in Faulkner's "The Bear"). Gardner is, in the words of
his close friend Dickey, "one of the most profound scholars
I know."

90 John Gardner: A Defense Against Madness. Produced and
directed by Richard O. Moore. The Originals: The Writer
in America, PBS, 3 April 1978 (produced in 1975).
Each of Gardner's novels deals with a particular--though
not necessarily philosophical--problem and concerns some
basic dichotomy, such as law and order/rebellion. SD
concerns the breakdown of American civilization and the
implications of Sartre's existentialism, which "is
essentially paranoid ... loveless ... faithless... [and]
egotistic." Although his novels are bleak, because
experience inevitably leads to a loss of faith, there is
always the possibility of love, e.g., Clumly's and Peeker's.
In JM "love is conspicuous by its absence," and in G even
the monster finally learns to love after resisting it for
so long. Gardner can identify with Grendel because he knows
the monster is wrong and why he is wrong. It is usually
more interesting to write about characters like Grendel

than those, like Chandler in Res, who already have the
right answers. In general there are three kinds of
characters in Gardner's fiction: those that "have given
in to the emotional war that is in everybody"--the
monsters (nihilists); the human beings; and the clowns,
who become monsters when they fail to become human. Henry
Soames is human because he does what he knows is right; he
holds in the monstrous emotions that are contained in his
monstrous body. That no man can win by his own efforts
alone--the doctrine of grace--is what Gardner has re-
tained from his Presbyterian upbringing. Concerning his
writing habits, Gardner says he writes whenever he can
and completes most of the work of composition during a
walking stage, telling himself the story over and over
until it is real in his mind; only then does he write it
down and begin to revise. Writers tell a very complicated
kind of truth: that "no decisions are possible because all
sides have some truth in them"; this is the truth we all
know "but can't afford to know." In places such as New
York and San Francisco, writers lose sight of the timeless
truths and concern themselves with the ephemeral. But in
southern Illinois (and the western New York of Gardner's
childhood), life is less complicated; as a result the
writer can devote himself to his complicated art. The good
teacher of creative writing should strive to help his
students to perfect their own styles. At the University
of Iowa Gardner wrote privately in order to avoid imitating
the work of the workshop faculty. (Gardner reads excerpts
from G, "The Ravages of Spring," JM, and "John Napper Sailing Through the Universe.")

91 Greenberger, R. E. "A Night with John Gardner: A Private
Eye and a Heroine Called Elaine." Pipe Dream (SUNY-
Binghamton), 7 April 1978, p. 17.
    "Shadows" has been in-progress for fifteen years and is,
like Gardner's other works, parodic. His detective is an
erudite alcoholic. The heroine does not appear in the
first 100 pages. (Greenberger adds that even in this parody,
Gardner's concern for his characters is strong; the novel
still requires further polishing and condensing , however.)

92 Prescott, Peter S. "Theft or 'Paraphrase'?" Newsweek, 91
(10 April 1978), pp. 92, 93B, 94.
    In a review published in the journal Speculum, Sumner
Ferris has pointed out Gardner's extensive and unacknowledged borrowings in LTC. Gardner, noting that Ferris does
not accuse him of plagiarism, defends his method as that of

a "popularizer" who is trying "to make...history come alive."
(See also Cacavas, "Gardner accused of foul play," Spectrum,
14 April 1978, and Gardner's interview with Dick Cavett,
16 May 1978.)

93   Fuller, Edmund. "A Novelist Calls for Morality in Our Art."
     Wall Street Journal, 21 April 1978, p. 17.
     Gardner grew up in a Presbyterian family, his father a
     "superb" and eloquent lay preacher. Although there are
     religious overtones to OMF, Gardner views religion as ethno-
     centric and "conservative," whereas art, a "hunting for real
     values," is universal and "radical." Among today's writers,
     Gardner considers himself "one of the best of a very
     mediocre crowd." He is optimistic about the future of
     fiction thanks to "a new generation of writers" who are not
     concerned with irrealism or nihilism but instead with the
     moral fiction Gardner espouses. (See also the annotation
     for this entry listed under "Reviews" of OMF.)

94   Howse, John. "Gardner's Paper Gives Insight into Fictional
     Process." East Tennessean (East Tennesee State University),
     21 April 1978, p. 6.
     A story's conflict can be resolved either with the
     character repeating his mistakes or with the affirmation
     of some universal value. (Much of the lecture, which
     Gardner read from a prepared text and which Howze criticized
     as "tedious," concerned a possible reworking of the Iliad.)
     According to Gardner, "wordless knowledge is the truth great
     fiction seeks out."

95   Moriarty, Elizabeth. "John Gardner: Good Fiction Sets
     Off a Dream." Johnson City (Tenn.) Press-Chronicle, 22
     April 1978, p. 3.
     Gardner likes most people he meets and usually tries to
     imagine the lives of his new acquaintances. He wrote JM
     in place of "Epic Conversation," a planned study of epic
     poetry. He believes there are no great contemporary
     American fiction writers. The major flaws of "mainstream"
     fiction are insufficient authorial interest in character
     ("frigidity"), unprepared-for effects ("sentimentalism"),
     and the intrusion of the author's personality or ideas
     into the fiction ("mannerism," to which Faulkner was
     sometimes prone). Good fiction creates a dream in the
     reader's mind; the focus is on character, supported by
     plot and setting. Gardner develops his characters intui-
     tively. During first revision, he adds details to deepen
     characterization and then later works to delete inexact
     lines.

96 Tyler, Ralph. "John Gardner: The Novelist-Critic Finds
   Most of Today's Fiction Puny." Bookviews, 1 (May 1978),
   6-9.
   OMF was begun in 1965 when it was unfashionable to attack
   Sartre. (Specifically, Gardner objects to Sartre's denial
   of history.) Gardner did not write it in anger and expects
   that the best of his fellow writers will react to it
   "intelligently." He wrote his forthcoming "book on how to
   write creatively" while recovering from surgery. Claiming
   that "mere intellectual entertainment" is not "serious art,"
   Gardner says that telling himself stories--not abstract
   reasoning--is his way of thinking out important questions
   and exploring implications. OL exemplifies this process:
   its inside-novel is "a model of how not to write.... It
   gives you clues how to read the real novel." Gardner
   denies that his sense of values derives from his rural
   upbringing. Briefly he describes his work habits (working
   slowly and on several novels concurrently), his other
   current interests (possibly writing for television and
   film, a radio talk show on the arts, and operas), and,
   noting that there are no truly first-rank Twentieth
   Century American novelists, cites those contemporary writers
   he most admires: Irving, Davenport, Cheever, Calvino, and
   Fowles.

97 Nugent, Tom. "Two Literary Lions Tangle." Baltimore Sun,
   2 May 1978, pp. B1, B6.
   Speaking at the invitation of program director John Barth
   to the Johns Hopkins Writing Seminars, Gardner distinguished
   between "primary fiction," which "analyzes the way things
   are in the world," and "secondary," which is "fiction that
   talks about fiction." The latter is useful in that it
   exposes artifice and preconceptions and thus forces the
   primary writer to become more inventive and penetrating.
   Barth, noting that the primary artist too writes "in the
   context of his eminent predecession," said Gardner was
   obscuring the issue since he was doing little more than
   talking about good fiction and bad. (For Barth's reply to
   Nugent's article and to OMF, see his letter to the editor,
   Baltimore Sun, 6 May 1978, p. A14.)

98 The Dick Cavett Show. Public Broadcasting System, 16
   May 1978.
   "Fiction writers have lost faith in fiction"--this is the
   premise of OMF, a work Gardner began in 1965. Since art
   and society influence each other--"they chase each other's
   tails"--the keynote in both today is despair. What fiction

should do is test values and embody its themes in believable
characters. Vonnegut's "cartoons" may be "wonderful" but
they are nonetheless a minor form of art. (In Western
culture, the epic forms the main literary tradition.) In
his own writing Gardner begins with the story clearly in
mind. Because his novels tend to read "slow," he
"jazz[es] them up with cartoon stuff." Most reviews are
not helpful to the writer and some can be harmful. One
reviewer of JM was so antagonistic that for a time Gardner
was unable to write, and another reviewer, Peter S.
Prescott, "hates me" and in his 10 April 1978 Newsweek
article misrepresented Gardner's response to Summer Ferris's
Speculum review of LTC.

99 Laskin, Daniel. "Challenging the Literary Naysayers."
Horizon, 21 (July 1978), 32-36.
    The wellsprings of Gardner's writing are "the Western
intellectual tradition" and, in his choice of genres, "the
trash tradition." His fiction is devoted to "keeping the
kid alive," i.e., the wholeness of the child, "the noble
self." Contemporary fiction, on the other hand, tries "to
make us comfortable with our betrayals"; its ironic detachment is characteristic of our age's cultural "adolescence."
OMF is intended for those readers who find such fiction
disappointing or who have been misled by the academic
critics into thinking that a "literary sideshow" (e.g.,
the fiction of Donald Barthelme) is actually "the Big
Tent" of true art. Of his own novel, SD, Gardner says
that the "large overtones" and "spiritual implications"
make it his "Big Fiction." In writing it he discovered "a
governing metaphysical system" he could believe in and then
pursue individual aspects of in his works. Currently he
is writing a novel which will be "a summary of everything
I've done, a recapitulation"; it will be the last of his
complicated philosophical fictions. Also in progress is
"The Art of Fiction" in which he explores the differences
between "primary" and "secondary" literature. As a
teacher of creative writing he will devote himself to
helping his students "shorten the time of apprenticeship."
(See also the annotation for this entry listed under
"Works About.")

100 McCullough, David W. "Eye on Books." Book-of-the-Month
Club News, August 1978, p. 16. Rpt. in People, Books &
Book People (New York: Harmony Books, 1981).
    "My position [in OMF] is not Christian. It's simpler than
that. Art. like medicine, should support what's healthy.

It shouldn't support despair," something New York City
writers seem unwilling to understand. Today's popular
writers "are head and shoulders above the serious writers,"
who, in Gardner's view, have been trivializing literature.
True art requires characterization, "ruminating" (which
Gardner does on late night walks), and "passionate affirmation without simplifying." (See also the annotation
for this entry listed under reviews of OMF.

101 Rutherford, Glenn. "John Gardner: A Writer Who Knows His
Craft." Louisville Courier-Journal, 15 September 1978,
p. E5. In edition 6 of the Courier-Journal, distributed
in Indiana, the interview was titled "John Gardner
Discusses What's Write with the World" and appeared on
p. B1.
Gardner, who calls himself a "fifth-rate, first-class
writer," says there are two classes of good literature:
works that are elegantly crafted and works such as the
Iliad, Anna Karenina, Moby-Dick, and "Bartleby the
Scrivener" that have a pronounced effect on the world.
In his own writing, Gardner composes for long, continuous
periods. Once while working on NM for three straight days,
he began hallucinating, a method that produces good fiction
but that he would not recommend. He also likes to put a
story aside for a time in order to return to it afresh.
He advises teachers in his audience at Indiana University
Southeast to encourage their students to read intensively
and to share ideas "until we blossom into something we're
proud of."

102 Allen, Bill. "His 'Vivid Dream' May Well Put You to Sleep."
Dallas Times Herald, 13 November 1978, pp. C1, C8.
At the Southern Methodist University Literary Festival,
Gardner read two of his stories: "The Literary Horror,"
written to "improve" the literary theories of William Gass,
and "Amarand." (Allen judges the former "inventive" but
"lacking character and life, forced in humor," soporific
and superficial. The latter story, although more realistic,
is "boring" and loosely written.) Although Bellow,
Vonnegut, Updike, and Mailer were criticized in OMF,
Gardner does like their work; Coover's fiction, however,
is "evil-spirited" and "anal compulsive."

103 Sinkler, Rebecca. "One Literary Giant, One Nasty Little
Dwarf." Today: The (Philadelphia) Inquirer Magazine, 17
December 1978, p. 6.
Opera and the novel are entirely different literary forms.
The former is "mythic" and should deal with the fantastic

and the familiar "old stories." With the story already
established the librettist can then concentrate on character.
Rumplestiltskin, like fairy tales, is interesting because
it is ambivalent as to what is fair; also, it frightens
and at the same time delights. Such art entertains and
improves its audience, says Gardner, who "looks more like
a village storyteller" than the brooding figure normally
associated with the modern artist.

104 Peyton, Terry. WUHY-FM (Philadelphia), 28 December 1978.*
   Gardner and Joseph Baber were interviewed during an
   intermission in the Opera Company of Philadelphia performance
   of Rumpelstiltskin. (Cited by Harry Harris, Philadelphia
   Inquirer, 25 December 1978, p. 9E.)

105 Christian, Ed. "Interview with John Gardner." New York
   Arts Journal, no. 14 (1979), 17-19.
   Excerpted from "An Interview with John Gardner" (1981).

106 Renwick, Joyce, and Howard Smith. "An Interview with John
   Gardner." Gargoyle, no. 11 (1979), 5-7.
   Revised for John Gardner: An Interview (1980).

107 Basler, George. "SUNY's Starting to Shine in Creative
   Writing--Gardner." Binghamton Press, 5 February 1979.
   Also published under the title "John Gardner sees a bright
   light for writing at SUNY" in Binghamton Sun-Bulletin,
   5 February 1979.
   Speaking at the Temple Concord in Binghamton, Gardner
   said that good fiction creates for us "a vivid and continuous dream" and forces us "to face up to things we can't
   face up to ourselves." Fiction must be honest and should
   be moral; it must support life rather than death. Revision
   is absolutely necessary. Because writing also depends on
   the writer's entering a dream state, writers often turn
   to drugs or alcohol either to enter this state or to come
   away from it. Currently Gardner is writing a novel and
   a screenplay (he has written three others, including one
   for Jane Fonda and Vanessa Redgrave), and is devoting much
   of his time to making the writing program at SUNY-Binghamton
   the best in the world. Gardner believes that writing, like
   painting and music, can be taught; students can learn not
   to make mistakes and in this way will be able to "release
   their genius."

108 LeClair, Thomas. "William Gass and John Gardner: A Debate
   on Fiction." New Republic, 180 (10 March 1979), 25, 28-33.

For Gardner, "Fiction is an enormously complicated language," the purpose of which is communication. Acknowledging that the creation of a beautiful object (fiction, for example) is "an affirmation of a kind," Gardner adds that fiction should chiefly be concerned with affirming the "true and good." To do this the writer must, by careful plotting, create "a vivid and continuous dream" in the reader's mind. In making fictional order out of life's chaos, the writer attempts to "understand" and "control" aspects of his own personality. Thus character is not, as Gass claims, merely "a linguistic location in a text" but "an apparition in the writer's mind" which, because fiction is both resonant and referential, requires the reader's empathetic response. Gass's own fiction is, in Gardner's judgement, mere "fiddling around," a waste of genius. In reply, Gass says that Gardner's views no longer apply; modern and contemporary fiction requires the reader's attending to page and line, not plot and character. Gardner, on the other hand, believes that the sophisticated academic reader is perhaps unable to see, in a simple fairy tale, for example, the obvious moral content. (Excerpted without attribution in New York Times Magazine, 8 July 1979, p.15; attributed 12 August 1979, p. 62.)

109 Ferguson, Paul F., John R. Maier, Frank McConnell, and Sara Matthiessen. "John Gardner: The Art of Fiction LXXII." Paris Review, 21 (Spring 1979), 36-74.
    Gardner eschews realism and is a philsophical novelist only in a limited sense. His chief interests in writing fiction are the dramatization of character and human values and the creation of "a feast of the senses" (including the imagination) of the reader. Unlike the academic fiction of such writers as Joyce and Updike, where narrative events are of little importance, Gardner maintains that fiction should be carefully plotted, entertaining, "overt," and should deal with what Aristotle termed energeia. Fiction should create a dream in the reader's mind--fine style need not interfere with this--and, without becoming didactic, should provide, as the Shaper does in G, a vision "worth pursuing." Critics should concern themselves with this vision, that is, with distinguishing true art from that which is either immoral or trivial. Of his own fiction Gardner comments on his nearly photographic memory and his "one real skill," "chasing implications to the wall." His fiction is autobiographical but not recognizably so (e.g., the conflict between order and anarchy characterizes both the fiction and the author). He notes that his "oral" style derives from his upbringing (in particular, his

father, early writings, and life on a farm are discussed)
and that his settings tend to be unobtrusively symbolic
(Batavia, for example, symbolizes a civilization's decline). He also mentions that his teaching has affected
his writing in three ways: it has provided him with source
material, has given him a sense of his audience, and has
been a humbling experience in that he has discovered how
many good student writers there are. (Includes a facsimile
manuscript page from Vlemk.)

110 Harkness, James. "Interview: John Gardner." The News
(SUNY), April 1979, Forum sec., pp. 1-2, 7-8.
Writing can be taught providing the teacher knows what
he is doing and is himself a published writer. Although
Gardner has not found it difficult to adjust to success,
he did find it difficult to get published at all early in
his career. His break came when William Gass mentioned
Gardner's name to editor David Segal. (Gardner also
mentions the sudden acceptance of non-realistic literature
following the success of the Beatles.) Today is an
especially good time for writers, owing to the number and
quality of the little magazines, which are far superior
to slick publications such as the New Yorker. Popular
fiction has its part to play as well; it helps subsidize
publication of serious work and can be, as in the case of
John Jakes's novels, entertainment of a high order. NM
was begun when he was nineteen; it is not the simple love
story he intended because he failed to strip away all of
the tricks he had included. Gardner does not feel that
the philosophy in his fictions is intrusive; rather, it
is part of the action. Whether or not the reader
recognizes the quotation from Sartre at the end of "The
Warden" is not important, for the story can be understood
emotionally as well as intellectually. In Gardner's view,
"morality has no conventions," but this does not mean that
Sartre's existentialism is therefore correct, for Gardner,
unlike Sartre, believes there is something that makes us
human and that our job is to find out what this is.
(Gardner acknowledges Sartre as a fine stylist and
admits that it is Sartre's early works of which he is
critical.) According to Gardner, Gass is "a profoundly
moral person" who, though he does not write immoral books,
does argue against the relevance of morality in art.
Gardner argues for moral criticism, which judges a work
according to the standards of truth and beauty; thus, to
judge Celine, as writer, a moral failure is to judge him
an aesthetic failure as well.

111 Summers, Patty, and Steven Riddle, "A Look at GMU's
    Writing Conference." Phoebe (George Mason University),
    8 (April 1979), 81-95.
    (Gardner's remarks are quoted in two of the article's
    subsections, "Symposium on Fiction," pp. 81-83, and
    "Conversation with John Gardner," pp. 83-85, and para-
    phrased in a third, "Integration of Genres," p. 85. The
    writing conference was held in January 1979; the other
    participants were Liz Rosenberg, Susan Shreve, Katherine
    Paterson, Victoria Rue, Honor Moore, Peter Klappert,
    Denise Levertov, Daniel Mark Epstein, Kirkpatrick Sale,
    Susan Wood, William McPherson, and Frank Conroy.) The
    writer's job is to create "a vivid and continuous dream
    in the reader's mind." To achieve this dream, he must
    establish his own narrative voice; to maintain it, he
    must not make any distracting slips in the mechanics of
    writing. Characters should not be confined to reality and
    should be developed by means of plot. Whereas "life is
    complicated, fiction is not." The writer, if he is to
    avoid mannered writing, keeps himself out of his fiction.
    He searches out "the logic of the story," i.e., what can
    be dramatized and what can be told. Effective writing
    teachers are those who understand and can articulate its
    techniques; genius cannot be taught. Before his own
    students begin to write stories, Gardner has them complete
    specific exercises. Dissatisfaction with the writing work-
    shop at the University of Iowa, the presence of "a great
    teacher," and similarities between Chaucer's poetry and
    Disney's cartoons are the reasons Gardner switched from
    the workshop to Chaucer. Thanks to his study of Anglo-
    Saxon and medieval literature, Gardner has discovered a
    variety of non-novelistic forms and techniques which he
    has adapted to his fiction: JM and Chaucer's "imitation
    epic" Troylus and Cryseyde; SD and Malory; G and Beowulf
    (and Sartre). It is this familiarity with "an ancient
    tradition" which distinguishes Gardner from such writers
    as Barth and Barthelme, who know contemporary fiction
    only.

112 Adelman, Beth. "Fiction's Improved Little with Time,
    Gardner Says." Binghamton Press [or Sun-Bulletin?], 23
    April 1979.
    Most writing today is bad, and the current interest in
    writing "doesn't mean anything for the serious writer."
    His students at SUNY-Binghamton are so talented that once
    he has taught them the "tricks" he knows, they become his
    equals; "That's how I decided to write in a way so
    complicated no one could do it because it was silly."

Gardner judges that some of his works are "great,"
others "mediocre," and the rest "bad." "Most of it is
luck." He took up the study of medieval literature because
he was a pacifist and did not want to fight in Korea.
Adelman reports that Gardner read "his latest short story,
'Rude Heads That Stare Asquint,'" at the Vestal Public
Library the week before, weaving "a tale of suspicion and
understanding between a writer and a deformed boy."

113 Harris, Daisy. "'Odd Couple' of One Mind on Writing."
Dayton Daily News, 27 April 1979, sec. 3, p. 31.
    Gardner and John Jakes, the principal speakers at the
Sinclair Community College Writers Workshop, spoke approvingly of each other's work. Jakes noted Gardner's clarity,
and Gardner cited Jakes's mastery of history and their
shared "visionary approach." All writing, Gardner claimed,
can be divided into two classes: the good, which draws the
reader in, and the bad, which distracts the reader.
"Everything in fiction exists for the character."

114 Krishner, Trudy. "Jakes and Gardner: 'We're Like Ice Cream
and Beefsteak,' Sometimes You Need One, Sometimes the Other."
Dayton Journal Herald, 28 April 1979, p. 33.
    Gardner and John Jakes, participants at the Sinclair Com-
munity College Writers Workshop, praised each other's work.
LTC is, Jakes said, history as it "was meant to be written."
Gardner cited Jakes's mastery of history and pointed to
their "simply celebrating different aspects of life"
(Krisher's title quotes Gardner). According to Gardner,
writing is "an escape from reality that turns you back to
reality rejuvenated"; it should produce "a vivid and
continuous dream in the reader's mind." Gardner advised
young writers to develop a single idea in each of their
works and to choose characters with "a fundamental idea
of how to get by in the world." Highly critical of commercial publishers (they publish such escapist works as
McKuen's poetry), he suggested the alternative of self-
publication and he reminded his audience to "be dependent
on your own integrity."

115 Grills, Robert. "Contemporary Author Emphasizes Mastery."
UT (University of Tennessee) Daily Beacon, 10 May 1979,
pp. 1, 6.
    Writing demands mastery and, like the drawing of a char-
coal sketch, revision. Although the writer must become
personally involved in his work, at times he must detach
himself and ask "Is that really true?" Gardner, visiting
Joseph Wood Krutch Lecturer, likens his own style to that
of a jazz musician: both work from an established form.

116 Renwick, Joyce, and Howard Smith. "An Interview with
     John Gardner." Lone Star Book Review, 1 (June 1979),
     5, 10.
       Excerpted from John Gardner: An Interview (1980).

117 Renwick, Joyce, and Howard Smith. "Last of the Radio Heroes:
     Novelist John Gardner Crusades for the High Art of Radio
     Drama." Horizon, 22 (July 1979), 67-68, 70-71.
       Excerpted from John Gardner: An Interview (1980).

118 Singular, Stephen. "The Sound and Fury Over Fiction."
     New York Times Magazine, 8 July 1979, pp. 12-15, 34-36,
     38-39.
       Gardner candidly discusses the break-up of his marriage
     (a clash of egos), the fifteen-year period he spent waiting
     to be published, his present idyllic life with Liz Rosen-
     berg, and the pressure he now feels to write following his
     bout with cancer. His teaching is time-consuming but a
     necessary duty: "Fiction is the only religion I've got."
     He briefly comments on Updike, Malumud, Mailer, Heller,
     and New Yorker fiction and reasserts his view that fiction
     must lead, must present "models of decent behavior." The
     remarks he made in OMF about great art always being af-
     firmative were, he now admits, not "quite sound." In the
     forthcoming "The Art of Fiction" he sharpens his point:
     by creating a vicarious experience for the reader, "great
     fiction ...helps us know what we believe, reenforces those
     qualities which are noblest in us, leads us to feel uneasy
     about our failings and limitations." Although he judges
     himself "a serious and careful philosophical novelist,"
     he acknowledges flaws in his novels. The reticence about
     sexual love so obvious in his fiction will be overcome in
     "Shadows," a novel-in-progress based in part on Liz
     Rosenberg. Whereas in previous novels Gardner was "learn-
     ing techniques," now he feels sufficiently established to
     go deep "down inside me" and just write "wonderful stories."
     (See the annotation for this entry listed under "Works
     About.")

119 Harvey, Marshall. "John Gardner: Considerations...."
     The Cresset, 42 (September 1979), 19-22.
       "Fiction should create heroic figures" and aim to
     discover "rules for behavior that will allow people to
     live in the world harmoniously." The writer should take
     risks but should also be aware that certain kinds of
     writing are better than others. In "The Old Men" Gardner
     tried to write a "satisfactory" novel but ended up saying

something he didn't really believe. He writes for "melody,"
ideas, and "vision." Because images play an important
part in his fiction, he tends to emphasize "physical details" and uses a cartoon technique in order to clarify
his characters (e.g., Clumly as a mole "burrowing into a
set of rules"). Several of his works (e.g., JM, WA, G,
and "The Ravages of Spring") have been partly composed in
dreams. Not a systematic reader, Gardner is interested
in philosophy, science, and Melville. He finds Celine
"brilliant" but "wrong-headed morally" and Hemingway un-
interesting. Much of his reading is devoted to gathering
background material for his fiction; he has had to read
up on computers for one novel-in-progress, "Shadows,"
and on psychohistory (which he doesn't like) for another,
"Rude Heads that Stare-squint." Asked about the bear in
OL, Gardner says he was drawing less on Faulkner than the
various myths in which the bear represents "the eternal
creature." To kill a bear is to separate oneself from
nature; by not shooting the bear at the end of the novel,
James Page reunites himself with his "emotional past."
The bear also is related to Ariah, but because it is a
symbol, or "feeling," its meaning cannot be entirely
specified. In general Gardner sees himself as a religious
writer concerned with "spiritual values," "individual ful-
fillment and social harmony."

120 Grey, Gene. "Writing Program His Dream." Binghamton
Press, 25 November 1979, pp. Cl, Cl4.
   Gardner is fully committed to making the writing program
at SUNY-Binghamton the nation's most selective. He plans
to establish a $1 million endowment, hire prominent
faculty, publicize the program, and increase the number
of students. A good writing program should develop student
talent in a verifiable way and should provide students
with a "support system," a community of writers and
teachers able to help the student market his work. In
Gardner's view, the reading public is "vast."

121 Forsman, Theresa. "The Novelist As Actor, Playwright,
Teacher." Binghamton Press [or Sun-Bulletin?], 25
November 1979, pp. Cl, C?.
   See annotation listed under "Works About."

122 Renwick, Joyce, and Howard Smith. John Gardner: An
Interview, New London Interviews #3. Dallas: New London
Press, 1980.
   Radio is "relatively inexpensive" and therefore superior
to television as a medium for high art--i.e., "something

that is totally entertaining" and which requires the total involvement (memory, imagination, emotions, and moral feelings) of the audience. Radio plays are not plays "simply read into microphones"; they are stories built "from the sound upward" (thus requiring close collaboration between writer and sound technician) and using sound "to create a vivid and continuous dream in the listener's mind." Since good radio plays, such as Barthelme's, need to be heard several times to be fully appreciated, they should be recorded for sale as well as aired. As Gardner says about his own "The Temptation Game" (winner of the Armstrong prize), "Your emotions understand it but your mind [doesn't at first]." Turning from his work for radio, Gardner notes that OMF was begun in 1964 but remained unpublished until his view became more widespread and his reputation established. It is intended for "people who love books" but find contemporary novels "boring, stupid, depressing, and shoddy." Although great fiction can be difficult (e.g., Joyce and Faulkner), the emphasis today on an academic fiction which can be taught rather than appreciated is wrong. In his own fiction Gardner develops an "emotional-intellectual world view." G concerns reason's denials and those affirmations that are necessary but can only be made on faith. The subject of KI is Gardner's "theory of art as a special kind of affirmation." JM deals with polarities, such as male-female, which are both basic and complementary. (Similarly used are Gardner's dragons, which symbolize "the creative-destructive principle" and evoke "the whole question of free will and determination.") Gardner revises his novels extensively--NM passed through twenty years of revision-- and is for most part satisfied with his published work. Art, in Gardner's view, involves the "interpenetration of the universal and the particular"; it teaches not by precept and reason but by the presentation of examples which are both persuasive and "thrilling." Fiction which deals with "manners" is better handled in the realistic mode, whereas that which concerns "morals" requires a fabulist treatment. Gardner works in both--even, as in NM, in a single work. Of his teaching Gardner says that he taught medieval literature because he loves it and because the teaching gave him the necessary time and finances to write his fiction. He teaches writing in order to help young writers and because his fiction is still not sufficiently remunerative. In teaching writing he emphasizes technique and exercises (not the pronouncements of OMF), commitment to excellence, the searching out of what fiction is, and the creation of that "vivid and continuous dream in the

reader's mind." Although he is a demanding and critical
teacher, he wants his students to believe ardently in
themselves as writers. (Briefly Gardner also notes differences in students enrolled in college writing courses
and those who attend Breadloaf.) Recently Gardner has
become interested in writing plays and scripts for television and film. He mentions that he finds it difficult to
write short stories (KI being comprised of "tales and fables
and weird forms"). Except for "The Art of Fiction" and
perhaps some reviews, he plans to write no more criticism.
He will concentrate on his novel "Shadows," which he likens
to Melville's Pierre: ". . . it's deep. The only question
is whether or not a person is sane to go on working on it."
Of other writers at the August 1978 Breadloaf workshop,
Gardner has special praise for Susan Shreve and Stanley
Elkin, "a genius and a pro" who is nonetheless "wrong" when,
in his fiction, he says that "love is an illusion."
(Excerpts from this interview appeared in Lone Star Book
Review, Horizon, and Gargoyle in 1979; wording occasionally
differs.)

123 Kakutani, Michiko. "Portrait of the Artist as a First
Novelist." New York Times Book Review, 8 June 1980, p. 39.
   "'I think this generation [of writers] is technically
far superior to the generation before it,' says John Gardner
.... 'Never before in history have we seen so many people
who are so good at what they do. The question that remains
is whether that technique is accompanied by a vision--a
vision that will endure.'"

124 Cryer, Dan. "John Gardner." L[ong] I[sland] Magazine
(Newsday), 22 June 1980, pp. 17-18, 30, 32-33, 35.
   Gardner is of two minds regarding literature: it is a
superfluous activity, a luxury; but it is also "wonderful"
in that it creates a captivating world in which the reader
feels entirely secure. Gardner writes for himself and, by
extension, for all readers like him. Because he is a
"trusting" person, his fiction is "accessible"; William
Gass, on the other hand, is an emotionally "guarded person"
who keeps his readers at a distance. Illustrations are
appropriate to Gardner's non-realistic works ("cartoon
realism"), such as NM, which was written over a twenty-year
period. Although he once hoped to make each of his novels
completely distinct, he now realizes that some repetition
is unavoidable. His favorite authors are Homer, Chaucer,
Shakespeare, the French playwrights, Tolstoi, Mann, Boll,
Melville, and especially Dickens, "because he's so much

50

like me, so brilliant and so stupid." Toni Morrison,
Charles Johnson, Ron Hansen, John Irving, and Maxine Hong
Kingston are among the best of today's many fine writers.
The fiction of Updike, Barth, and Philip Roth, however,
is marred by the contemporary emphasis on self-revelation
(as opposed to self-improvement based on careful revision).
OMF was a necessary but "misunderstood" book written to
distinguish "real art" from the realist middle-class novel
and the journalistic fiction of Mailer and Solzhenitsyn.
Bellow is "an interesting philosophical novelist," but his
work is not as immediately compelling as that of Joyce
Carol Oates. Although Gardner uses philosophy in his
fiction (MG, a novel-in-progress, concerns a philosopher
of aesthetics), he does not use it in order to make philosophical discoveries or to present an abstract argument.
FB (whose popularity in certain sections of the United
States baffles Gardner) is his most philosophical novel
and the one in which characters are only superficially
developed. Tolstoi's ideas on this novel's theme, good
and evil, interest Gardner "because they're so close to
mine and so false." Concerning his extensive literary
borrowings from writers such as Gass, Gardner likens his
works to "montages or collages" and calls the artist a
Nietzschean superman who is superior to society's prohibi-
tion against plagiarism. The artist's only responsibility
in this matter is that he transmute his "raw material,"
using it, as Joyce and Rauschenberg have done, in an
entirely new way. The artistic freedom Gardner took in
writing LTC may have been illegitimate, however, because
the laws of historical scholarship that he neglected are
quite different from the laws of art.

125 Sweeney, Louise. "John Gardner." Christian Science Monitor,
24 June 1980, sec. B, pp. 2-3, 11.
   The true artist loves books, emphasizes dialogue and
gestures rather than explanation, and is tolerant (bigoted
writers, such as Ayn Rand, repeat themselves endlessly).
Gardner, who became a medievalist because his fiction was
not being published, is firmly committed to the teaching
of writing (partly because so many writing teachers do
their students more harm than good) even though few of his
students have any real talent. Gardner's own work is
marked by careful planning and repeated revisions. For
his metaphysical mystery novel, "Shadows" (the title alludes to Plato's Republic), he has accumulated some
10,000 pages of notes. He has recently completed another
novel, "Nicholson's Ghost," with which neither he nor his
editor, Robert Gottlieb, is yet entirely pleased. Con-

cerning his writing habits, he notes that he works for
long hours and often late into the night; he prefers to
work on several projects concurrently in order to return
to his longer works with a fresh mind. Gardner, whose
friend and former colleague Edmund Epstein comments that
he is "constantly trying to explore his internal wilder-
ness" in an effort to understand himself more completely,
uses writing as a means to discover what he believes.
Examples of this process are the inside-novels in OL and
FB, a novel which suggests that although all men are
spiritual giants, in some the giant is transformed into
a monster. A religious writer, Gardner has "an absolute
profound sense of God in the world." He admires Tolstoi,
Melville, Oates and Austen (Emma is his favorite novel)
and cites his parents, who made literature an important
part of family life, as a major influence on his career.
His mother, for whom he has written a play, "Days of
Vengeance," speculates that the death of his younger
brother, Gilbert, may have led Gardner to live, in a
sense, two lives (thus his varied career and his immense
productivity). Gardner denies that he is the literary
hit-man described by Stephen Singular (see the 8 July
1979 interview). Concerning his two marriages, he says
the first was romantic but lacked fairness; the second is
more mature.

126 Grey, Gene. "John Gardner Novel Takes [...]." Binghamton
Press, 5 October 1980.
    Gardner's advice to Fred E. Bielenberg on adapting SD
for the stage was "to use what he could and throw out"
the rest. This Bielenberg did, eliminating characters
and entire sub-plots and creating a work that satisfies
Gardner, who is especially pleased with the set Bielenberg
designed. Even in its present form, the play, with its
cast of eighteen, would probably be too expensive to stage
professionally. Gardner, who has no interest in adapting
his own works, says the novel grew out of the social and
political situations of the 1960's and reflects his own
ambivalence about the period: "I felt it was worth getting
the word out for both sides." He chose Batavia for his
setting because of its small-town feel and the details he
could draw from his own background.

127 Burns, Alan. "John Gardner." In <u>The Imagination on Trial</u>:
     <u>British and American Writers Discuss Their Working Methods</u>.
     Ed. Alan Burns and Charles Sugnet. London and New York:
     Allison and Busby, 1981, pp. 40-50.
     <u>NM</u> was begun as a way of explaining western New York to
     a friend from New York City. Although the first draft was
     finished when Gardner was nineteen, the novel was not pub-
     lished until he was forty. During the revision what began
     as an imitation realist novel, a mask for Gardner's fabul-
     ation turned into a "gentler" work; the "foolishness" and
     triviality dropped out as Gardner became more interested in
     his characters and their situation. His characters begin
     as imitations of real people but suddenly come alive in
     their own right. This happened very quickly with Callie,
     with whom Gardner closely identified; similarly George
     Loomis began as a contrast with Henry but became more
     important and more developed as Gardner continued to write.
     Dreams are important to Gardner. <u>NM</u>, for example, concerns
     a dream he used to have about a mountain that seemed alive
     and that seemed alternately aware of and indifferent to
     Gardner. One of the stories in <u>KI</u> was a dream that Gardner
     had had, and the game of blind baseball in <u>Res</u> has an
     arresting dream-like quality. As a writer, Gardner utilize
     both his reason and his intuition. The "ability to be
     calmly critical" is, he says, his "most important faculty,"
     one which writers such as Elkin and Pynchon--both "geniuses
     lack; their works evoke a series of "brilliant images" but
     offer no climaxes. In fact, much of American fiction is
     well written but ultimately uninteresting because the
     writers are not concerned with the intuitive truth of their
     fictions. Gardner's own analytical nature derives from the
     Welsh singing and poetry contests of his youth where the
     competitiveness and criticism were directed towards one
     goal: achieving the best. (Gardner also notes that he
     uses his family as "a basic reference" for understanding
     the way people think and act.) His novel-in-progress,
     "Shadows," deals with the most fundamental human problem:
     what happens when you realize you can't save those you love

128 Tully, Jaqui. "Dialogues' Adaptation to Greet Novelist
     Gardner." <u>Arizona Daily Star</u>, 5 April 1981.
     In a telephone interview, Gardner, who will be visiting
     Tucson in a few days, spoke of John Bielenberg's dramatiza-
     tion of <u>SD</u>, which will be performed at the University of A
     zona, 6-12 April. Gardner was impressed by the play when
     it was first performed at SUNY-Binghamton. Although
     Bielenberg considers his work an adaptation, Gardner calls

it a "reproduction" in which several characters are combined and the focus is on a few key scenes. Gardner also
briefly discusses AL, "Shadows," which he has been working
on since 1974, MSS, which he hopes to have out by 1 May,
and the reading audience, which he feels is not reading
less.

129   Dudar, Helen. "Pen Names: The Written Confessions of John
Gardner." New York Daily News, 4 June 1981, p. M9.
Since he was eleven, Gardner has been haunted by "memory
flashes" of his brother's death; on the advice of a
psychiatrist he wrote about the experience and the result
of this "bibliotherapy" was "Redemption," a story that was
"extremely painful" to write. Gardner is now free of his
obsession and, following his marriage to L. M. Rosenberg,
of his need to make public appearances as a way of convincing himself he is loved. He also believes he has mel-
lowed since the publication of OMF. Although he does not
always reach the high standards he set for writers in that
book, he does so more often than some of his critics believe. His early works were often rejected by editors who
did not appreciate his "cartoon realism" (which has more
to do with Disney than with Isak Dinesen), and the New
Yorker continues to refuse his fiction (most recently
"Come on Back"). Gardner composes at night, the time
best-suited for the flow of dream images, but revises
during the day. He considers his teaching an aesthetic
obligation and has written a writing text called "The Art
of Fiction." Having successfully recovered from cancer
surgery, he has not become obsessed by death; life, he
says, is much more terrifying.

130   Mitcham, Judson, and William Richard. "An Interview with
John Gardner." New Orleans Review, 8 (Summer 1981), 124-
33.
Although Gardner agrees with Gene Lyons (Harper's, Feb.
1980) that he exudes a "vatic" air, he rejects Lyons' view
that writing cannot be taught (the mistaken romantic notion
of the artist as isolated genius) and points out that what
Lyons calls nepotism at Bread Loaf is a useful system in
which promising young writers are rewarded according to
merit. Gardner's early career proceeded much more slowly.
Writing against the tide of realism, he had completed four
novels before one was published. (It was William Gass,
whom Gardner had published in MSS, who mentioned Gardner's
name to his editor at New American Library, David Segal,
who in turn accepted Res.) Gardner also discusses the

reactions of certain writers to OMF--Elkin, Bellow, Mailer, Heller, Barth, Barthelme, and Updike--and identifies John Fowles' strength: brilliant dramatization of philosophical ideas, "convincing" characterization, strong plot, and style. Because Gardner writes about what he knows best, his fiction has very few black characters; he is nonetheless interested in the work of black writers Toni Morrison, Ishmael Reed, Charles Johnson, John McCluskey, Colleen McElroy, and Wesley Brown. There is also little sex in his novels, though Gardner, unlike Stephen Singular (New York Times Magazine, 8 July 1979), does not think this is a flaw. Asked about his review of Styron's Sophie's Choice, he says that in America evil, which derives from the feeling of being vulnerable, comes in two "styles": Southern-Gothic preoccupation with fallen grandeur and Northern repression. The "central antagonist" in his novels is death, and all his works until "Redemption" deal with guilt. Gardner's dislike of the romantic hero is one reason he writes so much for and about children and has joined the editorial staff of a new children's magazine. Good writers "express...the moral needs of their age"; great writers go beyond their age. Pynchon is "brilliant," "a great stunt man," but not a great writer. Some of Gardner's work fits his moral-fiction theory; FB does not. It is "my most immoral book...gloomy and gothic and funny in some of the wrong ways."

131   "Gardner Launches Magazine." Binghamton Sun-Bulletin, c. 18 September 1981.
      MSS is dedicated to the great writers and artists of the next generation and will publish the kinds of works most magazines "won't touch": long poems, plays, serial novels, etc. The work of young writers will gain a certain credibility by being published alongside the work of establishe figures; all works will be selected on the basis of the tastes of the editors (Gardner, Liz Rosenberg, and Ken Morrow). The magazine will be attractive, accessible, and entertaining, on the order of the old Saturday Evening Post. The first issue is currently available. (Slightly shorter versions of this item appeared as "Gardner Starts Magazine," Buffalo Courier-Express, 18 September 1981, p. A2, and "A Novelist and His MSS," New York Times, 19 September 1981, p. 15.)

132   Sachs, Sylvia. "Writing Should Be Upbeat, Novelist Says." Pittsburgh Press, 2 November 1981, p. Al.
      Speaking on moral fiction at Chatham College, Gardner said novelists can choose to affirm life or to deny it.

There are outlets for good fiction today, especially the
little magazines and university presses. Good instructors
can actually teach creativity and help student writers
correct their mistakes. Although television is addictive,
especially to people who have boring jobs, television
poses no threat to writers.

133 Winther, Per. "An Interview with John Gardner." English
Studies, 62 (December 1981), 509-24.
      Gardner has been especially interested in existential
philosophy because, he feels, most Americans are by their
nature existentialists. Recently he has been considering
Darwinism in a political-ethical sense--democracy and
goodness are more fit to survive than tyranny and evil--
which is what FB is about. Despite this optimistic view
and his Christian upbringing, Gardner's vision is essentially tragic. Among the early influences on his
writing, Gardner mentions Scott, Longfellow, the Bible,
and the Hardy Boys but not Chaucer, who was more a
kindred spirit than an influence. Metafictional techniques
are not inherently bad, though they can be misused as sub-
stitutes for thought and feeling or used imperfectly as
in "The King's Indian," where Gardner enters the story in
the guise of his persona, "John Gardner." In G, which
Gardner wrote before learning the Anglo-Saxon technique
of interlacing, the Shaper is "a noble hack" and Grendel
"the higher kind of poet." SD is "an architectonic novel"
in which parallel plots are used to achieve resonance and
in which echoes are heard of Faulkner, Joyce, Dante,
Malory, and Tolstoi. JM is more opera than novel; the
characters are unreal, the form intensely artificial.
It, G, and "The King's Indian" are Gardner's three
favorite works. NM is a pastoral novel in that it dramatizes complex problems in simple terms. The Goat Lady
(based on an actual person) represents the goat for which
the shepherd Henry cannot be responsible. The inside-
novel in OL parodies all "stupid fiction" in a Marx
Brother's way, making the reader see and laugh at the
stupidity. Vlemk began as a short "happy tale" criticizing
the views of William Gass, but in writing it Gardner found
his own theory of moral fiction changing slightly. The
story also became too long to read aloud, and this caused
Gardner to write "Amram," retitled "Nimram," a shorter
work that essentially makes the same points. FB follows
the structure of The Scarlet Letter: novel preceded by a
long introduction. Freddy writes his book as "a kind
of biblio-therapy" and learns that the world is not as
dangerous and inhospitable as he had thought. This is
why he gives his book to Winesap, who has accidentally
proven himself a kind man.

134 Johnson, Jay. "Writer's Block: Printing Delays Literary
     Magazine." Binghamton Press, 13 December 1981.
     The second issue of MSS will appear in January 1982
     instead of December 1981. Of the 1000 copies of the
     first issue, published in September, all but 20 have been
     sold. Most of the authors are local, and the acceptance
     rate is one in thirty. Experimental and pornographic
     manuscripts, even those of high quality, will be automat-
     ically rejected.

135 Christian, Ed. "An Interview with John Gardner."
     Prairie Schooner, 54 (Winter 1981), 70-93.
     "A story is the most valuable thing in the world,"
     Gardner claims, though whether or not it stems from some
     personal pain he is not sure. His fiction is influenced
     by medieval literature, which he finds Disney-like. He
     defends the ending of Res saying that although Chandler's
     "attempt to turn death into life misfires horribly,"
     others, especially his wife and daughter, form a healing
     bond. Agathon's problem is his inability to transcend
     mockery and absurdity and to accept the power of love
     and affirmation. This novel, in part derived from Plutarch
     and about the Vietnam War, is a moral fiction, and Peeker
     is its hero. WA and G are tightly organized novels; the
     former, however, lacks the "bridge between the tight
     realism and the mythic cartoon simplicity," and the latter's
     ninth chapter is weak. NM is an episodic novel. JM grew
     out of two scholarly works Gardner had begun: a transla-
     tion of Apollonius Rhodius and a study of epics. Although
     the Smugglers section of OL was conceived as part of the
     larger novel, Gardner had once considered publishing it
     separately ("That really would have been terrible"). The
     bear symbol was also part of the original plan; the ending,
     like the endings of his other novels, was not. Gardner
     uses "an approach to death" backdrop in his fiction for
     dramatic effect. His recurrent prison metaphor suggests
     the prison of logic and man's unwillingness to have faith
     in love. Although his characters are often clowns ("a
     Walt Disney effect"), they are never caricatures. His
     novels invariably develop in complexity: Grendel, for
     example, became more human and James Page less sympathetic
     than originally planned. Once Gardner gets an idea for
     a novel, he immediately begins looking for "the hot
     issues in the conflict." Some of his ideas for stories
     derive from his reading: The Ordeal of Sparta led to
     three short stories and a book on aesthetics yielded four

new works. Lately Gardner has been reading less. His
most recent fiction is a long tale called "King Gustav,
Lars Joren, and the Devil." Although G and SD are experimental works, Gardner is generally critical of the
experimental trend, which he sees as part of that fear
of emotion and of taking strong stands that has plagued
Americans at least since the Vietnam War. He advises
young writers to portray emotion accurately, write about
what they feel is important, pretend that fiction does
influence its readers' lives, revise their work, and
publish early. Gardner's own revisions are numerous and
are based in part on how his work sounds when read aloud.
Turning to the subject of moral fiction, Gardner denies
the validity of situation ethics, claiming the true
measure of conduct is love. Great literature (as distinct from that which is bad or merely "good") must be
hopeful; conversely, a cynical or even a satirical work
can never be great literature. Gardner briefly discusses
Hardy, Beckett, Woolf, Fry, Thomas, Cary, Barth (who
"parades despair"), Hawkes (whose dream is genuine), and
Gass (whose best work creates a dream in the reader's
mind, though too often Gass allows his language to overwhelm his material). This "mannerism" is one of "the three
great sins of contemporary writing"; the others are
frigidity and sentimentality. Gardner does not view himself as a didactic novelist; rather, he explores moral
questions in order to arrive at moral values.

136 Reilly, Charlie. "A Conversation with John Gardner."
Classical and Modern Literature: A Quarterly, 1 (Winter
1981), 91-109.
   Gardner writes for readers like himself, like the
earnest, even desperate reader he was as a child and
young man. He will not compromise his art to achieve
popular success. Although he selects his illustrators,
he does not dictate what they will draw. In modern and
postmodern literature, the reader is enticed into a subjective world, whereas in Gardner's work, the reader,
wihout being distracted from the story, is constantly
aware of the book's reality, partly as a result of the
illustrations. His major subject is, as Geoffrey Wolff
has pointed out, the relationship between freedom and
order, but this does not mean that the fiction is
written to conform to the theory. True inventors of
artistic forms--Homer, Bach, and Strauss, for example--
always derive more from their inventions than do their
imitators. However, writing about modern life from

within a traditional form enables the writer to see his
world in a new, otherwise unavailable way. In writing
JM, Gardner used Apollonius until near the end, when he
re-read Euripides, "a master of soap opera," and for the
first time recognized his brilliance. He could not merely
borrow from Euripides; he had to adapt Euripides to the
epic form. Sketching the history of medieval translation,
Gardner says that JM is a translation in the same way that
Chaucer's Troilus and Cressida is: each preserves its
source and adapts it to a modern age. (Gardner adds that
unlike the Barthelme-like Apollonius, he is neither
cynical nor nihilistic.) JM is written in "sprung
hexameters" because the rhythmic aspect of G (including
line-breaks) was destroyed when the manuscript was set
in type. The purpose of The Smugglers, which was begun
as a parody of the contemporary philosophical novel, is
in part to show how bad art can destroy a culture, as
Gardner explains in his Hudson Review essay, "Moral Fiction,"
just as good art can create a civilization, as in the case
of the Jews. Although NM was not begun as a pastoral,
Gardner eventually used elements of Vergillian and Christian
pastorals to bring his work together; the pastoral form
serves as a vehicle for discussion of contemporary issues,
the problematic relationship between the individual and
the community, and the ritualistic solution to this problem.
Claiming he does not write fiction from reference books,
Gardner says WA is as much about Sartre (whom he loves
and hates) as about ancient Sparta. The prison, he adds,
derives from Dante. His future projects include two
novels-in-progress (one about the ocean and another about
Rasputin, whose death catapulted Russia out of the Middle
Ages and into the chaos of the modern world) and his
teaching of writing (in which he emphasizes the writer's
obligation to society, an obligation that includes dedication to technique: "the ultimate morality is, in a sense,
getting the line right").

137 Coale, Samuel. "'Into the Farther Darkness'" The
     Manichaean Pastoralism of John Gardner." In John
     Gardner: Critical Perspectives. Ed. Robert A. Morace
     and Kathryn VanSpanckeren. Carbondale and Edwardsville:
     Southern Illinois University Press, 1982.
        See annotation under "Works About."

138 "John Gardner." Writer's Workshop: Transcripts. Columbia,
     S.C.: University of South Carolina and the South Carolina
     Educational Television Network, 1982, pp. 20-24.
        At the present time, a very intelligent literary realism
     is in vogue, but what really counts is good writing, not
     literary trends. Gardner began writing as a youth in

response to, or in competition with, the oral literature of his family. He decided to dedicate himself to writing while attending Washington University, where he was exposed to "real" and accessible writers such as William Carlos Williams. In revising his earliest novel, NM, he changed the style and the main character's name (originally Losch Soames), added one chapter and deleted several others. Noting that in its original form the novel was "grotesquely sentimental," Gardner says that the writer must deal with the emotions, not avoid them, but in such a way that they are portrayed correctly. He lengthened "The Wedding" section into an emotional, "tour-de-force" because he was angry over the unwillingness of publishers to accept his work. In fact, his one published story, "A Little Night Music," was only accepted because the Northwest Review had received a grant to publish work about Indians. Gardner's backlog at this time included Res, WA, SD, and G (which one editor said was, except for the violence, a "wonderful children's book"). Frustrated, Gardner began writing derivative poems, all of which were accepted. His break came when Gass mentioned Gardner's name to David Segal, who began publishing Gardner's boxful of fiction piece by piece, first at New American Library, then at Harper's, and finally at Knopf, which had previously "hated" Gardner's work. In Gardner's judgment, many writers worry "about publishing before they are ready to publish." What they should do is learn the basic principles of fiction-writing, which are actually very simple: use abundant and vivid details; create a "continuous dream in the reader's mind" (no distractions); revise carefully; and be concerned about characters and the plot, setting, etc., that contribute to good characterization. Plot exists only to allow the character to know, through his actions, who he is. And characters exist because of our "immense capacity for love and understanding," as a non-intellectual way to understand our world and ourselves. All characters are based, either consciously or unconsciously on real people. In SD, Will Hodge is based on Gardner's cousin Bill and both Clumly and the Sunlight Man on his uncle George. The writer observes human gestures and mannerisms around him in order to discover what they mean. (The desire for freedom and for order is inherent in a democracy; as a result, the confidence man is the most interesting character in American fiction.) Once the writer has mastered the basic principles, he should begin publishing his work, realizing that editors are solely concerned with literature's commercial possibilities. (In his

introduction to this interview, George Plimpton says that
the lesson to be learned from Gardner's career is, "Just
keep on writing...and eventually you'll find some measure
of success.) This interview was videotaped at the University of South Carolina and aired on Public Television in
the fall of 1982; it is scheduled to be re-shown in the
fall of 1983. Excerpts have been published in Overview:
Writer's Workshop (Columbia, S.C.: University of South
Carolina and the South Carolina Educational Television
Network, 1982, p. 7, and Contemporary Sources: Readings
from "Writer's Workshop" (New York: Holt, Rinehart and
Winston, 1982), p. 71. The interview is summarized in
Beth Littlejohn et al., "Writer's Workshop": Study Guide
(New York: Holt, Rinehart and Winston, 1982), p. 27, and
Overview, p. 22.

139 Ziegler, Heide. "John Gardner." In The Radical Imagination and the Liberal Tradition. Ed. Heide Ziegler and
Chris Bigsby. London: Junction Books, 1982, pp. 126-50.
   A man's life is largely determined, but within an
individual's given nature he is able to make certain
important choices. Henry Soames, for example, must be a
sensualist, but he can choose to become a responsible
sensualist, a lover of the "mutable world." George Loomis
fails to develop a responsible attitude toward things,
people, or himself. In OL, the ways James, Sally, and
Lewis live are individually satisfactory until they come
into conflict. The best way to respond to this conflict
is emotionally and involves adaptability and responsibility
to everything and everyone. Sally, for example, comes out
of her room not because she is submissive but because she
is concerned (though the changes in Sally's, James's, and
Lewis's personalities may only be temporary). Contemporary
American writers mistakenly view conciliation and traditional
values as threats to their freedom. Claiming to be
Nietzschean supermen, they nonetheless feel and complain
about a "great loss" they have in fact inflicted on themselves. It is necessary to observe rituals and at the
same time to discover true values by empathizing with
particular people in particular situations (as happens to
everyone in SD except Benson/Boyle). The narrowness of
our present "codes" is the subject of Gardner's early
novels. The search for a universal code, one that will
make man physically and spiritually healthy, is the subject
of the later works. Perhaps the universal code can only
be realized through pain and forgiveness. The fittest to
survive may very well be to those who are gentle and just.

The "KI" suggests that the best kind of human existence is one "where you are solidly in touch with the physical and you know the spirit is there." By spirit Gardner means a single, unifying life force, like, yet different from, the devouring white law Poe imaged at the end of Pym. As a parodist, Gardner works in a distinctly American tradition where the reader is asked to take seriously the content of the literary model, as in Poe's "The Devil in the Belfry," Melville's The Confidence Man and Pierre, and the works of Stephen Crane. In the first part of KI, Gardner deals with the pessimistic view of many modern writers, and in "John Napper Sailing Through the Universe" he presents an alternative vision: an imagined world. The "Queen Louisa" stories involve a naive affirmation. In "KI" the contrasting views of parts one and two are restated positively as a combination of the real and the imagined, of life and literature. Artists and priests are alike in that both want "to tell the world how to be." Priests and bad artists preach and proscribe. True artists, on the other hand, improve their world by imagining a better one. Gardner is drawn to non-realistic forms such as the tale because they are "efficient" ways of getting at the mysteries and deep truths of our lives.

140 Wigler, Stephen. "Gardner's Ghosts." Rochester Democrat and Chronicle/Upstate Magazine, 11 July 1982, pp. 15-20.
   Wigler sees Gardner as "a study in contrasts and contradictions." Concerning OMF, for example, Gardner is alternately angry, humble, and proud. He admits the writing is careless and the judgments overhasty, but he also believes the book was a necessary response to "the intellectual, New York City-oriented crowd" with its emphasis on a literature of hopelessness. Although Wigler calls him a conservative writer, Gardner mentions his innovative work, adding with some bitterness that it is this aspect of his career that has gone unnoticed. His non-realistic writings and cartoonish characters lend themselves to illustrations--illustrations which Wigler says give the books an old-fashioned look. As a child Gardner developed his imagination as an alternative to the boredom and solitude of farm work. His earliest stories concerned maidens and monsters. He agrees that he sees some people as monsters, some as clowns trying to be human, and finally others who actually are human. Gardner denies that Peter Mickelsson is an autobiographical character; rather, he is based on Gardner's close friend James Dickey. In technique, Gardner's novel-in-progress, "Shadows," will

be his most experimental work, while in values his most conservative. In it, all the conventions of the mystery novel will be carried to their logical end. Gardner's aim is to create a sense of "mass paranoia" in the characters as well as the reader and then "to work back to faith from that." Although Gardner criticizes the Presbyterian Church in which he was raised, saying it no longer emphasizes ethical choices and has become merely fashionable, his friend and collaborator Joseph Baber considers Gardner a deeply religious man and firm believer in a hierarchy of aesthetic and moral values. (Elsewhere in the article, Baber mentions Gardner's ambition and faith in himself prior to his popular and critical success and Gardner's emotional state at the time of his divorce from his first wife.) Gardner also discusses his indebtedness to the Internal Revenue Service (because he is unable to prove that the taxes were indeed paid, all his future writing is, in a sense, for the IRS). Wigler mentions Gardner's looking much older than his 48 years and, making special note of Gardner's reputation as a teacher, quotes Thomas Gavin on the help Gardner offered him at Bread Loaf. Russell Peck and Walter O'Malley, S.J., discuss Gardner's popularity among college and high school students. (The interview was conducted in June at Gardner's parents' farm in Batavia, N.Y., where Gardner had been helping with chores and rehabilitation since his father's stroke ten months before.)

141 Adams, Noah. All Things Considered. National Public Radio, 15 July 1982.
      There are two Mickelssons: the philosopher-rationalist and the one who plunges into chaos, oblivious to all warnings. Although not at all frightened for most of the novel, Mickelsson does begin to believe that his two ghosts are Luther's devils. The lingering of their situation and anger in the house is related to Nietzsche's "scary idea" of eternal recurrence. Although Gardner has never seen or felt the presence of a ghost, the area around Susquehanna makes him think of, or imagine, ghosts. Given that his father once sensed an ax murder occurring five miles away, Gardner does believe that such a feeling can be real.

142 Suplee, Curt. "John Gardner, Flat Out." Washington Post, 25 July 1982, pp. H1, H8-H9.
      Gardner has been "badly hurt" by negative reviews of MG, the New York literary establishment's revenge for his having published OMF, which was written in 1964 and which

he tried to tone down during an emotionally and physically difficult period in his life. Defending the book at one point and claiming "most of it I got wrong" at another, Gardner apologizes for some of his remarks and praises contemporary authors Barth, Updike, Fowles, Sol Yurick, Cynthia Ozick, Oates, and Heinrich Boll; his distaste for "New York fiction" remains strong, however. Thanks to OMF more novels about middle America are being published. MG, which draws on Bellow and Updike, was intended to be a thriller on various levels, including the intellectual and the spiritual. Facing a midlife crisis and hating his times, the self-destructive main character is both crazy and heroic; on a deep emotional level he and Gardner are one. Luther and Nietzsche are important to the novel in that the former denies the value of man's works while the other claims that only man's actions have value. The novel, on the other hand, suggests that what is needed is a woman's saving grace. Citing his grandmother's influence ("she made my world mythic"), Gardner says that as a writer he tries "to break down the distinction between reality and fiction." He also briefly discusses his parents, brother's death, academic career (twice fired), his becoming a public figure, the two screenplays he wrote but will not identify, several of his best known students, troubles with the Internal Revenue Service, and relationship with Susan Thornton. Currently he is editing MSS, directing You're a Good Man, Charlie Brown in Susquehanna, Pennsylvania, and continuing work on his novel "Shadows," which concerns "the way back to faith" and has many characters that are based on contemporary authors. Although he says he is too depressed to write--an artist whose greatness goes unappreciated, spending his time reading Stephen King--by the end of the interview Gardner is optimistic, ready to go "flat out."

142a Edwards, Bob. Morning Edition. National Public Radio, 15 September 1982.
   Although he is frequently criticized for not answering questions he himself raises in his novels, Gardner says that it is religion and philosophy that answer questions, not life and art. Writers deal with what interests them, and in Gardner's case this means using philosophy and history dramatically to see how they will affect the outcome. It is the story, not the philosophy, that is important. The basic purpose of fiction is "to take us right out of temporality, right out of this world, this universe, into the eternal sunlit world where novels take place." Illustrations, because they preclude reading a

64

story as if it were real, aids in this process. Gardner's
ranting characters, such as the Sunlight Man and James
Page, reflect the ranter in Gardner's personality. It is
their ranting style, not what they rant about, that should
interest the reader. While it is true that "every writer
has his own aesthetic" and at times must be concerned
with the texture of his prose, chiefly he must be interested in larger matters.

142b "A Poet: Motorcycle Kills Author, SUNY Professor John
Gardner." Syracuse Post Standard, 15 September 1982,
pp. Al, A8.
    Quotes from United Press International interview,
August 1982; see annotation under "Works About."

142c Heinemann, Bill. WSKG-FM (Binghamton, N.Y.), 19
September 1982. This interview was aired as part of a
Gardner "Retrospective," which also included a performance
of Gardner's "Songs for the End of the World" and readings
from SD.
    The novelist is a mimic and must write what his characters
dictate. Setting combines realistic and dream elements
(the latter must be carefully checked during the revision
stage). How to go into a hypnotic trance is one of the
techniques a writer must learn. Gardner would never revise any of his published novels and believes that Fowles's
revision of The Magus inferior to the original. (Gardner
also notes that Fowles's use of tricks in, for example,
The French Lieutenant's Woman, where the author observes
his characters on a bus; Gardner has a similar scene in
OL.) One test of a novel is reality; the culture enters
the fiction which in turn gives direction to the culture,
either directly or by filtering down to the level of
popular literature. Authors of morally responsible
fiction (e.g., Faulkner and Joyce) are themselves morally
responsible men. In their work "goodness prevails,"
whereas in the works of Spillane, Celine, and de Sade it
does not. Asked to name which of his works he likes best,
Gardner mentions KI, which he read chapter by chapter to
the dying Nicholas Vergette, his "dearest friend"; G
because it is so well liked by high school students; and
NM, because it is read by people who usually dislike
modern novels. Gardner always decides on the appropriate
medium for a work as soon as he has the initial story-
idea. Don Giovanni, he notes, is a great opera but, in
Joseph Losey's adaptation, a "terrible movie." Radio is
a better literary medium than television; radio productions

are less expensive, appeal to the audience's imagination, and have greater dramatic substance and continuity. As video cassettes become more of a force in the marketplace, the quality of television will improve. One important literary effect television has had is the way it has influenced the remarkable novels of Ishmael Reed. Concerning his own librettos, Gardner notes how closely he has collaborated with Joseph Baber, "a wonderful poet" whose personality is close to Gardner's. In their work, the music comes first, then the plot; the librettist submits to the demands of the music. Gardner believes that the translation of librettos, or any literary works, is always difficult and in the case of non-comic works inadvisable. Each language has its own special sounds: American English, for example, has black and Jewish components and a certain wryness that defies translation.

142d Kearney, Robert P. "September Darkness." [Published in an unidentified Minnesota newspaper sometime in late September or early October 1982.]
   See annotation under reviews of MG.

142e Beans, Bruce. "John Gardner's Last Interview." Today: The (Philadelphia) Inquirer Magazine, 17 October 1982, pp. 1, 18-21.
   Although he has recanted some of OMF, Gardner still maintains that great art "makes you whole" and that the literary establishment has made fashionable the cynical writer it says best represents the modern age. A writer who leaves his roots behind will never write an important work. While living in San Francisco, Gardner felt out of place among both his sophisticated academic colleagues and the literary crowd at City Lights. The move to Carbondale saved his sanity but undermined his marriage (Joan having been forced to abandon her promising career as a concert pianist). Even in Carbondale Gardner continued to drink excessively and to contemplate suicide. When he nearly died from cancer five years ago, it was not fear he experienced but distress, feeling that he was betraying his loved ones. (Joyce Carol Oates has commented on Gardner's "extremely complex personality," and his mother Priscilla has said he seems to be living two lives.) Despite the negative reception of MG (the reviewers' way of retaliating against OMF), Gardner believes it "a great novel" about contemporary issues and the agony of greatness. Mickelsson is not a self-portrait; rather, he is based on the poet James Dickey. Reviews of

MG so depressed Gardner that for a time he considered himself finished as a novelist. Even now he feels too drained
to continue work on "Shadows" (at present, 750 pages long);
instead, he is translating Gilgamesh. Although his editor,
Robert Gottlieb, has assured him his work will live on,
Gardner says that is not enough; he wants his recognition
now. Gardner also comments on his teaching, which he
calls a duty, and his marriages. (Beans briefly discusses
Gardner's family and funeral. His sudden death violated
one of Gardner's rules for writers: no unprepared for effects. The real tragedy of Gardner's death is his having
died while still under attack by his critics.)

142f Ferguson, Paul F., and John R. Maier. "A Conversation
with John Gardner." In Literary Interviews. Ed. Philip L.
Gerber. Forthcoming, State University of New York Press.
    The similarity of their personalities is what first at-
tracted Gardner to Chaucer, a writer who Gardner feels
"became a kind of metafictionist" in his late work. Gardner
says he uses traditional literary forms in order to achieve
"a sense of newness"; the narrator of JM, for example, is
modelled on Chaucer's narrators, and the in-progress "King
Gustav, Lars Joren, and the Devil" is consciously written
as "a boring, dry, stupid tract." Although Gardner is in
a way a metafictionist, chiefly he is a writer who, like
Bellow and Singer, is concerned with character, plot, and
creating "a vivid and continuous dream in the reader's
mind." On the genesis of some of his work, Gardner notes
that his children's stories began as Christmas presents for
his own children and were published at the suggestion of a
friend. ISM was written as "a response to a kid's situation"
like Bettelheim, Gardner believes "that fairy tales help
you solve your problems." Res began as a plot told to a
writing class, and G developed from a student's question
about Beowulf. The teaching of literature has often provided Gardner with the forms he uses in his fiction. The
teaching of writing, on the other hand, is both time-
consuming and, in that it makes him overly conscious of
technique, damaging to his own writing. Yet it is grati-
fying work and "a kind of duty." Of student writers
Gardner notes that there are a "few crippling defects":
the inability to see virtues as well as vices, being
emotionally inhibited, and being "caught up in Saturday
Evening Post language." Looking back on his career,
Gardner says that he "made it" but "at enormous expense."

Part II
Reviews

The Complete Works of the Gawain-Poet (1965)

143 Benson, Larry D. *Journal of English and Germanic Philology*, 65 (July 1966), 580-83.
An "energetic and convincing" translation.

144 *Choice*, 3 (June 1966), 306.
"The translations, sometimes free, retain the original tone, most of the original texts, much of the alliteration, and many of the other poetic devices and stanzaic forms."

145 Clark, Cecily. *Medium Aevum*, 36, iii (1967), 285-87.
Questions Gardner's interpretation of Gawain as a virgin and the making of the Green Knight into "more of a shape-shifter than ever he was in mediaeval romance." The translation is misleading and Gardner's tone "that of an amateur's uncritical self-confidence."

146 Cutler, Edward J. *Library Journal*, 90 (1 October 1965), 4078.
"... could hardly be improved."

147 Garmonsway, G. N. *University of Toronto Quarterly*, 36 (April 1967), 300-01.
Gardner's "modish energetic and symbolic approach ... tempts him to overplay his hand" in the introduction; his translation at times misses the original's sense.

148 Grigson, Geoffrey. "The Anonymity of a Great Poet." *Country Life* (London), 6 January 1966, pp. 42-43.
Gardner's "line by line rendering is not really in verse and not really a substitute" for the original poetry. But in bringing these poems together in a modernized version with "a firm and brilliant introduction," Gardner has performed a valuable service.

149 Howard, Donald R. *Speculum*, 42 (January 1967), 149-52.
The translation is "a poetic achievement in its own right." The introduction, though not without some "original suggestions," is "too personal" and at times erroneous.

150 Lumiansky, R. M. "The Old Made New." *New York Times Book Review*, 28 November 1965, p. 28.
The introduction is too long and too polemical; the translation is poetic and remains faithful to the original. Gardner is to be congratulated for making so much medieval poetry available to a modern audience.

151 Mehl, Dieter. Anglia (Tubingen), 85, i (1967), 87-89.
Metrical rather than purely lyrical, Gardner's translations are more exact and more elegant than previous ones.
The introduction is stimulating and well-researched but
too interpretive for an edition such as this.

152 Newstead, Helaine. Romance Philology, 22 (February 1969),
358-60.
Although the translation is good, the interpretations
stated in the introduction are too personal and "capricious."

153 "Notes on Current Books." Virginia Quarterly Review, 42
(Winter 1966), xviii, xx.
The translations are good, but "where did Gardner find
his four levels of interpretation, which contradict the
usual ones."

154 "Sir Gawain in America." Times Literary Supplement, 21
July 1966, p. 636.
Gardner mistranslates and shows little evidence of
scholarly research.

155 Wilson, R.M. Modern Language Review, 62 (January 1967),
108-09.
The translation is free but adequate; there is no attempt to duplicate the original's intricate metrics. The
arguments presented in the introduction are "occasionally
more ingenious than convincing."

156 Wilson, R. M. Modern Language Review, 67 (January 1972),
164.
Notes paperback issue.

The Resurrection (1966)

157 B., S. I. "The Impact of One Man's Death." Los Angeles
Times, 19 June 1966, "Calendar" section, p. 30.
This is "not an academic novel"; the philosophical
speculation of the first portion of the novel gives way
to a consideration of "human interest values." "... a
moving if incompletely realized first novel,... an
intensely personal work, a modern answer to Tolstoy's
pessimistic 'The Death of Ivan Ilyich.'"

158 Chicago Tribune.*
Quoted on back cover of Ballantine edition of Res; not
located in Chicago Tribune files.

159 Choice, 4 (May 1967), 288.
   "Vivid in portraiture, though it inclines to the
   grotesque." The style is awkward and the philosophical
   passages are "turgid."

160 Halio, J. L. Southern Review, ns 6 (Winter 1970), 250.
   Listed but not reviewed.

161 Hicks, Granville. "Strange Games and Sea Changes."
   Saturday Review, 49 (July 1966), 25-26.
   "Gardner ... seems to be hoping, as first novelists
   sometimes do, that the reader will understand what he is
   trying to do better than he does."

162 Kirkus Reviews, 34 (1 May 1966), 490.
   Gardner is more concerned with ideas than people. The
   novel is noteworthy for the description of setting and
   the pages dealing with Chandler's wife.

163 Mahoney, John. "Under Sentence of Death, a Teacher Learns
   Truth." Detroit News, 3 July 1966, p. G3.
   Res is "accomplished" art (its form is especially
   "impressive") and "commanding reading." The prologue--
   "a film clip"--reflects the entire novel. Minor characters
   are eccentric, gothic. The protagonist comes to understand
   the intensity and relevance of the seemingly insignificant
   and learns "the metaphysics of love."

164 Nelson, Elizabeth. Library Journal, 91 (1 June 1966),
   2872-73.
   The philosophical passages are integral to this novel
   about the "quest for philosophical truth" and the "search
   for identity and immortality."

165 New York Post, 18 June 1966.*
   Cited in Howell.

166 Turner, Alice K. "PW Forecasts: Paperbacks." Publishers
   Weekly, 205 (4 March 1974), 78.
   Gardner's novel, which is not at all "dry" or academic,
   has "hints of mythology, of the classical confrontation
   with death, with the Fates, with the orphic journey to
   Hades."

167 West, Paul. "New Fiction." Washington Post Book World,
   17 July 1966, p. 12.
   The novel is slow and too insistently philosophical except
   at the end where "the prose achieves a brief, symphonic
   intensity."

Papers on the Art and Age of Geoffrey Chaucer (1967)

168 De Vries, F. C. Neophilologus, 52 i (1969), 99-101.
What characterizes these essays is "... the deadly
solemnity, the dreary jargon, the stressing of ir-
relevanciers [sic], the parade of learning, and ... the
strange insensitivity to the tone of Chaucer's poetry."
Includes a lengthy discussion of Gardner's "The Case
Against the 'Bradshaw Shift.'"

169 Speculum, 43 (April 1968), 392-93.
Lists contents.

The Wreckage of Agathon (1970)

170 Baldwin, Barry. Library Journal, 95 (1 August 1970), 2716.
"More hysterical than historical," Gardner's novel "reads
like a parody of Mary Renault (perhaps it is?) and is a
total bore."

171 Bannon, Barbara A. "PW Forecasts: Fiction." Publishers
Weekly, 198 (13 July 1970), 149.
"A historical novel with a difference," one filled with
"irony and drollery" and suitable "for very special tastes
indeed."

172 Booklist, 67 (1 January 1971), 354.
A "skillfully crafted...parable on contemporary
experience"; the novel's "frequent anachronisms add
immediacy."

173 Boyd, Robert. "Books." St. Louis Post-Dispatch, 22
October 1970, p. E3.
Part historical fiction, part fantasy, Gardner's "darkly
comic" novel is disturbingly profound and provocatively
subtle. Agathon, "an opportunist who has squandered the
riches of his mental capacity," tells of his youth; Peeker
tells of his wreckage, and it is this awareness that makes
the book Peeker's.

174 Davis, L. J. "Was There a Greece?" Washington Post Book
World, 20 September 1970, p. 2.
Although Gardner handles tone and symbolism well, his

novel has a "threadbare" plot and seems to require that the reader have "a special knowledge." Moreover, "one is ... continually aware that one is reading a novel."

175 Elkin, Stanley. Back dust-jacket cover of Harper & Row edition of WA.
WA "is careful, informed and ultimately wise. Not the least of this book's several strange charms is that it manages--rare in fiction--to dramatize philosophic systems and to discuss the old hard questions in hard new ways. Agathon, Mr. Gardner's Seer, is something new--fiction's first dirty old gentleman. But for me the novel's outstanding quality is its pacing, here a flawless feat to make a reader wonder and a writer tremble."

176 Gass, William. Front inside dust-jacket flap of Harper & Row edition of WA.
WA "is one of the finest of our contemporary fictions: historical in form but deeply immediate in spirit, it possesses a remarkable unity of wit, thought, perception, and feeling."

177 Gordon, David J. "Some Recent Novels: Connoisseurs of Chaos." Yale Review, 60 (March 1971), 433-34.
Agathon, who seems drawn from the Socrates of the "Apology" and "Crito" as well as Joyce Cary's Gulley Jimson and Marguerite Yourcenar's Hadrian, "believes that in a world where truth is unknowable and where time's wreckage makes prisoners of us all, vividness of being is the highest wisdom." The novel's political background is "credibly dramatized" but the "liveliness" of the style is facile.

178 Kirkus Reviews, 38 (15 July 1970), 761.
"Although distended with celebration, the narrative offers some fine flights of inventive garrulity, impressive thoughts on important concerns ["the nature of reality, the relation of the individual to the scheme of things, the meaning of it all"], but not always succeeding on fictional terms."

179 Lehmann-Haupt, Christopher. "Looking for the Novelist." New York Times, 24 September 1970, p. 45.
"Anachronisms abound and perplex; Gardner's prose--and occasional dactyls--often reads like a 20th-century schoolboy's translation of the ancients; there are witty and obfuscating parodies of philosophies ranging from Aristotle's to Rousseau's." However, the parts are too discordant for the novel to succeed.

180 Midwood, Barton. "Fiction." Esquire, 75 (January 1971), 64, 69-70.
    Discusses the novel's historical and political background, as well as its contemporary literary and political allusions. Has special praise for the novel's lyrical passages.

181 "Paperbacks." Best Sellers, 31 (1 March 1972), 547.
    Notes Ballantine edition.

182 Pierpont, Phillip E. Best Sellers, 30 (1 February 1971), 477-78.
    As in Res, Gardner uses opposing points of view and a a plague metaphor. Agathon's death is anticlimactic, thus emphasizing the theme that both this life and the next one are without value.

183 Wernick, Robert. "Seer v. Slob." Time, 96 (9 November 1970), 86.
    Notes various contemporary allusions and the fact that Agathon quotes verbatim from Dryden's translation of Plutarch's "Life of Lycurgus" in "this sharp and provoking little antihistorical novel."

184 West, Paul. "Black Comedy in Ancient Sparta." New York Times Book Review, 15 November 1970, pp. 4, 65.
    Agathon is "a Visigothic Falstaff out of Diogenes by Rabelais" who believes that man has "a better chance of self-realization at the hands of chaos" than of order. The novel's second half is less interesting than the first.

185 Wolff, Geoffrey. "A Cell in Sparta." Newsweek, 76 (21 September 1970), 101-02.
    The novel is at once metaphysical and comic, more successful in the prison sections than in those recounting Agathon's history. Notes parallels to Sartre's No Exit and Heisenberg's uncertainty principle.

Grendel (1971)

186 Adams, Phoebe. "Short Reviews: Books." Atlantic, 228 (October 1971), 135.
    "Whatever else he has accomplished--and his intention is none too clear--Mr. Gardner has certainly found the ultimate antihero" in his "mod social satire."

187 Ashby, D. Science Fiction Commentary, 48-50 (October-100-01*
    Cited in Science Fiction Book Review Index, vol. 7 (1976).

188 Bannon, Barbara A. "PW Forecasts: Fiction." Publishers
    Weekly, 200 (19 July 1971), 117.
       "A superb short narrative"; "powerfully evocative."

189 Bateson, F. W. "Grendel and Beowulf Were Two Pretty Boys."
    New York Review of Books, 17 (30 December 1971), 16-17.
       "Mr. Gardner's G is interpretation and elaboration rather
    than translation--a sophisticated version of what Beowulf
    is ultimately about in modern terms." Grendel is the "most
    sympathetic figure" in the book for which one source may
    be The Tempest.

190 "Beowulf's Beast." Times Literary Supplement, 14 July
    1972, p. 793.
       Grendel "is Milton's Satan in infantile ridiculousness;
    what one of Kafka's heroes might have become if he had let
    out a scream of rage and revenge." At the end of the novel,
    Grendel "is delivered into hope," his final words are not
    a curse but a blessing. The novel's language "combines
    the rich, clotted feel of Anglo-Saxon rhythms with ironic
    contemporary colloquialisms."

191 Best Sellers, 32 (1 November 1972), 365.
       "A splendid reconstruction of the old legend as it
    seemed from the monster's side."

192 Booklist, 68 (15 December 1971), 353.
       "Sophisticated comedy that depicts Grendel as one who is
    continually disappointed in the reality as compared to the
    ideal he holds of man."

193 Boyd, Robert. "Heroic Ideals, Monster Values." St.
    Louis Post-Dispatch, 26 September 1971, p. C4.
       Despite what Gardner says in Esquire, October 1971, his
    humans are the monsters in G; the reader empathizes with
    the monster-narrator as Gardner points out, "graphically
    and relentlessly, the emptiness of honor, the seamy
    hypocrisy of human virtue." Like Capote in In Cold Blood,
    Gardner patiently examines the motives of his monster.
    The book is "an allegorical plea for an intuitive realiza-
    tion ... that heroism and monstrosity are alike human
    values and therefore a priori, and therefore deceptions
    we practice upon ourselves." The flaw in this book is
    typical of much recent fiction: the tendency to indulge
    in expository as opposed to dramatic philosophizing. None-
    theless, the novel is one of the best in years and its
    author, "already one of the best young writers in the
    country," possesses the style, the imagination, and the
    intelligence to become a great writer."

75

194 Boylan, Mildred. "'The Tenants' and 'Grendel'--Two
    Stories Well Told." Rochester Times-Union, 18 December
    1971, p. C13.
    Grendel is a charming monster; beneath [the novel's]
    lyricism is a very relevant message."

195 "Briefly Noted." New Yorker, 47 (18 September 1971),
    142-43.
    Gardner uses the monster as his mouthpiece.

196 Brown, Ruth Leslie. Saturday Review, 54 (2 October 1971),
    48-49.
    G is "more than a literary trick"; it is "a prose-poem."
    "Readers accustomed to the thin gruel of contemporary
    naturalism may feel that the author overindulges in verbal
    pyrotechnics. Let us be reminded that the English language
    is still a magnificent instrument of expression."

197 Compton, D. G. Books and Bookmen, 17 (September 1972),
    83-84.
    Notes the strong narrative, poetic language, and similar-
    ities to Ted Hughes's Crow.

198 Ditsky, John. "The Man on the Quaker Oats Box: Character-
    istics of Recent Experimental Fiction." Georgia Review,
    26 (Fall 1972), 297, 306-08.
    Couched as a reply to D. Keith Mano's review (New York
    Times Book Review below), Ditsky's remarks express a
    qualified acceptance of Gardner's experimental fiction and
    praise for the way Gardner draws the reader into the
    creative process.

199 Emergency Librarian, 9 (January 1982), 13.
    A captivating story of a monster torn by his own
    contradictory feelings and representative of "the dark
    side of us all."

200 Foote, Timothy. "The Geat Generation." Time, 98
    (20 September 1971), 89-90.
    The novel supports "the view that man is more naturally
    kin to Cain than Abel. Yet it is closer to a more enter-
    taining tradition--the literary monster made real because
    he has been made so human." Grendel resembles King Kong,
    Milton's Lucifer, and, in his having learned to swear from
    listening to men, Shakespeare's Caliban.

201 Green, Stephen. "The Monstrous Grendel Stalks Anew in Mr.
Gardner's Rewriting of Myth." The National Observer, 10
(2 October 1971), 27.
    A "sad and beautiful novel"; its style is contemporary,
but its mood is that of the heroic epic. "...Grendel dies
in style, his purpose and sense of humor never lost."

202 Harrell, Don. "Beowulf, from the Monster's Point of View."
Houston Chronicle, 10 October 1971, p. 14.
    Gardner's rendering of the Beowulf story is comic, but
its point is "ultimately serious." Grendel is a sympathetic
figure, no more a monster than the reader.

203 Howes, Victor. "Notes from the Underground." Christian
Science Monitor, 9 September 1971, p. 13.
    Grendel is a nihilist fighting all order; Beowulf, who
believes "in the self-renewing powers of the green world,"
is a positivist whose victory is no accident and whose
strength derives from his understanding of Grendel's
nature.

204 Hunter, Jim. "In the Cylinder." The Listener, 87 (29
June 1972), 874.
    "An impressive and orignal novel, philosophically not
far from Beckett."

205 Kennedy, Veronica M. S. Science Fiction Research Association Newsletter, 12 (June 1972), 4.
    G is not "gimmicky"; rather, it is a "disturbing yet
deeply satisfying" work that portrays Grendel sympatheticall
while still insisting upon his essential monstrousness.
As in Browning's "Caliban upon Setebos" and William
Golding's The Inheritors, Gardner's view of the alien
enables the reader to see his own world afresh. The novel
is ironic and ambiguous throughout, and the final sentence
emphasizes the relativity of good and evil.

206 Kirkus Reviews, 39 (15 July 1971), 762.
    As in his two previous novels, "Gardner demonstrates his
agility at juggling metaphysical notions while telling a
diverting tale"; "the dialogue is witty and has a highly
contemporary lilt."

207 Locke, Richard. "Grendel Is a Beauty of a Beast." New
York Times, 4 September 1971, p. 19.
    G is "an extraordinary achievement"; its prose recalls
Roethke and Hughes (Crow), and its theme echoes Nausea and

The Fall. Grendel himself resembles both the Frankenstein monster "filled with longing" and the monsters drawn by Maurice Sendak. Despite the book's weaknesses--loose subplots, "its forays into verse and drama," and an occasionally "too sweet" style--G proves that "Gardner has become a major contemporary writer."

208 Malm, Harry. Library Journal, 97 (15 March 1972), 1180-81.
Grendel "alternates between empathy and rage" in this "highly imaginative, well-crafted novel." (The review appears in the "Adult Books for Young Readers" section.)

209 Mano, D. Keith. "Beowulf from the Monster's Viewpoint." New York Times Book Review, 19 September 1971, pp. 6, 12, 14.
G "is another fierce blow struck against the realistic novel, the dead novel"; it is "myth itself." Grendel "has the mulatto's syndrome": he despises both his animal nature and his human side. Bored and hopelessly unique, Grendel learns that he is, as men define him, "sin personified: evil in a Manichean war he cannot avoid." Grendel's parting words are ambiguous--either curse or blessing. Although Gardner's dialogue is sometimes "too flatly contemporary and poised," his "metaphorical power" is "considerable."

210 Marsh, Pamela. "1971--Always the Unexpected." Christian Science Monitor, 26 November 1971, p. B3.
Mentions G.

211 Maslen, Elizabeth. "The Monster as Critic." Encounter, 40 (March 1973), 77.
"A fine medley of poetic phrase and workaday prosiness, heroic parody and pseudo-intellectual jargon"; similarly, the character Grendel is both poet and clown.

212 Monfried, Walter. "Whatever Happened to Beowulf." Milwaukee Journal, 11 October 1971, p. 3.
Chiefly, the review summarizes Beowulf.

213 Murray, Michelle. "'Lashings of Wit, Baroque Metaphor' ... It's a Winner." National Catholic Reporter, 8 (11 February 1972), 16.
The novel is at once philosophic, religious, and dramatic; its point is that "without death to throw them into relief, concepts such as heroism begin to seem foolish to the monster, who finds that he can take nothing seriously...."

214 "New and Recommended." New York Times Book Review, 26
    September 1971, p. 61. (Repeated through 10 October
    1971.)
        "Beowulf as seen by his victim, the fierce utterly alone
    monster, ultimately bestial yet conscious of his fate,
    evoked with harsh, brooding, mythic power."

215 "1971: A Selection of Noteworthy Titles." New York Times
    Book Review, 5 December 1971, p. 83.
        Lists G.

216 "Notes on Current Books." Virginia Quarterly Review, 48
    (Winter 1972), xix.
        In this novel, "Gardner has loosened his style somewhat,
    and his idea of the novel, but not his tight hold on
    ridicule, pain, absurdity, and death."

217 O'Hara, T. Best Sellers, 31 (1 November 1971), 355.
        Brief summary.

218 Prescott, Peter S. "Modest Monster." Newsweek, 78 (13
    September 1971), 102B.
        G "is not just the kind of facile revisionism in which
    'Little Red Riding Hood' is told from the wolf's point of
    view; it is instead a celebration and a conservation of
    what we most need in one of the greatest poetic myths we
    have. Lightly, if seriously done.... I cannot recommend
    it too highly."

219 Prescott, Peter S. "The Year in Books." Newsweek, 78
    (27 December 1971), 60-61.
        Brief notice adapted from Prescott's 13 September 1971
    review, above.

220 Sastri, P. S. Review in American Studies, no. 6 (June
    1974), 89-90.*
        Cited in Howell.

221 Schlueter, Paul. "Minutes." Christianity & Literature,
    21 (Fall-Winter 1971-72), 10.
        It was announced at the 28 December 1971 business meeting
    of the Conference on Christianity and Literature that
    Gardner would receive the Conference's annual book award
    for his novel G.

222 "A Selection of the Year's Best Books." Time, 99 (3 January 1972), p. 70.
    In G the "heroes of the epic are revealed as bloodthirsty murderers, thieves, and hypocrites."

223 Van Brunt, H. L. "The Headiest, Happiest Holiday Gifts: Books." Saturday Review, 54 (27 November 1971), 46.
    The monster's "point of view is as hilarious and refreshing as the author's prose."

224 Van Der Weele, Steve J. for the time being, 1, iii-iv (1973).
    Gardner's well executed retelling of the Beowulf story is analogous to C. S. Lewis's Till We Have Faces; Gardner reinterprets the epic through his modern sensibility without slighting the original, using the story as a backdrop for his "anthropological commentary." The nihilistic monster represents the counter culture; the Shaper is the establishment's poet laureate.

225 Waugh, Auberon. "Getting to Grips with Reality." Spectator, 229 (1 July 1972), 14.
    The novel is "elegantly written," marred only by the illustrations.

226 Whitmore, Priscilla. Library Journal, 96 (1 September 1971), 2670.
    Grendel is "a study of maniacal drive, fear, loneliness, and craving for communication." The placing of "carefully casual anachronisms" serve to create an "Ionesco-like atmosphere."

The Alliterative Morte Arthure [,] The Owl and the Nighin-

gale [,] And Five Other Middle English Poems in a Modernized

Version (1971)

227 Bestful, Thomas H. Speculum, 48 (January 1973), 142-46.
    The translations are well done, though in "The Owl and the Nightingale," Gardner often departs from the literal meaning ... because he seems compelled to put more life and color into a poem which has these qualities in abundance." In his commentaries, Gardner is "haphazard about fundamentals."

228 Choice, 8 (11 January 1972), 1451.
The translations substitute "modern gracefulness" for the original's "ruggedness."

229 Fry, Donald K. Library Journal, 96 (15 December 1971), 4097.
In his modernizations (rather than translations) of these medieval poems and in his "lively and sensible" introductory comments, Gardner has done "the general reader a real service."

230 Robbins, Rossell Hope. Anglia (Tubingen), 92, i-ii (1974), 231-34.
Highly praises the translations and introductory comments; includes a list of suggested changes. Also refers to G: the "overtones of Arthur's saint of St. Michael's mount" and its "highly cursus-ed prose" reminiscent of Ulysses.

231 Salus, Peter H. English Studies (Amsterdam), 54 (June 1973), 275-76.
"WA was a truly interesting academic novel; G, though briefer, was a better novel. Professor Gardner's 'translation' of Gawain ... was not as satisfactory. The volume at hand is even less impressive." The author should "stick to novels."

The Sunlight Dialogues (1972)

232 Adams, Phoebe. "Short Reviews: Books." Atlantic, 231 (January 1973), 100.
Gardner undertakes "to cram the whole history of Western civilization into New York State. It doesn't fit."

233 Bannon, Barbara A. "PW Forecasts: Fiction." Publishers Weekly, 202 (9 October 1972), 106.
"Although this will undoubtedly get much 'serious' discussion, a little symbolism goes a long way."

234 Barkham, John. "The Way We Are Now." John Barkham Reviews. Seen in typescript; published in various news-papers, including the New York Post (as noted in an attributed blurb on p. [750] of the Ballantine edition of SD).

This "impressive" work is traditional in its style and structure but contemporary in its depiction of the anxieties of the modern age and in its use of myth, which Gardner, unlike other contemporary novelists, employs "judiciously." The story, at once immediately intelligible and yet profound, is especially powerful in the confrontations between Clumly and the Sunlight Man. The Batavia setting is fully realized and entirely imaginative. Gardner has clearly emerged as a major novelist.

235 Bell, Pearl K. "Of Myths and Men." New Leader, 55 (25 December 1972), 13-14.
   Gardner succeeds in creating an "authentic portrait of small-town American life and the sinister currents that mislead the best and the worst of men." However, "the demonically comprehensive hubris of its ambitious author" results in the novel's chief flaws: the largeness of purpose, the "elaborate mythical superstructure," and the occasional "pomposity."

236 "Best Sellers." New York Times Book Review, 11 February 1973, p. 33.
   Fifteen weeks; through 20 May 1973.

237 Booklist, 69 (15 February 1973), 549-50.
   One-paragraph summary.

238 "Books About to Be." New York Times Book Review, 3 September 1972, p. 5.
   "John Gardner, who made a sympathetic figure of Beowulf's beast in 'Grendel[,] again plumbs the legendary in 'The Sunlight Dialogues,' which transmogrifies King Arthur's court to Batavia, N.Y., circa 1966."

239 Boyd, Robert. "A Whale of a Book, Perhaps A 'Moby Dick.'" St. Louis Post-Dispatch, 24 December 1972, p. F4.
   As in G and WA, Gardner writes of man's place in the universe, though here in a more prosaic setting. The novel's realism is the foundation for Gardner's perhaps overly complex speculations. Despite its incredible variety, the novel "has the driving suspense of a good, tight mystery story. "The ways in which the Hodges react to the Sunlight Man suggests the ways in which the novel impinges on the real world. The subplots and minor characters serve, as in Renaissance portraiture, to imply both the story's larger context and "the artist's

virtuosity." The novel is at once "magnificent" and troubling. Whether it is profound or merely "empty rhetorical gesturing" only time will tell.

240 Brady, Charles A. Buffalo Evening News, 16 December 1972, p. B8.
   Gardner's novel, which is more derivative than it seems, is part Faulkner, part "allegory of the human condition," and part Crime and Punishment. The fusing of metaphysics and physical reality is not entirely successful. Although an admirable intellectual work, it does not give us characters we can care about.

241 Bravard, Robert S. Library Journal, 97 (1 September 1972), 2751.
   "A sharp, flowing narrative prose that finds significance in the details of small-town activity yet is comfortable in handling large ideas." The characters are well drawn, and the story is enhanced by the allusions to medieval literature.

242 Breslin, John B. "A Prospect of Books." America, 127 (7 October 1972), 265.
   SD is "Gardner's transformation of King Arthur's Court."

243 "Briefly Noted." New Yorker, 48 (13 January 1973), 92.
   The novel is "a pastiche of childish romances"; the characters are more "types than individuals." Includes a paraphrase of and a quote from the publisher's notice which accompanied review copies: "In a notice issued by the publishers, Mr. Gardner writes that he belongs to the tradition of Robert Louis Stevenson and other romancers, as opposed to the realistic tradition of Henry James, and he goes on to explain that his book is 'mere art ... a book that imitates not life but certain kinds of books.'"

244 "Briefly Noted." Washington Post Book World, 26 November 1972, 15.
   "From the author of G, a novel about the conflict between a police chief who believes in absolute justice and a magician who believes in absolute freedom. Set in a small town in upstate New York."

245 Burgess, Anthony. "Our Current Plight Viewed in Symbol, Allegory." Chicago Tribune, 17 December 1972, sec. 9, p. 3.
   What prevents Gardner's philosophical concerns from becoming "pretentious" is his careful rendering of setting

and characters "viewed with the sharpness of hallucination."
The Hodges comprise a "dynasty of paternalistic land mag-
nates." Taggert is the novel's Merlin. Gardner's micro-
cosmic view of the contemporary American condition is good
in parts but disappointing as a whole. The novel is too
long and the illustrations undercut the book's seriousness.

246 Burton, Hal. "Horror in Batavia." Newsday, 12 December
1972, part II, pp. A10, A11.
SD mixes Gothicism and philosophy, horror and pity,
metaphysics and reality. The novel, over which there hangs
a Faulknerian sense of doom, mirrors the vastness and
latent violence of its Western New York setting. The concluding scene is especially powerful. This is a "very
fine book, written traditionally to shatter traditional
images."

247 Butscher, Edward. "The American Novel Is Alive and Well."
Georgia Review, 27 (Fall 1973), 393-97.
Gardner's "intense concern for spiritual and philosophical
values" marks this as a major American novel, "a total
allegory for contemporary America ... in which the Sunlight
Man labors desperately to restore illusion (art), to con-
vince the equally desperate Police Chief (and himself)
that the universe is neither absurd nor meaningless."
Nowhere does Gardner "violate the characters' integrity.
Each inner voice is distinct, true to itself...."

248 Cheuse, Alan. "Here Be Monsters." Nation, 216 (21 May
1973), 666-68.
SD "is as rich in points of view as it is in character
and narrative situations." Gardner's fiction "dramatizes
social fact by means of a narrative method that is modern
in its conviction of the illusory nature of textual
'reality' while it is traditional in that it keeps all the
force and feeling of the ancient Shaper-poet...." Includes
lengthy discussions of G and WA.

249 Choice, 10 (March 1973), 92.
Despite "a frivolous hocus-pocus surrounding the figure
of the Sunlight Man," this novel is "a striking advance
over the tour de force, G... because it is rooted in
human actuality."

250 Davenport, Guy. "Order and Disorder." National Review,
25 (2 February 1973), 158-59.
Davenport discusses the novel in terms of the older values
associated with the town and the modern, less human values

associated with the city. SD is like "a play made up almost entirely of subplots." Though the novel is too long, Gardner's prose is "bold, flexible," and "his mastery of vernaculars is superb." One possible source is the revolt of the Batavians against Nero's Roman Empire.

251 "Doomed All Ways." Times Literary Supplement, 23 November 1973, p. 1455.
SD is an "old fashioned chronicle ... in which is embedded a series of dialogues"; "... Gardner's bland gloom is less interesting than the frame in which it is set." The author's strengths are those of the tradi- tional novelist: "an ear for dialogue, firm control of a complex plot, and a perceptive presentation of family hatred and the curiously clever stupidity of the legal world." His weaknesses are "lapses into imprecise rhetoric ... and ponderous parentheses," "a taste for pseudo-tough Chandlerian metaphor ... and the occasional verbal infelicity."

252 Edwards, Thomas R. "A Novel of Large Risks and Achieve- ment." New York Times Book Review, 10 December 1972, pp. 1, 14.
Gardner is a "philosophical novelist" whose "allusive texturings aren't tricks--he sees that such tricks are empty without a full acceptance of the literal lives of his characters." Clumly is his "finest creation"; the "existential artist," the Sunlight Man, is the least interesting. (In the "Letters to the Editor" column, New York Times Book Review, 21 January 1973, p. 30, Sally Savage admonishes Edwards for failing to mention Napper's illustrations for Gardner's novel; Edwards replies that he worked from proof sheets which did not include the illustrations.)

253 Foote, Timothy. "Magic Realism." Time, 101 (1 January 1973), 60, 62.
Although the novel's "surfaces occasionally resemble All in the Family," the story derives more from the Divine Comedy, Revelations, The Rime of the Ancient Mariner, and the epic of Gilgamesh than from realism. The strength of the novel is Gardner's willingness to "affirm the banal and the ordinary," and its "master- piece" is "Clumly's final speech on law and order, which shapes and caps the book as Molly Bloom's soliloquy shapes and caps Ulysses."

254 Fuller, Edmund. "The Odd Secrets of the Lunatic
    Magician." Wall Street Journal, 6 February 1973, p. 20.
    "A deeply humane, affirmative book"; for Gardner truth
    "lies not in literal historicity but in the metaphors, the
    images of life." The novel is "rich in allusions," among
    them Shakespeare's Justice Shallow and Melville's Moby-Dick.

255 Gillott, Jacky. "Fiction " London Times, 18 October 1973,
    p. 16.
    SD is "infinitely demanding" but well worth the reader's
    attention. Its theme is the importance of community, and
    its subject is that community embattled, specifically under
    attack by the Sunlight Man, who "represents for every man
    or woman he meets, the terror that can most closely threaten
    their soul." Gardner's "greatest gift is his perception
    of the personality's infinite range."

256 Hill, William B. "Fiction." America, 128 (5 May 1973),
    420.
    The "story of a tormented soul" in which "the setting is
    important, because it is a small town ... and against its
    low profile the characters of the Sunlight Man and the
    simple police chief, whose depth is as great as his
    simplicity, loom very large."

257 Holleran, James V. "That 'Grendel' Man Returns with a
    Familiar Literary Smorgasbord." National Observer, 12
    (27 January 1973), 23.
    The novel's "derivativeness of incident and theme tends
    to eclipse the distinctions of the book--and they are many."
    Although the novel is complex, its message is "piously
    shopworn" and the Sunlight Man is its least interesting
    character.

258 Howes, Victor. "American Allegory: a Choice of Monsters."
    Christian Science Monitor, 20 December 1972, p. 11.
    SD "restates the Grendel theme--civilization as a choice
    between monsters--in a modern setting." It "reads like a
    cross between the social tapestries of Theodore Dreiser
    or James Gould Cozzens, and a medieval fiction of debate.
    Or William Faulkner gone north." Diffuseness is its
    chief weakness.

259 Kelly, Robert. "Absolute Existential Freedom Practiced."
    Fort Wayne News-Sentinel, 16 December 1972, p. WK4.
    Although this novel concerns the conflict between two
    idealists--Clumly (absolute justice) and the Sunlight Man

(absolute existential freedom)--it is "somehow the human
condition of trying" that seems to triumph.

260 Kirkus Reviews, 40 (1 October 1972), 1162.
   "A complex and difficult fable of curiously American
   relevance."

261 Knight, Susan. "A Babylonian in Batavia." New Statesman,
   86 (19 October 1973), 570.
   In this "attempt to mythmake America," Gardner "has
   aimed high and won." There are resemblances to Faulkner
   and to Nineteenth-Century novels. Gardner's language is
   "impressive," his symbolic details are used poetically,
   and "most forceful of all is the opposition of the
   dialogues themselves."

262 Lehmann-Haupt, Christopher. "Blood and Ideas in Batavia."
   New York Times, 15 December 1972, p. 45.
   For its clear portrait of contemporary life, its
   "metaphysical mystery," and "the boldness of his experiment,"
   Gardner's SD is superior to G and WA.

263 McCullough, David W. Book-of-the-Month Club News, Winter
   1973, p. 8.
   "A novel of Faulknerian complexity and involution by a
   novelist who, like Faulkner, creates his own grotesque world
   and makes it chillingly believable."

264 McLellan, Joseph. "Paperbacks." Washington Post Book World
   16 December 1973, p. 6.
   Restates "Briefly Noted" above.

265 McNatt, James F. "The Sunlight Dialogues: Mere Fiction?"
   Southern Review, 11 (Summer 1975), 716-20.
   SD is a "dialectical" novel--it is itself a process--in
   which Gardner "feels that the significant thought is
   imaginative, not just empirical and logical, and that therefore man will survive so long as he tells good stories."

266 Maddocks, Melvin. "Paleface Takeover." Atlantic, 231
   (March 1973), 98-101.
   The novel resembles a Galsworthy saga, "but, like a
   morality play, the novel constantly moves from specific
   people and events toward a sort of staged warfare of good
   and evil."

267 Maddocks, Melvin. "Reviewer's Choice," Life, 73 (1 December 1972), 24.
   Although this is a philosophical novel, "... there is nothing abstract or academic about Gardner's supernatural confrontations between the counter-culture and the system."

268 Manning, Margaret. "Love and Respect." Boston Globe, 18 December 1972.
   SD will stand comparison with Moby-Dick and The Sound and the Fury despite its weaknesses: too long, too rhetorical, too many subplots. Its strengths are characterization--especially the "brilliant and tiresome" Sunlight Man and Clumly, "a wonderful character who is forever growing and changing"--and its emphasis on pity.

269 Murray, Michael. Commonweal, 97 (12 January 1973), 332-34.
   "The novel is ambitious to a fault... The author has found no concrete, artistic center to the work with which to hold the themes together...." Equally blameworthy are the author's literariness, philosophizing (especially in the dialogues), and the characterizations of Clumly ("engaged in a quest too abstract") and the Sunlight Man ("a bore"). "...it is more By Love Possessed than Moby Dick."

270 "New and Recommended." New York Times Book Review, 17 December 1972, p. 25. Repeated through 7 January 1973.
   "A philosophical novel with mythic overtones set in Batavia, N.Y., and Camelot ["and Camelot" omitted from 17 December 1972 text], which explores the eternal conflict between freedom and order."

271 New York Times Book Review, 3 December 1972, p. 80.
   Notes forthcoming review, 10 December 1972, below.

272 "Notes on Current Books." Virginia Quarterly Review, 49 (Spring 1973), lvi.
   "A compulsive, artfully composed, intelligently conceived philosophical novel" despite its digressive subplots, over-abundance of characters, and "undeniable prolixity."

273 "Novel Done With Skill, Priest Says." Rochester Times-Union, 17 October 1973, p. B3.
   The Rev. Joseph B. Dorsey discussed SD at Rochester's main library. He praised Gardner's handling of sensitive issues, imagination, nineteenth-century scope, vivid

characterizations, poetic structure, and narrative power. The novel, which does not besmirch the author's native Batavia, is a detective story about "the redemptive power of love."

274 Pierpont, Phillip E. Best Sellers, 33 (1 June 1973), 104-05.
More than just a parody of earlier novel forms, SD attempts "to create an archetypal novel." The book has a "Faulknerian quality"; the characters are "real" (often based on people Gardner knows). One weakness is the inclusion of so many subplots.

275 Playboy, 20 (March 1973), 22.
"The best parts of the novel are the vignettes of the major-minor characters, where the author's style and insights are given scope. But Gardner has made this a novel of ideas, and while the ideas are valid enough, they labor in vain for artistic viability."

276 Prescott, Peter S. "Quest for a Birdbath." Newsweek, 81 (8 January 1973), 62, 64.
SD "is more fascinating in its parts than in its whole." The symbolism, much of which alludes to the stories of Gawain and King Arthur, leads to "nothing worth having, nothing that strengthens the story." The novel's overt literariness leads Prescott to say that SD reads more like a first novel than a fourth.

277 Pritchard, William H. "Long Novels and Short Stories." Hudson Review, 26 (Spring 1973), 233-34.
"However brilliant or stupid you may find it, it has a place somewhere down the line from Melville and James and Faulkner and other American writers of impossible books."

278 Rovit, Earl. "Some Shapes in Recent Fiction." Contemporary Literature, 15 (Autumn 1974), 549.
The realistic "police novel ... expands into an extended inquiry on the contemporary relationship between order and creativity--becoming as well a kind of morality play of allegorical gestures." Unfortunately, Gardner's style is not equal to his intelligence; although his interior monologues are quite good, "all the characters tend to think with Gardner's voice."

279 "A Selection of the Year's Best Books." Time, 101
(1 January 1973), 62.
"In the finest novel of the year wisdom and magic turn
a small American town into the metaphysical crossroads of
the modern world."

280 "SR Reviews Books: The Best of 1972--for Giving and Getting."
Saturday Review, 40 (2 December 1972), 80. Same notice
appears under the title "SR Recommends" in Saturday
Review of the Arts, 1 (6 January 1973), 85; Saturday
Review of the Arts, 1 (3 February 1973), 65; Saturday
Review of Education, 1 (13 January 1973), 73; Saturday
Review of the Sciences, 1 (27 January 1973; cover is dated
February 1973), 71; and Saturday Review of Society, 1
(20 January 1973; cover is dated February 1973), 61.
"The author takes on the complex texture of an American
small town, the motif of medieval romance, and the weighty
themes of freedom and entropy in his most important novel
to date."

281 Sudler, Barbara. "'Sunlight Dialogues' Is Top-Flight
Existential Novel." Denver Post, 24 December 1972, Roundup
sec., p. 14.
SD is "a medieval romance, a morality play, an existential
novel for our times," and its author is "the fashionable
darling of the Establishment." It is a novel that combines
suspense, Barth, Beckett, Cheever, and Fowles. The Hodge
clan, "imagined in Russian dimensions," is especially well
done.

282 Sipper, Ralph B. "Magic Tricks and a Torrent of Colloquies."
San Francisco Chronicle, 7 January 1973, "This World" sec.,
p. 29.
SD is "an unqualified spellbinder" and a major work of
serious fiction that successfully defines the contemporary
experience. Although erudite and intricately structured,
the novel is compelling and understandable and the plot
"straightforward."

283 "Some Notable Books of 1972." Washington Post Book World,
3 December 1972, p. 5.
As "Briefly Noted" above.

284 Tanner, Tony. "The Agent of Love and Ruin." Saturday
Review of the Arts, 1 (6 January 1973), 78-80.
Discusses similarities between G and SD, especially
their concern with entropy, suspicions about language, and

the parallels between Grendel and the Sunlight Man, the
Shaper and Clumly. The realism of SD is one of the novel's
attempts at depicting the artifice of order. "It is another comment on the achievement of this novel that we
can accept a small-town American cop talking metaphysics
and feel, not that realism has been lost, but that fiction
has gained." Gardner's (like Updike's) "straining for
self-vaunting but redundant simile" and the fact "that
some of the very long tirades detach themselves from the
speakers' characters" are the novel's weaknesses.

285 Taylor, Henry. In Masterplots Annual 1973. Ed. Frank N.
Magill. Englewood Cliffs, N.J.: Salem Press, 1974, pp.
353-56.
"In an age when fiction is seeking to go beyond its
traditional limitations, this novel exhibits, simultaneously, a mastery of realistic techniques, and an ironic
awareness of their inadequacy."

286 Thompson, Francis. "Batavia, Alas, Has No Good King."
Tampa Tribune-Times, 24 December 1972, p. C5.
SD is filled with literary echoes: in its self-reflex-
iveness and detective story form, the French nouveau
roman; in its portrayal of a monster (the Sunlight Man),
Beowulf and G; and in its tracing the fall of a great
family, Aristotle's definition of tragedy and Faulkner's
The Sound and the Fury.

287 Thwaite, Anthony. "Novels." Observer, 14 October 1973,
p. 38.
The novel is pretentious, hollow, inert and humorless.

288 Torgersen, Margaret. "Dialogues in Batavia." Rochester
Democrat & Chronicle, 3 December 1972, "Show" sec., p. 11.
Gardner is more than a local colorist; he brilliantly
links place and emotion, detail and history in a novel
that is "a superb story" and a good deal more. He
compassionately and fully understands his characters and
setting. The interwoven threads of the various characters' experiences are held together by Clumly (a
mixture of Ahab and Babbitt), who with "a pitying and
forgiving eye ... always sees both sides."

289 Turner, Alice K. "PW Forecasts: Paperbacks." Publishers
Weekly, 204 (22 October 1973), 112.
Notes Ballantine editions of SD, WA, and G in a boxed
set.

290 White, Edward M. "Shedding Light on Law and Order." Los
Angeles Times, 15 October 1972, Calendar sec., pp. 58-59.
A good editor might have transformed this "momentous
failure" into one of the year's best novels. The bloated
and "repetitious" passages of introspection--Taggert's
monologues and Clumly's stream of consciousness--are the
novel's major flaw. Freed of his philosophical concerns,
Gardner creates vivid portraits of his minor characters.

291 Wolff, Geoffrey. "Trench Warfare on the Borders of
Reality." Washington Post Book World, 24 December 1972,
p. 3.
The general subjects of SD make up "a longer list than
ever that hungry Faulkner dreamt of when he called for the
'old verities.'" The novel, like the list, is too long,
yet it "insists on being read at a single sitting" because
"despite its variety, it is a metaphor, an extended meditation on the trench warfare between freedom and order."

292 Wood, Michael. "New Fall Fiction." New York Review of
Books, 19 (19 October 1972), 33-37.
Despite the "purple prose" and "empty" similes, SD is a
novel of "tremendous authority and distinction." It has
a realistic base, but its strength derives from the creation of a self-contained fictional world. Moreover, the
breakdown of the Hodge family is reflected in the breakdown of the novel form. Gardner's theme is not, as in G,
waste versus order, but instead waste as "the result of
brave attempts to break out of order's limitations."

Jason and Medeia (1973)

293 Adams, Phoebe. "Short Reviews: Books." Atlantic, 232
(September 1973), 118.
Animadverts against Gardner's use of hexameter.

294 Bannon, Barbara A. "PW Forecasts: Fiction." Publishers
Weekly, 203 (30 April 1973), 53.
"... ambitious and impressive, but probably destined for
a somewhat special audience." Outline follows Euripedes
but in "contemporary terms."

295 Booklist, 70 (1 September 1973), 23.
"Superb"; "The portrayal of Jason as a politician, an
intellectual overcome by forces beyond his control and the
sympathetic delineation of Medeia as a woman haunted by a

terrible heritage and deeply wronged as a wife and mother"
are especially well done.

296 Boyd, Robert. "A Classical Arabesque." St. Louis Post-
Dispatch, 1 July 1973, p. 4D.
"The story seems no more than a handy medium for Gardner's
literary gamesmanship." The poem's most serious shortcom-
ing is "the banality ... of the poesy."

297 Bravard, Robert S. Library Journal, 98 (15 April 1973),
1307-08.
"A powerful and haunting novel that reads like a superb
translation of a primitive epic." As in G, "Gardner uses
a familiar past to illustrate and inform the present."
However, using "his contemporary self as the narrator"
causes some "dissonance."

298 "Briefly Noted." Washington Post Book World, 15 July 1973,
p. 15.
Notes the variety of myths and levels of meaning.

299 Carne-Ross, D. S. "Epic Overreach." New York Review of
Books, 20 (4 October 1973), 35-36.
"A full-scale literary disaster"; "Only prolonged quotation could do justice to the unflagging banality of
diction and imagination...." Also faulted are Gardner's
"shop-worn metaphysics," absence of narrative, and abundance of "stuffing." "The only moral I can discover in
this lamentable affair is that reviewers should take care
how they praise young and ambitious authors."

300 Choice, 10 (November 1973), 1382.
The poem derives from Greek and Hindu myths and employs
a distinctly modern poet-narrator as a framing device.

301 Crinklaw, Don. "Academic Literary Grooves." National
Review, 25 (23 November 1973), 1311-12.
Faults JM as an "academic fiction": derivative; too much
talk, too little action; "more fun to talk about than to
read"; "total disregard for the marketplace and little
interest in the reader."

302 DeFeo, Ronald. "Fiction Chronicle." Hudson Review, 26
(Winter 1973-74), 777.
The book is bloated and overly philosophical, its
language "feeble" and occasionally "foolish."

303 Dickstein, Morris. "Bizarre Invention, a Translation without an Original." New York Times Book Review, 1 July 1973, p. 4.
Approves "the local tactics of narration and verbal display" but criticizes Gardner's inability to handle human relationships, the triteness of his ideas, and his intruding (as Barth does in Chimera) a modern consciousness on his ancient material. As for why Gardner wrote JM: he "is a prolific and learned writer of amazing virtuoso dexterity, but with little power of judgment or depth of inspiration." (For calling Gardner an "overachiever," Dickstein was upbraided by Joyce Carol Oates in a letter published in the New York Review of Books, 4 October 1973, p. 37.)

304 Hall, Joan Joffe. "First Rate Narrative Verse." Houston Post, 5 August 1973.
Gardner's interweaving of various myths is written in "first class narrative verse, supple, varied, intelligent, charged." Medeia represents passion, and Jason the moral dilemma of choice and uncertainty. Gardner's unnecessarily erudite vocabulary and use of a modern narrator are the work's only shortcomings.

305 Kirkus Reviews, 41 (1 April 1973), 426.
"... impressive ... in its bookish, pseudo-Homeric way, but, finally ... rather overblown, unwisely incantatory, synthetic."

306 Kirsch, Robert. "Story of Jason and Medeia Retold in Epic Poem Style." Los Angeles Times, 18 July 1973, sec. 4, p. 4.
Gardner's story is powerfully and freshly told, "deep and convincing ... erudite but never pedantic." Like a dream, it creates "a mosaic" of reading, experience, and imagination. The "complex process" of love and the uncertain power of the supernatural are the major themes in this "fable not irrelevant to the politics of our time."

307 Library Journal, 98 (1 April 1973), 1198.
Gardner "attempts to restore to the tales their original grandeur and intensity."

308 Maddocks, Melvin. "The Sharks of Fate." Time, 102 (16 July 1973), 74.
Gardner's theme, especially in JM and SD, is "How can law and freedom be reconciled?" Betrayal is inevitable, as in "man's determination to renegotiate with what he has killed in others and in himself."

309 New York Sunday News.*
   Quoted in Ballantine edition of JM, p. [i].

310 Nye, Robert. "A Very Strange and Exciting and Entirely
   Original Book." Christian Science Monitor, 18 July
   1973, p. 13.
   Gardner is a writer who uses language as though he
   "just invented it." JM is a religious book about the
   power of love; ultimately it "defies rational analysis."
   Gardner, whose pitch is too high-keyed, adds "a
   tincture of Disney to the divine."

311 Pierpont, Phillip E. Best Sellers, 33 (1 October 1973),
   292-93.
   JM is "a re-creation--not a mere imitation or recast-
   ing." Pierpont, a former student of Gardner's, takes
   earlier reviewers to task for criticizing the author's
   use of "received myth," the book's "episodic quality,"
   and for failing to notice the "dream frame." The poem
   works on various levels--as story, as allegory, and as "a
   philosophic statement" of affirmative nihilism." Its less
   obvious sources are Chaucer's "Hous of Fame" and "The
   Knight's Tale," "The Song of Solomon," and personal
   experience.

312 Pittsburgh Press.*
   Quoted in Ballantine edition of JM, p. [i].

313 Prescott, Peter S. "Benom, Kumry and Ultion." Newsweek,
   81 (25 June 1973), 88, 90.
   "John Gardner is so talented that he can bring off, at
   least in part, anything he wants to write. It's what he
   wants to write that bothers me." Where Barth's imitation,
   Chimera, succeeds, Gardner's does not. Criticizes
   Gardner's use of obscure words, neologisms, and hexameters;
   " ... at best his verse is derivative, and at worst it is
   fruity."

314 St. Louis Globe-Democrat.*
   Quoted in Ballantine edition of JM, p. [i].

315 Slater, Ian M. Fantasiae, 3 (October 1975), 6-7.
   Faults Gardner for addressing parts of JM to readers
   familiar with Greek myths and other parts to an audience
   apparently ignorant of those myths. The review includes
   some detailed discussion of how Gardner used a number of
   his sources.

316 Thomas, Phil. "Gardner Goes Back to Greeks." <u>New</u>
<u>Orleans Times Picayune</u>, 19 August 1973, sec. 3, p. 11.
<u>JM</u> is as good as, perhaps even better than <u>G</u> and <u>SD</u>.
Its characters are real, its "free verse" well done, and
the use of the modern narrator "enables the reader to
observe the major characters while at the same time
being inside them." The one flaw is Gardner's occasionally
slipping into the modern idiom.

317 Walsh, Chad. "Linking the Archaic Past and the Present
in an Epic Poem." <u>Chicago Tribune</u>, 1 July 1973, sec. 7,
p. 3.
Gardner's Homeric poem succeeds despite its shortcomings.
The author fails to interweave his two story lines (Jason's
adventures and Kreon's daughter) successfully; his "revi-
sionist" portrayal of Medeia is "less believable" than his
other characterizations; Jason is more an observer
than a character; and the mixing of high and low diction
seems unintentionally comic. But "the importance of <u>JM</u>
goes beyond the particular book," pointing away from
contemporary poetry, which is heavily psychological, and
towards a poetry in which the story is more important
than the poet.

Nickel Mountain: A Pastoral Novel (1973)

318 Adams, Phoebe. "Short Reviews: Books." <u>Atlantic</u>, 233
(February 1974), 96.
"The latest novel by the author of the overwrought <u>SD</u>
is a return to his earlier, simpler style."

319 Allen, Bruce. "Up the Hill, Down the Hill." <u>Baltimore</u>
<u>Sun</u>, 27 January 1974, p. D5.
<u>NM</u> is a rewarding novel, a celebration of "plain love"
and marriage. Because it deals with the commonplace, the
novel is at first painfully slow-paced; gradually it becomes more interesting and culminates in an elegaic final
scene of great power. Henry, the main figure, slowly attains a full knowledge of life. The other characters
serve as contrasting "<u>exempla</u> of futility or failed
knowledge."

320 Bannon, Barbara A. "PW Forecasts: Fiction." <u>Publishers</u>
<u>Weekly</u>, 204 (1 October 1973), 77-78.
Gardner "writes beautifully and simply of life and death
and passion in unexpected places."

96

Barrett, Mary Ellin. "Cosmo Reads the New Books."
Cosmopolitan, 176 (February 1974), 44.
" ... a wonderful misshapen valentine of a novel."
Setting and characters are well drawn; ordinarily trite
material is transformed into a "dazzling" story.

322 "Best Sellers." New York Times Book Review, 20
January 1974, p. 29.
Ten weeks; through 14 April 1974.

323 Booklist, 70 (15 February 1974), 632.
" ... Henry's slow transformation by responsibility."

324 Boyd, Robert. "Righteous Obligations." St. Louis Post-
Dispatch, 23 December 1973, p. 4C.
Henry "is the epitome of the grotesque hero of whom
Gardner ... is so inordinately fond." The novel's
language, characterizations, and physical appearance are
its strengths; its chief weakness is that "it suffers
from its parentage"--its having been written while Gardner
was in graduate school.

325 Boylan, Mildred. "Henry Soames Is the Latest of John
Gardner's Heroes." Rochester Times-Union, 23 February
1974, pp. D5, D8.
Like the Sunlight Man, Henry is "intense," honest, and
"courageous," though not as loquacious. His "nagging
ailment is loneliness." Whereas Callie is "uncomplicated,"
Henry is complex. Although the plot is low-key and
repetitive, the reader does become emotionally involved
in the lives of the characters.

326 Brady, Charles A. "Gardner Tackles Pastoral Novel."
Buffalo Evening News, 5 January 1974, p. A14.
What little "genuine Gardner" there is in NM is very
good, but this novel concerning a Chaucerian May-December
marriage includes too many diverse elements to be entirely
successful. The concluding cemetery scene and the "macabre"
portrait of Simon Bale are especially well done.

327 Breslin, John B. "Winnowing the Word Harvest." America,
129 (6 October 1973), 250.
Reviewed with Joyce Carol Oates's Do With Me What You
Will; "both deal with lives transformed by the emergence
of an unexpected capacity for love."

328 "Briefly Noted." New Yorker, 49 (21 January 1974), 94.
Despite the detailed realism, there is no depth to the
characters, and Gardner "fails (like the book's phonily
old-fashioned illustrations) to ever fully capture the
reader's imagination."

329 Cheuse, Alan. "Real Coffee, Ideal Coffee." Nation, 218
(15 June 1974), 759-61.
"John Gardner has attempted once again the paradoxical
task of speaking for the speechless and feeling for the
numbed." In this "marvelously composed" novel of simple
style and simple subject, "sentiment is Gardner's good,
sentimentality his evil."

330 Choice, 11 (April 1974), 258.
"Only Joyce Carol Oates has written in recent times as
well of the business of 'silent majority' living"; where
her characters struggle against life, Gardner's "have found
a way to come to terms with living" in this novel of "plain,
exact prose."

331 Christian Century, 92 (14 May 1975), 502.
The story is good though "rather wild and incoherent at
times."

332 Cockshutt, Rod. Raleigh News and Observer.*
Cited in Cockshutt's review of KI. Raleigh News and
Observer, 2 February 1975.

333 Daillie, R. Quinzaine Litteraire, 1976, p. 8.*
Cited in Arts and Humanities Index, 1976.

334 DeFeo, Ronald. Commonweal, 99 (1 March 1974), 536-37.
"Bloated language," Gardner's "incessant preaching,"
and philosophical ideas that are "merely recorded, not
dramatized" are the weaknesses of WA, G, and SD. NM,
though it has none of these faults, still fails as a
result of inadequate characterization.

335 "The First Books of Christmas." Washington Post Book
World, 8 December 1974, p. 8.
A one-sentence summary of Skow's review, below.

336 Foote, Timothy. "Signs of Life." Time, 102 (31 December
1973), 55-56.
"Among the considerable afflictions of the serious novel
these days are fear of banality and a horror of sentiment.
However skillfully they are written, there is often not
enough at stake in contemporary novels to keep the mind

and heart alive." But in NM Gardner, like Sherwood
Anderson, "is willing to sound boring and simple-minded
in an attempt to reinvest [cliches and soap opera
characters] with a kind of truthfulness and passion."

337 Fuller, Edmund. "An Unlikely Shepherd Tends His Human
Flock." Wall Street Journal, 30 January 1974, p. 10.
" ... no finer fiction is being written in America,
currently, than the richly varied novels of John Gardner."
Soames is "not an antihero" but the hero of a novel "rich
... in supporting figures."

338 Hill, William B. "Fiction." America, 130 (4 May 1974),
348.
NM is a successful pastoral; the use of numerous minor
characters is "a mode that by now has become a Gardner
convention."

339 Hirsch, Foster. America, 130 (27 April 1974), 336-37.
Although "a sophisticated fable, a complex pastoral,"
NM "is the author's least dazzling and most human performance." Gardner "assembles his materials casually."
His characters are "noble peasants"; Henry in particular
is "like the bartender of literary tradition ... a
listener."

340 Howe, Linda. "This 'Nickel Mountain' Is Solid Gold."
Rochester Democrat & Chronicle, 24 February 1974, p. H6.
Gardner's "literary modesty," nineteenth-century sense
of narrative, and creation of characters the reader can
care about make this an excellent novel, one that is
serious yet not without a "crazy twist" to keep the
seriousness in perspective. Neither innocent nor stupid,
Henry is "an argument for unselfinterested human love" in
this novel about "urban paranoia." (NM is listed among
"Rochester best sellers" on same page.)

341 Howes, Victor. "John Gardner's Stop-Off: 'Pastoral
Romance in Middle America." Christian Science Monitor,
30 January 1974, p. F5.
Links Gardner to Updike and Cheever "as one of the
presiding portrayers of life in late 20th-century America."
His story is "fundamentally religious," "an investigation
of the ways we are our brother's keeper." There are
similarities to soap opera and to Sidney's "Arcadia" in
Gardner's plotless "novel, or romance."

342 Jones, A. Wesley. In Masterplots Annual 1974, Ed. Frank
N. Magill. Englewood Cliffs, N.J.: Salem Press, 1975,
pp. 273-77.
Review includes an extended analysis of the novel's
structure and, in relation to Res, a discussion of the
confrontation-with-death theme. According to Jones, NM
represents seven years of growth on the author's part.

343 Kirkus Reviews, 41 (1 October 1973), 1122.
"Sort of like Our Town, an old-fashioned tableau--and
as plain as a pinewood coffin." The novel's design is
similar to that of Res.

344 Kisor, Henry. "... Gardner's Triumph of Humanity."
Chicago Daily News, 22-23 December 1973, Panorama sec.,
p. 6.
Gardner's "old-fashioned faith in humanity" pits him
against the modern culture; his books involve "religious
experience that does not demand religious belief." (Kisor
notes that NM may be an early novel.)

345 LaSalle, Peter. "Compassionate Encore." National
Observer, 13 (12 January 1974), 21.
The only flaw in this essentially realistic novel is
Henry's being too obviously symbolic; otherwise, it is
proof of Gardner's "compassionate, probing intelligence,
and real craftsmanship."

346 Lehmann-Haupt, Christopher. "John Gardner Down to Earth."
New York Times, 20 December 1973, p. 37.
Briefly traces Gardner's meteoric career and mentions his
pyrotechnic style; the reviewer prefers the simple style
of NM and notes the novel's thematic similarity to Cheever's
Bullet Park.

347 Leonard, John. "1973: An apology and 30 Consolations."
New York Times Book Review, 2 December 1973, p. 2.
"John Gardner (playing it straight for once in a
pastoral novel called 'Nickel Mountain')."

348 Lhamon, W. T. Jr. Library Journal, 98 (1 November 1973),
3283.
"Conservative of character in a world that makes that
effort hard, this is a serious novel by a still-
developing talent." His characters "find no answers and
some are randomly, suddenly, inanely snuffed without
dignity. Puzzling life, they create idiosyncratic
systems...."

100

349 Lhamon, W. T. Jr. "Old Tidings." New Republic, 169 (15
December 1973), 25-26.
    NM suffers from its twenty-year composition. The first
half stresses the modern view of "having the nerve to ride
horror down"; the second half is fashionably postmodern,
emphasizing man's indignity and cheapening Gardner's conservative approach to character in the novel's first half.

350 Lomas, Herbert. "American Fiction--I." London Magazine,
ns 15 (October-November 1975), 109-10.
    "John Gardner ... seems to have written that unlikely
thing right now, a novel based on traditional moral frame-
works, tentatively Christian." Throughout the novel there
is "a religious debate ... about practical Christianity and
theoretical Christianity," the upshot of which is that the
characters "begin to lose their guilt in humility." One
reason the novel is so interesting is Gardner's "narrative
power."

351 Manning, Margaret. "Life Silhouetted by a Neon Sign."
Boston Globe, 7 January 1974.
    Gardner "transmutes the everyday into universal terms"
in a novel that is "no simple idyl."

352 Millar, Sylvia. "One Fat Saviour." Times Literary Supplement, 13 December 1974, p. 1420.
    "Each of the novel's eight sections deals with one
significant event which alters the consciousness of the
characters." Henry is a Christ figure, carrying "the
sins of the world symbolically, in the form of fatness
and heart disease."

353 Murray, G. E. "The Blue Plate Special." fiction
international, 2/3 (1974), 124-26.
    Discusses similarities and differences between NM and
SD, two early works only recently published. NM "makes
memorable that which is easily forgotten or buried amid
the dazzling ruins, allusions, and techniques of SD."
"Clumly endures the banality of evil.... Soames shores
against the evil of banality." Gardner's defense "of
everyday mediocrity" is not fashionable, "yet sentimentality in the hands of Gardner becomes a force."

354 "New and Recommended." New York Times Book Review, 16
December 1973, p. 17. Repeated through 13 January 1974.
    The novel "evokes the eternal pastoral, the magic of
change, the goodness of man."

355 "1973: A Selection of Noteworthy Titles." New York Times
Book Review, 2 December 1973, pp. 76-77.
Gardner "plays it straight for once, and demonstrates
that a gritty realistic novel can, in the grinding against
each other of characters and events, yield permanent values."

356 Norris, Hoke. "A Feeling for Men and Women, for the Turning of the Earth and the Changing of the Seasons."
Chicago Sun-Times, 23 December 1973.
A "naturalistic novel" with some "needless muddying of
the style." "Second-hand Faulkner" yet nonetheless moving.

357 Pumphrey, Martin. "Measuring the Considerable Distance
Gardner Has Come." Chicago Tribune, 16 December 1973,
sec. 7, p. 1.
NM, a reworking of an early short story, suggests that
Gardner is abandoning his recent "idiosyncratic" vision
and is returning to a "more human set of relationships."
This novel presents contemporary American issues through
the filter of Gardner's personal vision and again evidences
his wide learning and resonant style. Like Res, it concerns death and change as Gardner explores "the existential
fears ... at the edges of the routine patterns of daily
life."

357a Ray, Lila. "John Gardner: A Writer of Epic Simplicity."
Span (India), March 1976, pp. 36-38.
The grim life described in NM is far from that usually
found in traditional pastoral; nonetheless, NM does
celebrate the world. The lyrical wedding scene adds a
touch of "idyllic distinction," and Henry and Callie are
portrayed as nearly mythic characters. Neither pessimistic nor sentimental, NM is a humble, "nickel" tale of
American life in which Gardner draws on material overlooked by other contemporary American authors. G, on the
other hand, deals with the extraordinary. Its narrative
method is an "astonishing" imaginative feat and its style
"as dark as its theme." Despite the differences, both
novels evidence the "absence of provincialism" and
abundant local color that place Gardner squarely in the
Washington Irving tradition. Gardner, however, goes
well beyond Irving's cosmopolitanism to affirm "a common
and homogeneous humanity." (Excerpt from G appears on
pp. 32-35.)

358 Rogers, Michael. "Briefly Noted." Rolling Stone, 14
    March 1974, p. 75.
      Ultimately Gardner "runs into the problem of how one
    writes about boring and inarticulate people without be-
    coming boring or inarticulate oneself."

359 Skow, Jack. "Time's Slow Reverie." Washington Post
    Book World, 31 March 1974, pp. 1, 4.
      In NM, Gardner's protean style becomes pastoral,
    "meaning, I suppose, that all the beasts in its country
    landscape are tame and that the reader can afford to
    dream a bit without worrying that he will be savaged."
    The author's "intention ... is to portray time."

360 Spacks, Patricia Meyer. "Fiction Chronicle." Hudson
    Review, 27 (Summer 1974), 288-92.
      "But the experience of reading NM is less compelling
    than it should be, because Henry and his friends exist too
    clearly for the convenience and at the disposal of the
    author who has created them." Henry "is, rather too
    insistently, a Christ figure" and the novel's moral is
    "too romantic."

361 Stade, George. "The Truths Under Our Noses If Our Noses
    Are Not in the Air." New York Times Book Review, 9
    December 1973, p. 5.
      Gardner's "pastoral invocation of 'whatever might be up
    there to watch over fools and children'" celebrates
    literature's "ancient forms" and succeeds in making the
    reader believe in both the forms and the "permanent truths."

362 Stone, Elizabeth. Crawdaddy, May 1975, p. 80.
      Rejecting contemporary pessimism as "too limited,"
    Gardner prefers to believe in human love and dignity.
    He chooses and modifies those genres--myth, epic, and,
    in SD, the "tall-tale-cum-parable"--most amenable to his
    faith in man's potential. NM, in so far as it concerns
    "soulsick grotesques in a bleak December world," is an
    ironic pastoral. By avoiding sentimentalism and by in-
    sisting on Henry's ridiculousness, Gardner makes his novel
    and his vision of the dignity of love convincing.

363 Thwaite, Anthony. "Marital Favorites." Observer, 17
    November 1974, p. 33.
      This "simple (I don't think deceptively simple)
    chronicle" is better than SD because Gardner is "more
    in control."

364 Washburn, Martin. Village Voice, 24 January 1974, p. 31
    NM is brilliant and deep, "and it might be entirely com-
    pelling were it clear what reality its characters are
    grounded in."

365 Wood, Michael. "Flirting with Disintegration." New York
    Review of Books, 21 (21 March 1974), 19-22.
    NM contrasts with the anxiety-laden novels of our time.
    Its theme is that "Guilt is damaging, but the thought of
    the rule of sheer chance is intolerable." The novel dis-
    plays Gardner's "gift for making stories ask balanced,
    intricate questions," yet it is not entirely successful
    in so far as the author occasionally uses his characters
    for his own purposes.

The Construction of the Wakefield Cycle (1974)

366 Axton, Richard. Medium Aevum, 47 (1978), 181-82.
    In this "engagingly" written and "enthusiastic" work for
    non-specialists, Gardner shows himself to be "appreciative
    of verbal craftsmanship" and willing "to venture value
    judgments"; often, however, he sidesteps important issues
    and resorts to generalizations.

367 Blanch, Robert J. Comparative Drama, 11 (Summer 1975),
    177-79.
    However "admirable" Gardner's objectives may be, "his
    criticism is frequently marred by simplistic reasoning,
    unsubstantiated statements, and misinterpretation." The
    explanation of the plays' "typological underpinnings" is
    noteworthy, but "his arguments for the existence of
    numerous 'typic' double entendres" are not. Includes a
    list of corrections of "major scholarly blunders."

368 Cawley, A. C. "The Master's Hand." Times Literary
    Supplement, 22 November 1974, p. 1324.
    Gardner's assumption that there was a single Wakefield
    master is neither new nor proven, and he is incorrect
    in believing a major theme to be the conflict between God
    and Devil (the actual conflict being between "earthly
    representatives of the civitas Dei and civitas terrena").
    However, Gardner "is very much alive to the poetic and
    dramatic qualities of the Wakefield cycle and writes
    splendidly about the darker pageants."

369 Choice, 11 (January 1975), 1630.
    Written in Gardner's typically "precise and unpre-
    tentious style."

370 Heinemann, Frederick J. Library Journal, 99 (1 December
    1974), 3133.
    This is an informative and provocative work. Gardner,
    who "only occasionally overexplicates," is most successful
    "when demonstrating the relation of individual pageants to
    the whole cycle."

371 Poteet, Daniel P., II. Journal of English and Germanic
    Philology, 74 (October 1975), 572-74.
    Gardner's book is largely a collection of individual
    essays. There are "sensitive" readings of the plays and
    a number of "provocative insights." However, the study is
    inconsistent and at times in error; it confusingly com-
    bines general and specialized discussions and does not
    prove its thesis that one poet wrote the entire cycle as
    a ritual agon.

372 Stevens, Martin. "The Art of the Medieval Mystery Play."
    American Scholar, 44 (Winter 1974-75), 151-56.
    Gardner errs in accepting "the outworn notion of progress
    in literary forms" and in holding the medieval mind (here
    and in G) in "apparent low esteem." He fails to support
    his contention that the cycle is the work of a single
    master and too readily dismisses the dramatic value of
    the Wakefield plays in favor of the purely literary.

The King's Indian: Stories and Tales (1974)

373 Ackroyd, Peter. "Blood and Thunder." Spectator, 235 (1
    November 1975), 572-73.
    Only a very patient reader will finish this collection
    of "overblown" tales.

374 Allen, Bruce. Library Journal, 99 (15 October 1974), 2619.
    The point of Gardner's "eclectic existentialism" and
    "neo-Ruritanian romances" is that "'a wise man settles for,
    say, Ithaca.'"

375 Bannon, Barbara A. "PW Forecasts: Fiction." Publishers
    Weekly, 206 (21 October 1974), 46.
    Gardner's book, which may have been influenced by John
    Barth, is "a puzzling, ambitious effort perhaps fully
    understood only by himself."

376 Barnes, Julian. "Semi-Bold." New Statesman, 90 (31
October 1975), 550.
Despite all the moving back and forth between levels of
meaning in the title story, there may be "nothing much
there all along." Lewis Carroll may be one of Gardner's
sources.

377 Barras, Leonard. "Short Stories." London Times (Sunday),
7 December 1975, p. 41.
Gardner's collection is "a virtuoso exercise in
mimicry.... The burlesque fairy tales are the most engaging in intrinsic appeal" and "The Ravages of Spring"
is the author's most accurate impersonation.

378 Booklist, 71 (15 February 1975), 595.
The stories blend reality and fantastic "mirror-images"
of reality.

379 Boyd, Robert. "Like THIS in Our Time?" St. Louis Post-
Dispatch, 1 December 1974, p. C4.
Although abruptly broken off, the title story is
brilliantly written. The remaining pieces range from the
"shopworn" ("The Warden") to the delightful ("Tales of
Queen Louisa") to a "memoir" ("John Napper").

380 Brady, Charles A. "Many Echoes Run in Gardner Tales."
Buffalo Evening News, 11 January 1975, p. C8.
Although the collection is "a magnificent sounding board
for [literary] echoes," only the five stories in "The
Midnight Reader" section are all that good. Fink's il-
lustrations are sumptuous, "a breathtaking tour-de-force."

381 Cherry, Kelly. "Gardner's Characters Give Fiction Back
Its Intelligence." Chicago Tribune, 1 December 1974,
sec. 7, p. 3.
"What Gardner does so successfully, and what too many
writers in America today fail to do, is to examine and
dramatize philosophical motives." "The Warden" has
Descartean implications and the title story deals with
"free will and its relation to time."

382 Chicago Daily News.*
Quoted on back cover of the Ballantine edition of KI.

383 Cockshutt, Rod. "Gardner Needs To Lie Fallow." Raleigh
News and Observer, 2 February 1975.
Gardner is in danger of wasting his time and talent on
such exercises as these stories. Except for the "straight-

106

forward and touching" "Pastoral Care," the collection
constitutes "rank show-off-manship." "The Tales of Queen
Louisa" is too fantastic; the mixture of Melville, Coleridge, Homer, Stevenson, Conrad, and others in the title
story is overly rich; and the "verbal jostling is over-
done."

384 Crain, Jane Larkin. Saturday Review, 2 (8 March 1975),
25-26.
"Gardner's sly and exuberant affection for his literary
models, coupled with his own meticulous craftsmanship and
inventiveness" may mask the fact that there is really
nothing going on below the surface of his "pyrotechnic
eclecticism." "Pastoral Care" and "John Napper" are the
collection's best pieces.

385 DeFeo, Ronald. "A Sweet Tooth for Philosophy." National
Review, 27 (28 February 1975), 234-35.
"KI surprises me on two counts. One, that a writer of
Gardner's sophistication could settle for such philosophical and literary doodling. And two, that so many critics
could be charmed with the performance. This kind of encouragement Gardner surely does not need."

386 Derrickson, Howard. "Dazzling Tales from Gardner." St.
Louis Globe-Democrat, 4-5 January 1975, p. D4.
Gardner is a dazzling and highly lyrical writer whose
range encompasses the gothic and contemporary "ethical-
problem fiction." "KI" and "Pastoral Care" are both moral
tales. The "whimsically ethical" Queen Louisa stories,
which derive from Lewis Carroll, are less interesting than
the Poe-like "The Warden" and "The Ravages of Spring" and
the Browningesque "The Temptation of St. Ivo." "John
Napper" is the climactic work. A recurring situation in
these stories is the protagonists' having to face nearly
overwhelming odds.

387 "Editors' Choice." New York Times Book Review, 22
December 1974, p. 17. Repeated through 29 December 1974.
Gardner is an exciting writer, adept at both fabulous
and realistic narrative.

388 Edwards, Thomas R. "Academic Vaudeville." New York
Review of Books, 22 (20 February 1975), 34.
This is a book by, about, and for teachers of literature.
"I can only hope that it has done this immensely gifted

writer some good to get these things [especially the
Barthian self-consciousness] out of his system."

389 Fowler, Doreen. "Some Art-ificial Reflections."
Memphis Commercial Appeal, 5 January 1975, sec. 6, p. 6.
Instead of the realist approach of most contemporary
writers, Gardner is unabashedly romantic. His "spectacu-
larly beautiful" stories stress the "artificiality of
creation" and as a result disrupt the reader's willing
suspension of disbelief. The stories are not, however,
meaningless literary toys. "The Temptation of St. Ivo,"
for example, concerns the paradoxical human hunger for
both freedom and order.

390 Garfitt, Roger. "Fiction and Fabulation." Times Literary
Supplement, 12 December 1975, p. 1477.
"The fabulists are restoring to the novel the theological
dimension of the epic, but the pantheon is deserted and
epic turns inevitably to farce." The best story in the
collection is the least fabulous, "Pastoral Care." The
title story parallels Pynchon's Gravity's Rainbow in a
number of ways.

391 Gelfant, Blanche H. "Fiction Chronicle." Hudson Review,
28 (Summer 1975), 309-11.
As hoaxes the stories are fun, as parodies "unsurpass-
able"; the best ones are "Pastoral Care" and "John Napper."

391a Girault, Norton. "Under the Big Top with John Gardner."
Norfolk Virginian-Pilot, 5 January 1975, p. C6.
Gardner is a dazzling writer, and "KI" is a sea story
"to top all sea stories," a work that can be read on
various levels. The title, which refers to an ancient
chess stratagem rediscovered in the Twentieth Century by
Aron Nimzowitsch, suggests that the old ways are the best.
Thus, the narrative method of KI: the recycling of authors,
works, and styles as a way of saving the reader just as
the King's Indian saves Jonathan Upchurch both physically
and spiritually. KI is also an argument for the return of
illustrated fiction. Fink's "serious, haunting" drawings
complement Gardner's "rambunctious, campy-comic, and
ironic stories." The illustrations at the end of "The
Temptation of St. Ivo" adds to the story a dimension only
hinted at in the text.

392 Gray, Paul. "American Gothic." Time, 104 (30 December
1974), 56.

Gardner is "a fabulist with a heart." The recurrent
situation in this collection is "traditionalist meets
anarchist; an inherited past must defend itself against
a plotless future."

393 Grumbach, Doris. "Fine Print." New Republic, 171 (21
December 1974), 24.
"Close to perfection in its invention and imagination."

394 "Esquire Recommends." Esquire, 82 (August 1974), 28.
Lists KI.

395 Friedman, Alan. "A John Gardner Spectrum, from Gothic
Horrors to Romantic Realism." New York Times Book Review,
15 December 1974, pp. 1-2.
Although "Gardner is in many places too cunning for his
own good," a "straightforward," "enormously appealing"
story such as "Pastoral Care" is finally unsatisfying because it lacks the magic of the other, more fantastic
tales. The review also discusses G, SD, NM, and Res.

396 Harris, Michael. "A Limitless Shadow." Washington Post
Book World, 12 January 1975, pp. 1-2.
Gardner is less "the individual artist" than "the intellectual in touch with a tradition, who is skilled enough
to connect us with the past"; this is an especially
valuable skill in our contemporary age of "lost traditions
and broken connections." Conversely, Gardner's "chaos-
figures" serve to "open the doors of possibility" to his
"order-figures."

397 Howes, Victor. "Gardner's Tales Roam Allegoryland."
Christian Science Monitor, 19 December 1974, p. 10.
Gardner is "firmly committed to the old-fashioned virtues
of story-telling." Although there is too little characterization and too much philosophizing, these stories, whose
sources include Thurber and E. B. White, are still entertaining. In them Gardner suggests that reality "is an
agreed-on myth."

398 Kennedy, William. New Republic, 171 (7 December 1974),
19-20.
"Gardner is the Lon Chaney of contemporary fiction";
"illusory life ... is the dominant theme here." "John
Napper," though "a slight story," is a "key to Gardner's
psyche: he is not Napper but he wishes he were."

399 Kirkus Reviews, 42 (1 October 1974), 1075.
"Gardner's subject is imagination."

400 Lamperti, Claudia. Win, 11 (30 January 1975), 17.
KI will appeal to lovers of fantasy. Gardner "makes
liberal use of tradition, carving out his own version
with psychological depth and without losing integrity of
plot and philosophy."

401 Levine, George. "The Name of the Game." Partisan Review,
42 (Spring 1975), 291-97.
Gardner's best fictions are those in which the play
aspect is on the surface--G and, perhaps his finest work,
"The King's Indian"--and that evidence his faith in narrative as "the way to say yes to life." The "characteristic movement" in his work is "the convention asserted,
the convention tested and apparently found wanting, the
convention reasserted." (Levine also discusses NM, SD,
and G.)

402 McCullough, David. "Eye on Books." Book-of-the-Month
Club News, Spring 1975, p. 6.
Gardner, believing books should be appealing and
"wonderful objects" (as they were when he was growing up),
prefers that his books be illustrated; his editors permit
this "eccentricity" because of Gardner's popular appeal.
Upon first being asked to illustrate KI, Herbert L. Fink
said, "'There's no way my images for your stories could be
the ones you intended.'" The final engravings, however,
delighted Gardner.

403 Mallalieu, H.B. Stand, 17, ii (1976), 74-75.
The collection is original, not merely a pastiche. In
the best stories, "illusion creates reality."

404 Mella, John. "Fresh Fiction and Old Forms." Chicago Sun-
Times, 15 December 1974, p. C9.
It is the reader who becomes the King's Indian, "tricked
into acceptance of the universe." Gardner's narrator may
derive from Conrad.

405 Moody, Minnie Hite. "You May Not Dig, But Still Read On."
Columbus Evening Dispatch, 26 January 1975, sec. i, p. 6.
Gardner is a difficult, erudite writer, a "creator" of
works that are hard to classify and, at first, understand.
The best story is the collection's simplest, "Pastoral Care."

406 Murray, G. E. "In a Magic World with John Gardner."
Milwaukee Journal, 19 January 1975, sec. 5, p. 4.
KI is an "exceptional collection" by an entirely
original author. The common theme in the nine stories is
"survival in the face of accepted cynicism and despair."
Although the reader will not always agree with Gardner's
vision, the stories are all "great fun."

407 Murray, James G. Critic, 33 (March 1975), 71-73.
The philosophizing is intrusive and too often narrative
line is sacrificed for the sake of narrative voice. These
faults are outweighed, however, by the book's virtues:
Gardner's "intelligent, witty sensibility and sensitivity,"
his "sense of the absurdity of life," and his "invitation
to read." Browning is one of Gardner's sources.

408 Neilson, Keith. In Masterplots Annual 1975. Ed. Frank N.
Magill. Englewood Cliffs, N.J.: Salem Press, 1976, pp.
164-66. Rpt. in Survey of Contemporary Literature, ed.
Frank N. Magill, rev. ed. (Englewood Cliffs, N.J.: Salem
Press, 1977), pp. 4036-38.
Gardner is "a superb storyteller," especially in the
title story and "The Warden." His "Tales of Queen Louisa"
recalls Cabell's Poictesme romances and "The Temptation of
St. Ivo" probably derives from Browning's "Soliloquy in a
Spanish Cloister."

409 New York News.*
Quoted in Ballantine edition of KI, p. [i].

410 "1975: A Selection of Noteworthy Titles." New York Times
Book Review, 7 December 1975, p. 62.
Lists KI.

411 "Paperbacks." Washington Post Book World, 7 March 1976,
p. 8.
Ballantine edition. "The tang of vocabulary and action
is precisely right."

412 Parrill, William. "'Words and Pictures in Closest Harmony.
Nashville Tennessean, 12 January 1975, p. F6.
Gardner is "the most gifted American writer" in recent
years, but he lacks "restraint." Like Barth, Borges, and
Garcia Marquez, he bases his fiction in myth--less cleverly
than Barth but more seriously. But his best stories are
his more realistic ones, especially "Pastoral Care."

413 Rogan, Helen. "Whoops and Gasps." Bookletter, 1 (14 April
1975), 3-4.
Despite "moments of monumental unreadability" in Gardner's
books, reviewers continue to note his "promise," presumably
because of his "rampant writerishness: his obsession with
form, his literary in-jokes and elaborate imitations."
This quality is most noticeable in KI. "Short stories bring
out the worst in Gardner, for when he's not being arch,
he's plunging headlong into romantic agony."

414 Smith, R. T. "Short Stories from Two Masters of Literary
Magic." Charlotte Observer, 12 January 1975, p. B8.
Gardner's stories always and successfully combine "compelling plots," metaphor, allegorical action, and character.
In KI he creates "a book of nightmares" in which the subject is the difficulty of a man's making choices in a
world where the distinctions between good and evil are
blurred. (Reviewed with The Ebony Tower, by John Fowles.)

415 Thompson, Francis J. "Hedge against Inflation." Tampa
Tribune-Times, 26 January 1975, p. C5.
Gardner's stories are fun even for readers unfamiliar
with the works Gardner is parodying. The best is "Pastoral
Care," Gardner's second retelling of Beowulf. The author's
literary gamesplaying, including entering his own writing,
is as much a medieval as a modern technique. Gardner will
soon be recognized as a major writer.

416 Thwaite, Anthony. "Faculty in Ferment." Observer, 9
November 1975, p. 27.
These "pointless" parodies suggest "cleverness that
smells of the lamp or the creative writing course."

417 Vick, Judy. "Gardner Tells Varied Tales Well."
Minneapolis Tribune, 13 April 1975, p. D10.
Gardner is a master storyteller, as inventive as Lewis
Carroll, as descriptive as Dickens, and as horrifying as
Poe. The stories in this collection nearly cover the
literary spectrum. All are pleasurable; the title piece
is "profound."

418 Walker, Paul. Luna Monthly, 59 (November 1975), 21.
"Brilliant, moving, hilarious, wonder-filled yarns,
each with an existential sting."

419 White, Edward M. "John Gardner Jumps the Track." Los
Angeles Times, 2 March 1975, "Calendar" sec., p. 66.
Gardner has allowed his success to outstrip his promise;

his new book "is an absolute and total bust." While his intentions are "noble," his "execution is painfully inept, dull and pretentious." The only sign of craftsmanship in the book is the illustrations.

The Construction of Christian Poetry in Old English (1975)

420 Choice, 12 (September 1975), 841.
At times Gardner "superimpose[s] modern aesthetic principles upon older texts."

421 Greenfield, Stanley B. Modern Language Quarterly, 36 (December 1975), 426-28.
Contains numerous misreadings and factual mistakes, the latter suggesting that Gardner does not know the scholarship he cites.

422 Hill, Thomas D. Anglia, 95, iii-iv (1977), 498-500.
Gardner is "sympathetic" towards the poetry and familiar with recent scholarship. The book is, however, insufficiently developed, given the controversial nature of several of Gardner's views, and evidences hasty preparation, "insufficient attention to detail," and a "tendency to argue without considering the ramifications."

423 Hunter, Johanna. English Studies, 58 (August 1977), 350-53.
This is for the most part a "persuasive account of the progress of Anglo-Saxon Christian style" (the chapters on riddles and Beowulf being exceptions) but marred by numerous errors.

424 Keenan, H. T. Library Journal, 100 (1 November 1975), 2054.
"Clever, but often misleading" and marked by "superficial generalities."

425 Parr, Judith Tanis. Christianity & Literature, 26 (Fall 1976), 52-53.
Gardner's ideas require further development. His discussion of Beowulf is interesting but hardly definitive, and his chapter on circular allegory is too general.

Dragon, Dragon and Other Tales (1975)

426 Bartley, Edward. Best Sellers, 36 (April 1976), 29-30.
The morals in these subtly structured fables are "well worth considering."

427 Bulletin of the Center for Children's Books, 29 (March
   1976), 109.
      The stories have a coy, comic-strip style. Occasionally
   the irony becomes too heavy and "disrupts the narrative
   flow."

428 Cole, William. "Children's Books: The Best of the New
   Season." Saturday Review, 3 (29 November 1975), 30.
      Gardner seems to have enjoyed writing these "peculiar"
   tales.

429 D'Ammassa, Don. Delap's Fantasy & Science Fiction Review,
   3 (June 1977), 11-12.
      Gardner's style, a mixture of the traditional and the
   contemporary, makes these stories successful. They are
   witty and inventive, an amusing combination "of sarcastic
   satire and anachronistic spoof."

430 Elleman, Barbara. "Children's Books." Booklist, 72 (15
   January 1976), 684.
      Gardner uses the classic form of the fairy tale but
   gives it his own ironic twist.

430a Filiatreau, John. "Children: A Perfect Audience."
   Louisville Courier-Journal, 7 November 1976, p. E7.
      See annotation under Gudgekin.

431 "Kirkus Choice." Kirkus Reviews, 44 (1 January 1976), 6.
   Listed.

432 Kirkus Reviews, 43 (1 October 1975), 1129.
      The four tales are "disarmingly witty and polished" but
   "a bit thinner than we'd expect from the author of G and
   occasionally descending to the level of adult archness."

433 "1975: A Selection of Noteworthy Titles." New York Times
   Book Review, 7 December 1975, p. 66.
   Listed.

434 "Outstanding Books of the Year." New York Times Book
   Review, 16 November 1975, p. 55.
   Listed.

435 Philadelphia Inquirer.*
   Quoted on dust-jacket of KH.

436 Providence Sunday Journal.*
   Quoted on dust-jacket of KH.

437 "Recommended Paperbacks." Horn Book, 53 (June 1977), 329.
   Lists Bantam edition.

438 Ridley, Clifford A. "Last Minute Shopping? Quality Will
   Out." National Observer, 14 (27 December 1975), 17.
   G was "clearly a warm-up for Dragon, a book that will
   appeal to both adults and children.

439 School Library Journal, 25 (February 1979), 28.
   See annotation under CB.

440 Silvey, Anita. Horn Book, 52 (April 1976), 154.
   Gardner's motifs are traditional, "but the sly, laughing
   asides" are his own.

441 Woods, George A. "For the Older Children." New York
   Times, 20 December 1975, p. 25.
   Gardner tells his "original and irreverent" tales "with
   tongue-not-too-far-in-cheek."

442 Yardley, Jonathan. New York Times Book Review, 16
   November 1975, p. 29.
   These mythic stories have a "contemporary ring" and
   "morals with a twist." "Happy endings are reached, but
   through human rather than heroic means."

Gudgekin the Thistle Girl and Other Tales (1976)

443 Bevington, Helen. "Once Upon a Time and Ever After."
   New York Times Book Review, 14 November 1976, p. 28.
   These stories are too adult. Gardner retains the fairy-
   tale form but takes "liberties that are sly, humorous,
   ironical."

444 Bulletin of the Center for Children's Books, 30
   (February 1977), 90.
   "Sophisticated humor"; "shaky in structure."

445 Canella, Mary Laska. Best Sellers, 36 (March 1977), 386.
   A book for all ages, possibly "a classic in children's
   literature."

446 Cole, William. "Children's Books: The Best of the Season."
Saturday Review, 4 (27 November 1976), 34.
"Modern, hip fairy tales--eerie, inventive, funny."

446a Filiatreau, John. "Children: A Perfect Audience."
Louisville Courier-Journal, 7 November 1976, p. E7.
In these "offbeat, joyous stories," the characters exist
"in a loony world where anything's possible and virtue always prevails." As in his books for adults, Gardner brings
the reader face to face with the magical. (Reviewed with
Dragon.)

447 Kirkus Reviews, 44 (1 October 1976), 1093.
"Disappointing"; Gudgekin lacks the "sparkle" of Dragon
but suffers from the same "coyness."

448 Mercier, Jean. "PW Forecasts: Children's Books."
Publishers Weekly, 210 (4 October 1976), 74.
Noted as a Junior Literary Guild selection; "fantastic
fun."

449 Philadelphia Inquirer.*
Quoted on the dust-jacket of CB.

450 Ridley, Clifford A. " ... Good Children's Books."
National Observer, 15 (25 December 1976), 15.
" ... grand stories, altogether true to the child's firm
conviction that nothing makes any sense."

451 Saturday Review, 5 (27 May 1978), 66.
Lists Bantam edition.

452 School Library Journal, 25 (February 1979), 28.
See annotation under CB.

453 Stein, Ruth M. "Book Remarks." Language Arts, 54 (March
1977), 330.
To traditional motifs, Gardner brings his "no-nonsense
approach." There is the "same rich, offbeat humor" as in
Dragon; the illustrations, however, are "superfluous."

454 Westways, 68 (December 1976), 68.
"Wacky wit"; "flashes of the modern world intrude on the
fairy tale form."

October Light (1976)

455 Adams, Phoebe-Lou. "Short Reviews: Books." Atlantic,

116

239 (January 1977), 93.
Gardner "can do it all [character, plot, style, and
ideas]." Both stories in OL concern "guilt and evil and
the value of life which endures in spite of these things."

456 Askins, John. "Updike and Gardner: Getting to Know Us."
Detroit Free Press, 9 January 1977, p. C5.
Updike's Marry Me and Gardner's OL, along with Woiwode's
Beyond the Bedroom Wall, focus on the mundane and reflect
a shift in American life from self-assurance and exuberance
to contemplation and values. Both books are characterized
by "fine writing," "humane tone," careful characterizations, and "minutely observed detail." Neither, however,
is its author's best work. OL is too sentimental and includes a useless inside-novel.

457 Bannon, Barbara A. "PW Forecasts : Fiction." Publishers
Weekly, 210 (11 October 1976), 86.
"Will undoubtedly be hailed as a major work of fiction."

458 Barkham, John. John Barkham Reviews. Unattributed
clipping.
OL is Gardner's "most impressive" fiction. It includes
an old-fashioned novel conjoined with a contemporary story,
interesting digressions, richly textured prose, and Currier
& Ives-like "scene-painting."

459 Bedell, Thomas D. Library Journal, 102 (1 March 1977),
630.
This is "a strong and lovely book, probing deeply into
the soul and profoundly touching the reader." An inventive
work, it includes a "marvelous" inside-novel.

460 "Best Sellers." New York Times Book Review, 30 January
1977, p. 33.
Ten weeks; through 17 April 1977.

461 "Best Sellers of the Year." New York Times Book Review,
4 December 1977, p. 111.
OL has been on the best sellers list for ten weeks.

462 Bookletter, 6 December 1976, p. 15.*
Cited in Howell.

463 Booklist, 73 (1 November 1976), 391.
   The novel deals with life "as a contest of wills" and
   with the "contrast between the pastoral and the sordid."

464 "The Books of Christmas: Two." Washington Post Book World,
   12 December 1976, p. 1.
   "John Gardner is a story-telling novelist, as rollicking
   as Dickens and as ribald as Fielding, with affinities to
   earlier centuries."

465 "The Bookshelf." Changing Times, 32 (April 1978), 43.
   Lists Ballantine edition.

466 "Briefly Noted." New Yorker, 52 (14 February 1977), 122-23.
   The novel is "a kind of counterpoint examination of the
   contemporary and the traditional Bicentennial America,"
   weakened by The Smugglers section, and "characteristically
   peculiar."

467 Choice, 14 (March 1977), 62.
   Gardner has emerged "as a significant American novelist";
   he tells his story "in a flexible, conversational prose
   that advances the narrative effortlessly."

468 Clapperton, Jane. "Cosmo Reads the New Books."
   Cosmopolitan, June 1977, p. 8.
   The story of the Pages is "scaldingly intelligent"; The
   Smugglers is "a cynical melodrama."

469 Coale, Sam. Providence Journal, 27 March 1977, p. H16.
   Despite the novel's modernist self-consciousness,
   Gardner remains faithful to "the dramatic focus of his
   work" and the reality of his characters. The inside-novel
   affects Sally's rebellion and is used by Gardner to comment
   on the confrontation between brother and sister. As in SD
   Gardner evidences a Faulknerian "sense of doom, locale and
   family intrigue" in which each event leads directly to another. As in NM, there is the pastoralism and sharp vision
   of Robert Frost. This "sumptuous" novel reveals not a
   concept of fiction but "a human world made universal by
   its suffering, its limitations, its glimpses of possible
   forgiveness."

470 Coppel, Alfred. "Strange Novel of Allegorical Protest."
   San Francisco Chronicle This World (magazine), 2 January
   1977, p. 32.
   The author of so rich and rewarding a novel as WA has,

in OL, written an extraordinarily dull book: preachy, allegorical, ponderously symbolic.

471 DeMers, John. "Growing Old in Vermont." New Orleans Times Picayune, 9 January 1977, sec. 3, p. 10.
"Insight and language" make this simple story complex. The characterizations, descriptions, and rendering of passing time are especially well done. The one flaw is Gardner's having made the story too long by including the inside-novel, which is "impossible to connect" with the main action.

472 Dickey, Edward. Best Sellers, 36 (March 1977), 380.
Perhaps "the most significant contribution to the American Bicentenary," Gardner's novel helps to explain the relationship between present and past in America.

473 "Editors' Choice." New York Times Book Review, 2 January 1977, p. 2. Through 6 February 1977.
A brief paragraph drawn from the more approving comments in Towers' review below.

474 Elliott, George P. "Fiction and Anti-Fiction." American Scholar, 47 (Summer 1978), 406.
This is Gardner's best fiction, marred, however, by the inexplicable insertion of a "punk-novel."

475 Ferrell, Talshian. "October Light: Two Novels: One Boring, One Brilliant." In These Times, 1 (19 January 1977), 17.
Only the inclusion of the hodgepodge "sub-novel" and of reminiscence that impedes the narrative flow mar this otherwise impressive novel. Gardner's powerful and exciting "main story" is vividly described and effectively evokes the American past.

476 Filiatreau, John. "A Family Battle That Ends with Wisdom and Change." Louisville Courier-Journal, 9 January 1977, p. D5.
Although Gardner may be the finest American writer today, his "strained literariness," in SD for example, can be annoying. This trait, coupled with the inside-novel, nearly dooms OL, a book saved by Gardner's masterful language. Dr. Alkahest is the one character in The Smugglers that is well done.

477 Forbes, Cheryl. "Up from Decay." Christianity Today, 21 (18 February 1977), 28.

"As a satire on the pseudo-philosophical pot-boiler,
[The Smugglers] is nearly successful. But as a trigger
for Sally's memories of the past, it is farfetched."

478 Ford, Stephen. San Francisco Review of Books, February
1977, pp. 29-30.
Although Gardner obviously "cares about writing," OL
is not an especially interesting book. Its two stories
fail to cohere; oddly enough, The Smugglers is the more
interesting: a serious writer's attempt at writing trash
fiction. The Vermont story, which concerns the "momentous"
consequences of mundane acts, is peopled with "caricatures"
rather than convincing characters.

479 H., R. R. "Now in Paper." Bookviews, 1 (June 1978), 17.
Despite occasional excesses, this is an "impressive"
work, "an allegorical and symbolic novel."

480 Halio, Jay L. "American Dreams." Southern Review, 13
(October 1977), 840-42.
Although the end may be a bit sentimental, this story of
compromise is Gardner's "best so far."

481 Harkness, James David. "The War between the Pages."
Bookletter, 6 December 1976, p. 15.
OL deals with the schizophrenic American spirit. Gardner,
one of today's finest writers, is eloquent, skillful in
his use of dialect, characters, and pastoral elegy and in
drawing the line where the ordinary and the surreal inter-
sect. The overt philosophizing of the earlier novels is
less obtrusive in OL, a book that will appeal as much to
the reader's head as to his heart. Its one flaw is The
Smugglers, "a literary red herring" served up to Sally as
"metaphysical junk food."

482 Hendin, Josephine. New Republic, 176 (5 February 1977),
30-32.
OL, like Gardner's other fiction, deals with the role of
the modern hero; though his fiction is action-filled, the
author himself suffers from "moral paralysis" and "is too
much a product of the times he condemns. He is cynical
about the aims of heroes." His male characters lack "a
sense of masculine purpose" and are unable to use their
"power in the service of a worthwhile cause." (The review,
with few changes, is included in Hendin's Vulnerable
People.)

483 Hepburn, Neil. "This Lunar Beauty...." _Listener_, 98 (25
August 1977), 254.
   The _Smugglers_ section is preferable to the story of the
   Pages, which is marred by sentimentality.

484 Hicks, Granville. _American Way_.*
   Cited in Book-of-the-Month Club "Featured Alternate"
   circular for _OL_; review not located in _American Way_ files.

485 Kendall, Elaine. "Gardner's Literate Feast on the Gravy
   Train." _Los Angeles Times Book Review_, 19 December 1976,
   pp. 1, 12.
   _OL_ succeeds at two levels: as accessible popular literature and as serious art. Its two stories "become not only
   contrapuntal, but complementary" by the end of the novel.
   There is considerable humor, and the use of the Vermont
   dialect is sparing but effective.

486 _Kirkus Reviews_, 44 (1 October 1976), 1110.
   The inside-novel serves as "a philosophical counterpoint
   to the big quarrel" and is "merely skimmable. In fact,
   much of the main novel seems adrift in its riches."

487 Leavis, L. J., and J. M. Blom. "Current Literature 1977."
   English Studies, 59 (October 1978), 448-49.
   _OL_ is a rarity among recent American novels in that it
   treats its subject, America, genuinely and correctly.
   This makes it all the more "irritating" that Gardner
   should "waste so much energy" writing _The Smugglers_, which
   he intends both as "hilarious rubbish" and as a meaningful
   commentary on the story of James and Sally.

488 LeClair, Thomas. "Updike and Gardner: Down from the
   Heights." _Commonweal_," 104 (4 February 1977) 89-90.
   Bellow, Updike and Gardner "have resisted language games
   and the apocalypse of fact" and have preferred narrative
   and "the possibility ... of transcendence." _OL_ is thematically similar to _Mr. Sammler's Planet_ but is spoiled by
   The Smugglers ("a Pynchonized _Dog Soldiers_ with a sci-fi
   ending"). The inside-novel is "too long to work as parody
   and too meager to be taken seriously"; it is also "inconsistent" in that it is not morally affirmative.

489 Lehmann-Haupt, Christopher. "Books of the Times." _New
   York Times_, 1 December 1976, p. C21.
   This "dark pastoral comedy" is Gardner's "most compelling

novel," evidence that he is continuing to move steadily
away from a fiction in the service of philosophy to a more
purely fictional form. The novel-within may be a self-
parody of Gardner's earlier allegorical books.

490 Lipez, Richard. "Yankee Stamina." Newsday, 30 January
1977, "Ideas" sec., p. 23.
OL is Gardner's "most accessible and most enjoyable
novel," a work about the Yankee mind and the uses of
memory. The Smugglers is a splendid parody of trash
fiction.

491 Littlefield, William E. Kliatt Paperback Book Guide, 12
(Spring 1978), 6.
Characterization and language are especially strong in
this "exploration of what life has to teach and reteach us."

492 Logan, William. "Fiction within fiction: John Gardner
and the Accidents of Life." Chicago Tribune Book World,
12 December 1976, p. 3.
"OL has neither the complexity of characterization that
enlivened SD and JM nor the mythic invention that transformed G. The tediousness that threatened his other novels
is often triumphant here." However, OL "nearly ends re-
deemed by its pathos." The Smugglers section "turns the
book into a novel partly about the effects of reading."

493 Long, Fern. "Stormy Autumn of Their Lives." Cleveland
Press Showtime Magazine, 24 December 1976, p. 20.
The immensely knowledgeable Gardner uses his novel to
express his opinions of the contemporary culture. It is
a well-written book, in some ways Gardner's best, filled
with the author's sympathetic understanding of his two
older characters. The Smugglers story parodies popular
romances and gothics but also hints at some underlying
meaning (Dr. Alkahest's name, for example, refers to the
alchemist's universal solvent).

494 McPherson, William. "The Proof Is in the Pudding."
Washington Post Book World, 2 January 1977, p. 1.
"A good and rather old-fashioned story--rollicking,
ribald, truly imaginative the way Dickens, for example,
is truly imaginative, and real." Also, this hopeful novel
has philosophical and theological dimensions. It "hinges,
like a well-made play, on a single dramatic question: how
will Sally be lured from her room and brother and sister
be reconciled?"

495 Maddocks, Melvin. "Making Ends Meet." Time, 108 (20
    December 1976), 74.
    Except for the novel's affirmative ending--"more determined
    than logical"--Gardner nearly masters all his various roles
    in this book: "spoofer of pulp fiction," "composer of
    Kierkegaardian monologues," "mini-historian," and "pastoral
    poet." The Smugglers "comes dangerously close to upstaging
    OL."

496 Manning, Margaret. "John Gardner: Superb Writer in a Class
    with Updike and Bellow." Boston Globe, 5 December 1976.
    OL is "a serious religious novel," "the best novel of
    the year." Gardner "is a superb writer who shuns apocalypse,
    and who is affirmative about America."

497 Morgan, Edwin. "Coming to Terms with Trash." Times Literary
    Supplement, 12 August 1977, p. 977.
    Gardner is best at "manipulat[ing] our sympathies back
    and forth between brother and sister." He is less success-
    ful in keeping his "what-is-a-novel debate on the boil."

498 Morton, Kathryn. "Prime Materials Mixed into a Stew."
    Norfolk Virginian-Pilot, 23 January 1977, p. C6.
    Like NM and SD, OL "is long, confusingly formed, and
    philosophical." The novel is filled with rich scenes,
    though none is developed at any length. The rapid cutting
    from scene to scene may have been intended to suggest
    "diffusion, disparity, disinterest, keeping feelings dis-
    tanced and distracted"; the effect, however, is of "prime
    materials, merely thrown together."

499 Murray, G. E. "Once More, a Gardner 'Big Picture' Novel."
    Milwaukee Journal, 16 January 1977, sec. V, p. 4.
    Tradition, values, and the human condition are Gardner's
    concerns. Although OL lacks the lively philosophizing of
    SD and the "human warmth" of NM--two of the best novels of
    the decade--its themes and powerful prose make it one of
    Gardner's finest achievements. In it, Gardner not only
    juxtaposes two stories and two kinds of art, he also
    juxtaposes past and present. In Gardner's view, "people
    are what they remember."

500 Nordell, Roderick. "'October Light' Shows Literary Daring."
    Christian Science Monitor, 8 December 1976, p. 33.
    The novel, which has affinites with the work of Norman
    Rockwell, shows "quiet literary daring."

501 "Notable Books of 1976." Booklist, 73 (1 April 1977),
    1152.
    The "value of endurance" is the novel's theme.

502 "Notes on Current Books." Virginia Quarterly Review, 53
    (Spring 1977), 62.
    "A dramatic narrative that unfolds in perceptive counter-
    point. The focus is sharp, the descriptions are vivid,
    the thematic messages ring true without sentimentality,
    heroics, or trivialization."

503 Olson, Clarence E. "Never Too Old to Hurt." St. Louis
    Post-Dispatch, 26 December 1976, p. E4.
    "At a basic level, the novel explores 'one's potential
    for becoming a victim, and one's potential for becoming a
    destroyer.'" The characters are fully realized; there is
    little plot, however, and, in The Smugglers, "little
    apparent purpose."

504 Ostermann, Robert. "Through the American Psyche."
    National Observer, 16 (29 January 1977), 21.
    "Gardner is carving new lines in the features of the
    American mythology he has already searched out in SD and
    NM." Sally and James insist that "experience has but one
    face" and only perhaps at the end do they discover what the
    youth Terence does: "everything together, 'life's monstrosity
    and beauty.'"

505 Paulin, Tom. "Captain Fist." New Statesman, 94 (22 July
    1977), 123-24.
    "This is a brilliantly imaginative novel, whose comic
    pessimism negates both the foundations and the surfaces
    of American society."

506 Prescott, Peter S. "Moonlight in Vermont." Newsweek, 88
    (29 November 1976), 104.
    "Within the welter of words, symbols, gassy speechifying
    and half-hatched allegories there was once, I suspect, a
    good lean novel, but I can't find it now."

507 Pritchard, W.H. "Merely Fiction." Hudson Review, 30
    (Spring 1977), 158-60.
    This is "Gardner's strongest and sanest" fiction. It
    "is regionally so alive, morally so decent and interesting,
    that its special features (epigraphs, novel-within-novel,
    artificial chapter titles, illustrations) may be endured

as lively notions necessary to release this novelist's
story-telling propensities."

508 Prothro, Laurie. "Books in Brief." National Review, 29
(15 April 1977), 452.
Gardner's ingenuity is "excessive" and "the book drags,"
especially The Smugglers sections. But "his marvelous
poetry" makes the novel "almost worthwhile."

509 R., D. H. West Coast Review of Books, 3 (March 1977), 28.
OL "reads well but not easily." Gardner's language is
so clear and expressive that the illustrations are superfluous. In this human saga, James Page is "inhumanly hard
working."

510 "Random Notes." National Review, 28 (26 November 1976),
1299.
"Worth looking into."

511 Ravitz, Abe C. "Choosing Up Sides for Geriatric Warfare."
Cleveland Plain Dealer, 26 December 1976, sec. 5, p. 28.
"With affection, humor, and sympathy Gardner has brought
to life a provocative statement of idealism and reality
as they collide" and the resulting accommodation of reason
and emotion. He makes ingenious use of the novel-inside-
the-novel device in order "to maintain the energy of
Sally's revolt."

512 Ray, Lila. "Life's Little Ironies." Literary Half-Yearly,
19 (January 1978), 172-80.
OL is a serious story told in an entertaining and comic
manner. The Smugglers is "an extravagant strip cartoon"
and the entire novel a "pyrotechnical tour de force" in
which Gardner turns the particular into the universal.

513 Reed, Kit. "Too Much Extra Freight." New Haven Register,
2 January 1977, p. D4.
It is disconcerting to have Gardner admit in advance
that his story is not entirely original--more artifice than
art. The battle between the Pages is "fairly interesting,"
and the "interwoven" story of James's son has a not unappealing mythic quality. But the material borrowed from
other authors adds little to the story, and the inside-
novel, a potentially fascinating device, merely distracts
the reader. The Smugglers is "self-indulgent, over-long,
fragmented, incompletely thought out, and overloaded with
"symbolic and allegorical freight."

514 Rubenstein, Roberta. "Unlocking Two Lives." Progressive, 41 (February 1977), 59-60.
   In this "wonderfully rich" book, "the antagonists discover how each has contributed to (and also shared) the deepest griefs of their respective lives." The inside-novel "deliciously thickens the plot."

515 Rush, Michael. "Reviewers' Choices: Summer Reading." Christian Century, 94 (18 May 1977), 482.
   The novel is "at once chilling and warming, neatly wrapped in a Vermont backdrop."

516 Sage, Lorna. "The Corn and the Moonshine." Observer, 24 July 1977, p. 29.
   Gardner may be playing the part of the country-reciter who tells other people's poems. The juxtaposing of the two stories is successful.

517 "A Selection of Noteworthy Titles: 1977." New York Times Book Review, 4 December 1977, p. 34.
   Listed.

518 "Short Reports." London Times (Sunday), 28 August 1977, p. 35.
   Like much of American fiction, Gardner's work, especially OL, is overwritten. The "confused account of an old woman's rebellion against male tyranny set off against a book-within-a-book" is typically American. Here Gardner's verbal "brilliance" becomes "a tidal wave of verbiage" which "drowns the humanity of the characters."

519 Stone, Elizabeth. "John Gardner Writes Two Novels for the Price of One." Village Voice, 27 December 1976, 70-71.
   Examination of Gardner's earlier works suggests that he imitates various literary forms in order to "keep the reader from the comfort of total engagement" and total meaning (Gardner's meaning being derived chiefly from feeling rather than reason). The juxtaposing of the two novels in OL frees Gardner from the explanations which marks his previous fiction; in this sense, The Smugglers may be self-parody.

520 Stuttaford, Genevieve. "PW Forecasts: Paperbacks." Publishers Weekly, 212 (14 November 1977), 64.
   Lists Ballantine edition.

521 Swindell, Larry. Philadelphia Inquirer.*
    Quoted on back cover of the Ballantine edition of OL;
    Book-of-the-Month Club "Featured Alternate" circular for
    OL lists the reviewer's name.

522 Tinniswood, Peter. London Times, 28 July 1977, p. 10.
    An uneven book--alternately "straightforward" and "complex,'
    stylistically brilliant and ponderous--"saved by the boldness
    of its conception and the high professional skills of its
    author."

523 Towers, Robert. "John Gardner's Strong, Somber, Symbolic
    Novel." New York Times Book Review, 26 December 1976,
    pp. 1, 16.
    Gardner has "a too well-stocked mind"; his style is "more
    histrionic or mimetic than instinctively novelistic." The
    strengths of OL are characterization and the dramatizing
    of the chief conflicts. Insistent New-Englandliness,
    overt symbolism, "sub-novel," and being "theme-ridden"
    are its weaknesses.

524 Van Laan, James R. In Magill's Literary Annual 1977. Ed.
    Frank N. Magill. Englewood Cliffs, N.J.: Salem Press,
    1977, pp. 580-83.
    The review is devoted chiefly to The Smugglers and its
    relation to the story of the Pages. Includes an untrust-
    worthy "Sources for Further Study" that the editor says
    will be revised in the second printing.

525 Wood, Michael. "The Not-So-Light Fantastic." New York
    Review of Books, 23 (20 January 1977), 59-61.
    It is uncertain just what Gardner is doing in this book
    other than trying--and failing--to animate cliches and the
    novelistic form.

526 "The Year's Best." Time, 3 January 1977, p. 82.
    Lists OL, Gardner's "best novel yet," in which "a spoof
    of pulp fiction [is placed] inside a philosophical mono-
    logue on good and evil."

The King of the Hummingbirds and Other Tales (1977)

527 "Book Remarks." Language Arts, 55 (February 1978), 215.
    Style rather than content will either "attract or turn
    off readers" to Gardner's "off-beat fairy tales."

528 Cole, William. "Children's Books: The Best of the Season." Saturday Review, 4 (28 May 1977), 31.
    "Hip fairy tales" from the "super-productive" Gardner.

529 English Journal, 68 (November 1979), 24.*
    Cited in Children's Book Review Index, vol. 6 [1980] but not located.

530 Karlin, Barbara. "Kids." West Coast Review of Books, 3 (May 1977), 39.
    Dragon "was a superb tour de force," but Gudgekin was entirely unsuccessful. The new collection is "snide", ironic, and thoroughly enjoyable.

531 Mercier, Jean. "PW Forecasts: Children's Books." Publishers Weekly, 211 (11 April 1977), 78.
    More "delicious nuttiness" from Gardner; "The Pear Tree" takes the traditional fairy tale to new heights.

532 Mercier, Jean F. "PW Forecasts: Children's Books." Publishers Weekly, 215 (23 April 1979), 80.
    "The Pear Tree" is "Gardner at his nuttiest best."

533 Morris, Theodore C. "Witches, Gnomes, Dragons." St. Louis Globe-Democrat, 9-10 April 1977, p. A12.
    Like Dragon and Gudgekin, Gardner's new collection successfully combines magic, mysticism, and humor. The blend of old and new stamps these stories as originals.

534 "New in Children's Paperback." Washington Post Book World, 11 March 1979, p. F2.
    "Charming and goofy" tales.

535 Rosen, Lois, et al. "Once Over." English Journal, 68 (November 1979), 74.
    These brief, simple tales concern the magical and the mysterious.

536 School Library Journal, 25 (February 1979), 28.
    See annotation under CB.

537 Sheils, Merrill, and Frederick V. Boyd. Newsweek, 90 (18 July 1977), 92.
    Although Gardner's stories are not at all like traditional fairy tales, "none of the magic that captivates youngsters is missing."

538 Viorst, Judith. "Children's Books." New York Times Book
    Review, 17 April 1977, p. 50.
      "Irreverent, sophisticated and sometimes somewhat
    confusing."

539 Weinkauf, M. Science Fiction and Fantasy Book Review,
    1 (July 1979), 83.*
    Cited in Science Fiction Book Review Index, 1979.

The Poetry of Chaucer (1977)

540 Allen, Bruce. "Two Paths for The Pilgrim." Newsday, 10
    July 1977, "Ideas" sec., p. 23.
      Although Gardner adds little to what scholars already
    know about Chaucer, he does point out areas of interest
    they have previously overlooked. This critical study,
    which could have been included in a shortened version of
    LTC, will appeal to some general readers. (Reviewed with
    LTC.)

541 Barbato, Joseph. "John Gardner on Geoffrey Chaucer."
    Chronicle of Higher Education, 14 (25 April 1977), 17.
      Gardner's study is susceptible to criticism from
    medievalists. (Reviewed with LTC; see also the annotation
    listed under "Interviews.")

542 Butler, Maeve. Minneapolis Tribune, 22 May 1977.
      This book broadens and deepens the portrait of Chaucer
    found in Gardner's biography. The discussions of various
    aspects of medieval culture are especially well done.

543 Choice, 14 (July-August 1977), 680-81.
      The book is "lively" but has no "consistent unifying
    view." There are various proofreading errors and some
    "intemperate remarks" about other Chaucerians. "To be
    used with caution."

544 "A Christmas Potpourri." Wall Street Journal, 15
    December 1977, p. 20.
      Listed.

545 Clemons, Walter. "The Great Geoffrey." Newsweek, 89
    (11 April 1977), 99-100.
      Gardner's views are stimulating and his reading of The
    Canterbury Tales original; his "scholarship is solid and
    thorough, but he wears his mortarboard at a rakish tilt.
    ..." (Reviewed with LTC.)

546 Donaldson, E. T. "Soliloquy in a Chaucerian Cloister; or, Philippa Perses." Yale Review, 67 (October 1977), 100-06.
Gardner is "very strong" in his discussion of nominalism but becomes preachy when he turns to Chaucer's Neoplatonism. His readings of the non-Canterbury poems are good but not at all original. The "hurried and huddled" chapter on The Canterbury Tales "is organized--when the author remembers-- around the medieval theory of the tripartite soul, which seems a learned device for explaining the obvious." In sum, Gardner's eclectic approach results in "overrichness" and "confusion." Donaldson includes a two-page discussion of factual errors found in the two books. (Reviewed with LTC.)

547 Fry, Donald K. "Boisterous Irreverence, Chaucerian Sympathy." Library Journal, 102 (15 April 1977), 925.
Neither scholars nor general readers will be pleased with this book. Gardner's analysis of technique is sharp, but he uses secondary materials too selectively and often "rambles" in discussing philosophy and patristic commentary. (Reviewed with LTC.)

548 Fuller, Edmund. "As Sane a Man as Ever Walked in England." Wall Street Journal, 20 April 1977, p. 24.
Brief mention. (Reviewed with LTC.)

549 Garbaty, Thomas J. "Literature." Thought, 53 (March 1978), 110-12.
Gardner's book is "challenging" in its emphasis on Chaucer's nominalism and in its demanding extensive familiarity with the poetry "for the reader not to be mis- led." It is "frustrating" in its obscurity, convoluted readings, display of learning, and "obsession with sexual puns." And it is "annoying" in its insistence that only Chaucer's audience (and Gardner) understood him. Al- though the book is at times persuasive, there is "also much grasping at tenuous straws."

550 Hanning, Robert W. Georgia Review, 31 (Fall 1977), 732-35.
The expectations raised by the appearance of two works on Chaucer by a scholar-critic-novelist of Gardner's stature "are constantly thwarted by Gardner's method of presenting (and obscuring) basically sound critical ap- proaches to Chaucer that he shares with other contemporary scholars." His synthesis of the Kittredge/Donaldson and the Robertson strains of Chaucer scholarship results in successful readings of individual poems, but his self-

professed aim "'to follow where the poems lead'" and not
develop any one critical point adds up to "inconsistency
and irresponsibility" as well as the book's "fatal weakness," Gardner's "hit-and-run allegorizing." (Reviewed
with LTC.)

551 Johnston, Albert H. "PW Forecasts: Non-fiction."
Publishers Weekly, 211 (31 January 1977), 72.
Gardner's "impressive critical study" involves "close
textual analysis" and brings to light "a strikingly
'modern'" Chaucer.

552 Josipivici, Gabriel. "The Temptations of Chaucer." New
York Review of Books, 24 (28 April 1977), 18-22.
Despite his "enormous enthusiasm" and "boundless confidence," both of Gardner's books are "disappointing" because they are solely concerned with presenting "Gardner's
Chaucer." PC is "too dense and too thin," i.e., filled
with material already known and lacking anything either
new or substantive about the poetry. Although Gardner
claims he has no point to make, he nonetheless "drives
rather hard" his "strange argument" that Chaucer is very
much a kind of modernist writer. (Reviewed with LTC.)

553 Kirkus Reviews, 45 (1 January 1977), 28.
Gardner's aims are "excellent," but his book is flawed
by "factual vagueness" and the "unselective" accumulation
of details; "his broader insights are dissipated when he
attempts to apply them closely."

554 Kirsch, Robert. "Second Thoughts on Divisions in the
Chaucerian Mind." Los Angeles Times Book Review, 1 May
1977, pp. 1, 13.
Gardner should have published the single work he had
originally planned, for in dividing it into two books he
also divided himself into two kinds of writer: the popular
and the academic. PC "is clearer, better organized, easier
to read than the biography," which "is overblown and
faintly condescending in its folksiness." Still, Gardner
does provide a useful "overview" of recent scholarship,
and despite the fact that "the poetry is the poet's
biography," he "does capture the irrepressible man."
(Reviewed with LTC.)

555 McVeigh, Terrence A. America, 136 (21 May 1977), 469-70.
Gardner is "eclectic and pragmatic" in his use of
secondary sources. His readings are "informative,"

131

"independent," and "aggressive" but not always persuasive. His allegorical readings based on the scheme of the tripartite soul are "mechanical" and his "defense" of tales such as "Sir Thopas" is "idiosyncratic." (Reviewed with LTC.)

556 Marvel, Bill. "Chaucer: The Poet as Finagler." National Observer, 16 (16 April 1977), 25.
    PC is not directly considered. (Reviewed with LTC.)

557 Mersand, Joseph. English Journal, 69 (March 1980), 81-82. Gardner's two books "raise the level of American Chaucerian scholarship considerably." PC is a "masterful" interpretation. Fully versed in medieval theories of composition and in Chaucer's various foreign sources, "Gardner performs the brilliant feat of showing how Chaucer utilized his source material to create new works of art." (Paperback issue; reviewed with LTC.)

558 Milosh, Joseph E. Cithara, 17 (November 1977), 58-60. The often jesting tone of this book may offend some scholars but doubtless would have appealed to Chaucer. Gardner's "stands on critical questions are consistently clear" and his readings "perceptive." Although his conclusions are "conventional" (as is to be expected in a comprehensive study), his insights are stimulating, even if not always entirely persuasive. Gardner's judicious eclecticism and "pervasive" scholarship are noteworthy, but what chiefly distinguishes his book is "the creative imagination of the experienced literary artist" which he brings to bear. Students and scholars of both Chaucer's and Gardner's work will find this book of "lasting" importance.

559 Modert, Jo. "Gardner As Ringmaster to Chaucer the Clown." St. Louis Post-Dispatch, 10 April 1977, p. D4. Instead of Chaucer's "life-as-a-pilgrimage" theme, Gardner interpolates "his own modern life-is-a-circus." His "conversational" style succeeds better in PC than in the biography, except in those passages where he scornfully attacks critics with whom he disagrees. The ornamented letters which introduce each chapter were drawn by Gardner. (Reviewed with LTC.)

560 Morrison, Theodore. "The Gardner's Tale." The Guardian Weekly, 116 (17 April 1977), 18. See next entry.

561 Morrison, Theodore. "The Gardner's Tale." <u>Washington Post Book World</u>, 27 March 1977, p. E5.
Both books "are lively, imaginative, completely unstuffy in style, and learned"; however, Gardner's allegorical, Neoplatonic readings of the poems are untenable. (Reviewed with <u>LTC</u>.)

562 Mudrick, Marvin. "The Blind Men and the Elephant." <u>Hudson Review</u>, 30 (Autumn 1977), 426-36.
"Not satisfied with inventing Chaucer's life, Gardner turns psychocritic and ... invents Chaucer's poetry, e.g. as it was affected by the politics of the time." Available evidence, however, suggests that Chaucer was much more a private poet than either Gardner or Donald R. Howard believes. (Reviewed with <u>LTC</u>.)

563 Muscatine, Charles. "The Poet's Table." <u>New York Times Book Review</u>, 24 April 1977, pp. 13, 38-39.
<u>PC</u> is "less innovative and less satisfying" than the biography. Gardner's exegetical analysis and penchant for analogizing is often "over intricate, far fetched and, finally, cold." Moreover, in "dealing with Chaucer's worst poems ... Gardner almost perversely dumps Christian exegesis and replaces it with a similar if opposite ingenuity: "that they are "'intentionally bad art.'" (Reviewed with <u>LTC</u>.)

564 Patterson, Lee W. "Writing about Writing: The Case of Chaucer." <u>University of Toronto Quarterly</u>, 48 (Spring 1979), 263-82.
In this book a confident Gardner "adopts an historical stance so foursquare as to seem simple commonsense," yet as historicist criticism his work "is deficient in every respect." Errors of fact, including misquotations, and "interpretive howlers" abound. The contention that Chaucer's irony derives from nominalism is unconvincing and unsubstantiated. The discussion of Neoplatonism depends on an absurdly vague definition of the term, and his "cracking of the <u>Canterbury Tales</u> is not much fun to watch," offering "at best a set of vaguely medieval bright ideas that are in no single instance subjected to the rigorous details of the text." Teachers of undergraduates "will rue the day this book first appeared on the shelves of the university library."

565 Peck, Russell A. <u>Criticism</u>, 20 (Winter 1978), 66-68.
The book is "impressive" despite Gardner's hurried final chapter on <u>The Canterbury Tales</u>, his failure to support his

point about nominalism, the various factual errors, and its being less a unified book than "a compendium of sensible discussions." Especially good are Gardner's command of secondary materials, his readings of individual poems, and "responsiveness to Chaucer as a manipulator of words and observer of people."

566 Rothschild, Victoria. "A Choice of Two Chaucers." Times Literary Supplement, 13 January 1978, p. 43.
Although he intends this book as an introduction to Chaucer's poetry, Gardner ("a master of the throwaway line and the unsubstantiated aside") depends almost exclusively on secondary materials, provides no means for following up leads, and includes a number of "blatant inaccuracies." Especially unconvincing is the claim that Chaucer's poetry reflects his acceptance of nominalism. (Reviewed with LTC.)

567 Shaw, Mildred Hart. "Bookshelf." Grand Junction (Colorado) Sentinel, 6 November 1977, Westworld sec.
"A persuasive synthesis" of recent scholarship and as much "a stirring, poetical experience" as reading Chaucer's own work.

568 Shoaf, R. A. Modern Philology, 77 (February 1980), 317-20.
Instead of opening up new ground in Chaucer studies, PC is "a harmful regression" in which Gardner, as he did in LTC, turns the medieval poet into "a Twentieth-Century upper-Middle Class Liberal." Gardner's oversimplified idea of nominalism is used to "camouflage" his fuzzy readings of individual poems. His book is rife with factual errors, entirely dependent on secondary sources, and so methodologically naive as to suggest "the absence of long personal contact with the dense spiritual complexity of his subject."

569 Swindell, Larry. "Life and Lore of a Paradoxical Teller of Evergreen Tales." Philadelphia Inquirer, 8 May 1977.
Both the biography and the critical study are honestly presented, well thought out and amiably written; the latter "is a triumphantly appreciative, judicious guided tour through the major works...." (Reviewed with LTC.)

The Life & Times of Chaucer (1977)

570 Adams, Phoebe-Lou. Atlantic, 239 (May 1977), 101.
    "The author makes no claim to original scholarship. He
    has synthesized available, but scattered, material with
    intelligence and grace."

571 Allen, Bruce. "Two Paths for the Pilgrim." Newsday, 10
    July 1977, "Ideas" sec., p. 23.
    Gardner's inferences concerning Chaucer's life are
    "lively and ingenious." The book is, however, repetitive
    and Gardner's language is unnecessarily indulgent.
    (Reviewed with PC.)

572 Austin, Richard. Month (London), 11 (June 1978), 213.
    The book is "lovingly constructed" and elegantly readable
    (although "plainly written for American readers"). It is
    the first biography to present Chaucer "whole": as man and
    artist. Its only flaw is the "comparisons with modern
    society that jar a little."

573 Barbato, Joseph. "John Garnder on Geoffrey Chaucer."
    Chronicle of Higher Education, 14 (25 April 1977), 17.
    "Non-scholarly" and thus susceptible to criticism from
    medievalists; nonetheless, the book is "eminently readable"
    and "an engrossing narrative." (Reviewed with PC; see also
    the annotation listed under "Interviews.")

574 Barnard, Judith. "Geoffrey Chaucer's Lusty, Gutsy Life
    and Times." Chicago Daily News Panorama, 2-3 April 1977,
    p. 7.
    Gardner's brilliance and humanity are fully evident in
    this book which is fleshed out with careful and plausible
    extrapolations from the few known facts. One problem is
    that Gardner's John of Gaunt is more vividly realized than
    his Chaucer. Another is Gardner's having unnecessarily
    limited his audience by failing to translate more of the
    poetry than he does. But these are not serious flaws.

575 Beam. Alvin. "Ride Gardner's Time Machine, the Flying
    Chaucer." Cleveland Plain Dealer, 3 April 1977, sec. 4,
    p. 26.
    General readers will have some difficulty with the Middle
    English; otherwise Gardner's book is very well done, in-
    cluding the passages of "controlled invention." His

rendering of Chaucer's death, "a subtle masterpiece with
its touch of Chaucerian deep seriousness and complexity
and humor," is especially good.

576 <u>Booklist</u>, 73 (15 March 1977), 1060.
A brief approving paragraph.

577 "Books Briefly." <u>The Progressive</u>, 41 (June 1977), 44.
Written somewhat in the style of a picaresque novel,
Gardner's biography is the first to treat Chaucer in light
of recent discoveries about the poet's age. The book is
aimed not at the specialist but at the general reader already familiar with Chaucer's poetry.

578 "Briefly Noted." <u>New Yorker</u>, 53 (25 April 1977), 149-50.
"Learned, long-winded, and exuberant."

579 Burgess, Anthony. "Chaucer, American Style." <u>Observer</u>,
20 November 1977, p. 28.
Since so little is known about Chaucer's life, the
novelistic liberties taken by Gardner in writing this
biography are acceptable, even necessary, but nonetheless
objectionable to a British audience (for whom this book is
very clearly not intended). In commenting on the later
poetry, Gardner, writing very much in the "post-Joycean"
tradition, seems correct in his judgments. "The Gardner
Chaucer squares with the poems, and is tougher, more
subtle" than the Chaucer known to many readers.

580 <u>Choice</u>, 14 (February 1978), 1644.
The discussion of the marriage group is "provocative,"
but Gardner is to be faulted for his mingling of fact and
fiction and, in his discussion of John of Gaunt's relationship to Chaucer, his reliance on George Guion Williams's
unscholarly <u>A New View of Chaucer</u>.

581 Christopher, Michael. "Days of Thorns and Roses." <u>US
Catholic</u>, 42 (August 1977), 50-51.
Gardner succeeds "brilliantly" in sketching Chaucer in
the context of his age; his is "the kind of book you can
dip into almost anyplace and read with pleasure."

582 Clark, Lindley H., Jr. "A Christmas Potpourri of Books."
<u>Wall Street Journal</u>, 15 December 1977, p. 20.
Listed.

583 Clemons, Walter. "The Great Geoffrey." <u>Newsweek</u>, 89
(11 April 1977), 99-100.
This stimulating, scholarly and "very appealing investi-
gative biography" includes "a rich context of fourteenth-
century English history and social detail." Only the
novelistic sections are weak, in fact "banal." (Reviewed
with <u>PC</u>.)

584 Cowen, Janet M. <u>Review of English Studies</u>, ns 29
(November 1978), 471-72.
Using an approach that is "unashamedly speculative,"
Gardner has failed to make use of relevant recent studies,
has used secondary material in misleading ways, and has not
supported his hypotheses.

585 Dannenfeldt, Karl H. <u>History: Review of New Books</u>, 6
(February 1978), 79.
Chiefly a summary of major points in the biography with
a few (generally naive) evaluative comments (e.g., pointing
out that the excerpts from Chaucer's poetry have not been
modernized).

586 Dolan, Terry. "Ye Novel Viewe." <u>Hibernia</u>, 10 February
1978, p. 25.
In this "extraordinary concoction," Gardner's strength--
his confidence--is also his weakness. Celebrating Chaucer's
life, he turns "conjectures into facts" and attempts to
resolve all uncertainties.

587 Donaldson, E. T. "Soliloquy in a Chaucerian Cloister; or
Philippa Perses." <u>Yale Review</u>, 67 (October 1977), 100-06.
Of Gardner's two recent studies of Chaucer, <u>LTC</u>, although
reminiscent of a boy's biography, is probably the more useful volume. The novelistic passages are clearly ineffective
some are sentimental while others are used to add local
color. Donaldson includes a two-page discussion of
factual errors in the two books. (Reviewed with <u>PC</u>.)

588 "Editors' Choice." <u>New York Times Book Review</u>, 1 May
1977, p. 64. Through 22 May 1977.
"Scholarly, loving recreation of the poet and his day."

589 Ferris, Sumner. <u>Speculum</u>, 52 (October 1977), 970-74.
Gardner's book "disappoints the great expectations with
which it was anticipated." "Inadequate and unscholarly"
both as biography and as criticism, it includes a number

of passages "closely paraphrased" without appropriate
acknowledgement. The one thing to its credit is the
author's enthusiasm which, however, perhaps "led him into
writing and publishing before he was properly ready"; the
resulting work is "ultimately ... a disservice to its
author, publisher, and readers" and in no way supplants
Marchette Chute's Geoffrey Chaucer of England as the best
non-academic biography of the poet. (See also Peter S.
Prescott, "Theft or 'Paraphrase'?," Newsweek, 10 April
1978.)

590 Frankis, P. J. Notes and Queries, 27 (June 1980), 248.
Making free with history and even geography, Gardner has
written "a kind of historical novel" in which the setting
is made cosily suburban. It is unlikely that his book,
which may have been intended for young readers, will lead
to an accurate "and sympathetic reading" of Chaucer's
poetry.

591 Fry, Donald K. "Boisterous Irreverence, Chaucerian
Sympathy." Library Journal, 102 (15 April 1977), 925.
Gardner's book is a comprehensive synthesis of available
material and, where no material is available, fiction. He
draws his characters "vividly and sympathetically." His
"boisterous irreverence, occasional homely diction and
purple passages and unfashionable cheerfulness" will make
the book appealing to general readers and unappealing to
scholars. (Reviewed with PC.)

592 Fuller, Edmund. "As Sane a Man as Ever Walked in England."
Wall Street Journal, 20 April 1977, p. 24.
This new book attests to Gardner's skills as both novelist
and scholar.

593 Geylio, Michael. Grand Rapids Press, 17 April 1977, p.
F2.
Gardner handles the historical material well but adds
nothing to Chaucer's biography.

594 Gohn, Jack Benoit. "A 'Faction' Contends with the Great
Geoff." Baltimore Sun, 17 April 1977, p. D5.
Since Gardner is careful to distinguish his facts from
his imaginative renderings, his "two-pronged" approach to
Chaucer's biography succeeds both in elucidating the poet's
life and his poetry. Gardner's work is "innovative and
ingenious" as well as an excellent "synthesis" of existing
materials.

595 The Griffin (The Readers' Subscription Service), 27 (May 1977), 3-5.
A promotional write-up for the May "Main Selection."

596 Hanning, Robert W. Georgia Review, 31 (Fall 1977), 732-35.
Mentioned as "even more wayward" than PC. (Reviewed with PC.)

597 Hitchcock, James. Critic, 36 (Fall 1977), 74-76.
This "highly speculative" biography is "more trite than boldly creative." Gardner's chief difficulty arises when he attempts to place Chaucer in his age; Gardner seems "to dislike the Middle Ages," and his understanding of Wycliff is "imprecise." Ultimately, the book is "a flower of the 1960s--a piece of 'relevant' scholarship."

598 Homer, Frank X. J. America, 136 (7 May 1977), 428-29.
A vivid recreation of Chaucer's age and "a lively portrait" of the poet.

599 Howes, Victor. "A Novelist Fills in History's Blanks." Christian Science Monitor, 20 April 1977, p. 23.
"This is speculative biography, but based on careful assumptions." Gardner may not always be correct, but even if he doesn't always document "the 'real life' Chaucer" he does excite interest in Chaucer the man, "the born survivor."

600 Johnston, Albert H. "PW Forecasts: Nonfiction." Publishers Weekly, 211 (31 January 1977), 72.
"Gardner's scholarly but absorbing biography provides a clear-eyed, human portrait of Chaucer as man and poet" and should stimulate readers to renew their acquaintance with Chaucer's poetry.

601 Josipovici, Gabriel. "The Temptations of Chaucer." New York Review of Books, 24 (28 April 1977), 18-22.
Despite Gardner's "enthusiasm" and "boundless confidence," the book is "disappointing" and presents solely "Gardner's Chaucer." It is an overt popularization fleshed out with "potted intellectual and political history" and fictional hypotheses. (Reviewed with PC.)

602 Kirkus Reviews, 45 (1 February 1977), 134.
Gardner's work is enthusiastic ("filled with a likable spirit of freewheeling evangelism"), polished, and "force-fully written." But his fictionalizing is not successful and "his attempts to fit the poetry into his biography are often high-handed."

603 Kirsch, Robert. "Second Thoughts on Divisions in the Chaucerian Mind." Los Angeles Times Book Review, 1 May 1977, pp. 1, 13.
Reviewed with PC; see annotation.

604 Laut, Stephen J. Best Sellers, 37 (July 1977), 121.
Gardner's chief fault is that he "never aims at a specific audience." A number of Gardner's conclusions are unconvincing (e.g., concerning Chaucer's marriage and alleged peculation), but his scholarship, "insights" into the poetry, and "imaginative talent" make the book worthwhile.

605 Lehmann-Haupt, Christopher. "Books of the Times." New York Times, 23 March 1977, p. C23.
The book is "popular literary biography of the highest order." Gardner, whose imagination is well-suited to the task, provides a vivid reconstruction of Chaucer's age and a useful summary of recent Chaucer scholarship. That Gardner does not help the reader through the Middle English sufficiently is the reviewer's sole "quibble."

606 Leneghan, R. T. "Medieval People." Michigan Quarterly Review, 17 (Winter 1978), 102-07.
Gardner does not deal adequately with either Chaucer's religion or the security enjoyed by the elite classes. Nonetheless, the biography is satisfactory in that it provides "a convincing and responsible account" of Chaucer in his social milieu. There is nothing objectionable in Gardner's shifting between the roles of biographer and novelist because he is "scrupulous" in keeping the two voices distinct.

607 McCormick, Jay. "'Chaucer': Full of Intuitions." Detroit News, 19 June 1977, p. L2.
Gardner uses the age of Chaucer to flesh out lacunae in the poet's thin biography. The result is a pleasurable work "of scholarly probabilities and the novelist's intuitions."

608 McVeigh, Terrence A. America, 136 (21 May 1977), 469.
Gardner is "eclectic and pragmatic" in his use of secondary sources; his style is "lively" and self-assured, and his method includes "a touch of poetic license." (Reviewed with PC.)

609 Marvel, Bill. "Chaucer: The Poet as Finagler." National
    Observer, 16 (16 April 1977), 25.
    Gardner's fictionalizing (a method Chaucer "would very
    much have liked") and the parallels he draws between the
    Fourteenth and Twentieth Centuries are especially well
    done. For the general reader there is a helpful abundance
    of details concerning the spiritual and intellectual life
    of Chaucer's age. (Reviewed with PC.)

610 Mersand, Joseph. English Journal, 69 (March 1980), 81-82.
    Gardner's two "books raise the level of American
    Chaucerian scholarship considerably." The biography de-
    picts the life Chaucer may have lived, one that is in
    accordance with the few available facts and which illumin-
    ates the poetry. (Reviewed with PC.)

611 Modert, Jo. "Gardner as Ringmaster to Chaucer the Clown."
    St. Louis Post-Dispatch, 10 April 1977, p. D4.
    Gardner's book is so "loaded with faults common to
    pseudo-intellectual works for mass consumption" as to seem
    like The Smugglers story in OL, intentionally bad art. The
    padding is obvious (a one-volume "Life, Times, and Poetry"
    would have been better), the sources are out-of-date,
    quotations are either misused or awkwardly inserted, some
    of the allusions to modern literature are "ridiculous,"
    and, as in PC, Gardner substitutes his life-as-circus
    theme for Chaucer's life-as-pilgrimage. (Reviewed with PC.)

612 Morris, Robert K. "A Parfit Gentil Knight." St. Louis
    Globe-Democrat, 7-9 May 1977, p. D4.
    Gardner succeeds in bringing Chaucer's age to life,
    largely as the result of novelistic devices used to sup-
    plement the scholar's facts. Although he never allows the
    historical novelist free reign, Gardner will probably find
    few admirers among academic readers.

613 Morrison, John F. Philadelphia Evening Bulletin, 3 April
    1977, sec. 2, p. 4.
    No mere "fictionalized history," this scholarly work is
    further proof of the prolific Gardner's versatility.

614 Morrison, Theodore. "The Gardner's Tale." Guardian Weekly
    116 (17 April 1977), 18.
    See next entry.

615 Morrison, Theodore. "The Gardner's Tale." Washington Post Book World, 27 March 1977, p. E5.
Except for Gardner's handling of the charge of raptus brought against Chaucer and forming his Chaucer in a too Neoplatonic mold, this biography, as well as its companion volume, is "lively, imaginative, completely unstuffy, and learned." (Reviewed with PC.)

616 Mudrick, Marvin. "The Blind Men and the Elephant." Hudson Review, 30 (Autumn 1977), 426-36.
Gardner's psychobiography is a fabrication; what he calls "'using the tricks of a novelist'" really amounts to "filling in and faking." (Reviewed with PC.)

617 Muscatine, Charles. "The Poet's Table." New York Times Book Review, 24 April 1977, pp. 13, 38-39.
Rather than a continuous life-story, Gardner has written "fresh and adventuresome" "periodic snapshots" that make up a "marvelously persuasive case" for Gardner's view of Chaucer. The novelistic sections are "charmingly" done, but the parade of scholarly details, the lack of finish, the lapses into the "idiom of the TV popularizer," and the "many debatable points and some mechanical errors" are to be faulted. (Reviewed with PC.)

618 "New in Paperback." Washington Post Book World, 23 April 1978, p. E2.
The Vintage paperback is listed.

619 "Notes on Current Books." Virginia Quarterly Review, 54 (Winter 1978), 14, 16.
Like his novels, Gardner's biography is marred by "overwriting and cuteness." He is often "uncritical" (e.g., he accepts "the untenable theory that the Gawain-poet was one John Massey"), his scholarship is "unreliable," and his writing tends towards the "sensational."

620 "Paperbacks: New and Noteworthy." New York Times Book Review, 23 April 1978, p. 43.
The Vintage paperback is listed.

621 Quinton, Anthony. "Long before Shakespeare." Saturday Review, 4 (16 April 1977), 46, 48.
Gardner's biography has several flaws: little is said of "Chaucer as a literary man," Gardner's "literary infelicities that are intended, no doubt, to put the reader at

ease," the disunity and unrelatedness of its parts, and
the appended guide to Middle English pronunciation. "A
book about the world of Chaucer with a narrowly biographical chapter might have served better."

622 Rothschild, Victoria. "A Choice of Two Chaucers." Times
Literary Supplement, 13 January 1978, p. 43.
    Like PC, the biography "derives its authority almost
entirely from secondary material," but unlike the
companion volume, LTC is of some value to students of
Chaucer, especially in Gardner's surveys of the historical
and social milieus. However, Gardner is incorrect in believing Chaucer attended Oxford and was influenced by the
nominalists. Gardner is also to be faulted for his
platitudinous tone, shifting from biographer to novelist,
careless scholarship, and "the flatness of the imaginative
writing." The biography is further evidence of Gardner's
efforts, beginning with G, "to bring medieval literature
out of its Pre-Raphaelite mists into the adolescent world
of the Tolkien reader." (Reviewed with PC.)

623 Rowland, Beryl. Queen's Quarterly (Kingston), Winter
1978-79, pp. 719-20.
    This is a popular rather than scholarly biography, one
that will interest its readers in Chaucer and his poetry.
Gardner is familiar with Chaucer scholarship, draws generally accurate conclusions, organizes his book "brilliantly
quotes his sources skillfully (the plagiarism charge is
overblown), and spices his work with a "cynicism compatible
with contemporary taste."

624 Sachs, Sylvia. "'Chaucer' a Medieval Study." Pittsburgh
Press, 10 April 1977, p. G10.
    Although Chaucer remains a rather "cardboard figure" in
this biography, Gardner's skills as a "literary detective"
result in "a stunning picture" of the medieval age in which
parallels to our own times "are hard to miss."

625 Scattergood, V. J. "English Poetry." British Book News,
May 1978, p. 411.
    Although the author's spirit and enthusiasm are evident,
his biography is unreliable, abounding with remarks "made
as if they were demonstrably true but for which there is
no evidence."

626 "A Selection of Noteworthy Titles: 1977." New York Times
Book Review, 4 December 1977, p. 15.
    Listed.

627 Setnik, Susan E. Kliatt, 13 (Winter 1979), 30.
This handsomely produced book is both scholarly and
pleasurable and includes a helpful appendix on pronunciation. (Review of the Vintage paperbound issue.)

628 Skow, John. "Bloody As Could Be." Time, 109 (16 May
1977), 96, E3.
Despite Gardner's clowning manner, this is not "a
slight book." Its readers "may find themselves hooked
on Chaucer. For those who do, Gardner has thoughtfully
and simultaneously provided a sterner volume of criticism:
PC."

629 Stuttaford, Genevieve. "PW Forecasts: Paperbacks."
Publishers Weekly, 213 (20 February 1978), 126.
The Vintage paperback will be issued in April.

630 Swindell, Larry. "Life and Lore of a Paradoxical Teller
of Evergreen Tales." Philadelphia Inquirer, 8 May 1977.
Other than the passages of novelistic "whimsy," which
should have been omitted, this biography succeeds both as
scholarship and in interesting the reader in Chaucer.
Both the biography and the critical study are honestly
presented, well thought-out, and amiably written.
(Reviewed with PC.)

631 Tablet, 4 February 1978, p. 108.
Gardner's "chatty" book is "harmless, fairly informative,
the next best thing to a competent 'historical novel.'"

632 "This Week's Arrivals." Christian Century, 94 (27 April
1977), 412-13.
A "popular literary biography."

633 Whitman, Alden. "A Book to Explain Chaucer's Poetry."
Chicago Tribune Book World, 17 April 1977, p. 3.
Gardner's book is "lively, wise, witty, and ... immensely wordly [sic]"; his novelistic speculations are
intelligent and illuminating.

634 Williams, David. "Fourteenth Century Fixer." London
Times, 8 December 1977, p. 10.
In this broad, rather than narrowly specialized biography,
Gardner places Chaucer in his age "with great authority
and readability, and creates a character we can believe
in." The scholarship is "sound" and the writing "vivid."

635 Williams, David. "Soft Back, Hard Centre." <u>Punch</u>, 278
(23 January 1980), 165.
   Gardner fleshes out the few known facts of Chaucer's
biography with a careful rendering of the poet's "setting"
and a justifiable use of the novelistic imagination.

636 Williams, Raymond. "The Englishness of Chaucer."
<u>Guardian Weekly</u>, 118 (15 January 1978), 22.
   The biography is "provocative," and though it does not
itself contribute significantly to our understanding of
medieval culture, it is indicative of the "effort to apply
specialized work on this difficult period to more general
and now crucially important cultural questions." The
novelistic sections, however, are "tushery" and "evasive."

637 Wilson, A. N. "Gee, It's Geoffrey." <u>New Statesman</u>, 94
(25 November 1977), 735-37.
   Gardner is "the Walt Disney of Chaucer scholarship";
Chaucer, however, is not amenable to such treatment.
Gardner might have written an historical romance about
Chaucer on the order of <u>G</u>; instead he wrote a book that
is wholly neither fantasy nor scholarly biography.

<u>A Child's Bestiary</u> (1977)

638 <u>AB Bookman's Weekly</u>, 60 (14 November 1977), 2820.
   "Full of both fun and lots of blank white space for
crayon work by inspired tots."

639 <u>Bulletin of the Center for Children's Books</u>, 31
(February 1978), 92.
   The verses are "flippant and often witty," but the col-
lection is "uneven."

640 Clemons, Walter. "Armida Had a Nasty Eye." <u>New York
Times Book Review</u>, 25 December 1977, p. 7.
   Gardner "has an uncertain ear, and I am not sure he
always means to be as awkward as he sounds." (Reviewed
with <u>ISM</u>.)

641 Cole, William. "Children's Books: Best of the Season."
<u>Saturday Review</u>, 5 (26 November 1977), 40.
   "Superior nonsense."

642 Flowers, Ann A. <u>Horn Book</u>, 54 (February 1978), 62.
   The verses, "humorous and wryly sophisticated," recall
Hilaire Belloc and Ogden Nash.

643 Geringer, Laura. School Library Journal, 24 (October 1977), 111.
  Gardner's philosophizing becomes occasionally "too abstract, but there are enough good satiric jabs ... to reward readers willing to browse through more than once."

644 Herne, Betsy. "Children's Books." Booklist, 74 (1 December 1977), 612.
  Despite some sophisticated joking and irreverence, most of the verses "are just easygoing good fun or clever observations...."

645 Kirkus Reviews, 45 (1 September 1977), 936.
  "Sly, sparkling fun."

646 Mercier, Jean. "PW Forecasts: Children's Books." Publishers Weekly, 212 (12 September 1977), 132.
  A "merry book" for "all ages."

647 Millar, Neil. "Ode to a Giraffe Who Munches the Sun." Christian Science Monitor, 3 May 1978, p. B4.
  Though "for all ages," "some readers may feel uneasy about the author's concept of the Deity as fallible and human."

648 Milton, Joyce. "Sweet Bards of Youth." Washington Post Book World, 13 November 1977, p. 4.
  The quick changes of pace, the "thoroughgoing morality" without any preaching, the "bumptiously irreverent" tone, and the fact that "the pretensions of mankind, including its anthropocentric attitude towards religion, come off second best to the behavior of beasts" make this a completely "satisfying" book.

649 Reading Teacher, 32 (October 1978), 46.
  The collection will be useful in language arts and creative writing classes, grades 1-4.

650 School Library Journal, 25 (February 1979), 28.
  In Dragon, Gudgekin, and KH, Gardner reshapes traditional fairy tales into his "own existential world view....coyly mocking the values that fairy tales assert." ISM is "tiresome." CB is better because Gardner is "able to smirk less and jest more."

In the Suicide Mountains (1977)

651 Adams, Phoebe-Lou. "PLA." Atlantic, 240 (November 1977), 104.
"Deftly told and makes a sound point."

652 Booklist, 74 (1 September 1977), 22.
This is an "often delightful, but at times tired story" for adult readers.

653 Bulletin of the Center for Children's Books, 31 (April 1978), 126.
The plotting is unevenly paced; the "style is witty, sophisticated, occasionally verbose, often intricate."

654 "Children's Books." Bookviews, 1 (December 1977) 22.
A compassionate and "thoroughly believable" novel.
(Same as Publishers Weekly, 5 September 1977.)

655 Clark, Jeff. Fantastiae, 6 (February 1978), 7.
The novel's mood is as awkward as the book's boxy shape. Gardner has "gracefully adapted and interpolated" the Russian fairy tales into his text.

656 Clemons, Walter. "Armida Had a Nasty Eye." New York Times Book Review, 25 December 1977, p. 7.
In general, "a moody, uneven book" that will be of more interest to adults than to children. Gardner has reworked his sources successfully and the characters of Armida and Chudu are well done. The adventures, however, lack interest. (Reviewed with CB.)

657 Cosgrave, Mary Silva. "Outlook Tower." Horn Book, 54 (April 1978), 194-95.
The tale is "exuberant and hilarious." The Russian fairy tales Gardner has borrowed have not been "enhanced by the adaptation."

658 Dirda, Michael. "Brief Notes." Washington Post Book World, 20 November 1977, p. 5.
Gardner's "elegantly told story ... reflects the serious theme and light-hearted tone of Chaucer and Sir Gawain and the Green Knight." By defeating the dragon, which represents consciousness without self, the three main characters "learn to reconcile their own warring natures."

659 English Journal, 67 (February 1978), 79.
ISM is suitable for courses on fantasy and legends.

660 Geringer, Laura. School Library Journal, 24 (December 1977), 54.
Summary of plot.

661 Kirkus Reviews, 45 (15 August 1977), 868.
"Trendy" but except for the opening section and the author's "word magic," the story is not successful.

662 Thomases, Jeanne B. Kliatt, 15 (Winter 1981), 12.
Gardner successfully combines the themes and characters of traditional fairy tales with a contemporary setting. The result is a story filled with "silliness, non sequiturs, and magic."

663 Mercier, Jean. "PW Forecasts: Children's Books." Publishers Weekly, 212 (5 September 1977), 73.
A compassionate and "thoroughly believable" novel for readers of all ages from "Gardner of the boundless imagination and crazy wit."

664 "New in Paperback." Washington Post Book World, 2 November 1980, p. 12.
In this "fable about appearance and reality," the three main characters defeat materialism (the dragon) and "impure spirituality" (the six-fingered man).

665 "Notes on Current Books." Virginia Quarterly Review, 54 (Spring 1978), 67.
ISM, the fifth of Gardner's so-called children's books, is not entirely suitable for young readers.

666 "Paperbacks: New and Noteworthy." New York Times Book Review, 31 August 1980, p. 19.
Brief summaries of book and Clemons' review above.

667 Schaeffer, Susan Fromberg. "A Fabled Land of Heroic Dragons." Chicago Tribune Book World, 16 October 1977, pp. 1, 4.
"Probably the perfect parable, or fairy tale, for our introspective time. Beneath its properly fantastic surface, Gardner takes on our current preoccupations with women's roles, feminism generally, the search for self-fulfillment, even the search for happiness through the religion of the prominent 'born-again' Baptist."

148

668 School Library Journal, 25 (February 1979), 28.
    See annotation under CB.

669 Thomas, Phil. "John Gardner Pens Suicide Mountains for
    Young Readers." Southern Illinoisan (Carbondale), 8
    January 1978, p. 31.
    Gardner cleverly turns the family world "topsy-turvy"
    in this well-told story for readers young and old.

670 Wiehe, Janet. Library Journal, 102 (August 1977), 1677.
    "A delightful diversion, a wise and funny fairy tale
    for grown-ups."

671 Wolfson, Barbara. "A Memorable, Magical Tale." Newsday,
    4 December 1977, "Ideas" sec., pp. 24, 21.
    Gardner's message--that the world is not always as it
    appears to be--is not original, but his treatment is. In
    his previous books for children, Gardner was merely coy;
    in ISM he is "the natural storyteller" of KI, telling old
    stories in order to prove "timeless truths." Significant
    issues are raised in this "morality tale." Although some
    readers may object to a book about suicide for children,
    fairy tales traditionally deal with questions of life and
    death, good and evil.

On Moral Fiction (1978)

672 Aldridge, John W. Rev. of Vulnerable People, by Josephine
    Hendin. New Republic, 179 (16 September 1978), 26-28.
    In contrast to the "willed optimism" of Hendin, who
    "believes that our novels in their negativism or in spite
    of it somehow reflect 'the richness, excitement and hope
    of American experience during the past thirty years,'"
    Gardner finds their "programmatic angst" to be "a perver-
    sion of the truth." What had been a necessary "adversary
    position" previously adopted by the novelist has in recent
    times become "a fashionable dogmatic stance"; against this
    negativism Gardner rightly calls for a life-enhancing art.

673 Aloff, Mindy. Dance Magazine, 54 (September 1980), 56.
    The attacks on postmodernists for their immorality,
    "defective eye," and poor taste by critics such as Gardner
    and Clement Greenberg have not been convincing.

674 Apple, Max. "Merdistes in Fiction's Garden." Nation, 226
    (22 April 1978), 462-63.
    The strength of OMF derives from Gardner's "sincerity"

and its "eloquence" from his "self-consciously" chosen "simple language" (which only rarely becomes "solemnly tedious"). Gardner's "literary blindspot" is his "failure to see the reality within the exaggeration, the moral within the 'trivial.'" Moreover, the "literary emergency" Gardner speaks of does not really exist; the audience for the experimental fiction Gardner finds so prevalent is in fact quite limited.

675 Atlantic Monthly, 241 (June 1978), 99.
OMF, "though loosely organized and somewhat arbitrary, nonetheless contains a good many interesting and tough-minded judgments."

676 Beardsley, Elizabeth Lane. Journal of Aesthetics and Art Criticism, 37 (Winter 1978), 226-28.
Despite a number of insightful philosophical remarks, the book is, in general, "a blend of strong rhetoric and weak conceptual thought." Gardner's discussion of the contemporary celebration of freakishness is useful, though like the rest of the book, it suffers from his belief that imaginative literature is superior in moral value to non-fiction, his equating the artist's vision with moral vision, and his failure to see the way fiction contributes "to an understanding of moral complexities, as contrasted with moral inspiration."

677 Birnbaum, Milton. "Affirming Art." Modern Age, 23 (Spring 1979), 204--6.
Gardner, like Solzhenitsyn, is right in calling attention to today's "moral miasma." OMF suffers not from what Gardner says but how he argues his case. There is no "careful analysis" either of the causes of art's decay or of contemporary writers (in a book about today's literature, too many pages are devoted to Dante as "'our model moral artist'"). Also, Gardner is often hyperbolic in what he claims for art, occasionally wrong (as in turning Homer into an overt moralizer), and sometimes guilty of "lapses into puerile breeziness and solecisms." Yet better "a good cause badly presented" than "a bad one consummately delivered."

678 Booklist, 74 (15 April 1978), 1312.
Gardner's well-supported argument is "refreshingly controversial," "emphatic but not strident."

679 "Books Briefly." Progressive, 42 (July 1978), 44.
Gardner's "overstatements are embarrassing and his

metaphoric arguments frustratingly vague." OMF is a ruthless book, "more a zealous expose than an important contribution to artistic criticism."

680 "Bookviews Choice." Bookviews, 1 (May 1978), 42.
Setting high standards for art, Gardner has written a "provocative book about the nature and validity of creativity."

681 Buckmaster, Henrietta. "Gardner: Down with Today's Fashionable Opacity." Christian Science Monitor, 8 May 1978, p. 26.
Gardner is fully aware of the "range" of the writer's various roles--poet, priest, seer--and he confirms the power of fiction and the artist's isolation from which that power develops. His remarks on the contemporary literary scene are illuminating. "His morality is never moralistic."

682 Cahill, Daniel J. "Moral Crossroads." Novel, 13 (Spring 1980), 323-25.
Gardner's Aristotelian argument is forceful and humanely tolerant. Unlike other contemporary writers, he lets us know where he stands concerning his colleagues. Although he may be right that what passes for literature and art today is mere "verbal agility," he fails to realize that while many literary experiments may be spurious and worthless, others can lead us to "unforeseen discoveries."

683 Cahill, Daniel J. World Literature Today, 53 (1979), 686.
Making critical judgments about the moral worth of literature is the unfashionable position taken by Gardner in his boldly argued OMF, a work that is as daring and skillful as it is "generous and humanistic."

684 Campbell, Charles. Journal of the American Academy of Religion, 47 (June 1979), 349-50.
Gardner is "an intelligent and perspicacious critic," but his book, though insightful, is built upon "vague definitions." It is poorly organized and impractical in its approach, written by a man who is chiefly "a dreamer, a humanist, and most of all an artist."

685 Caplan, Brina. Georgia Review, 32 (Winter 1978), 935-38.
What Gardner holds up as "'the Good' seems to represent no more than the promptings of John Gardner's own good heart"; as a result much good fiction simply cannot measure

151

up to the rather personal and unduly narrow standard he has established.
In asking why do so many contemporary writers lack moral commitment, he raises an important cultural question, but instead of answering it, "he continually wanders away in search of 'eternal verities.'"

686 Carroll, David B. In Magill's Literary Annual 1979. Ed. Frank N. Magill. Englewood Cliffs, N. J.: Salem Press, 1979, pp. 511-15.
Gardner addresses a serious issue but in a "cryptic and overpersonal way." While his criticism of John Cage's music is valid, his discussion of literature dismisses authors without analyzing them, omits others who seem appropriate (e.g., Kesey), and allows no room for ironic moralists such as Heller. The second half is repetitive and sometimes vague and commonplace; the "Art and Insanity" chapter is "simply strange."

687 Carter, Albert Howard III. Studies in Short Fiction, 16 (Summer 1979), 242.
Gardner raises important issues and sheds light on his own practices as a novelist, but his tone is too dogmatic and "condescending" and his argument too "repetitive" and at times (as in his discussions of Slaughterhouse Five and Something Happened) flatly wrong.

688 Choice, 15 (November 1978), 1208.
"A refreshing and salutary corrective to a literary establishment so concerned with fads and textual criticism that it seems to have lost sight of art as a moral statement."

689 Clark, John R., and Anna Lydia Motto. Thought, 55 (June 1980), 240-44.
Gardner is "simply rhetorical, proscriptive, and viscerally personal"; his idea of goodness is "generalized, pious, and myopic"; and his argument is slovenly written, "arrant nonsense."

690 Coale, Sam. "The Eternal Verities Get a Defender." Providence Journal, 7 May 1978.
Gardner is "basically" correct "in this cranky, perceptive, and often shrill diatribe." However, in dismissing most contemporary writers Gardner is wrong, mistaking the literary expression of nihilism and despair for support.

691 "Coming Next Month." Bookviews, 1 (March 1978), 33.
Gardner makes some strong comments about the "failure
of morality" in contemporary literature.

692 Davis, Lennard J. "Cultivating a Moral Garden." New York
Arts Journal, no. 10 (1978), 25-26.
Gardner's call for moral art is condescending in its approach to its readers, philosophically naive, reductive
("For Gardner it is all rather simple--when you're right,
you're right"), and blatantly ahistorical--mere "camouflage for Gardner's real purpose, his attack on fellow
writers. His moral righteousness is especially curious
in light of the "moral lassitude" of his near plagiarism
in LTC.

693 Epstein, Joseph. "Rx for the Novel." Commentary, 66
(July 1978), 57-60.
Gardner is especially strong in describing the process
of art and the relation of this process to morality and in
making clear "the need for a criticism of fiction that is
judgmental." His weaknesses are the "scatter-shot"
criticism of fellow writers and his failing to see the
similarity between Bellow's views and his own.

694 Feld, Ross. "Motives for Metaphor." Harper's, 257
(October 1978), 89-93.
Gardner's argument is most appealing when he is discussing writers such as Barth. But for the most part Gardner
is too much concerned with "procedure." Welty has a
clearer understanding of what fiction is and is not.
Gardner's position is a curious blend of ethical culture,
liberalism and conservatism, troubling in its humorless-
ness and "barely blanketed competitiveness." (Reviewed
with William Gass's The World Within the Word and Eudora
Welty's The Eye of the Story.)

695 Flower, Dean. "Fiction Moralized." Hudson Review, 31
(Autumn 1978), 530-35.
This "book of complaints" does include several appealing
views but is doomed by its many flaws: Gardner's unper-
suasiveness, his insecurity in dealing with major talents,
his anti-intellectual bias, carelessness, self-righteousness, and inability to admit that art can "instruct by
negative example."

696 Fuller, Edmund. "A Novelist Calls for Morality in Our
Art." Wall Street Journal, 21 April 1978, p. 17.

OMF "is an important book, indeed a must, for all who care about the art of fiction and are disturbed at its present state." (See also the annotation for this entry under "Interviews.")

697 Gaffney, J. "Christian Ethics." America, 143 (15 November 1980), 312-13.
    Its shrillness aside, OMF is a much-needed book and is consistent with Gardner's morally based fiction.

698 Gillenkirk, Jeffrey. "Surely Goodness and Mercy." In These Times, 2 (31 May 1978), 23.
    In these loosely connected essays, Gardner posits a "medieval code" that amounts to "totalitarian optimism." His view is noble but hopelessly out-of-date. Instead of "trying to forge myths of post-industrial man," Gardner chooses to "conjure the pre-industrial version."

699 Gow, Haven B. Christianity and Literature, 28 (Fall 1978), 54-56.
    Gow approvingly summarizes Gardner's view of true art as life-affirmation and as a search for values. Like Eliot and Babbitt, Gardner proves that true art can be distinguished from fake on the basis of "rational and intellectually defensible grounds."

700 Graff, Gerald. "What Has Gone Wrong with Fiction?" The Chronicle of Higher Education, 16 (8 May 1978), 21.
    Roger Sale (New York Times Book Review, 16 April 1978) is wrong in believing that the tone of OMF disqualifies it from serious consideration. Despite Gardner's unconcern for "careful demonstration" and his writing more as a literary journalist than an academic scholar, Gardner does succeed in exposing the various "self-deceptions" of contemporary fiction and criticism.

701 Gramm, Kent. Theology Today, 35 (January 1979), 515-16.
    Gardner "assumes what some might call a prophetic stance in regard to 'post-modern' culture." Of special interest are his comments on fellow writers.

702 Green, Martin. "Tromping on Babies." Commonweal, 105 (18 August 1978), 535-36.
    Gardner's historical perspective is faulty in that the "tradition" he harks back to is not at all as clearly established as he would have us believe. Moreover, Gardner fails to develop precise critical views or to consider a truly moral writer like Philip Roth.

154

703 Hanscom, Leslie. "A Hip Defense of the Square View of Art."
Newsday, 2 April 1978, "Ideas" sec., p. 14.
What Gardner has done is to think out and express what
many readers--academic critics not included--"instinctively
feel": that most of today's serious fiction is "a miserable
experience to read."

704 Harris, Robert R. Bookviews, 1 (May 1978), 60.
Gardner's book is intensely and intelligently argued,
sure to appeal to readers disappointed by recent academic
fiction. However, Gardner is occasionally "pig-headed,"
and the book's second half tends to be "abstract and
repetitive."

705 Hoffman, Michael J. "Themes, Topics, Criticism." In
American Literary Scholarship: An Annual/1978. Ed. J. Albert
Robbins. Durham, N.C.: Duke University Press, 1980, p. 431.
Gardner apparently wrote OMF to correct "the excesses of
contemporary literature and criticism," especially obscur-
antism. His stance is "impassioned" and "strikingly anti-
modernist" but at times "almost hysterical in tone." A
little of his argument goes a long way.

706 Howard, Maureen. "A Cry for Authenticity." Quest 78, 2
(May-June 1978), 71-72.
OMF is "accessible criticism"; its arguments are as appealing" as Gardner's concern is "genuine." Yet however
"reasonable" Gardner's "middle-class outrage" may be,
there is a certain philistinism in his views. His humor-
lessness, his "odious ranking of fellow writers, and his
failure to consider the questions of audience and artistic
intention are among his faults. Filled with slogans and
contradictions, his book reads "like a bull session,"
instead of a reasoned appeal for authenticity. A much
better treatment of this subject is Iris Murdoch's The
Sovereignty of Good. (Review concludes with a paragraph
on Gardner's story, "Stillness": "a rich story, unstylish,
and very, very good.")

707 Janssens, Uta. "The Artist's Vision: John Gardner."
Dutch Quarterly Review of Anglo-American Letters, 9, iv
(1979), 284-91.
OMF is "basically a collection of essays, written
separately and for different purposes." It is less a
challenge to writers and critics than a "manifesto"
offering insights into Gardner's own fiction, a

"theoretical pendant" to OL in which the author resembles his cantankerous character, James Page. Gardner seems unaware that his views form a part of a tradition extending from Dr. Johnson to Lionel Trilling. His most important point is the defining of philosophical fiction as a way of thinking.

708 Johnson, Diane. "Two Novelists Offer Homely Wisdom and Plain Talk." Chicago Tribune Book World, 30 April 1978, p. 3.
Although occasionally "too reactionary," too full of "homely wisdom," Gardner is most persuasive "where he seriously addresses a large and complicated subject. ..." (Reviewed with Eudora Welty's The Eye of the Story.)

709 Johnston, Albert H. "PW Forecasts: Nonfiction." Publishers Weekly, 213 (20 February 1978), 114.
"His anti-modernist polemic contains much that is wrong-headed ... and ... is repetitious, especially the aesthetic generalizations of the second half. Nevertheless, this is an important, salutary, much needed [and provocative] critique."

710 Kazin, Alfred. "Moral John Gardner." Esquire, 89 (9 May 1978), 35-36.
Kazin has high praise for Gardner's fiction and is in sympathy with the views propounded in OMF. As a critic, however, Gardner is not original, is "sometimes petty" and (as in his praise of John Fowles) forgetful that ideas alone do not make great art. The chief deficiencies of OMF are Gardner's failure to explain "why literature is deteriorating in our distracted society" and the fact that the issues he raises "are more urgent than the way Gardner handles them."

711 Kellman, Steven G. Modern Fiction Studies, 24 (Winter 1978-79), 650-54.
Even though his bold Jeremiah occasionally lapses into Tartuffe, Gardner succeeds in presenting a "counterpoint" to the arid "jargon and tedium of much recent criticism."

712 Kirkus Reviews, 46 (1 March 1978), 282.
OMF is at once "profound and petty." "Excessive and self-limited as Gardner's 'rules' for moral fiction may be, they do illuminate the lousiness of much of today's writing, they do remind us of the viability of some centuries-old models, and they will provoke a good deal of healthily furious literary fisticuffs."

156

713 Kirsch, Robert. "John Gardner Disestablishes Establish-
    ment." Los Angeles Times Book Review, 30 April 1978,
    pp. 1, 8.
    This is a serious and long-needed critique of the con-
    temporary arts and criticism, a salutary, even exemplary work
    for the general reader as well as the professional critic.
    Although at times "trapped by his own imperatives,"
    Gardner is right in his assessments of current fiction, in
    his approval of some popular writing, in rejecting the
    view that today there is no audience for art, and in noting
    that criticism should be concerned with art and that art
    should be concerned with life.

714 Laskin, Daniel. "Challenging the Literary Naysayers."
    Horizon, 21 (July 1978), 32-36.
    See the annotations for this item listed under "Inter-
    views" and "Works About."

715 LeClair, Thomas. "Moral Criticism." Contemporary Litera-
    ture, 20, iv (1979), 508-12.
    Despite Gardner's "earnest force," his willingness to
    articulate unfashionable "feelings and tastes many dis-
    gruntled readers share," and his "common sense view," his
    argument is seriously weakened by his "inconsistent defini-
    tion of moral fiction," his naivete, and his straight-
    jacketing solemnity.

716 Lehmann-Haupt, Christopher. "Books of the Times." New
    York Times, 3 May 1978, p. C21.
    The author "has a flair for writing about the big ideas
    in a charmingly homespun way." His is "a lively per-
    formance," but one having too little foundation. While
    Gardner may be correct about postmodernism, he is not
    convincing when he criticizes cultural relativism or the
    instability of the universe.

717 Levy, Laurie. Chicago, 27 (August 1978), 168-71.
    "Gardner is insufferably demanding, pompous, verbose"
    but most of the time correct. What is most controversial
    is his subjective criticism of fellow writers. Although
    he "will be derided" for his views, there are many in-
    novative writers who agree with the position Gardner has
    taken. (Review includes significant misquotation.)

718 McCaffery, Larry. "The Gass-Gardner Debate: Showdown on
    Main Street." Literary Review, 23 (Fall 1979), 134-44.
    Gardner is preachy, condescending and philosophically

naive; his views are carelessly thought out and reactionary,
and his book is filled with "easy, unsupported assumptions."
Concerned chiefly with message, Gardner can never appreciate either the rigor of Gass's philosophically based
criticism or his "notion of the recovery of life through
art." (Reviewed with William Gass's The World Within the
Word.)

719 McCullough, David W. "Eye on Books." Book-of-the-Month
Club News, August 1978, p. 16.
   Quotes OMF and, at length, Gardner. (See entry under
"Interviews.")

720 Madrick, Jeffrey G. "Taking the Measure of Modern Letters."
Business Week, 24 July 1978, p. 11.
   Although "abstract," "windy," and "careless" in his
failure to acknowledge other critics, such as Leavis, who
have taken a similar position, Gardner is "particularly
strong when [he] angrily debunks myths about literature
that have evolved into respectability in recent years."

721 Mandeville, Helen I. Modern Schoolman, 56 (May 1979),
379-80.
   Gardner's book is sophomoric, pseudo-philosophical,
preachy, and directed at no clearly defined audience.
Simply dismissing authors out of hand, he seems to prefer
realism to fabulation and to leave no room for any art that
is not "great." His canonization of the artist implies
"a strangely totalitarian view of art."

722 May, John R. Horizons: Journal of the College Theology
Society, 5 (Fall 1978), 283-85.
   This "very disappointing book" is "a jeremiad rather than
a work of serious criticism." Gardner is to be faulted
for his anti-intellectualism, his questionable judgments
of other writers, his redundancy, and his failure to devise
"a far more subtle hermeneutic to get from novel to affirmation...."

723 Morace, Robert A. New Mexico Humanities Review, 1
(September 1978), 58-60.
   "Gardner's insouciance towards his audience" is the
book's most serious flaw. Points out specific instances
of careless proofing, editing, writing, and thinking and
suggests that Gardner revised previously published views
in order to create a more strident tone in OMF.

724 O'Connell, Shaun. "Critical Condition." Massachusetts
Review, 22, i (1981), 185-202.
   Gardner is a present-day Matthew Arnold, a reactionary
recoiling from equivocation and the styles of the 1960s.
His ideas are appealing until he puts them to practical
use; then they appear snobbish. His speculations are left
undocumented, and his definition of life is "rigid and
restricted." Ultimately, OMF "fails because it is
arbitrary, ill-reasoned, and recklessly written."
Gardner's position is more effectively argued by Eugene
Goodheart in The Failure of Criticism.

725 "Paperbacks: New and Noteworthy." New York Times Book
Review, 9 September 1979, p. 49.
   Listed, with brief description.

726 Patrick, Anne E. Journal of Religion, 59 (July 1979),
369-70.
   The author's preference for generalizations renders his
book useless both for the student of contemporary fiction
and the student of contemporary theology. Gardner raises
an important topic--secular morality--but handles it in
so "superficial, opinionated" a way as to invite "hasty
dismissal."

727 "Random Notes." National Review, 30 (14 April 1978), 476.
   Gardner's book "tells some plain truths."

728 Romano, John. "The New Traditionalists." New Leader, 62
(17 December 1979), 7.
   In their attacks on postmodernism, Gardner's OMF and
Gerald Graff's Literature Against Itself may help to return
literature and criticism to a needed sense of responsibility
The problem with Gardner's argument is his failure to understand the difference between "moral teaching" and "moral
concern," as exemplified in Nineteenth-Century realism.
As a result his "extraordinarily well-written" book posits
the "philistine" notion that in the final analysis a book
should be judged by its moral thesis.

729 Rovit, Earl. Library Journal, 103 (1 April 1978), 753.
   The book is "repetitive," "impressionistic," and
"preachy"; the comments on individual contemporary writers
are, however, "shrewd and worthy of attention."

730 Sale, Roger. "Banging on the Table." New York Times Book
Review, 16 April 1978, pp. 10-11.

OMF "is a book of pronouncements," views that are both "old-fashioned" and "predictable." Although Gardner pretends to be John the Baptist, his tone is more "jesting" than prophetic. His book is not the "'careful criticism'" he calls for; nor is it, "for all its solemnity, a serious book."

731 Schott, Webster. "The Sound and the Fury." Washington Post Book World, 23 April 1978, p. E3.
This book is a useful corrective to the hyperbole which characterizes most evaluations of contemporary fiction. Gardner's "panoramic Reader's Digest concepts of Truth, Beauty, and Goodness" will cause us to "think more clearly about what counts in art...." However, his view is both "idealistic" and narrow. Moreover, Gardner's contention that art changes us runs counter to the historical evidence, which makes clear that we change art, not the other way around. "Gardner can't give us a theory of art that rises from modern knowledge, so he makes one based on discarding the very art this knowledge has created."

732 Schwartz, R. L. "Criticism." Minnesota Daily (University of Minnesota), 1 May 1978, pp. 12-13.
Following a long and balanced summary, Schwartz points out that Gardner's theory is sound but his application is mean-spirited and unconvincing. Although OMF is an intelligent and provocative book, too much of it is devoted to attacking the bad, too little to advocating the good. Moreover, Gardner defines the moral artist inconsistently, first as the Homeric bard and later as the mad Romantic poet.

733 Simon, Jeff. "Gardner's Table Pounding Saps Intellectual Force." Buffalo News, 21 May 1978, p. G4.
Approves of Gardner's attacks on trivial fiction and "pseudo-scientific" criticism, but not his "ill-tempered tendency towards pronouncement." One paragraph discusses the decision by the University of Buffalo not to appoint Gardner to a faculty position.

734 Steiner, Robert. American Book Review, 3 (November-December 1981), 5-6.
It is surprising that a book so weightless and so poorly argued should be the focus of so much recent attention. Gardner's literal-minded approach to "language and the reading process serves a truly self-satisfied humanism." His flacid definition of morality is ultimately utilitarian,

as befits his notion of the writer's obligation to democracy. Gardner fails to understand the moral implications of language, of structure, and of the relations between writer and reader, writer and tradition. At the opposite pole is Gass, who, understanding how language creates meaning, rejects Gardner's idea that there are beliefs which all men must share. (Reviewed with Gass's The World Within the Word.)

735 Swanson, Roy Arthur. Canadian Review of Comparative Literature, 7 (Fall 1980), 452-65.
   Like most moral critics, Gardner mistakenly identifies morality with truth, both of which, in OMF, derive their authority from the author's personal views rather than from the absolutes he frequently invokes. OMF includes little that is profound, much that is perverse and intellectually "flabby." (Swanson includes a four-page list of selected errors.) The publication of OMF has had one salutary effect: "Reviewers now appear less timid about recognizing Gardner's mediocrity."

736 Thomas, Brian. American Spectator, 12 (January 1979), 28.
   Gardner fails to explain the precise "relation between art and morality." He assumes universals without bothering to define them and consequently resorts to "buzz-words." He interprets fictional narrators too literally and writers such as Barth and Pynchon too superficially. Although he knows the ultimate standard for art "is aesthetic, not moral," he argues for precisely the opposite view.

737 Towers, Robert. "Good Grief!" New York Review of Books, 25 (20 July 1978), 30-32.
   The argument of this book is certainly worthy, but its method is not. Gardner's Protestant tone, broad and reductive definitions, and slighting of the role of the unconscious in art are to be faulted. The "intrusive moralism" evident here mars all of Gardner's fiction except G.

738 Tucker, Carll. "A Huzzah for Happy Endings." Saturday Review, 5 (1 April 1978), 56.
   Gardner is for affirmation and happy endings and for more of a layman's rather than an academician's, criticism of literature. He argues that moral art requires no intellectual justification; it "attempts to be both accessible to its audience and truthful to a higher vision of what the world ought to be." Thanks to Gardner, we can watch

a romantic comedy and not feel "inclined to apologize for liking it."

739 Vine, Richard. "On Fictional Morality." Salmagundi, 44/45 (Spring-Summer 1979), 262-66.
Gardner is certainly "on to something" and so deserves our attention. However, his argument adds only anger to what has already been said by Ortega y Gasset in The Dehumanization of Art, but in light of the state of the arts today, anger may be necessary. Ultimately, however, Gardner is naive; he fails to convince because he knows too little, or too distantly, that sense of cultural and personal disintegration that has led to the creation of truly moral fiction by, for example, Dante, Tolstoi, and the writers of the 1920s.

740 Walla, Tom. Critic, 37 (October 1978), 3-4.
The book is poorly organized and reaches a number of inappropriate conclusions, e.g., making the presentation of ideals "a necessary pre-condition" of art and viewing literature as either good or bad. Still, "this is a provocative, stimulating and rewarding book." (Walla, it should be pointed out, misunderstands entirely Gardner's idea of the process of art; thus his objection to Gardner's supposed "necessary pre-condition.")

741 Wells, Robert W. "Between the Lines." Milwaukee Journal, 14 May 1978.
The review consists chiefly of excerpts; it concludes noting the need for this book to be read by the general public.

742 Williamson, Chilton, Jr. "The Democratic Scribe." National Review, 31 (30 March 1979), 425-28.
Gardner is "a mediocre novelist of some reputation"; his OMF has been "handled gingerly" by reviewers, whose ambivalence reflects their own "depraved" sense of art and weak "moral sense."

743 Wolcott, James. "A Cloud of Smoke and a Hearty Hi-Ho Silver." Village Voice, 23 (10 April 1978), 52-53.
The Public Broadcasting System series The Originals presented Gardner as "a honey-tempered bohemian," but in fact he is a reactionary "in danger of becoming the poet laureate of the era Pauline Kael has dubbed 'Eisenhower II.'" His OMF is a "murderous" attack on modernism; it

differs from similar attacks published in the New York
Times Book Review only in its overt sentimentality.

744 Wolff, Geoffrey. "They Shoot Fish in a Barrel, Don't They?"
New Times, 11 (24 July 1978), pp. 66, 69, 71.
   For the past eight years Gardner has been engaged in a
one-sided debate with William Gass over the purpose and
nature of fiction. In his 1970 reply to Gass's essay,
"The Concept of Character in Fiction," Gardner was
"respectful and scrupulous." But in OMF Gardner is in too
much of a hurry to be either. Rehashing old ideas, the
pontificating Gardner himself writes an "immoral" book,
one which lacks the "precision and demonstration" and
"commitment to the job of work at hand and not to slogans
or proclamations" of what is truly moral.

Rumpelstiltskin (1978)

745 Choice, 17 (April 1980), 219.
   Gardner's language is simple and efficient and his
characters are clearly realized. All three of his librettos
suffer from "occasional jarring lapses of taste and tone."
As retellings of familiar stores, only Rumpelstiltskin is
successful, chiefly as "a mild and pleasant work" for
children. Melodramatic touches mar Frankenstein and William
Wilson. The latter is Gardner's "most serious and ambitious"
operatic work, though even here there is more of Gounod's
Faust than of Poe's philosophical tale.

746 Smith, Patrick J. "Three Opera Librettos." Lone Star Book
Review, 1 (January-February 1980), 14, 36.
   Gardner mistakenly asks that his composers follow the
librettist's lead. The librettos are self-indulgent and
annoyingly arch literary games; the best is Rumpelstiltskin.
The prefaces are marred by errors and Gardner's "lack of
rigor." In general, the three librettos will appeal chiefly
to Gardner's "fans." (Reviewed with Frankenstein and
William Wilson.)

Frankenstin (1979)

747 Choice, 17 (April 1980), 219.
   See annotation listed under Rumpelstiltskin.

748 Smith, Patrick J. "Three Opera Librettos." Lone Star Book
Review, 1 (January-February 1980), 14, 36.
   See annotation listed under Rumpelstiltskin.

William Wilson (1979)

749 Booklist, 75 (15 December 1978), 652.
"Primarily an esoteric item for collections specializing
in literary ephemera."

750 Choice, 17 (April 1980), 219.
See annotation listed under Rumpelstiltskin.

751 Johnson, Eric W. Library Journal, 104 (15 January 1979)
195.
This libretto "does manage to exist by itself"; the text
is "sometimes mordant, sometimes romantic, always with an
undercurrent of terror and hopelessness."

752 Smith, Patrick J. "Three Opera Librettos." Lone Star
Book Review, 1 (January-February 1980), 14, 36.
See annotation listed under Rumpetstiltskin.

Vlemk the Box-Painter (1979)

753 LeGuin, Ursula. "Where Giants Roam." Washington Post Book
World, 23 March 1980, pp. 1, 5.
Instead of a major story, Gardner has written a minor
"allegory" in which he turns some of his ideas from OMF
into narrative form. In that book, he claims that
"accuracy of detail" is not "'necessary to the fabulous'";
in this he is wrong and it is precisely his mannered slips
in the details of Vlemk (the anachronisms in particular)
that are especially objectionable. "If only Gardner had
told it with faith in its reality, if only he had honored
his fable with confidence in its truth!" (Reviewed with
FB.)

754 M., S. San Diego Magazine, 32 (April 1980), 72-73.
Gardner's fairy tale is serious but not preachy; it is,
however, rather tiresome.

755 Shields, David. "John Gardner's Vlemk the Box-Painter."
Chicago Review, 32 (Spring 1981), 122-25.
Vlemk is not the kind of moral fiction that Gardner, in
OMF, says involves process, exploration, and discovery.
Rather, it is precisely the kind of programmatic,
didactic art that Gardner calls immoral. It merely il-
lustrates the thesis of OMF.

Freddy's Book (1980)

756 Adams, Phoebe-Lou. "PLA." Atlantic, 260 (April 1980),
    p. 129.
    "Freddy's tale is so constructed that a reader can find
    in it almost any social, political, or aesthetic principle
    he fancies, raising the suspicion that Mr. Gardner is
    simply playing a prank on his more earnest admirers."

757 Allen, Bruce. "Immoral Romance?" Sewanee Review, 89
    (Winter 1981), vi, viii.
    Despite some promising materials, including the
    characterization of Lars-Goren, FB has too much talk and
    too little narrative thrust. The author of OMF seems to
    be "misleading us to accept Freddy's nihilistic conclu-
    sions." Perhaps Gardner intended this puzzling and un-
    satisfying novel as an ironic Chaucerian "romance written
    by the wrong kind of romancer...."

758 Appel, David. WKYW (Philadelphia), n.d.
    Gardner has tried valiantly but unsuccessfully to
    combine gothic and mythic elements in a "metaphysical folk
    tale designed for very special tastes."

759 Ashton, Elizabeth. "Gardner: The Devil Is Dead and There's
    a Giant in the Attic!" Houston Chronicle, n.d.
    In this "teacherly" novel, Gardner sets out tantalizing
    images and philosophical clues for the reader to hunt down.
    Freddy's tale "is its own excuse"; in fact, the entire novel
    may simply be "dressing for the provocative last chapter"
    which poses the existentialist question anew.

760 Askins, John. "Some Monsters." San Jose Mercury News,
    15 June 1980.
    Gardner has more sympathy for monsters than for humans,
    perhaps because he believes himself an outcast. As a
    result, readers do not become sufficiently interested in
    his characters; nor do they feel compelled to think out
    the philosophical questions Gardner raises.

761 Auslander, Steve. "'Freddy' Weaves Tall, Devilish Story."
    Arizona Daily Star, 4 May 1980.
    FB does not epitomize OMF; instead, it is a "great" work
    showing flashes of brilliance. Gardner is a "superb"
    stylist and creator of personalities. Tonally, the two
    parts are virtually identical.

762 Baldwin, Doug. "Freddy's Fabulous Book." <u>Washington Daily</u>
(University of Washington), 23 April 1980, p. 14.
Most of Freddy's tale is an entertaining and well written
folktale, but the last fifty pages are preachy, cliche-
ridden, and unresolved. Gardner thought himself equal to
writing Dostoievski's Grand Inquisitor scene. Oddly, the
novel is remarkably similar to the literary gamesplaying
Gardner attacked in <u>OMF</u>.

763 Bannon, Barbara A. "PW Forecasts: Fiction." <u>Publishers</u>
<u>Weekly</u>, 217 (1 February 1980), 102.
In this "fanciful" but distinctly minor work, "Gardner
twits some favorite targets and evokes a murky mythology
with chilling effect."

764 Barkham, John. <u>John Barkham Reviews</u>. Seen in typescript;
appeared in various newspapers.
"A minor jeu d'esprit, another demonstration of its
author's versatility and obsession with ancient mythology."
<u>FB</u> can be interpreted any way the reader chooses.

765 Bedell, Thomas. "Fiction." <u>New Age</u>, July 1980, pp. 58-59.
This "morality tale" is overstuffed with metaphysical
debates, symbolic possibilities, and literary play, but it
is also an entertaining tale with an especially vivid
Devil.

766 Blei, Norbert. "Fan Letter for Freddy." <u>Milwaukee Journal</u>,
4 May 1980.
This is a good, perhaps even a great novel; the prose
sings and Gardner succeeds in shaking the reader out of
his accustomed ways of thinking. The novel fails, however,
to the degree that it is an academic game and the metaphysics overwhelm the novel's humanity.

767 <u>Booklist</u>, 76 (1 March 1980), 929.
The opening section is provocative but undeveloped, the
second is "tedious," and the pairing of the two is
"artificial and unsatisfactory."

768 "Books for Summer Reading." <u>New York Times Book Review</u>,
8 June 1980, pp. 24-25.
A two-sentence summary which notes that Winesap "hears"
Freddy's story.

769 Brady, Charles A. "Here's a Devil Who Speaks with a Nordic
Accent." <u>Buffalo News</u>, 20 April 1980, p. E8.
This novel, perhaps drawn in part from Dante, Isak

Dinesen, M. R. James, and Chaucer, does not, despite its many fine features, "add up to an admirable whole." The second part either fails to develop the themes of the first or develops them "mechanically." Gardner's moral--that "Man is his own devil, and needs no other"--is tediously developed. "We could have done with more of Freddy"--"a better-natured, housebroken Grendel"--and less of the Devil.

770 Campbell, James. "Undue Artifice." New Statesman, 102 (6 November 1981), 21-22.
    Despite a few imaginative sections, the novel is generally unsuccessful, especially the thin characterization in the second part, and the absence of connection between the two parts.

771 Carter, Ron. "Novel a Tantalizing Failure." Richmond Times-Dispatch, 27 April 1980.
    After a good start, the novel becomes a tedious fantasy capable of being interpreted in numerous ways. The ideas in Freddy's tale are individually interesting but are never brought together into a coherent whole and have little bearing on the novel's first part.

772 Clark, Jeff. Library Journal, 105 (1 March 1980), 635-36.
    FB is "one of Gardner's most subtly moving and persuasive fictions on life and its conduct, without the precious tidy moralism sometimes present in his other work." The two stories are successfully conjoined--the first concerns "the volatile relations" between the three main characters; the second "is a haunting psychological-historical romance."

773 Clark, Tom. "'Freddy's Book' Is Medieval Story-Within-the Story." Denver Post, 13 April 1980, Roundup sec., p. 32.
    Although elaborately and cleverly constructed, FB is "essentially an intellectual curiosity piece." The inside-story, which recalls Dinesen, Tolkien, and Bergman, combines medievalism and contemporary relativism; it is far better than the "contrived preamble."

774 Coale, Sam. "Devilish Doings in Old Sweden." Providence Sunday Journal, 6 April 1980.
    Although Gardner's latest novel derives in part from Chaucer, it is also very clearly in the romance tradition of Hawthorne. In his "rich tapestry, the 'universal alchemy' of Gardner's complex vision and muscular, gothic-imbued prose, all options remain open; magic is reborn into a modern world flattened by its own sad rational despairs...

775 Cosgrave, Mary Silva. "Outlook Tower." Horn Book, 56
(December 1980), 677.
Summary.

776 Cruickshank, Ken. "Gardner's Book Isn't as Good as
'Grendl' [sic]." Jacksonville Times-Union and Journal, 13
April 1980.
FB is finely written, but the plot lacks direction.
Perhaps Gardner uses Freddy in the first part to explain
his own failure in the long historical tale. Only the
illustrations make this book worth buying.

777 Cryer, Dan. "Eight Feet Tall, Monsters All." Baltimore
News American, 6 April 1980.
FB and G deal with the same general subject. FB, which
recalls Bergman's early films, is written in a prose that
is at once supple, plain, and moving; the gothic sections
are frighteningly real. This "subtle" tale leaves the
reader wondering whether Freddy represents the ambiguity
that Winesap, the rationalist, cannot admit.

778 Cryer, Dan. "John Gardner's Monstrous Myth." Newsday,
27 March 1980, part II, p. 2.
G is "a parable of modern man as monster"; FB deals with
a similar mythic world. A subtle, in some ways "baffling"
work, FB is also "powerful" and rewarding. Gardner seems
to suggest that Freddy is the ambiguous aspect of life
Winesap refuses to acknowledge and that Lars-Goren can
no more succeed in killing the devil than man can hope to
capture reality by means of language. Both attempts are
necessary, however, if human existence is to have meaning.

779 Cultural Information Services, 28 April 1980, p. 12.
Some readers will find the philosophical questions
interesting, and others, more ambitious, will try to puzzle
out the connections between the novel's two parts.

780 Cunningham, John R. "'Freddy's Book' Winner for Storyteller Gardner." Pittsburgh Press, 27 April 1980.
This rewarding novel mixes fantasy and reality and
concerns the consequences of human fortitude.

781 Curtis, Kim. "Battles Between Man-Devil Informative."
Fort Wayne News Sentinel, 24 May 1980.
More confusing than boring, FB might make sense to some-
one who wants to study it rather than read it; the novel
raises questions but fails to answer them. Parts of
Freddy's tale are good, but a little of it goes a long way.

782 Dachslager, Earl. "Gardner's Tale Within a Tale Doesn't
    Live Up to Its Promise." Houston Post, 23 March 1980,
    p. AA14.
    Gardner fails to synthesize his various elements:
    natural and supernatural, historical and fantastic, spiritual
    and political, and the halves of his book. Freddy seems
    merely an excuse for his story. The illustrations are far
    more impressive than Gardner's disappointing novel.

783 DeFrange, Ann. Oklahoman, 29 June 1980.
    In retreating into his world of fantasy, Gardner has made
    his vision too narrow. After an intriguing beginning, the
    novel becomes boring and predictable. The interesting story
    Gardner did not write concerns Freddy.

784 Dorenkamp, John H. Worcester (Mass.) Sunday Telegram, 11
    May 1980.
    Freddy's tale is not about Sweden but about Freddy, and
    it is intended to be read psychologically. By making
    Winesap not entirely likable, Gardner forces the reader to
    a more complex understanding of Freddy's personality. This
    is not a book for passive readers.

785 "Editors' Choice." New York Times Book Review, 30 March
    1980, p. 30. Through 27 April 1980.
    "A fabulous 16th-century land that mirrors the balance
    of good and evil is the heart of this novel within a novel:
    a challenging exercise in literary game-playing that is
    entertainment high and bright."

786 Erickson, Barbara. "Freddy Fries Effete Literates."
    Richmond (Calif.) Independent & Gazette, n.d.
    Freddy's tale criticizes a society characterized by
    Winesap's smugness and his failure to face reality, con-
    front evil and slay it. Brask parallels Winesap; both
    recall Sol Ravitz in SD. Lars-Goren resembles Henry Soames
    in NM; both instinctively know the difference between
    right and wrong.

787 Erie (Penn.) Times, 18 May 1980.
    A confusing but nonetheless fascinating novel; Gardner's
    Devil is "one of the most convincing in modern literature."

788 Ewing, James. "Book Beat." Nashville Banner, 2 February
    1980.
    Prepublication notice.

789 "Fiction of the Week." Augusta (Georgia) Chronicle, 8 May 1980.
    Gardner succeeds in recreating the world of Sixteenth-Century Sweden and in using fantasy to establish Freddy's "secret anguish."

789a Filiatreau, John. "Gardner: Dullness in a Moral Mask." Louisville Courier-Journal, 13 April 1980, p. E7.
    FB is "an extraordinarily artificial book" whose sole excuse for being is so that Gardner can make several points about morality in literature. More essay than novel, FB is not at all compelling and, in its repeated allusions to "Jack and the Bean-Stalk," painfully obvious. The author is, like his character Winesap, a dilettante.

790 Fink, Rita. (Newspaper not identified.)
    Both parts of this interesting novel concern Gardner's favorite theme of good versus evil. Despite the author's rich language and "immaculate descriptions," the purpose of Freddy's tale and of the novel in general is unclear.

791 Forbes, Cheryl. "John Gardner: Remnants of Morality in Modern Fiction." Christianity Today, 24 (10 October 1980), 46-47.
    Gardner's morality does not conform to orthodox Christianity but does prick the Christian reader's conscience. FB is essentially a theological novel about the nature of evil, the existence of God, scripture, and the Reformation. A "brave," finely written work, it raises significant questions about lust, greed, and power both in and out of the church.

792 Fowler, Doreen. "The Devil's Due." Memphis (Tenn.) Commerical Appeal, 23 March 1980, p. G6.
    Although in technique and method FB recalls G, "KI," and OL, it is, except for the opening section, uncharacteristically lifeless. The philosophical debate of part two--the search for the devil becoming the search for truth--raises numerous questions but provides either answers that are too simple or no answers at all.

793 Fuller, Edmund. "The Psycho-History of a Boy/Monster/Genius." Wall Street Journal, 14 April 1980, p. 24.
    FB again proves "the immense diversity" of Gardner's subjects and methods. Despite its originality, gothic imagery, intellectual play, and satire, the novel is disappointing: too much is left unsaid and the idea that

170

Freddy could have written the novel ascribed to him is
untenable.

794 Gardner, Kit. <u>Charleston</u> (S.C.) <u>Evening Post</u>, 27 April
1980.
The novel "is complex and charming, though long on
morality and short on substance" and "irreparably divided."
The Devil is "oddly appealing."

795 Garyantes, Diane. "Of the Devil, Kings, Bishops and
Knights." <u>Daily Collegian</u> (college not identified), 20
June 1980.
The "loose ends" dangling at the end of the novel will
leave readers feeling unsatisfied. However, the novel is
vividly written; Brask's cynicism adds zest to the novel,
and it is "refreshing" to think that someone as virtuous
as Lars-Goren might actually exist.

796 Goldenberg, Judi. "Legend of Devilish Intrigue."
<u>Richmond News Leader</u>, 2 July 1980.
Gardner's strengths are characterization, command of
various literary styles, humor, and willingness to
experiment, to take seriously the novelist's duty to entertain the reader and to tackle major issues without simplifying them or preaching. In <u>FB</u> "his impatience with his own
talent" leads him astray, causing him to abandon Winesap
and "direct storytelling" prematurely.

797 Granetz, Marc. <u>New Republic</u>, 182 (19 April 1980), 36-37.
"Profoundly disappointing," <u>FB</u> is more "sermon" than
novel. The novel-with-the-novel device has "no structural
interest" and neither story is rewarding. The first is
"slick" and without any of that "discovery by process"
Gardner says characterizes moral fiction; the second is
boring, its characters "difficult to care about."

798 Gray, Paul. "Devil's Due." <u>Time</u>, 115 (31 March 1980), p. 8
Following an "irresistible beginning," the novel thwarts
its readers' expectations, becoming less narrative and more
argumentative. Gardner never becomes preachy, however, and
the "novel's failure to satisfy is almost offset by its
power to disturb." The book's medieval world is, like the
modern age, "theologically muddled," but despite the confusion the characters understand that eventually "the
labyrinth of morality will yield the proper path of
behavior."

799 Grumbach, Doris. "A Boy-Man Monster Talks of the Devil."
Los Angeles Times Book Review, 27 April 1980, p. 4.
Despite Gardner's "persuasively fine" writing, FB is a
minor work. Its second part includes many "excellent
stretches of ideation that save the arid retelling of
history," yet it is less interesting than the first part
"promised to be." It is a novel which echoes Chaucer and
Twain ("The Mysterious Stranger") and is narrated "in
Gardner's own familiar instructive tone."

800 H. "Gardner's Latest Is a Tall Tale about Two Too-Tall
Men." Long Beach (Calif.) Independent/Press Telegram,
18 April 1980, p. Bl4.
Deep, readable, and delightful, FB will enhance Gardner's
esteemed position in American literature. Freddy's tale
is a "metaphysical folk tale," at once childishly simple
and psychologically, philosophically, and mythically
complex.

801 Halio, Jay. "Fiction and the Malaise of Our Time."
Southern Review, 17 (Summer 1981), 626-27, 630.
Although Freddy is not a "credible" character, his story,
which shows how belief can overcome the contemporary
malaise, is powerful. Gardner is among those whose work
disproves Alfred Kazin's pessimistic view of contemporary
American writers (New Republic, 18 October 1980). Instead
of being trapped in the present, Gardner "respect[s]
legitimate authority and dare[s] to dream."

802 Hand, Judson. "Gardner Spins a Tale of Genius and Giants."
New York Daily News, 9 March 1980.
"Gardner's new novel is deep, highly readable and, in
general, a delight. It will enhance his position as one of
the country's most admired writers."

803 Harris, Roger. "The Book Shelf." Newark (N.J.) Star
Ledger, n.d.
A well-written and portentous story which follows
Gardner's characteristic "half-mythic formula."

804 Hilton, Earl. "On Evil, Devil and Despair." Chronicles
of Culture, September-October 1980, pp. 30-31.
Freddy's tale, which has some of the "stylized simplicity"
of a fairy tale, is mistitled, for it is not about the
Macbeth-like Gustav Vasa but the Devil and Brask, who
represent despair, and Lars-Goren, who is not a simple,
static character. Despite appearances, FB is not an

example of literary narcissism, and whatever Gardner's
borrowings, his themes are his own: the price of power,
man's influence on others, and moral responsibility. The
novel is flawed in two ways: the unnecessary opening
section and, in striving to clarify his own views,
Gardner's having made Brask too didactic a character.

805 Houston, Levin. "Scandinavian History Recounted by
    'Freddy.'" Fredricksburg (Virginia) Free Lance Star Town
    & Country Magazine, 5 April 1980.
       The unifying threads in Gardner's writing--the combination
    of medievalism and contemporaneity, his sympathy for mis-
    fits--appear in FB, which may be Gardner's "most mysterious"
    book.

806 Howes, Victor. "Mini-Epic Couched in a Riddle: (We're
    Probably Not Supposed To Ask Why)." Christian Science
    Monitor, 2 April 1980, p. 17.
       FB it not, as the dust-jacket proclaims, a novel inside
    a novel but instead "an epic introduced by a novella."
    Why Gardner has chosen to structure his novel in this way
    is neither made clear nor, "since Freddy's book is vastly
    more interesting than Freddy," is the answer especially
    important. Freddy's book is "a tale, half history, half
    metaphysics," which concerns a king who, like Grendel, is
    "'cut off from heaven by boredom and despair'" and who
    plays an Ingmar Bergman-chess game in which "King takes
    Bishop."

807 Hunt, Marianne. (Unidentified Regina, Saskatchewan, news-
    paper), 3 May 1980, p. 10.
       In this compelling novel, Gardner draws parallels between
    Freddy's life and the artist's place in society, but he
    fails to connect his two narratives and leaves many points
    unresolved; perhaps he is contemplating a sequel.

808 Jaffe, Harold. American Book Review, 3 (January-February
    1981), 9-10.
       Gardner "is an excessively prolific writer of middling
    fiction, ill-tempered polemics, and occasional scholarship"
    whose most recent novel, despite a promising parodic open-
    ing section, fails both in design and in workmanship.
    While his nostalgia for past orders is artistically tenable
    his treatment is wooden and unconvincing.

809 K., B. L. <u>Kliatt</u>, 16 (January 1982), 21.
As with Gardner's other works, more questions are raised
than are answered; "as in Kafka's works, there are no set
answers." A book for "inquiring readers" and courses on
myth and medieval literature.

810 Kalpakian, Laura. "Gardner's Book: Sound, Fury, But What
Do They Signify?" <u>Miami Herald,</u> 30 March 1980, p. M7.
Gardner is a talented writer, but <u>FB</u> is a "smug,"
"murky" novel. In <u>OL</u> he used an inside-novel to advantage,
but the purpose of Freddy's tale is impossible to define.

811 Kellythorne, Walter. "Nightmare in Black and White."
<u>Victoria</u> (Canada) <u>Times</u>, 3 May 1980, p. 43.
"A nightmare collage" as stark as a Bergman film.

812 Kelso, Dorothy H. "Gardner Uses Classic Ingredients."
<u>Quincy</u> (Mass.) <u>Patriot Ledger</u>, 19 May 1980, p. 15.
Gardner's aim is unclear (to create a "distant mirror"
of the modern age? a Shakespearean study of leadership?),
and his characters are preachy, their voices indistinguish-
able from the author's. Freddy's tale is far less interesting than either the opening section or Biamonte's
illustrations.

813 <u>Kirkus Reviews</u>, 48 (1 January 1980), 21-22.
The novel is written in the familiar Gardner style--
"disingenuous, didactic, well-worded but flat"--and filled
with all his "pet peeves"--"organized religion, writers like
William Gass, a philosophical relativism, and literature's
city slickers." In general the novel continues the "preaching and feuding" of <u>OMF</u>. Freddy may be "a Gardner self-
portrait."

814 Kisor, Henry. "New Fiction for Spring." <u>San Francisco
Examiner</u>, 18 February 1980, p. 18.
The publication of <u>FB</u> in March should provoke numerous
attacks by those writers whom Gardner "libeled...as
ethical morons" in <u>OMF</u>.

815 Kline, Betsy. "This Gentle Monster a Renaissance Man."
<u>Kansas City Star</u>, 30 March 1980, p. E10.
Gardner succeeds in writing a novel that "strives to be
be many things at once." The story of Lars-Goren's
triumph is "a sensitive, suspenseful study of intellectual
man and his battle over his emotions to strive for what
is right" even when moral action "is meaningless in a

cruel world." FB is quite unlike other modern novels and
is all the better for being so.

816 Krisher, Trudy. "Freddy's Book: An Admirable Effort That
Doesn't Work." Dayton Journal Herald, 3 May 1980, p. 24.
Attempting a great deal, Gardner achieves very little.
Graduate students will mine Gardner's vast load, but the
general reader will soon be bored by an emotionally arid
work that sacrifices character to philosophy. Freddy is
more interesting than the story Gardner has him fashion
to reflect his situation.

817 Kubal, David. "Fiction Chronicle." Hudson Review, 33
(Autumn 1980), 447-48.
The novel's prologue is "very promising," but Freddy's
tale is nothing more than a "modernist attack on rational,
liberal humanism." This is especially odd in light of
Gardner's militantly anti-modernist stance in OMF. Instead
of affirming moral and aesthetic values, FB supports anti-
intellectualism and primitivism and evidences Gardner's
distaste for "the democratization of the mind."

818 Larson, Charles R. "Siamese-Twin Tales, One from the Pen
of a Giant." Detroit News, 13 April 1980.
The point of Gardner's literary tricks in FB is not
clear. Has he blurred the distinction between the two
parts to draw out the psychological aspects of his story
or is he simply teasing the reader? Does Freddy give Winesap
the manuscript, hoping the professor will psychoanalyze it?

819 LeClair, Thomas. "The Clatter of Moral Fiction." Saturday
Review, 7 (29 March 1980), pp. 53-54.
Instead of creating that "'vivid and continuous dream'"
which Gardner, in OMF, said fiction must create, FB, like
OL, is merely "another argument for but failure to write
the fiction that will ravish us into innocence, make us
listening children as we read." The three major characters
in the novel's "prologue" reflect aspects of Gardner's own
character: Agaard "is the medieval scholar who knows the
worst about the world"; Winesap is Gardner "the mimetic
novelist and critic"; and Freddy is Gardner the "literary
misfit." (The Freddy-character in part two, Lars Goren, is
"the knight of moral fiction who debates a William Gass-
like bishop of empty rhetoric.") In his recent works,
Gardner, "one of our noisiest writers," is "bumptious and
careless of fact, quick to judge and slow to credit, satisfied with simplification, proud of volubility."

820 LeGuin, Ursula. "Where Giants Roam." <u>Washington Post</u>
   <u>Book World</u>, 23 March 1980, pp. 1, 5.
      This "brilliant," finely illustrated book is reminiscent
   of Ingmar Bergman and Isak Dinesen. The killing of the
   Devil, one of the "most convincing devils" in recent literature, "is an event of great dramatic power and originality
   and of most devious and echoing implications." In sum,
   "The tale left me mystified and satisfied to the highest
   degree. Who could ask for anything more?" (Reviewed with
   <u>Vlemk</u>.)

821 Lehmann-Haupt, Christopher. "Books of the Times." <u>New</u>
   <u>York Times</u>, 12 March 1980, p. C26. Rpt. in <u>Minneapolis</u>
   <u>Tribune</u>, 23 March 1980, p. G14.
      Except for the final scenes and "an austere and cryptic
   majesty reminiscent of Ingmar Bergman's film 'The Seventh
   Seal,'" the second part of <u>FB</u> is less successful than the
   first. More troubling, as in <u>OL</u>, is just how the two parts
   connect. Freddy obviously represents "the artist in relation to conventional society," and his story is exactly
   the kind of history in the form of fairy tale his father
   condemns. (In it Bishop Brask serves as Gardner's mouth-
   piece.) "But what does all this add up to?"

822 Lodge, Sally A. "PW Forecasts: Paperbacks." <u>Publishers</u>
   <u>Weekly</u>, 219 (8 May 1981), 252.
      This sardonic fantasy is not Gardner's best work.

823 Logan, William. "Gardner's Book: Myth with Lapses of
   Imagination." <u>Chicago Tribune Book World</u>, 16 March 1980,
   sec. 7, p. 1.
      "Freddy's Book" may originally have been intended as a
   story for children to which Gardner, hoping to pass it off
   as adult fiction, then added "a convenient introduction."
   The attempt fails because "Freddy's Book" lacks "weight";
   moreover, Gardner's "arch prose, simple-minded philosophy,
   and condescending tone," as well as his "perfunctory,"
   simile-laden writing, all work against the book's success.
   The novel is not merely "inconsequential," however.
   Portions are plagiarized ("verbatim transcription and
   crude paraphrasing") from Michael Roberts' <u>The Early Vasas</u>
   and Ingvar Andersson's <u>A History of Sweden</u>. "Whether he
   writes too fast, is simply lazy or lacks a transforming
   imagination, Gardner's unacknowledged copying is inexcus-
   able." (See also Gardner's letter in response to this
   review and Logan's reply, both 13 April 1980.)

824 Lorenz, Cecilia. "'Freddy's Book' Blends Fantasy, Mystery, Humor." _Oakland Sunday Magazine_, 19 October 1980, p. 7.
FB is a challenging, entertaining, and satisfying novel: humorous, poignant (in its treatment of Freddy's situation and the Swedish rebellions), and, best of all, the way Gardner creates Freddy and then projects his psychology on the tale Freddy writes. (Lars-Goren surely speaks for Freddy when he says "Evil is life itself.") For the reader, FB is the "ultimate detective story."

825 Love, Spencie. "Gardner Monster Allegory Doomed on Two Counts." _Washington Star_, 23 March 1980, p. C10.
FB is a hurriedly written and distinctly unsuccessful work composed of a short satire and "a murky philosophical allegory." The static narrative, lifeless characters, reliance on history, and order vs. chaos theme are the hallmarks of its author, who may be more a "popular philosopher" than a novelist. The bishop is the most interesting character.

826 Lutz, Fred. "A Scandinavian Tale." _Toledo Blade_, 27 April 1980, p. F8.
Gardner's novels never seem to fulfill the promise with which they begin. As Gardner said of Mailer in _OMF_, his imagination "is almost always better than what he can find to do with it." Except for a number of sloppily written sentences, the opening part is fairly good, but the second is a literary game whose purpose is not at all clear. Still, Gardner is always interesting, even when he fails.

827 McGoogan, Kenneth. "Knights, Monsters and Satan Himself." _Calgary Herald_, 10 May 1980.
A "serious, thought-provoking and entertaining" novel. Philosophically, the novel's structure--the naturalistic opening and Freddy's "metaphysical folktale ... a sophisticated morality play"--is justified. Believing that each man must be responsible for making choices involving good and evil, Gardner forces the reader to take Winesap's place and draw conclusions about Freddy's work. Aesthetically the novel fails, however; the connections between its parts are "tenuous" and the reader, forced to assume Winesap's role, feels "baffled, cheated, vaguely dissatisfied."

828 Maney, Brian. "'King Gustave [sic] and the Devil': Gardner's Book within Book." _The Ram_ (Fordham Univ.), 18 September 1980, p. 9.

The purpose behind the self-consciously ironic opening section is unclear. Freddy's tale is better: "absorbing, well composed and witty." Brask, its most interesting character, is the vehicle for Gardner's various specula- tions on art, history, language, and good and evil. Though imperfectly drawn, the Devil provides a measure of objectivity. The major problem with FB is that it teases meanings without actually making any of them clear.

829 Manning, Margaret. "Gargantuan Gardner Tale." Boston Globe, 17 March 1980, p. 26.
Gardner is an affirmative and intellectual writer who creates strong characters and who has a "style both straightforward and lyrical." FB, however, is "slightly off": a too-simple, broken-backed work in which the most interesting character is not Gardner's spokesman, Lars- Goren, but the evil Bishop Brask. The Devil "is a monu- mental bore."

830 Mazzarella, Merete. "En Moralitet om Onskan" [On the Morality of Evil]. Bonniers Littera Magasin, 50 (December 1981), 387-89. In Swedish.
Review of Gustav Vasa och djavulen [Gustav Vasa and the Devil], trans. Thomas Preis, published in Sweden by Norstedts, 1981. An American is hardly qualified to con- struct a readable work of historical fiction about a period that would give even a Scandinavian writer great difficulty. Gardner's handling of the political situation as a power struggle between good and evil is incredibly trite, with the exception of Bishop Brask's interesting existential commentary. It is questionable whether Gardner's Devil is totally evil or whether anyone would have benefitted from his destruction. Although the novel is not inter- esting either as historical fiction or for its theme, Gardner's openness and mocking equivocation make it worth- while reading.

831 Mellors, John. "Beloved Countries." Listener, 106 (31 December 1981), 827-28.
The "self-deprecating" humor of the first part is pleasing; Freddy's historical tale would have been better had Gardner left the Devil out.

832 Middleton, Harry. "A Fairy Tale of Castles and Monsters." Figaro, 8 September 1980, sec. 2, p. 18.
Despite similarities to the "haunting" ISM, FB is moral fiction at the expense of storytelling. The fine opening

section is followed by a dogmatic and digressive lecture
involving no risk or challenge or mystery and offering
nothing new: Gardner again tells us "that action, while
only a gesture, is at times perhaps the only moral choice
we have." The novel's two parts neither fit together nor
interest the reader individually. Freddy is used to show
the limitations of Winesap's world-view. Reading FB is
like reading children's literature with Mother Goose
holding a gun to your head.

833 Milazzo, Lee. "Gardner's New Book within a Book." Dallas
Morning News, 16 March 1980, p. G4.
      FB recalls Gardner's earlier fiction: a "deceptively"
simple surface, monsters, ambivalent northern setting,
philosophical debates. The novel seduces the reader;
Freddy's tale successfully combines fantasy and history,
past and present in a projection of his personality.

834 Minutaglio, Bill. "A Monster Story in Two Parts."
Express News (unidentified city or town near Washington,
D.C.), 23 March 1980.
      Gardner cheats his readers and misdirects his energy and
abilities. FB's first part--a horror story written in the
familiar Gardner mode--is too short, and the second part--
"straightforward history" for the most part--is too long
and provides no insight into Freddy's personality. In
FB Gardner advocates psychohistory and combines it with
myth.

835 Murray, James G. "Fiction in the (Very) Low 80s: An Early
Retrospective with (Mostly) Regrets for the Future."
Critic, 39 (December 1980), 1-4.
      FB evidences Gardner's "accustomed intelligence and wit."
His spoofing is amiable but unsuccessful and his double-
story technique is "glaringly artificial."

836 Northouse, Cameron. "John Gardner." Lone Star Book
Review, 1 (May 1980), 1, 3.
      FB is not, as the review in the New York Times [Book
Review] implies, a "recantation" of OMF. Nor is it "a
conventional novel," fable, short story cum novella, or
novel-within-a-novel; in fact, the style is far less
important than the message. Freddy's approach, which combines Agaard's traditionalism and Winesap's trendiness,
parallels Gardner's. In this view, fiction is "a
rehearsal for actual day-to-day existence. Both understand that contemporary chaos is not an external but an
internal state which man can control.

837 "Notable Books of the Year: Fiction." New York Times Book
Review, 30 November 1980, p. 48.
    According to this one-sentence summary, Winesap "hears"
Freddy's story.

838 Observer, 17 January 1982, p. 31.*
    Cited in Book Review Index (1982).

839 O'Hara, J.D. "The Banality of Fiction." Nation, 230 (15
March 1980), 310-12.
    Such "eloquent monsters" as the green knight and Dr.
Frankenstein's enable us "to see ourselves as the others,
the outsiders, see us." Whether Freddy serves us in this
way is doubtful. He "is an industrious dullard and no
writer" who "can't comprehend the implications of his own
story, much less contrive a lucid discussion of them."
Gardner's purpose in this is never made clear. We can't
"expect revelations from Freddy" and receive from Gardner
no "revelation of Freddy." In fact, we never know who is
responsible for the numerous errors and inconsistencies
which dot Freddy's tale. Are they purposeful? Are "the
turgidity and banality of the opening section" similarly
purposeful? The "blatant exhibitionism of [Gardner's] great
themes, . . . the glaring presence of his daring fictional
devices (which whole shoals of sci-fi writers manipulate with
more skill) ... [and] the undemanding leadenness of his
prose" hardly add up to art. "Freddy's sad work" is much
less successful than the legend of King Krogold in Celine's
Death on the Installment Plan.

840 Olson, Clarence E. "There's a Moral to the Monster." St.
Louis Post-Dispatch, 30 March 1980, p. C4.
    Gardner's moral "tends to be lost in the art of the story,
or surfaces as rhetoric rather than substance." Thus, for
example, the evil Bishop Brask is far more interesting than
the good Lars-Goren. Instead of a fiction of craftsmanship
and "moral commitment," FB is a hastily written, though still
pleasurable, "diversion." But then, Gardner is always better
read for "fun" than "moral improvement."

841 Ousley, Cellastine. Best Sellers, August 1980, p. 167.
    Brief summary, concluding: although the novel is difficult
to "understand or read," the illustrations are interesting.

842 "Paperbacks: New and Noteworthy." New York Times Book
Review, 31 May 1981, p. 55.
    An "entertaining" and "challenging exercise in literary
game playing." According to the two-sentence summary,
Winesap "hears" Freddy's tale.

843 Pastoret, M. C. "Gardner's Triumph." Cleveland Plain
Dealer, 13 April 1980, p. C15.
   This "deftly achieved" novel includes "a gracefully
styled morality tale" that, because it seems to acknowledge
the triumph of evil, appears to contravene Gardner's own
view of moral fiction. Actually, however, FB suggests that
the individual chooses to be good or evil or indifferent.
Winesap chooses to rise above his age and befriend Freddy,
who in turn makes his friendship's offering to Winesap.

844 Peacock, Allen H. "Johnny's Gardner's Book: Murky Yet
Still Wonderful." Baltimore Sun, 27 April 1980.
   Although Gardner proved himself an intolerant and mean-
spirited critic in OMF, as a fiction writer he is, in his
preoccupation with evil and the individual's responsibility
to society, the successor to Melville, Poe, Emerson,
Thoreau, and especially Hawthorne, whose allegorical reworkings of the past Gardner's works clearly resemble.
FB is enjoyable but not entirely satisfying; the two parts
are not sufficiently conjoined, and the nihilistic ending
is rather uncharacteristic.

845 "Pick of the Paperbacks." Christian Science Monitor, 8
June 1981, p. 25.
   One paragraph summary focusing on the Agaards.

846 "Picks and Pans." People, 28 April 1980, pp. 9-10.
   Figuring out the relationship between Freddy and his tale
is a challenge readers do not have to take up to enjoy FB,
which succeeds on the merits of Gardner's "idiosyncratic and
graceful" writing alone.

847 Pintarich, Paul. "Monster Weaves a Medieval Web." Sunday
Oregonian (Portland), 13 April 1980, p. C4.
   In the second part, the reader is locked out of the
Twentieth Century and consequently feels unsettled despite
Gardner's narrative skill, imagination, and historical
knowledge. Good and evil are distorted by Freddy, who in
his fictional Lars-Goren achieves "the ultimate satisfac-
tion of bringing good into the world." FB is a strong
novel, though like OMF, it will probably be attacked.

848 Richman, Robert. "Beat the Devil." Village Voice, 25
(10 March 1980), 45.
   FB clarifies and corrects the opposing definitions of
moral fiction--as "explicit didacticism" and as discovery
--in OMF. Lars-Goren, the book's hero, is not merely a

moral absolute; rather his goodness is tried in a series
of "existential 'tests,'" which serve as "the moral transcriptions of Gardner's intuition of real-life pressures."
His juxtaposing of medieval and modern worlds is only
"slightly awkward, perhaps even necessary, because the
idea of moral exploration is "foreign to the contemporary
cultural landscape." Moreover, the conclusion of the
medieval tale ingeniously returns the story to present
time.

849 Romano, John. "A Moralist's Fable." New York Times Book
Review, 23 March 1980, pp. 1, 26-27.
   Gardner's new book again evidences the fact that the
author is at war with himself: the fabulist versus the
moralist. His "brand of morality, with its characteristic
stress on strength of will, turns out to be incompatible
in practice with the softer charms of storytelling."
FB is "entertainment high and bright"; the opening section
is "enthralling," and the conclusion "a marvelously virtu-
osic piece of narrative'; and the characters Brask and Gustav
are "persuasive." Although Gardner's method "of defining
evil in terms of its ineradicability" saves his moral from
being "platitudinous," the programmatic second part makes
the reader "feel downright resentful." (Romano bases several
of his comments on Heinrich Zimmer's psychological study
of folktales and myths, The King and the Corpse, a work
he feels Gardner must surely know.)

850 Sale, Roger. "Stranger than Nonfiction." New York Review
of Books, 27 (29 May 1980), 39.
   The novel is broken-backed and only slightly more interesting in its second part (which may derive from Chaucer's
"The Pardoner's Tale"). Even in this second part "the work
suffers because the mythology he is using is the modernist
myth of nostalgia for a lost unity given us by the very
people Gardner would wish literature to circumvent, Henry
Adams, Eliot, Pound, Yeats.... To tell the kind of tale
Gardner wants to tell, The Waste Land is a better medium
than [the allegorical] FB."

851 Sales, Joseph E. "A Fairy Tale Look at Morality."
Rutgers Daily Targum (Rutgers the State University, New
Brunswick, N.J.), 12 September 1980.
   In FB Gardner proves that a fairy tale can be significant
art. Using the alliance of Lars-Goren and Brask to parallel
his relationship with his father, Freddy "creates a vision
of hope to counter his father's despair."

852 Seib, Kenneth. "'Freddy' Hailed as Gardner's Best."
Fresno Bee, 4 May 1980, p. G9.
Gardner's "obsessive themes" recur in FB: each man's
"monstrous isolation," the past-haunted present, the
dream-like clash. Accessible yet at the same time not
easily comprehended, FB is Gardner's best novel and the
year's most important publication.

853 Sermon, Charles. "Gardner Falls Short in 'Freddy's Book.'"
Columbia (S.C.) State, 30 March 1980.
A "leaden, lifeless" work given over to Gardner's "making
ironic moral headway," FB has none of the humanity of OL.

854 Shaw, Mildred Hart. "Monster Son Turns Author." Grand
Junction (Colorado) Sentinel, 30 March 1980, Westworld
sec.
The use of the inside-novel here is more acceptable than
in OL, though still not successful. Unfortunately, the
story Freddy writes seems beyond his abilities. Consequently, the reader, after untangling all the meanings, is
forced to ask, "Whose book is it?"

855 Shippey, T. A. "Giant the Jack-Killer." Times Literary
Supplement, 23 October 1981, p. 1231.
Although FB is the kind of book that seems to invite
dreary academic discussion, it is nonetheless "completely
enthralling." In this unfashionably optimistic "fable
about the rights and wrongs of humanism," Gardner again
takes the side of the underdog. The key to the novel is
the "deep-level nastiness" of Winesap, the giant who meets
his Jack, Freddy.

856 Signal (Special Interest Group Network on Adolescent
Literature), December 1980, p. 15.
One sentence summary; FB is noted as being for young
adults and up.

857 Sinkler, Rebecca. "A Contrived Way of Dispatching Our
Devils." Philadelphia Inquirer, 13 April 1980.
Freddy is Gardner's metaphor for the artist who
struggles beyond his monstrous wound to a sane vision of
human life. Interesting as Freddy's adventure tale and
Gardner's fable of the artist are (at least to a limited
audience), the novel fails because of its "contrived"
structure, which recalls the literary games Gardner
played in G and OL.

858 Sinkler, Rebecca. "On Books." Philadelphia Inquirer, 10
    February 1980.
    Gardner generously bestows two novels on his readers, one
    "a metaphysical fantasy."

859 Sommer, Anthony. "Gardner's 'Freddy': Thoughtful, Hollow."
    Phoenix Gazette, 29 March 1980.
    Despite similarities to earlier Gardner works and its
    depth and complexity, FB is not an especially satisfying
    novel--less humorous, more wooden than the author's pre-
    vious efforts. However, Gardner is an innovative writer,
    and the reader should not expect every experiment to be
    a success.

860 Spearman, Walter. "Lantern." Durham (N.C.) Sun, 23
    August 1980. (The column appears in six North Carolina
    newspapers and in the Danville [Virginia] Register.)
    Elegantly written but the inside novel is not used as
    effectively as in OL.

861 Stanley, Don. "Bergman in Disneyland." The Magazine
    (Vancouver?), 20 April 1980, p. 12.
    Some of FB derives from Dante and much of it from Disney
    cartoons and Bergman's films. The Devil, for example, is
    borrowed from Dante and is treated the way Disney treated
    Dumbo. Unfortunately, the novel raises more questions
    than it answers.

862 Strickland, Jill. The Bookshelf, radio broadcast, 15
    July 1980. Program no. 503. (Station not identified.)
    Long plot summary concluding: killing of the Devil is
    Lars-Goren's way of rejecting the idea that human life is
    meaningless; FB is a "deeply moral novel" that ingeniously
    combines history and adventure.

863 Supplee, Vinton. "'Freddy's Book': A Devilishly Delight-
    ful Novel within a Novel." Arizona Republic, 23 March
    1980.
    Each of the two cleverly and effectively written stories
    can stand on its own merits; together they "gain depth."
    Gardner's Sweden and Lars-Goren's struggle may derive from
    Bergman's The Seventh Seal, but the novel's plot is
    original.

864 Tatum, Bil [sic]. [Springfield, Missouri?] News Leader,
    4 May 1980.
    Despite some occasional oversimplification, FB is "a

184

rich and haunting novel both entertaining and intellectual.
Each of its two parts complements the other and comments
on human nature and morality. The Devil is especially
well done.

865 Ten Harmsel, Larry. Grand Rapids Press, 6 April 1980, p.
11. Printed in slightly different form as "Good Morals
Can't Help Bad Fiction." Greensboro (N.C.) Daily News,
27 April 1980.
Perhaps the key to this confusing and badly conceived
novel is Lars-Goren, who represents the idea of father-
hood in an extended sense: the enduring power of human
love in the face of evil. The "almost satanic confusion
of incidents" may have been intentional, Gardner's way of
forcing the reader to consider the question of good and
evil for himself.

866 Thomas, Phil. "Gardner Novel Is Two in One." Omaha
World-Herald, 20 April 1980. This Associated Press release
also appeared, in a shorter version, under the title "New
Novel Has A Split Personality." Durham Morning Herald, 20
April 1980.
The writing is quite good, but the joining of the two
stories is forced.

867 Toussaint, Karen. "Pondering Charm." [Unidentified newspaper serving Havre-de-Grace, Maryland], 2 July 1980.
The "elusive charm of ISM recurs in FB, an enjoyable,
though perhaps insubstantial novel "rich with allegory,
mysticism and intrigue." Freddy's tale is especially
fascinating.

868 Tyler, Anne. "Gardner Wrestles Anew with the Devil."
Chicago Sun-Times Book Week, 9 March 1980, p. 11. Rpt. as
"Eight-Foot Baby Tells a Witty Gothic Fairy Tale." Van-
couver Sun, 21 March 1980.
As in ISM, Gardner again proves himself "a master storyteller." His brilliant new novel combines the suspense,
plot, and conflict between good and evil associated with
fairy tales with a serious purpose and fully drawn
characters (the monster and the Devil are particularized
and therefore believable). The powerful philosophical
debates in the second part do not undermine the narrative
tension.

869 Walters, Ray. "The Bounteous Spring of 1980." New York
Times Book Review, 27 January 1980, p. 11.

"Gardner, long a player of metaphysical literary games, describes how an awkward young man creates in 'Freddy's Book' a 16th-century Scandinavia that mirrors his own anguish and desires."

870 Weigel, John A. "'Freddy' Spins Complex Allegory of Good, Evil." Cincinnati Enquirer, 27 April 1980.
   Not himself believing in Freddy's fable, Gardner seems to have written in FB his own literature of exhaustion.

871 Willis, Jim. "His Fans Know He Can Do Better." Northwest (N.J.) Daily Record, 22 June 1980, p. H17.
   Readers familiar with Gardner's work will find this novel confusing, inconclusive, and rather unenlightening; new readers will be put off by the double-novel structure. Despite the promising beginning, the novel soon falls victim to the thinness of the characterization and the uncertain relationship between Freddy and his tale.

872 Winter, Douglas E. Fantasy Newsletter, 3 (August 1980), 11.
   An original and brilliant novel, both entertaining and thought-provoking. The two parts echo each other. Freddy's tale, which deals with "a critical watershed in history," has a hero worthy of the Scandinavian sagas.

873 Witherspoon, Mark. "Monster Poses Metaphysical Questions." Wichita Falls Times, 4 May 1980.
   FB entertains the reader and at the same time asks him to "question some of life's platitudes." Freddy's tale argues that man's actions have intrinsic value only and is made all the more intriguing in that it follows the consciences of two characters--Brask and Lars-Goren.

874 Wyatt, Robert. "John Gardner's Tale of Devil's Death an Account to Ponder and To Love." Nashville Tennessean, 16 March 1980, p. F10.
   This "unusual" and "magical" novel is morally ennobling. Instead of the search for self-fulfillment which preoccupies many contemporary writers, Gardner deals with larger themes. The novel does have several flaws: the "dangling" introduction, Brask's speeches which supplant narrative action, and the simplistic killing of the Devil.

875 Yenser, Jon K. "Gardner Has Written Better Novels." Jackson (Miss.) Clarion Ledger/Daily News, 11 May 1980, p. H5.
   In many ways a typical Gardner work, FB is, however, much

186

less successful than his "less affected" fictions. The
novel seems to contravene one of the rules set down in
OMF, that characters must not be used to propound the
author's predetermined message.

The Art of Living and Other Stories (1981)

876 Allen, Bruce. "From Gardner, Short Stories Dimmed by
Abstractions." Christian Science Monitor, 24 June 1981,
p. 17.
Gardner's fables of art and morality are generally unsuccessful. "The Joy of the Just" is repetitious, pointless, and dull, and "Vlemk" is "an interminable allegory."
The title story, which uses the medieval forms of the
knightly quest and the formal debate, is more satisfying.
The best story, "Come on Back," neither defends nor examines art; it is art, less a story than "a loving portrait."

877 Bannon, Barbara A. "PW Forecasts: Fiction." Publishers
Weekly, 219 (27 March 1981), 41.
"Gardner is in top form in these tales of living in real
and imaginary worlds." "The Music Lover," and "Vlemk"
(a "lovely fable") are individually mentioned.

878 Betts, Doris. "A Tale of Two Storytellers." Washington
Post Book World, 3 May 1981, pp. 5, 13. Also published
as "Tales of Two Storytellers: Gardner and Carver." New
York Daily News, 14 May 1981, pp. M4, M12.
Gardner and Raymond Carver have quite different concep-
tions about what fiction is and what its effects should
be. Gardner creates persuasive situations but often forces
his stories to bear the weight of an aesthetic theory already made "tediously clear" in OMF. "Vlemk" is too long,
"The Joy of the Just" reads like a very bad Eudora Welty
story, and "The Problems of Art" is "expository" and
"sophomoric." "Come on Back," "Stillness," "The Music
Lover," and "Nimram" are truly moral fictions (rather than
mere platforms for Gardner's theory). Carver's reader
remembers the author's style; Gardner's stories are
clumsier, but his reader remembers them for the stories
themselves and the people in them. (Reviewed with Carver's
What We Talk About When We Talk About Love.)

879 Bolotin, Susan. "A Preview of Spring Books." New York
Times Book Review, 25 January 1981, p. 13.
AL is forthcoming this spring.

880 "Books for Vacation Reading." New York Times Book Review, 31 May 1981, p. 26.
    The stories concern the "theme of art and its vexed relation to life."

881 Boyd, Robert. "Gardner-Dazzling and Quirky." St. Louis Post-Dispatch, 6 December 1981.
    An uneven but nonetheless "indispensable" collection. "The Joy of the Just" and "Nimram" are especially weak. The more autobiographical stories are better, and the title story successfully combines autobiography and aesthetics.

882 Braverman, Millicent. "A Word on Books." KFAC-AM/FM (Los Angeles), 10 June 1981.
    AL provides a good introduction to Gardner's "literary, yet wholly accessible fiction." Whether dealing with the mythic or the contemporary, Gardner treats the same general subject: mortality.

883 Champlin, Charles. "Breathing Life into the Short Story." Los Angeles Times, 19 May 1981, sec. 5, p. 6.
    What is most impressive in Gardner's fiction is the way he explores his past life in western New York. His characteristic fabulism and mastery of various narrative voices are evident in AL, a collection marred by the author's aloofness. The stories seem "exercises in style and voice"; moreover, their excessive length undermines the short story form.

884 Charleston (S.C.) Evening Post, 10 July 1981.
    "Well told and enjoyable."

885 Chesney, Allen. "Gardner's Latest Collection." Chattanooga News Free Press, 24 May 1981.
    The stories are precisely written, "delightful and haunting." The fantasies are not escapist and are made convincing by means of detail. Especially noteworthy are "Vlemk," "Trumpeter," and two realistic stories, "Redemption" and "Stillness."

886 Choice, 19 (September 1981), 79.
    Although at times too moralistic, too concerned with theme at the expense of character, these stories are imaginative, intelligent, and exhilarating. Each one moves "toward some purifying or transcendent moment."

887 Clark, Lindley H., Jr. "A Christmas Potpourri of Books."
Wall Street Journal, 2 December 1981, p. 28.
A varied collection by a major writer.

888 Coale, Sam. "Oddball Insights in 'Art of Living.'"
Providence Journal, 31 May 1981.
Gardner is least successful in preachy, allegorical
fairy tales such as "Vlemk." His best stories are those
"grounded in his resonant rural realism" in which the
commonplace is transformed into a comprehensive human
vision.

889 Collier, Peter. "John Gardner's Wizardry Brings His Art
to Life." Chicago Tribune Book World, 24 May 1981, p. 1.
Compelling narrative, imaginative extravagance, and an
undercurrent of myth and fable characterize the fiction
of John Gardner, "one of our brainiest writers." AL concerns not only the writer's craft but also the art of
characters who must live "in the shadow of dread." The
title story is Gardner's metaphor for the writer's task:
to make something that is both appealing and right. Making
life interesting is what Gardner does best; the finest
stories in this collection are "Nimram," "Redemption,"
and "Stillness." Less successful are such "tendentious
and self-indulgent" pieces as "Vlemk."

890 Dorenkamp, John N. "An Uneven Lot." Worcester (Mass.)
Sunday Telegram, 31 May 1981.
Despite his craftsmanship and versatility, Gardner is
not always a pleasure to read; his vision is sometimes too
bleak, his prose too excessive ("Vlemk"), and the narrative clotted by too many questions ("The Art of Living").
More successful are "Stillness" (depicting a woman's
nostalgia, fear, regret, and ultimate acceptance), "Come
on Back" (lightly and delicately told), and "The Joy of
the Just" (a wry comedy).

891 "Editor's Choice." Atlanta, August 1981, p. 56.
One-sentence description.

892 Ehresmann, Julia M. "Upfront: Advance Reviews." Booklist,
77 (1 March 1981), 870.
These stories are "disquieting" and "caringly, carefully
crafted." Some are quasi-autobiographical, others are
Germanic, and a number deal with the line between fantasy
and reality.

893 Ely, Hank. "Good and Evil: An Unflinching Look." <u>Winston-Salem Journal</u>, 24 May 1981, p. C4.
   Although Gardner is sometimes prone to make his aesthetic and philosophical points at the expense of his narrative (e.g., "The Library Horror"), his strength is his willingness to inspect the darkest and most despairing of moments without flinching. Better to see reality as it is, he implies, than to be deluded. Thus the delight he takes in deflating egos (e.g., "Nimram"). There is less humor in these stories than in Gardner's earlier works. The most successful union of narrative and philosophy is "Redemption," in which Gardner examines various and generally inadequate ways of coping with death.

894 Evenchik, Arthur. "In His Pursuit of the Moral, John Gardner Misses the True." <u>Baltimore Sun</u>, 24 May 1981.
   "The relationship between what we imagine and what we are" is Gardner's subject. The collection's best stories--"The Music Lover," "Vlemk," and "The Joy of the Just"--seem to unfold in the telling. Most of the others are lifeless exercises in moral fiction. In the title story, for example, Arnold Deller is nothing more than Gardner's puppet. Such stories are false at their center and cannot be saved by the author's craftsmanship. Gardner's strength lies in storytelling, not philosophy.

895 Fones, [?]. "Varied Looks at John Gardner." <u>Jackson</u> (Miss.) <u>Clarion Ledger-Daily News</u>, 28 June 1981, p. F7.
   Gardner can "turn pure fantasy into believable reality," as in the title story, which is "too outrageous to be fantasy." Some of Gardner's fans may find the collection disappointing; except for "The Joy of the Just," the stories seem incomplete.

896 Fuller, Edmund. "Box Painter, Ax Murderer, Imperial Dog." <u>Wall Street Journal</u>, 29 June 1981, p. 20.
   Gardner is one of the finest and most surprising writers in America today, in part because of the inventive way he combines borrowed material. Many of the ten varied and sometimes autobiographical stories deal with the therapeutic value of art. The best is "Vlemk," "a rich fairy tale for grown-ups."

897 Gardner, Kurt. "Collection by Gardner Has an Odd Balance." <u>Charleston</u> (S.C.) <u>Evening Post</u>, 12 July 1981.
   Whether real or mythical in setting, the stories all deal with the human as existing "somewhere between the dreadful

and the beautiful." Gardner's characters overcome their
sufferings by learning "the art of living with adversity."

898 Garrett, George. "American Short Fiction and the Literary
Marketplace." Sewanee Review, 91 (Winter 1983), 112-20.
   In this omnibus review of short-story collections published in 1981 and 1982, Garrett concludes that while all
the collections are competently written, the best are
those published by university and small presses rather
than the large commercial houses, such as Knopf. Works
such as AL are published not because of literary excellence
but because of the author's reputation as a novelist. That
only three of Gardner's ten stories had been previously
published [according to information supplied on the copyright page] proves that the collection did not have to
compete in the literary marketplace, as did most of the
stories published by the non-commercial presses.

899 Goldenberg, Judi. "Sillitoe, Gardner Cover Variety of
Subjects." Richmond News Leader, 17 June 1981.
   The stories are various in form and style, unpredictable,
humorous, and entertaining without being preachy. The key
question raised by Gardner is, how is the artist different
from other people? "Vlemk" depicts the orneriness of the
artist; "The Joy of the Just" portrays a woman who turns
vengeance into art. (Reviewed with Alan Sillitoe's The
Second Choice.)

900 Gorra, Michael. "John Gardner against the Wall." San
Jose Mercury News, 24 May 1981, Tab sec., p. 32.
   Gardner's literary experiments are not entirely admirable; having mastered craft, Gardner has lost his soul.
The three New York stories are his best, the most Gardner-
like. But in "The Joy of the Just" he is unsuccessfully
imitating Welty. "Vlemk" is "gimmicky"; its comedy is
undercut by ponderous meditations on art. More successful
are those stories in which the theorizing is made a part of
the larger whole, as in the talk of the "half-crazed" cook
in the title piece or the descriptions of dance in
"Stillness."

901 Griffin, Edward. "Gardner Bats .500 with New Stories."
St. Louis Globe-Democrat, 13-14 June 1981.
   "Nimram" shows Gardner at his best, a writer few can
equal. "Come on Back," "Vlemk," and "Redemption" are
slightly less successful. Weakest are "The Library Horror"

(perhaps left over from KI), "The Joy of the Just"
(watered-down Welty), and the gruesome, implausible
title story.

902 H., B. H. "Gardner Stories Please." Anniston (Alabama)
Star, 5 July 1981.
    A diversified yet unified collection by a writer "working
at the top of his form." Many of these stories include a
strong gothic element; the best is the title piece.

903 H., R. Chattanooga Times, 16 May 1981.
    "Beautifully crafted and literate," though perhaps super-
ficial.

904 Harris, Roger. "Gardner Lifts the Short Story to New
Heights." Newark (N.J.) Star Ledger, [?] April 1981.
    The collection includes the best new short fiction to be
published in recent years. Unlike Gardner's novels, which
are sometimes cumbersome in their use of myth, his stories
are less mythic and more effective. "Vlemk," the collection's most ambitious work, is perhaps the best Gardner
has ever written; its moral is "graceful and accurate,
didactic without being preachy, involved but never obscure."
"Come on Back" is a simpler story, noteworthy for its
"unmatched lyric delicacy."

905 Hill, Douglas. "Between the Moral and the Possible."
Macleans, 94 (8 June 1981), 51-52.
    Gardner, "a romantic moralist," is "at his fluent, wide-
ranging best" in this collection. Writing a "graceful,
unstudied prose," he proves himself a master of narrative
voice and "the economical opening." His stories focus on
moments of crisis presented in vivid images and "sharp-
edged memories."

906 Kelly, Robert. "Author Uses Seamless Dexterity." Fort
Wayne News Sentinel, 18 July 1981, p. W10.
    Gardner is a superior writer. His endings provoke the
readers' imaginations and cause them to consider the stories
even after the actual reading is over.

907 Kipp, Julie. "Gardner Puts Hope in Honest View of Human
Scene." Denver Post, 5 July 1981, Roundup sec.
    Gardner is deep, hopeful, and honest; his theme is
redemption through the art of loving, and his means for
effecting this redemption are various, for what counts,

Gardner suggests, is the result. Because it is a fairy tale for adults, "Vlemk" is both long and complex. "Trumpeter" depicts a conscious all-is-well belief and an unconscious questioning of that belief. Gardner's characters are both real and symbolic.

908 Kirkus Reviews, 49 (1 March 1981), 301-2.
   Gardner, the artist-philosopher, has written stories that are skillfully done but "generally unaffecting." "Stillness," "Come on Back," and "The Joy of the Just" are more emotionally appealing than the other seven, which seem written for artists rather than for the general reader.

909 Kreyling, Michael. Studies in Short Fiction, 19 (Winter 1982), 77-79.
   The art of living, which is the art of living morally, involves reconciling self and other, individual and society. In "Nimram," Gardner places his characters in a moral arena but "tantalizingly" withholds judgment. In "Redemption" the main character is saved when he chooses art instead of guilt. "The Music Lover," "The Library Horror," and "Vlemk" experiment with the styles of Mann, Poe, and Grimm. "Come on Back" invests a familiar plot "with genuine feeling" and a sure sense of people and place. The central event in the title story clashes with the effect Gardner is trying to achieve. In the collection as a whole, Gardner is the author as workman offering what he knows "to an audience in whom he believes."

910 Kucera, Barb. "Gardner at His Best in 'The Art of Living.'" [Unidentified newspaper near LaCrosse, Wisc., and Two Harbors, Minn.], n.d.
   Fantasy borders on reality in these superbly described stories, each of which focuses on the characters' emotions. The only weak story is "Vlemk," which has neither the humor nor the enchantment of Gardner's "masterpiece," G.

911 Leary, Lewis. "Gardner's Collection Has Staying Power." Chapel Hill (N.C.) Newspaper, 21 June 1981.
   Gardner's stories are more substantive, more suggestive, and more memorable than most. His vision of a world made up of memory, dream, and realism, of sorrow and pleasure is every reader's as well. The stories are distinct in form and subject yet coalesce into a larger, more embracing whole. "Vlemk" is "a delightfully ridiculous tale" filled with tricks. "The Art of Living" is a story of "simplified loyalty" better than any that Steinbeck ever wrote.

912 Lutz, Fred. "Corny Moral Message." Toledo Blade, 13
September 1981.
Like Oates, Gardner writes hastily and sloppily, often
indulging in the fabulous to avoid the difficulties of
realism. Although imaginative, he does not attend sufficiently to his craft; instead he moralizes. One notable
exception is the moving story "Nimram," which recalls NM
and SD.

913 McMahon, Allan. "A New Collection of Gardner Magic."
Fort Wayne Journal-Gazette, 17 May 1981, p. D10.
Ten "expertly written" and absorbing stories by a
"master" storyteller. "Vlemk" is a fantasy of the highest
order.

914 Manning, Margaret. "The Slippery Slope of Life." Boston
Globe, 4 May 1981.
Gardner knows life can be terrible, but he refuses to
give up hope. Possessing a prodigious intellect, a lucid,
lyrical style, and a firm sense of characterization, he
has proven himself a major contemporary writer, the Melville of the Twentieth Century. Love, vengeance, fantasy,
fear, madness, and tenderness are his themes; the old and
the new, the mythic and the realistic are his subjects.
"Redemption" rings true to life. "The Art of Living,"
which is about love, may seem implausible, even gruesome
to some readers.

915 Morton, Mary. "John Gardner Paints Fictional Worlds
Brilliantly." Nashville Banner, 19 September 1981, p. A5.
Gardner's fictions are accessible and entertaining, at
once humorous and serious; beneath the surface lurks the
author's moral sense. "Vlemk," for example, is more than
a charming fairy tale; "it tells us about ourselves and
the way others see us."

916 Moynahan, Julian. "Moral Fictions." New York Times Book
Review, 17 May 1981, pp. 7, 27-28.
AL, like OMF, concerns the relationship of art and life.
Unfortunately, Gardner, like the later Tolstoi, seems to
force his fiction into a theoretical mold, as in the collection's worst piece, "Vlemk." The technically inept
title story reads like a failed novel, while other stories,
including "Nimram" and "Redemption," are marred by Gardner's
"lurching style of excessive ... parenthetical remarks."
"Come on Back" is the most accomplished story in AL.

917 Nicholls, Richard E. "Cogent, Straightforward Tales from
John Gardner." Philadelphia Inquirer, 14 June 1981, p. L14.
Gardner's "generous vision" and "straightforward style
is especially welcome in an age of literary puzzles and
"verbal stunts." His major theme is the power of art to
"lift us out of desperate situations." Out of "modest"
experiences, Gardner draws "plain truths." "Come on Back"
is affectionately written, carefully detailed, and "richly
metaphoric."

918 "Notable Books of the Year." New York Times Book Review,
6 December 1981, p. 34.
Listed.

919 Nykor, Lynda. "Stories Illustrate Magic in Joy and Pain."
London (Ontario) Free Press, 3 October 1981.
Gardner sees the various arts as part of the richness of
life. The reader respects him as "one of those rare few
who, while seeing and understanding everything, never quite
lose their innocent optimism."

920 Peacock, Allen H. "Lackluster Collection of Murky Gardner
Stories." Cleveland Plain-Dealer, 19 July 1981.
Except for "Redemption," the stories are "uninspired
and hollow," written to the formula set forth in OMF, "a
pedantic, nasty and finally ridiculous diatribe." "Nimram"
has an unconvincing ending; the title story is "macabre";
"Trumpeter" and "Vlemk" are either didactic or pointless
and have the kind of characters for which Gardner has
criticized Pynchon.

921 Pintarich, Paul. "Mystery, Humanness Mix in 'Art of
Living.'" Sunday Oregonian (Portland), 10 May 1981.
Mixing the medieval and the contemporary, Gardner writes
stories of survival, of characters who either have defeated
or are struggling with their demons. Against the darkness
and mystery, which he does not entirely dispel, Gardner
posits "a thoughtful humanness and complex simplicity."
"The Joy of the Just" shows "how misplaced good becomes
the most profound evil," and "Vlemk" depicts the struggle
for perfection in an imperfect world.

922 Reed, Ronald. "A Narrator's Different Drum." Fort Worth
Star-Telegram, 10 May 1981.
These "superb" stories "explore the junction between the
real and the ethereal," the mythic or the artistic. In
several, the line between these realms is uncrossable

("Nimram"), in others blurred ("The Library Horror"), and in others nonexistent ("Vlemk"). Less accessible than some contemporary writers, Gardner forces the reader to think in other than a purely modern way.

923 Rheinheimer, Kurt. "Moral Fiction: Gardner's Latest Stories Rich, Carefully Developed." Roanoke Times, 25 October 1981.
Gardner's moral fictions, "carefully and slowly developed, rich of detail and nuance, move across relatively small distances with a genuine thoroughness of treatment and thought."

924 Rice, Doug. "Gardner Blends Life and Art." Pittsburgh Press, 24 May 1981.
These stories of "the tension and peaceful coexistence" of art and life, are slowly developed and carefully controlled. In them, reality gives way to dream states and tranquility to troubling mystery as Gardner, one of our finest writers, probes human life.

925 Ridley, Clifford A. "Gliding among the Disciplines." Detroit News, 10 May 1981, p. J2.
Gardner is skillful, prolific, and proficient in various literary forms.

926 Sanders, Scott. "Gardner's Stories: Are They Both Moral and Visionary?" Chicago Sun Times, 10 May 1981, Book Week sec., p. 24.
"Guilt, vengefulness, mortality, and ... the powers of art" are Gardner's subjects. Half of the stories are moral fictions if by the term we exclude Gardner's criterion that the artist be a visionary and emphasize art as a struggle against chaos. In the other stories, including "Vlemk" and "Trumpeter," the problems of art do not emerge from the problems of living; instead, Gardner manipulates his material in an obvious and tedious manner.

927 Saunders, Tom. Winnipeg Free Press, 20 June 1981, Leisure sec., p. 5.
Gardner is equally adept in realism and fantasy. His greatness derives from his "discernment," intellect, and "limpid style." The "deceptively simple" stories in AL are not his best work, but they are challenging, pleasurable, and "brilliantly told."

928 Seib, Philip. "Not-So-Short Stories: A Rare Misstep by John Gardner." Dallas Morning News, 21 June 1981.

A disappointing collection. The plots "wander purpose-
lessly," and the writing is in general undisciplined. The
successful passages only make clear how badly Gardner has
failed in rushing these stories into print.

929 "Short Stories Show John Gardner's Art." Fredricksburg
(Virginia) Free Lance-Star, 16 May 1981.
Certain elements recur in Gardner's fiction: myth,
folklore, mysticism, and his sympathy for his grotesque
yet gentle, vulnerable characters. Many of the stories in
AL recall Dinesen and Fowles. The best one is "The Joy of
the Just," which is both humorous and horrifying. An
economical writer, Gardner is weakest in longer stories,
such as "KI" and "Vlemk." "Come on Back" and "The Art of
Living" (with its "shocking" ending) belong to the "New-
Yorker nostalgia school."

930 Simon, Jeff. "Gardner at His Worst and Best." Buffalo
News, 10 May 1981, p. E7.
Gardner the imaginative writer ("Trumpeter," "The
Library Horror," and parts of "Vlemk") succeeds, but Gardner
the "thinker, relentless didact and pastoral realist" is a
bore. He tries to appear "cosmopolitan and knowing" but
fails, sometimes getting his facts wrong, as in "The Music
Lover" where he attributes a concerto for percussion to
Bartok.

931 Starr, William W. "Collections Include Themes about Music,
Black Women." Columbia (S.C.) State, 10 May 1981.
The stories are "delightfully and imaginatively varied."
"The Library Horror" and "Redemption" are the two best;
"Vlemk" is entertaining but overlong. (Reviewed with Alice
Walker's You Can't Keep a Good Woman Down.)

932 Stevens, Peter. "Gardner's Style a Bit Too Clever."
Windsor (Ontario) Star, 29 August 1981.
A disappointing collection from a gifted writer. The
stories are "too stylistically contrived" and lifeless;
the narrators are unconvincing. "Trumpeter" and "Vlemk"
are especially weak.

933 Stuart, Candace. "Variety of Artists Inspired by Brush
with Death." South Bend (Indiana) Tribune, 26 July 1981.
The artists in these stories become acquainted with
death and incorporate this experience in their craft.
Arnold Deller, for example, teaches those around him to
overcome their instincts and to love as a matter of policy.

Gardner's strength is his ability to turn a simple plot
into a complex tale. His weakness is a tendency towards
the trite and the predictable. The woodcuts enhance
Gardner's "macabre fairytale style."

934 Tampa Tribune-Times, 24 April 1981.
In his "witty" story, "The Joy of the Just," Gardner
deliberately misquotes Proverbs 21:15.

935 Thomas, Jane Resh. "Gardner and the 'Fiction of Ideas.'"
Minneapolis Tribune, 11 May 1981, pp. G14-G15.
Least pleasurable are the stories in which ideas play the
central part, e.g., the Hawthornesque "Vlemk" and "The
Library Horror," which quotes Susanne Langer. Perhaps
Gardner intended to contrast these stories with "Redemption"
and "The Joy of the Just," which are less philosophical,
more aesthetically satisfying.

936 Thomas, Phil. "Stories by Gardner Are Lively Reading."
Associated Press Newsfeatures.
Gardner is a writer who never repeats himself and always
maintains the highest literary standards. AL, however, is
an uneven collection. Stories such as "Vlemk" seem self-
indulgent and ponderously philosophical. "Nimram,"
"Stillness," and "The Art of Living," which may upset some
readers, are far better.

937 Thompson, Kent. "Intimations of Morality." Books in Canada,
10 (August-September 1981), 9-10.
Art, as Gardner defines it in his title story, is "an act
of love" that continues and extends the literary tradition
and achieves a degree of commercial success. G is art; AL
is not, the stories merely serving to illustrate ideas.
Since Gardner's aim is to instruct his readers, the fairy
tales "Vlemk" and "Trumpeter" are more successful than the
more realistic fictions. Many of the stories employ "flat
popular stereotypes" or weakly echo better works (e.g.,
"The Joy of the Just" and O'Connor's "A Good Man Is Hard
to Find.")

938 Tyler, Anne. "Little Miracles: In Gardner's Fine Stories,
Questions in the Stillness." Detroit News, 10 May 1981,
p. J2.
AL is "bounteously packed with plots and people and ideas."
The variety of narrative forms and tones distinguishes it
from most collections, which are often "repetitious" and
"predictable." "Vlemk" is a "masterpiece": inventive,

198

humorous, and fully rounded. What unifies the ten stories
is the way Gardner stops the action and allows his characters "to state their concerns."

939 Walch, Bob. "Diverse Stories by Gardner." [Unidentified
newspaper], n.d.
Although generally well written, the first five stories
have weak endings. The second five are more successful:
longer, greater development of plots and characters. The
best is "Vlemk," which recalls Pinnochio, Pygmalion, The
Picture of Dorian Grey.

940 Weinberger, Andy. "American Genius--Eloquent Yet Inscrut-
able." Los Angeles Herald Examiner, 5 July 1981, p. F6.
Gardner has intelligence and literary genius, but he has
grown complacent. The stories in AL are well crafted but
inert and unambitious, the plots merely excuses for Gardner's
metaphors. He traps his characters in embarrassing situations, leaving them to work their own way out. The title
story is undermined by Gardner's incessant lecturing.

941 Wiehe, Janet. Library Journal, 106 (July 1981), 1442.
"Ten impeccably styled stories, more intellectually
elegant than affecting," about the artist, his art, and
his life.

942 Winston, Iris. "Fantasy, Realism and Twists of Irony."
Calgary Herald, 18 July 1981, p. F10.
A varied collection mixing fantasy and realism. Description is Gardner's strength; endings are his weakness. His
stories are less successful than his novels.

MSS A Retrospective (scheduled for 1981 but never published)

943 Booklist, 76 (15 May 1980), 1338.
A strong collection; profits will be used to publish new
work in future volumes.

944 McDonald, William. "Literary Revival." Lone Star Book
Review, 1 (January-February 1980), 14, 31.
MSS was a short-lived little magazine (three issues)
which grew out of the literary ferment of the San
Francisco area in the early 1960s and which published
early work by Oates, Gass, and Hawkes. The new MSS re-
prints a number of the original pieces and will be
followed by new issues which will publish work by today's

fiction writers, poets, photographers, and graphic artists. (Quotes Gardner's introduction.)

Mickelsson's Ghosts (1982)

945 Abbott, Scott. "Mickelsson's Mormons." Sunstone Review (Salt Lake City), 2 (September 1982), 1, 30-33.
Gardner's fiction and his call for moral literature have been well received by Mormons, who will find MG much less appealing both for its explicit sex and its portrayal of Mormonism. To a degree, Gardner's criticism of Mormonism, especially its colorlessness and business-like approach, is merited. Moreover, it is not Gardner but his characters that rail against Mormonism. In fact, a careful reading makes clear the characters' views are prejudices intended by Gardner to suggest the characters' failings. In this "novel about epistemological and ethical uncertainty," Gardner dramatizes the plight of a man who has no communal values upon which to base his ethical decisions, in part because communal groups such as Mormonism have become mass movements rather than storehouses of moral values.

946 Adams, Phoebe-Lou. "Short Reviews." Atlantic, 250 (July 1982), 94.
In burdening his protagonist with so many problems, that are metaphors for today's social problems, Gardner only arouses in his reader "numb disbelief"; "the disasters cancel each other out and become meaningless."

946a Bann, Stephen. "Plots." London Review of Books, 4 (4-17 November 1982), 22.
MG is at once an example of what Todorov calls "the uncanny" and also a campus novel," one which "is not essentially satirical." Especially well done are Gardner's handling of his "fluctuating point of view," his exploration of the hero's disengagement from and involvement with others, Mickelsson's relationship to his house and rural community, and the development of seminar topics into "the obsessional themes of Mickelsson's inner voice."

947 Bannon, Barbara A. "PW Forecasts: Fiction." Publishers Weekly, 221 (9 April 1982), 44.
MG is philosophical meditation, exploration of love, and ghost story all in one "engrossing" novel that is as "rich in feeling as in thought." It may be Gardner's "most impressive work since SD."

948 "Barth and Gardner Give Professors Top Billing in New
    Novels." Chronicle of Higher Education, 25 (1 September
    1982), 33.
    Excerpts from MG and Barth's Sabbatical.

949 Betzner, Ray. Newport News (Va.) Daily Press, 18 July
    1982, sec. 6, p. 1.
    Gardner's combination of autobiography, murder mystery,
    ghost story, and philosophical tract is not entirely success-
    ful (the murder mystery does not fit the larger context
    and the sex scenes are of the kind one finds in the letters
    column in Penthouse magazine), but the autobiographical
    elements and the fine prose testify to Gardner's importance
    and stature. Like other Gardner heroes, Mickelsson is a
    bit mad. His major problems are his ability to empathize
    so fully and his inability to express his own feelings.

950 Booklist, 78 (1 April 1978), 985.
    Gardner's portrait of Mickelsson is "imaginative and
    persuasive"; unfortunately, the "lame" climax fails to
    resolve either Mickelsson's personality or Gardner's novel.

951 Boyd, Robert. "John Gardner's New Puzzle." St. Louis
    Post-Dispatch, 20 June 1982.
    MG and SD are comparable works; both are "breathtaking,
    audacious, vast in conception, meticulous in surface de-
    tail ... and complicated beyond the common understanding."
    MG is too didactic to be called a novel and too clumsily
    structured to be treated aesthetically. Although the
    settings, characters and sentences are well done, Gardner
    does not seem to take seriously the issues he raises;
    there is no reason for the reader to take the novel any
    more seriously.

952 Brady, Charles A. "Passing Grade for Gardner's Prof."
    Buffalo News, 4 July 1982, p. G7.
    MG is an "ambitious melange"—an intricate if perhaps
    not entirely successful ghost story. Gardner's sources
    include Dostoievski, Bulwer-Lytton, Yeats, and Arthur
    Conan Doyle. Mickelsson is in many ways the "little man"
    found in many contemporary fictions. Gardner's portrait
    of Jessica Stark is "beautifully done." The controversy
    occasioned by the new novel may have less to do with
    aesthetics than with Gardner's attack on liberal ideology.

953 Brady, Charles A. "Gift Books: Santa Has Plenty to Choose
    From." Buffalo News, 12 December 1982, p. H14.

MG, "on the whole" Gardner's best novel, is one of the twelve novels listed.

954 Braverman, Millicent. "A Word on Books." KFAC-AM/FM (Los Angeles), 9 July 1982.
Gardner is an author worth reading, but MG is not; the novel is "overdrawn, pretentious, obscure and unsatisfying," "too ponderous to be really entertaining."

955 Broyard, Anatole. "Books of the Times." New York Times, 12 June 1982, p. 15. Also published in the International Herald Tribune, 28 June 1982; Omaha World-Herald, 20 June 1982; Toledo Blade, 8 August 1982, p. C6; Wichita Falls Times, 4 July 1982.
MG offers a reader what a good novel should: not the irony and disillusionment of most contemporary works, but characters worth caring about, fully realized geographical and human settings, and ideas worth contemplating. Mickelsson's "teetering between self-realization and ruin" is compelling; he takes chances and makes mistakes in an attempt to find what is humanly sufficient. Rebuilding his house is the prelude to or substitute for self-transformation. The women in the novel are representative: Ellen of the people Gardner attacked in OMF, Donnie of anarchic sex, Jessica of a somewhat chilling utopian love. Only the ending is flawed--less a conclusion than a wild and perplexing overflowing.

956 Burdick, Barbara. "Mickelsson Haunted by Ghosts. Monterey (Calif.) Peninsula Herald, 4 July 1982.
Gardner sensitively and insightfully portrays a middle-age man's attempt to free himself from his past. The "richly textured flashbacks," "vivid imagery," "innovative style," and the author's deep knowledge of man's nature are among the novel's many strengths.

957 Butler, Robert. Bestsellers, September 1982, pp. 215-16.
Despite its rather shopworn plot, MG is a lively and compelling novel. Settings and characters (especially Mickelsson, Donnie, and Lawler) are fully realized. Although the plots are numerous and at times "melodramatic," even "preposterous," the reader never loses sight of Mickelsson, a Gargantua-Hamlet-Herzog figure, "whose bizarre adventures speak to all of us." Ultimately, MG is a subtle yet powerful religious novel of the fallen man's search for salvation. As a successful combination of the real and the magical and for drawing universal

significance from particular circumstances, MG deserves
the highest praise. Gardner is clearly "a contemporary
novelist of the first rank."

958 C., N. West Coast Review of Books, 8 (November 1982), 43.
Gardner blends "an intricate plot, artful language,
characters of great depth and subtlety and philosophical
concepts into a scary, absorbing story" of the kind John
Cheever would have written had he turned to horror fiction. The connection Gardner makes between community and
psychic ability slowly takes on great significance. The
philosophical references reenforce a story that is "at
once grittily real and sublimely supernatural."

959 Cantor, Hal. "'Ghosts' Better Left in Closet." Spring-
field (Missouri) News Leader, 25 July 1982. Also published in Burlington (Vermont) Press, ? July 1982. Gannett
News Service.
Parts of this novel are interesting and well-crafted,
and the setting and characters are well-drawn. But it is
impossible for the reader to care about Mickelsson, whose
philosophizing and imagined debates are boring. Gardner's
contrasting story elements refuse to jell, and the surprise
ending is unconvincing.

959a Carroll, James. "Critics' Christmas Choices." Commonweal, 109 (3 December 1982), 658.
"How can people so gifted for the truthful and beautiful
use of language live such sad unbeautiful lives?" is the
question Gardner raises. Mickelsson's agony is clearly
Gardner's own and is like Job's in all respects save that
it derives from Mickelsson's own self-destructiveness.
The writing is brave, humorous, and compassionate, a
pleasure to read.

960 Clapperton, Jane. "Cosmo Reads the New Books."
Cosmopolitan, July 1982, p. 34.
This "masterly" novel has "a terrifying climax" and ends
with Mickelsson's acceptance of "the benign phantoms that
surround us all."

961 Clark, Tom. "Now It's Gardner: Success, for Writers, One
Big Cry." Denver Post, 30 May 1982, p. R13.
Recently it has seemed that new novelists are turning
out better books than established writers such as Gardner.
The philosophizing in his intellectual ghost story is pre-
tentious, boring, and obtrusive. Much more effective is

his handling of setting, which is affectionate, evocative, substantial, and "less elevated."

962 Coale, Sam. "Mickelsson's Ghosts Haunts the Soul-Searcher." Providence Journal, 25 July 1982.
   Gardner uses his novel to think out solutions and compromises, resolving some predicaments and mysteries while leaving others "mystic and unnerving but not loose-ended." The balance of idealism and philosophic terror, as well as the fully realized settings and characters, are among the many strengths of this "sprawling, sumptuous" novel. Even though the novel is at times "too talky," the talk is always "rich, eloquent, poetic."

963 Coale, Sam. America, 147 (2 October 1982), 176.
   MG is a moral fiction of the Manichean confrontations epitomized in the dual nature of the main character and even in the novel's form: philosophy, on the one hand, and murder mystery, on the other. Despite the apparent resolution at the end, Gardner leaves the reader doubtful, brooding on an idealism that can be both necessary and demonic.

964 Coghill, Neil. Charlotte Observer.
   MG is "a psychological quest-romance" to answer the question, how is the ethical person to act in an unethical world? In fashioning an answer, Gardner creates Mickelsson's interior monologues as a complex ghost story and his personal life as a fairly straightforward detective story. Mickelsson is haunted by the ghosts of the Spragues, by his failings, by Jessica Stark (whose "changes from avatar to lover to friend are the linchpins of MG"), and most interestingly, by the ghosts of philosophers (though here the story becomes clotted by the dense and numerous philosophical passages). Although the two parts of the novel do not always mesh, they do "offer different pleasures for different readers."

965 Cohen, Andy. "Gardner's 'Ghost' Goes Thud." Binghamton Press, 20 June 1982, pp. Cl, C5.
   MG is "a ponderous mistake" for reasons that are obvious enough in the novel's opening sentence: overlong, labyrinthine, distracting in its details, and unrewarding. Gardner uses gimmicks to keep the reader from realizing the emptiness of both his story and his characters. Only the two-page scene involving the deaf lawyer is enjoyable.

966 Cowart, David. "Despite Prolific Output, Gardner's
   Novels Good." Columbia (S.C.) State, 11 July 1982, p. B10.
   All of Gardner's novels are good and some, including MG,
   are "superb." MG will appeal to both the general and the
   serious reader. Those interested in the philosophical
   aspect of modern problems will be strongly attracted to
   Mickelsson, whose "prospects for survival are ultimately
   theirs." In the treatment of sexual relations, MG represents "a major advance" in Gardner's fiction.

967 "Critics Give 'Ghost' Slight Praise." Binghamton Press,
   20 June 1982, pp. C1, C5.
   Quotes from reviews by Wolcott, DeMott, Broyard, and
   Edmund Fuller.

968 Cryer, Dan. "Gardner's Philosophizing Chokes His Plot."
   Newsday, 24 June 1982, pt. II, p. 2.
   Gardner writes brilliantly of father concern, the end of
   love, the beauty of philosophy, systems that once worked,
   and approaching bankruptcy. But on the whole, the novel
   sinks under the weight of melodrama and philosophical
   babbling. Gardner leaves too many questions unanswered,
   sweeping them aside in a final and unsatisfying melodramatic flourish.

969 Dale, Don. "Chasing the Ghosts of Gardner's Hybrid."
   Arizona Daily Star, 12 September 1982.
   Although Mickelsson is "too cerebral" and too attracted
   to the unusual, he is nonetheless representative of man,
   the hybrid animal-angel. His main problem is the failure
   to achieve objectivity. Gardner's problems are his slow
   opening section and his occasionally trying "too hard to
   conjure authenticity out of obvious fabrication." Gardner
   succeeds in making the reader care about Mickelsson and
   believe that there are "constants in life" to keep us from
   slipping into chaos.

970 DeMott, Benjamin. "A Philosopher's Novel of Academe."
   New York Times Book Review, 20 June 1982, pp. 1, 26.
   Like other Gardner novels, this extremely long work deals
   in part with a man's intellectual life. Mickelsson's philosophical speculations spring from the facts of his daily
   life. Late in the novel the rift between philosophy and
   plot widens, the novelist's voice becomes less flexible,
   and Gardner's novel of sensibility plus mystery tale becomes "a standard-brand thriller with a queer Gothic hum
   in the background."

971 Disch, Thomas M. "Books." (Magazine not identified.)
     This "incredibly prolix" novel--perhaps Gardner's dullest--
     will only appeal to "the more plodding students" in creative
     writing classes who believe in the virtue of literary imita-
     tion. Gardner's ghosts are as lifeless as "his other dot-to-
     dot characters"; their one saving feature is that they do
     not deliver philosophical lectures.

972 Domnarski, William. "Beleagured Prof Fends Off Demons."
     Hartford Courant, 1 August 1982, p. E10.
     Gardner succeeds in bringing together his many plots,
     though this could have been accomplished in fewer pages.
     The novel is less ambitious than uncontrolled, and the
     ghosts more distracting than effective. Despite the tedious
     classroom scenes and Gardner's discursive sentences, MG
     is enjoyable and the protagonist likable.

973 Duhamel, P. Albert. "Gardner's 'Ghosts' Major Work."
     Boston Herald American, 13 June 1982.
     This "corking good mystery story," a "major work" by one
     of America's few hopeful writers, deals with the important
     issues of post-Nietzschean philosophy. "Gardner writes with
     a fierce moral passion" about those who substitute illusion
     for reality, e.g., Lawler, a mixture of Mormonism and
     Nietzsche's superman.

974 Dunne, Mike. "Gardner Creates Ghosts for Thinking Readers."
     Sacramento Bee, 1 August 1982, Forum sec., p. 4.
     MG is not always easy to read and not entirely engrossing
     (too many philosophical digressions and too much of the
     hero's self-pity), but it is well-crafted and filled with
     sensitively drawn characters, keen insights, "snappy epi-
     grams and philosophical tidbits," downhome philosophizing,
     splendid descriptions of eyes, and forcefully developed
     apparitions. A thinking man's horror story, MG is in fact
     several stories in one: love, mystery, philosophical,
     psychological, and autobiographical. Too mainstream to be
     required reading in college courses and too cerebral to be
     dismissed, MG testifies to Gardner's "skill, range and
     energy."

975 Edlen, Lorena. El Paso Times, 11 July 1982.
     Mickelsson is a believable hero. The philosophical
     passages can be skimmed over.

976 Elkins, Mary Jane. "John Gardner Shows a Light Beyond
     the Philosophical Tunnel." Miami Herald, 1 August 1982,
     p. E7.

Several of Gardner's books, including WA and SD, begin
promisingly enough but end up trying the reader's patience.
MG is more successful, "an exasperating but deeply pleasurable novel." Mickelsson's spiritual crisis is partly
personal and partly the crisis of modern man. The truths
Gardner affirms are the "unfashionable, homely values" of
decency, responsibility, and community. In many ways, MG
dramatizes OMF. Gardner is weakest when philosophizing
and strongest when he sticks to storytelling.

977 Fay, Michael. "Gardner Pulls a Stein on Moral Fiction."
Calgary Herald, 4 September 1982, p. G5.
The simple story of Mickelsson's restoration of the farmhouse, which recalls Pirsig's Zen and the Art of Motorcycle
Maintenance, has a finely detailed setting and richly,
sympathetically drawn characters. Mickelsson binds the
novel together, and flashbacks deepen its meaning. Gardner's
"bizarre and trendy plot twists," reminiscent of Stephen
King, John Irving and John Barth, are objectionable,
especially in light of Gardner's criticism of fat, empty
books in OMF. Like Gertrude Stein, he has conceived a
theory but failed to put it into practice.

978 Fox, Thomas. "Ghosts in the Attic." Memphis Commercial
Appeal, 11 July 1982.
The writing is sometimes excessive and indulgent but
always filled with vivid and interesting characters,
dialogue, and philosophical ruminations. Although Gardner
can be faulted for the rush of disjointed and inchoate
suggestions at novel's end and the failure to pursue interesting subplots and minor characters, he succeeds in making
Mickelsson "as real as the ghosts in his window."

979 Fuller, Edmund. "An Ambitious, Morally Searching Murder
Mystery." Wall Street Journal, 14 June 1982, p. 20.
This is a flawed novel: too many narrative loose ends;
a hasty, unbelievable conclusion; and surrender to "fashionable modes of soft-porn and sacrilege." Nonetheless, MG
is far more ambitious and morally searching than other
contemporary works.

980 "Ghosts Haunt Hero of Gardner's Novel." (Newspaper Not
Identified.)
An ambitious, difficult, but rewarding "novel of thought"
to be read for its "lapidary" style rather than for its
substance. Showing his imaginative range and command of
setting and characters, the erudite Gardner can be forgiven
"his obsession with myth and allegory." His ghosts "move

mysteriously between the real and the unreal."

981 Gilder, Joshua. "Things That Go Glunk in the Night."
New York Magazine, 14 June 1982, pp. 62-63.
    Suspicions about Gardner both as novelist and as critic
that were raised by OMF are confirmed by MG, a novel of
"narrative slovenliness and intellectual cowardice."
Plots and ideas (each with its own "anti-idea") proliferate
beyond either the reader's or the author's comprehension.
The moral issues raised are either simplistic or simply
cancelled out, and the ending is ridiculous.

982 Girault, Norton. "A Haunting, 'Metaphysical Mystery' by
a Master Novelist." Norfolk Virginian-Pilot/Ledger Star,
11 July 1982.
    MG is both serious and fun. Its vivid characterizations
distinguish it from most mystery stories. The tragi-comic
Mickelsson, a Jekyll and Hyde figure, is saved, in part,
by "the rejuvenating force of community." Following the
death of the fat man, the narrative tension increases as
Gardner explores the conflicts between individual and
society, anarchy and order, liberal and conservative,
feeling and thinking.

983 Harris, Robert R. "What's So Moral about John Gardner's
Fiction? Saturday Review, 9 (June 1982), pp. 70-71.
    Many critics seem to have accepted Gardner's claim that
he is the American Tolstoi or Dostoievski despite the fact
that as a thinker he is merely a dilettante, as he proved
in OMF. OL won the National Book Critics Circle award when
Gardner's workmanlike writing and "simplistic ruminations"
were mistaken for profundity. MG, a soporific, confused,
and "maddeningly talky" novel, proves that Gardner is not
original, either as a thinker or as a novelist. Mickelsson's
trite ideas are the author's own. Moreover, the writing
is at times careless, at times (in the case of the ghosts,
for example) simpleminded. As a philosophical novel, MG
is, therefore, a "sham." Stripped of its excesses, it might
have made a good Raymond Carver story.

984 Harris, Roger. "Books." Newark (N.J.) Star Ledger, 27
June 1982.
    Gardner once had the ability to bring his characters and
novels to life, but except for the short stories, his recent
fictions are "murky" and ineffective. Some of MG is
brilliant, but most is pretentious and tedious.

985 Hayes, E. Nelson. "Bookcast." _Boston Ledger_, 12-19
July 1982, p. 17.
_MG_ and Barth's _Sabbatical_, two "unreadable novels cor-
rupted by too much learning and too little life," are the
kind of fiction Gore Vidal disdains. Gardner's philosophical ideas are elementary.

986 Heward, Burt. "Moralistic Writer Views Breakdown and
Ghosts." _Ottawa Citizen_, 17 July 1982, p. 34.
It is ironic that the author of _OMF_ should create in
Mickelsson "the least heroic, most unmoral protagonist
imaginable." Although Gardner's handling of marital
problems is quite good, the novel as a whole fails: verbose, badly structured, crudely written, the parts failing
to coalesce meaningfully.

987 Housto, Levin. "Gardner Novel Disappointing." _Fredricks-
burg_ (Virginia) _Free Lance Star_, 12 June 1982, Town &
Country sec., p. 8.
_MG_ is even more self-indulgent and undisciplined than
Gardner's other novels. The boring conclusion fails to
tie up the many loose ends of a work filled with narrative
contradictions. Still, Gardner's writing is, as always,
exciting and therefore worth reading.

988 Kearney, Robert P. "September Darkness." [Published in an
unidentified Minnesota newspaper sometime in late September
or early October 1982.]
OMF is that rare work of literary criticism that is read
and discussed by non-academic readers. Although Gardner's
main thesis was not inflammatory, both the book and its
outspoken author were often attacked, at times unfairly
(as in Wolcott's review of _MG_). Such critics overlook
Gardner's genuine concern, evident in, for example, his
willingness to participate, for free and out of a sense
of social responsibility, in the University of Minnesota's
conference on Artist's Response to the Nuclear Arms Race.
("It's my duty," he told conference organizer David
O'Fallon.) His last novel, _MG_, is at once humorous (scenes
of "sexual slapstick") and suspenseful. In it, Gardner
proves himself a keen observer of the fraudulent. His approval of "certain informed intolerances" in _OMF_ accounts
for his attacks on Mormons and the IRS. That Mickelsson,
a philosopher, is less accessible than Gardner's other
major characters (e.g., James and Sally in his best work,
_OL_), is somewhat disappointing. The "sense of things unrealized" that characterizes the ending of _MG_ also characterizes Gardner's life, cut short at age 49.

989 Kennedy, Joseph Patrick. "Gardner: The Life of the Mind in an Old Chevy." Houston Chronicle, 4 July 1982.
It is easy to fault Gardner for the scope of MG, a novel about a man trying to live the life of the mind while maintaining his everyday existence. But Gardner is to be praised for having written a novel that is not ponderously philosophical but, instead, exciting and readable.

990 Kenneson, James. "John Gardner's 'Dangling Man' Tailed by Ghosts." Indianapolis Star, 18 July 1982.
MG deals with a recurrent subject in American literature: the intelligent man whose life is falling apart. The philosophy is an integral part of this rich novel, one of the most ambitious to have appeared in quite some time (even if it is not quite as serious as Gardner intended it to be).

991 Kirkus Reviews, 50 (1 April 1982), 435.
Gardner's "most personal, most ambitious" as well as his "most shambling and ultimately incredible" novel. Although Mickelsson is interesting and the writing often quite good, "Gardner's Tolstoyan intention" (to curse and bless at the same time) is undermined by "ludicrousness, fatigue ... sloppiness" and Gardner's choosing to rail against anything and everything.

992 Kisor, Henry. "Of Ghosts, Mad Academics and John Gardner." Chicago Sun-Times, 23 May 1982, Book Week sec., p. 28. Rpt. in slightly altered form as "Gardner's 'Ghosts' Lack Good Haunts," Buffalo Courier-Express, 27 June 1982.
Gardner's philosophical novel is not boring but neither is it convincing. Although MG contains some of Gardner's best writing, the "massive metaphysical weight" that Gardner imposes is too much for Mickelsson's disordered mind to bear. The reader cannot be sure about Mickelsson's insights or the purpose of the ghosts, and the ending seems out of Stephen King rather than John Gardner. Still, the setting is well drawn and Gardner's risk-taking far more praiseworthy than the technical successes of many other contemporary writers.

993 Leary, Lewis. "'Mickelsson's Ghosts': View of Madness and Personal Ghosts." Chapel Hill (N.C.) Newspaper, 20 July 1982.
MG is difficult and possibly too demanding; perhaps "a magnificent, though perhaps loquacious, failure." Whether the madness in this novel is in the world or in Mickelsson alone is impossible to tell.

994 McDowell, Rita. "Ethics Professor's Conscience Found Unreliable." South Bend (Ind.) Tribune, 29 August 1982.
As the "veneer of socialization and ethics" cracks,
Mickelsson discovers that the real test of experience is
reality itself. This "noteworthy" novel includes an
abundance of characters and enough plots for several lesser
works.

995 Manning, Margaret. "Luther and Nietzsche and Sex and
Violence." Boston Globe, 30 May 1982, pp. All-Al2.
Gardner's sometimes heavy-handed preoccupation with myth,
ritual, and mystery is forgivable because the knowledgeable
Gardner tells stories worth reading. Part thriller, part
philosophical novel, MG is "a compelling, nervous, perhaps
overwritten" work that requires the reader's close attention. The main character seems "a middle-aged Thomas Wolfe,
groaning one moment, yawping the next," and in his relationship with the teenage prostitute, he resembles a
character in a bad novel. Belief is one of his gifts;
"paranoia, guilt, indecisiveness and an erotic temperament"
are his others. The novel's undergraduate classroom scenes
are "grimly funny."

996 Mason, David. "Academic Influence Intrudes Too Much in
Gardner Novel." Seattle Times, 15 August 1982, p. F9.
Novels about professors are rarely compelling, and MG is
no exception despite Gardner's attempt to make his character believable. There is too much talk and too many allusions and plot complications (including a pulp-novel
climax), and too little interest in Mickelsson at the end.
Gardner might have succeeded better had he sought to be
profound within the ghost story he writes so well.

997 Merritt, Robert. "Gardner's Novel Shows Top Form."
Richmond Times-Dispatch, 6 June 1982, p. G5.
As in his other works, Gardner combines strong narrative
"with involuted rambling." Part philosophical meditation,
part exploration of love and self-worth, MG is Gardner's
passionate attempt "to understand the most overwhelming
human fears." Besieged by metaphysical questions,
Mickelsson, whom the reader sees from within, grapples
with the ghosts of both the living and the dead in Gardner's
most ambitious and perhaps his best work yet.

998 Milazzo, Lee. "Right, Wrong and 'Ghosts' in All Guises."
Dallas Morning News, 27 June 1982.
Attacking Gardner has become fashionable, and MG
certainly invites criticism (it is diffuse, convoluted,
and "lumpy"). Yet Gardner's imagination, energy, "weeping

style," risk-taking, and memorable, if not entirely understandable title character make MG an "absorbing" work. The
sexual scenes may be worthless, but passages depicting
Mickelsson's disgust are forceful. Gardner's main problem
may derive from his having drawn on too many sources.

999 Miles, Jack. "Examining the Virtuous Crime, Gabbily."
Los Angeles Times Book Review, 30 May 1982, p. 4.
 At the center of many philosophical novels lies "the
philosophical crime, the crime that raises questions."
In MG the question is how human worth is to be assessed.
Although the novel is deep, it is not enjoyable. Both
Gardner and his tiresome protagonist are too talkative;
in fact, the novel reads as if it was dictated rather than
written.

1000 Miller, Steve. "Ghosts in the Machine." Michigan Daily,
1 October 1982.
 In his final novel, Gardner plays the roles of novelist
and critical thinker against each other to show how
Western man's philosophical and religious traditions direct
him through his life. On a stage at once autobiographical
and fictional, Gardner acts out his major theme: thought
versus action. The novel gradually shifts from the external world to the internal as the tension increases
until Mickelsson finally returns from the brink of disaster.
The book is necessarily long because, despite appearances,
it concerns much more than one man's mid-life crisis. Although at times too much about ideas and "too arty or too
amazing," MG still holds its own as a ghost story and as a
novel worth reading and pondering.

1001 Milligan, Bryce. "Gardner Explores Man's Sanity." San
Antonio Express News, 22 August 1982.
 Gardner wrote MG not to make a philosophical point but
to dramatize "the demise of a rationalize man." MG is,
therefore, to be praised rather than faulted. Even as
the Odysseus-like Mickelsson lapses into sentimentality
and sexual fantasy, he holds tenaciously to logic.

1002 Mitgang, Herbert. "The Books of Spring '82." New York
Times Book Review, 24 January 1982, p. 3.
 Gardner is one of the "pros" whose new work, about a
professor's disordered life, will be published this
spring.

1003 Montrose, David. "A Dream in Decline." <u>Times Literary Supplement</u>, 22 October 1982, p. 1156.

A literary craftsman, Gardner weaves his various narratives "into a compelling novel that is always more than its (rather conventional) parts." "Unobtrusively well-written, slowly but absorbingly developed," <u>MG</u> rivals Gardner's best work, <u>G</u>. <u>MG</u> shows the influence of Oates's <u>The Hungry Ghosts</u>, Updike's Rabbit Angstrom, and most importantly Bellow's Tommy Wilheim and Herzog. Although Mickelsson's murder of the fat man is not entirely convincing, Gardner deftly deploys red herrings throughout the novel and "neatly" ties together his various narratives. The one unsolved question is, what will Mickelsson do with his freedom? Using "ideology" as a unifying theme, Gardner understands man's need for some code that will make reality meaningful. The novel's final paragraphs suggest, however, that Jessica may be for Mickelsson "another false grail."

1004 Moore, Richard. "'Mickelsson's Ghosts': Compelling Story, Well Told." <u>Huntsville</u> (Ala.) <u>Times</u>, 29 August 1982, p. D8

Like many other American works, <u>MG</u> seems to be "an experiment in the fusion of forms." Gardner aims high and achieves a great deal. He dramatizes his ethical concepts in three ways: choosing a professor as his protagonist and (less effectively) a university as his setting; using a mystery plot borrowed in part from Dostoievski; and, most successfully, employing gothic romance to keep the reader's interest as unease turns first to dread and then to "pure terror." There is a great deal to Mickelsson ("mickle" means "much"), perhaps too much, but that hardly matters in so suspenseful a tale as this. (Lawler, Moore adds, is the novel's Grand Inquisitor as well as the incarnation of Luther, Nietzsche, and Kierkegaard.)

1005 "Notable Books of the Year." <u>New York Times Book Review</u>, 5 December 1982, p. 46.

Brief description drawn from DeMott's review.

1006 Nugent, Tom. "Novel As Rummage Sale." <u>Baltimore Sun</u>, 20 June 1982.

<u>MG</u> resembles an old-fashioned novel or, even more, a vast rummage sale. Some of the overabundance is interesting, but most is tedious. The farmhouse reminds the reader of how well Gardner once used this kind of setting. He should put his "considerable skills" to better purpose.

1007 Peacock, Allen. "John Gardner, Visionary." Cleveland Plain Dealer, 8 August 1982, p. C18.
   In his Job-like struggles, Mickelsson is portrayed sympathetically, even humorously. His rage reflects Gardner's attacks against his own real-life enemies. To the academic story Gardner adds "a potboiler of the first a rank," perhaps as a concession to "literal-minded readers." Although the two stories remain separate until the end of the novel, the combination is nonetheless "satisfying" and proves that Gardner is clearly in the tradition of "visionary American authors" Poe, Melville, Emerson, Thoreau, and especially Hawthorne, who juxtaposed the light and the dark, the real and the fantastic. Eventually, Mickelsson conquers evil and finds his salvation in Jessica Stark.

1008 Pearson, Ian. "The Lapses of an Engaging Teacher." MacLean's, 95 (5 July 1982), 50.
   Gardner's strength has been the "unsentimental celebration of human community" in his effectively dramatized stories and novels. But MG succumbs to the didacticism that endangers Gardner's brand of moral fiction. Had Gardner chosen a less academic protagonist, the reader would have been spared the boring philosophizing and would have been permitted to deduce the novel's moral message from the dramatic action. As written, the novel's "thoughtful and imaginative plot" is overwhelmed by the numerous passages of abstract thinking.

1009 Perrin, Noel. "Narcissus in Academe." Washington Post Book World, 16 May 1982, pp. 1-2.
   This is "an exceptionally bad book by an exceptionally good author" in need of some self-control. Infatuated by his main character, Gardner becomes indulgent and careless. There are too many themes and inconsistencies and the "density of detail" is overrich and ineffective. Jessica is a fantasy figure, a female Mickelsson.

1010 "Picks and Pans." People, 18 (6 September 1982).
   A cleanly written and rewarding novel. "Gardner's genius lies partly in his ability to blend ... elements into whole plots."

1011 Platt, Kathy. "'Ghosts' Story Line Is Tripled." Oklahoman, 3 October 1982.
   MG is three stories in one: novel, mystery tale, and an easy-to-understand philosophical discussion of modern man's predicament. (A brief obituary follows the review.)

1012 Podhoretz, John. "Landscape Fiction: John Gardner's Shot at The Great American Novel." American Spectator, October 1982, pp. 17-18.
     MG is "a long, sprawling, intensely serious work" having no clear focus. Gardner's best writing occurs when Mickelsson confronts those things that others take for granted. Gardner lavishes attention on every detail but fails to distinguish the important from the unimportant; instead of helping the reader understand the times (something Gardner is well-equipped to do), Gardner buries him under a mountain of indiscriminately described details. Conversely, in his attempt "to show man on the brink of self-destruction," Gardner fails to transform the abstract into the dramatically concrete. Gardner's problem is evident in CMF where he claims that the artist does not actually know what he is doing: thus his character Mickelsson never develops: except for a few lucid moments, he is crazy throughout the novel.

1013 Raskin, Jonah. "Haunting Mountain of a Novel." San Francisco Chronicle, 30 May 1982, Review sec., pp. 1, 7.
     Readers of Gardner's "innovative novels" know that he does not propound Moral Majority values, and MG proves that a novel can be both moral and intelligent without boring the reader. In fact, MG, the author's "most ambitious" work since SD, is "absolutely gripping." Gardner makes the unreal real as he once again shows that "the road to Beauty lies through the fields of Bestiality." In some ways recalling Hawthorne's and Melville's, MG also reminds the reader of Doris Lessing's The Golden Notebooks, in, for example, the protagonist's "inner collapse" and subsequent return to the "redeeeming textures of everyday existence."

1014 Reefer, Mary M. "Author's Words Return To Haunt Him." Kansas City Star, 27 June 1982, p. J1.
     MG is not a moral fiction; it does not affirm life nor instruct nor establish heroic models. MG combines philosophical speculation and a ghost story, but only the latter succeeds; the other is digressive moral dressing.

1015 Rodman, Selden. "Gardner's Last Novel." New Leader, 65 (4 October 1982), 18.
     It is not clear that Mickelsson is a moral man and Gardner a serious intellectual. Mickelsson feels responsible for others, but Gardner never explains the reasons for his character's tremendous guilt. (Nor does he explain how his many mysterious goings-on fit into his plot. Gardner seems to believe that Mickelsson, having su fered so much, deserves anything he can salvage.

1016 Seaton, R.M. "Engrossing Ghost Story Delights." Coffey-
ville (Kansas) Journal, 18-24 July 1982, p. D3.
   As "absorbing" a novel as can be found; an unusual ghost
story in which the apparitions are "incidental" to
Mickelsson's mental disintegration. It is clear that
Gardner leads "a fantastic life ... of the mind."

1017 Shaw, Barrett. "Haunting but Strenuous." Louisville
Times, 24 July 1982, p. E4.
   MG is a difficult but rewarding novel, "as bulky and
morose ... as complex, human and unpredictable" as its
protagonist. The novel succeeds on various levels, most
notably the human. Mickelsson descends "into an ethical
abyss" and struggles "back to human community." His mid-
life crisis is the town's, the nation's, and the world's.

1018 Sinkler, Rebecca. "A Great Novelist's Faculty Has Done
Him In This Time." Philadelphia Inquirer, 13 June 1982,
Books/Leisure sec., p. 3.
   Until now, Gardner has kept the two sides of his personality apart: the storyteller and the sermonizer. However,
in MG, an academic novel of the worst kind, the two voices
are confusingly mixed. Mean, middle-brow, middle-class,
and oversexed, Mickelsson is a familiar character in
American fiction (Bellow, Roth, Updike), but Gardner's
telling of his tale is monumentally tedious.

1019 Smith, C.W. "Intellectual Musings Smother Gardner's
'Ghosts.'" Dallas Times Herald, 11 September 1982.
   MG is a cross between Herzog and The Amityville Horror.
Although Mickelsson leads an exceedingly troubled life,
the novel is "awesomely dull." His tedious intellectual
musings and personal ruminations smother all of the story's
"dramatic possibilities." MG is also self-indulgent. Like
a number of other academic writers, Gardner wants to be a
man of letters rather than a "humble novelist." Had
Mickelsson been a more interesting, less pedantic character who examined his own emotional immaturity and himself as the cause of his own problems, MG might have
succeeded.

1020 Spearman, Walter. "The Literary Lantern." Southern
Pines (N.C.), 14 July 1982. Column appeared in six other
North Carolina newspapers and the Danville (Va.) Register.
   MG is "overlong, overwritten, and overphilosophical."
It is marred by excessive detail, "ramshackle structure,"
and the dreams and ruminations that impede the narrative

flow. Even the few scenes of real action are not tailored properly to the larger story.

1021 Thompson, Francis J. "Disbelief Comes Hard." Tampa Tribune-Times, 13 June 1982, p. C5.
A "delightfully ironic novel." Perhaps Mickelsson only imagines the Danites, whose existence is otherwise unbelievable.

1022 Tinsley, Anne Miller. "Major Novelists Going Audacious." Fort Worth Star-Telegram, 11 July 1982.
Alternating between guilt and rationalization, Mickelsson is the ghost of his former self. The novel is excessive and sprawling. There are too many themes and philosophical references (of the undergraduate sort) and too much "overkill" (as in the several classroom scenes).

1023 Towers, Robert. "So Big." New York Review of Books, 29 (24 June 1982), 17-18.
Except for G, Gardner is most successful when writing in the realistic mode. The occasional lapses in taste and judgment that resulted in FB and the Smugglers sections of OL are also present in MG, where Gardner unsuccessfully combines various plots and genres. The academic, love, and ghost stories are insubstantial and lack dramatic tension. Too much of the novel is given over to "the indiscriminate, underdramatized parade of ideas"; the novel does not add up to what Gardner apparently intended: a major contemporary statement. Despite a number of well written scenes and lovingly detailed descriptions, this "ambitious" novel fails as a result of "slipshod construction and uncontrolled garrulity."

1024 Toye, Randall. "Gardner Writes a Haunting Story." Spectator (Canada), 28 August 1982, p. 42.
The meaning of Gardner's ghosts is left for the reader to decide. Gardner creates "a haunting and provocative context" and a protagonist worth caring about.

1025 Tsunoda, Waka. "John Gardner's Latest an Intellectual
Pleasure." Torrance (Calif.) Daily Breeze, 30 July 1982.
Rpt. as "John Gardner Creates Remarkable New Novel,"
Monterey (Calif.) Peninsula Herald, 15 August 1982, p.
C6.
An outstanding literary achievement, MG evidences
Gardner's dramatic and intellectual skills, lucid prose
style, and ability to describe emotional nuances. MG
provides the reader with "a rare emotional and intellectual
pleasure."

1026 W., C.F. Santa Cruz Sentinel, 10 September 1982.
Some of the ghosts in this novel are supernatural;
others are psychological. The more Mickelsson uses
philosophy to expel his ghosts, the more lost he becomes,
for the solution Gardner posits is one based on magic,
hope, belief, and love. Philosophical breadth, the range
of the hero's problems, and the thickening of the plot
help make this a "great novel." MG is not a work for the
lazy or squeamish reader.

1027 Waters, Earl. "Gardner Takes a Walk on the Dark Side in
Novel." Chattanooga Times, 28 July 1982.
The main characters of SD and MG are alike in that their
thinking tends to wander. SD, however, is a much more
hopeful book. Several minor characters in MG are more
interesting than Mickelsson: Donnie, Tim, and Tinklepaugh.

1028 Weelejus, Ed. "Ghost Story." Erie (Penn.) Times, 6
August 1982.
Gardner's storytelling skill and his occasional social
reportage carry the reader through this "overlong" and
at times too philosophical novel. Mickelsson is as
haunted as the farmhouse he buys in order to escape madness and violence by reverting to his youth on the farm.

1029 Wiehe, Janet. Library Journal, 107 (15 May 1982), 1010.
The restoration of farmhouse and life are the themes of
MG, a novel that is as substantial and appealing as SD.
Gardner contrasts the rural and academic settings and the
two women who, each in her own way, save Mickelsson.

1030 Woiwode, Larry. "Gardner's 'Ghost' Story a Philosophical
Spellbinder." Chicago Tribune Book World, 13 June 1982,
pp. 1, 6.
MG is a work of spellbinding realism. The characters
are memorable; the settings vivid; the classroom scenes

exceptionally well done; the structure shapely; literary, philosophical, and historical echoes are integrated "seamlessly" into the story and discrete elements deftly woven into motifs. As Mickelsson (his name means "much," "great") encounters reality and drifts into the "value-free objectivity" he scorns, Gardner gradually unwraps his narrative "boxes within boxes." The novel's chief flaw is that the prose is occasionally obtrusive, not always equal to the author's serious purpose.

1031 Wolcott, James. "Core Curriculum." Esquire, June 1982, pp. 134, 136.
    Gardner is an ambitious academic novelist whose new novel is long on weighty themes, short on polished style. That the "slack and uninspired" writing may be intentional does not make the reading any more enjoyable. The language is at times "unintentionally comic," the sex scenes cliched, the references to Nazism inappropriate, and the philosophizing sloppy. Gardner's Jessica Stark may derive from the Harlequin romance, Jessica Stark, Nurse on Patrol.

Best American Short Stories 1982 (1982)

1032 "And Bear in Mind." New York Times Book Review, 19 December 1982, p. 24. Continued through 2 January 1983.
    Listed as a recent book of "particular ... interest."

1033 "Notable." Time, 120 (6 December 1982), 92-93.
    Almost all the stories in this "quirky collection" are worth rereading. "As John Gardner's valedictory, it's really something."

1034 Schreiber, Le Anne. "Books of the Times." New York Times, 11 October 1982, p. 19. Also published in the Louisville Courier-Journal, 14 November 1982, p. E7.
    The "intellectually demanding fiction" Gardner attacked in OMF is no longer fashionable, and in his "Introduction" to this collection Gardner's disfavor now falls on a more appropriate kind of literature: cold, ironic stories of people's unhappy lives. Of the stories he has selected, one is sentimental, one is horrifying, and at least ten are "remarkably daring and original."

1035 Spencer, Elizabeth. "Experiment Is Out, Concern Is In."
New York Times Book Review, 21 November 1982, pp. 7, 49.
Gardner's "outspoken and discursive" introduction
"invites immediate response and even disagreement," for
Gardner has based his selection on personal taste and the
belief that experimentation is out (as is a fiction of
manners) and a new, unironic seriousness and "frank engagement with life" is now in. His actual choices, however, do not always evidence Gardner's rationale for
selecting them.

On Becoming a Novelist (1983)

1036 Banks, Russell. Dust-jacket of Harper & Row edition.
"It's clear, after reading OBN, that we lost more than
a powerful novelist when Gardner died. We lost a powerful teacher as well."

1037 Broyard, Anatole. "Books of the Times." New York Times,
5 May 1983, p. C30.
Gardner may be overly fond of the literary mainstream,
several of his distinctions may be doubtful, especially
those concerning which writers are sensitive to language
and which are not, and his comment about contemporary
criticism may be ungenerous in light of the way his own
books have been favorably received. Still, OBN is a useful book for the common reader who will learn from it to
appreciate novels on an entirely new level. Moreover,
Gardner's ideas can be applied to life, to preserve its
strangeness and to keep it from becoming too "workshoppy."

1038 Coale, Sam. "John Gardner's Guide to Being a Novelist."
Providence Journal, 22 May 1983.
The best part of OBN is Gardner's demonic vision of art
and the artist. His attempts to be entirely rational re-
sult in a text that at times cancels itself as it goes.
The how-to advice is mere "window-dressing."

1039 Delbanco, Nicholas. Dust-jacket of Harper & Row edition.
"John Gardner's book is worth a thousand pictures of
the writer writing--bemused, puffing a pipe, one hand on
the keyboard, one in his hair. John was a devoted teacher,
and those of us who witnessed his generous attention must
be grateful for these pages and his ongoing example. OBN
evokes the life of the writer, the student, the teacher

as few other documents can; it gives rise to while
describing 'vivid continuous dreams.'"

1040 Engel, Peter. "Nonfiction in Brief." <u>New York Times
Book Review</u>, 10 July 1983, p. 17.
<u>OBN</u> is Gardner's "primer" for would-be writers and "a
testament to his belief that great novelists are not born
but made."

1041 Grossman, Elizabeth. "The Art of Never Quitting."
<u>Newsday</u>, 30 May 1983, Ideas sec., p. 2.
Gardner's advice is "simple" and "straightforward," if
at times obvious. The presentation is "honest and cogent,"
and the tone suggests his not wanting to sound "preachy,
pretentious or condescending."

1042 Matthews, William. Dust-jacket of Harper & Row edition.
"John Gardner was as impelled to teach as he was to
write; in some way his students recognized instantly,
writing and teaching were for him two parts of a single
and seamless investigation. His brave voice is audible
in every sentence of this book."

Part III
Reviews of Books to Which
Gardner Contributed

The Secret Life of Our Times: New Fiction from Esquire, ed.

Gordon Lish (1973)

1043 Bannon, Barbara A. "PW Forecasts: Fiction." Publishers
Weekly, 204 (3 September 1973), 50.
Gardner is one of the "eminently serious" authors in-
cluded in the collection.

1044 Booklist, 70 (15 November 1973), 320.
Gardner is one of the well-known authors included in
the collection.

1045 Choice, 11 (March 1974), 80.
Unlike the other contributors to this collection,
academic writers Barth and Gardner do not meet "live"
competition because they are read in university writing
courses where the reading lists are narrowly selective.
Moreover, Barth and Gardner seem to have substituted
"literary traditions and influences" for "complexity of
characterization." (See also Studies in Short Fiction
review below.)

1046 Kosinski, Jerzy. New York Times Book Review, 13
January 1974, p. 30.
Gardner approaches his theme, the individual's search
for identity, in an "utterly detached manner."

1047 Purcell, James Mark. Studies in Short Fiction, 11 (Fall
1974), 443-44.
Barth and Gardner are the collection's two academic
writers. In "The Temptation of St. Ivo" the reader is
not at all surprised by the confessor's revelation;
Grendel makes a "bourgeois-liberal assault" on society.
(See also the Choice review above.)

1048 Weathers, Winston. "Experiential Surprises, Wonderful
Wordings." Southwest Review, 59 (Winter 1974), 94-97.
The collection includes a number of today's best
writers. "The Song of Grendel" is one of the finest
pieces, "vigorous, joyous, pyrotechnical"; "The
Temptation of St. Ivo" is among the least successful.

1049 Yardley, Jonathan. "Wonderful Stuff." New Republic, 169
(8 December 1973), 29-30.
The stories are competent but, except for Barth's, not
truly interesting.

Forms of Glory: Structure and Sense in Virgil's Aeneid, by

J. William Hunt (1973)

1050 Gordon, C. D. Queen's Quarterly, Autumn 1974, pp. 472-73.
      Hunt's "'intrinsic approach'"--and Gardner's approval
      of it--is wrong for it ignores the poem's cultural context.

The New Fiction: Interviews with Innovative American Writers,

ed. Joe David Bellamy (1974)

1051 Baker, William. Antioch Review, 33 (Summer 1975), 115-16.
      Lists Gardner as one of the "serious professionals"
      interviewed.

1052 Gelfant, Blanche. "On Interviews." Contemporary
      Literature, 17 (Winter 1976), 110-16.
      Briefly quotes and discusses Gardner's comments on
      fiction as celebration, on literary borrowings, and on
      fiction as distinct from reportage.

1053 Samet, Tom. "Rickie's Cow: Makers and Shapers in
      Contemporary Fiction." Novel, 9 (Fall 1975), 66-73.
      Gardner's view of contemporary fiction is similar to
      Barth's irrealism and Scholes's fabulation. The true
      hero of G is the storyteller, the Shaper. Like many other
      writers included in this collection, Gardner has a dis-
      torted sense of the history of the novel.

1054 Vidal, Gore. "American Plastic: The Matter of Fiction."
      New York Review of Books, 23 (15 July 1976), 36. Rpt.
      in Matters of Fact and Fiction (New York: Random House,
      1976), pp. 117-19.
      Of all the writers interviewed in The New Fiction,
      Gardner is one of the most "truculent" and "much more
      intuitive and authentic than the usual academic browser"
      in myth. However, his view that university writers form
      the mainstream of American fiction and that they tend to
      be more affirmative than non-academic is ridiculous.

Anglo-Saxon Poetry: Essays in Appreciation, ed. Lewis E.

Nicholson and Dolores Warwick Frese (1975)

1055 Pheifer, J.D. Review of English Studies, ns 29 (August
     1978), 327-28.
     Briefly summarizes Gardner's essay and points out his
     misinterpretation of the name Hygelac.

Superfiction, or The American Story Transformed, ed. Joe David

Bellamy (1975)

1056 Publishers Weekly, 208 (21 July 1975), 71.
     The collection includes Gardner's "fanciful" story,
     "Queen Louisa."

Wedges and Wings: The Patterning of Paradise Regained, by

Burton Jasper Weber (1975)

1057 Choice, 12 (July-August 1975), 686.
     Contra Gardner, this book is not for the general reader.

1058 Lieb, Michael. "Three Monographs on Milton: An
     Assessment." Modern Philogy, 74 (November 1976), 207.
     Gardner is wrong to say this is a book for the general
     reader and to defend Weber's slighting of Milton scholar-
     ship as a "blessing."

1059 Maclean, Hugh. Journal of English and Germanic Philology,
     75 (July 1976), 435.
     Gardner's remark that this is not a book for specialists
     is "misleading."

Pages: The World of Books, Writers and Writing, ed. Matthew

J. Bruccoli and C. E. Frazer Clark (1976)

1060 Filby, P. W. RQ, 18 (Winter 1978), 213.
     The collection includes a number of "fine" essays,
     including Gardner's.

The Red Napoleon, by Floyd Gibbons (1976)

1061 Choice, 13 (December 1976), 1294.
      Gardner is correct; this novel is not a literary
      masterwork.

1062 Mullen, R.D. "Books in Review." Science Fiction Studies,
      4 (November 1977), 321.
      Gardner's afterword evidences his being "wholly un-
      familiar with the future-war story and its yellow-peril
      subtype."

Music from Home: Selected Poems, by Colleen McElroy (1976)

1063 Booklist, 73 (15 December 1976), 586.
      Agrees with Gardner's assessment that McElroy's is a
      "real" voice.

Conversations with Writers, ed. Bruccoli and Clark (1977)

1064 Millichap, Joseph R. Modern Fiction Studies, 25 (Summer
      1979), 332.
      Gardner's comments on the links between his criticism
      and his fiction are "perceptive."

The Pushcart Prize, III: Best of the Small Presses, ed. Bill

Henderson (1978)

1065 "The Bookshelf." Changing Times, 33 (August 1979), 23.
      Gardner is one of the "recognized masters" included
      in the collection.

1066 Choice, 15 (October 1978), 1053.
      The selection of essays, which includes Gardner's
      "Moral Fiction," is especially strong.

1067 Contoski, Victor. Library Journal, 103 (1 April 1978), 755
      Gardner's essay "is alone worth the price of the book."

1068 Fisketjon, Gary. "Here Comes Everybody." Village Voice,
      5 June 1978, pp. 68-69.
      Gardner is one of the "Big Name" authors included in
      the collection.

1069 Gordon, Mary. "Small Press Showcase." Washington Post
     Book World, 23 July 1978, pp. 1, 4.
        Gardner's essay should have been omitted from the col-
     lection since the book from which it is drawn, OMF, has
     received considerable attention. The same space could
     have been devoted to some less accessible work.

1070 Johnston, Albert H. "PW Forecasts: Nonfiction."
     Publishers Weekly, 213 (13 March 1978), 103.
        The kind of seriousness Gardner discusses in "Moral
     Fiction" is evident in the items selected for this col-
     lection.

1071 Kirkus Reviews, 46 (15 February 1978), 220.
        Gardner's "Moral Fiction" is a "companionably reaction-
     ary sermon."

1072 Littlefield, William E. Kliatt: Young Adult Paperback
     Book Guide, 13 (Fall 1979), 27.
        The collection includes "major" essays by Gardner and
     Adrienne Rich.

1073 Reuven, Ben. "A Wellspring of Good Writers." Los
     Angeles Times Book Review, 20 August 1978, p. 3.
        Pushcart Prize III answers the question Gardner poses
     in "Moral Fiction": how can literature save us?

1074 Sealock, Barbara. "Small Wonders From Small Presses."
     Christian Science Monitor, 13 November 1978, p. 21.
        Gardner's "Moral Fiction" is "a substantial piece of
     prose wisdom."

Homer's "Iliad": The Shield of Memory, by Kenneth John

Atchity (1978)

1075 Choice, 15 (September 1978), 860.
        Notes Gardner's "disdainful comments" concerning the
     work of Homer scholars.

1076 Combellack, Frederick M. Classical Journal, 74
     (December 1978-January 1979), 171, 173.
        Gardner's enthusiasm for this book is unwarranted.
     (The reviewer assumes the editor is not the Gardner of
     Common Cause.)

1077 Rhorer, Catherine Campbell. Yale Review, Winter 1979, 297.
Gardner wrongly approves of Atchity's writing as if "the
Homeric question" did not exist.

The Best American Short Stories 1978, ed. Ted Solotaroff and

Shannon Ravenel (1978)

1078 Reuven, Ben. "Short Stories: Exaggerated Rumors of
Death." Los Angeles Times Book Review, 26 November 1978,
p. 6.
Among the "veterans of the short story wars" included
in this collection, Gardner is one of the "marksmen."

1079 Romano, John. New York Times Book Review, 26 November
1978, p. 99.
Inclusion of writers like Gardner make this a collection
"worth having." In "Redemption" Gardner makes use of a
"grabber" opening.

1080 Wood, Michael. "This Is Not the End of the World."
New York Review of Books, 25 (25 January 1979), 28-30.
Wood does not include "Redemption" among the seven best
stories in the collection. Most of the stories are
"workmanlike" but fail to develop any real characters.

Kingship and Common Profit in Gower's "Confessio Amantis," by

Russell A. Peck (1978)

1081 Farnham, Anthony E. Speculum, 55 (January 1980), 166-69.
This book deserved a more perceptive reading by its
editor (Gardner) and publisher. Gardner's "bland statement" that the book is not for specialists is "offensively
patronizing."

John Gardner: A Bibliographical Profile, by John Howell (1980)

1082 American Notes & Queries, 19 (October 1980), 31.
Gardner's "Afterword" is a significant commentary on
the attitude of the writer towards his bibliographer.

1083 Choice, 18 (December 1980), 180.
Mentions Gardner's "self-conscious afterword."

1084 Kelly, Richard J. Library Journal, 105 (1 October 1980),
2068.
Gardner's "Afterword" is candid, witty, and "self-
effacing."

1085 Kiernan, Robert F. Literary Research Newsletter, 6
(Summer 1981), 124-26.
Since Gardner is not a major author, it is "pretentious"
to accord his "hackwork" the importance Howell's "honor-
ific" and "unnecessary" bibliography gives it.

1086 Morace, Robert A. Studies in the Novel, 14 (Spring 1982),
119-23.
Corrects a number of Howell's citations, adds several
new items (primary and secondary), and quotes from
Gardner's "Afterword." Also includes two errors, here
corrected. P. 120: "The Grave" appeared in QRL, 17 (1971)
and QRL 19 (1975); p. 121: "the year is 1973, not 1975."

1087 Rothman, David. Aspen Anthology, 10 (Winter 1980), 93.
While the academic community has responded to Gardner
either by denouncing or ignoring him, some writers have
expressed their hostility for what they feel is his un-
deserved success. To his credit, Gardner is one of the
only writers raising significant questions about the
nature of contemporary fiction. His "Afterword" to
Howell's bibliography lacks substance but does offer
useful glimpses into the author's personal life.

Becoming a Writer, by Dorothea Brande (1981)

1088 Ehresmann, Julia M. Booklist, 77 (1 April 1981), 1071.
Mentions Gardner's "critical foreword."

John Gardner: Critical Perspectives, ed. Robert A. Morace

and Kathryn VanSpanckeren (1982)

1089 Abbott, Scott. Sunstone Review (Salt Lake City),
September 1982.
Quotes from Gardner's "Afterword," which, though "no
great document," does serve "as ironic counterpoint to
the essays."

1090 Choice, 19 (November 1982), 428.
   Gardner's fictions are "strangely forbidding": academic,
intellectual, stilted, and "populated not by believable
characters but by cerebral phantoms." Contrary to what
Gardner says in his after "Afterword," these essays are
more interesting than his fiction; in fact, they generate
interest in the fiction.

1091 Kaufman, James. Los Angeles Times Book Review, 1 August
   1982, p. 7.
   Quotes from the "Afterword" by Gardner, whose "ambitious
novels ... carry a full complement of literary baggage for
critics to inspect."

In Praise of What Persists, ed. Stephen Berg (1983)

1091a Bayles, Martha. New York Times Book Review, 7 August
   1983, pp. 15, 18.
   Although all the contributors to this collection make
some connection between their experiences and their work,
only Gardner and Richard Hugo do so "clearly and com-
prehensibly."

Part IV
Works About
(other than reviews)

1962

1092 "Distinctive Short Stories in American Magazines." The
Best American Short Stories 1962. Ed. Martha Foley and
David Burnett. Boston: Houghton Mifflin, 1962, p. 428.
Lists "A Little Night Music."

1964

1093 "The Yearbook of the American Short Story: Distinctive
Short Stories, 1963." The Best American Short Stories
1963. Ed. Martha Foley and David Burnett. Boston:
Houghton Mifflin, 1964, p. 352.
Lists "The Edge of the Woods."

1965

1094 "Contributors." Perspective, 14 (Spring 1965), [2].
Gardner "has two novels coming out soon."

1966

1095 Thorpe, Willard. "Melville." In American Literary
Scholarship: An Annual/1964. Ed. James Woodress. Durham:
Duke University Press, 1966, p. 38.
Summarizes Gardner's "Bartleby: Art and Social Commit-
ment"; the religious allusions found by Gardner are "wild
conjectures."

1970

1096 "In Retrospect." Quarterly Review of Literature, 19,
iii-iv (1975), 3-4. "Retrospective" issue.
Gardner, Borges, and Coover are "intrepid innovators
and experimenters" who employ a poetic prose style.
Gardner's "The Grave" (reprinted on pp. 487-504) "is
remarkable, especially beside the scintillations of
writings like G, for its 'plainness,' its slow, low-
keyed strength."

1972

1097 Canaday, John. "Art: Napper's Illustrations for Novel."
New York Times, 16 December 1972, p. 27.
The Napper show at the Larcada Gallery in New York
consists of the illustrations published in SD and a

separate set of lithographs related to the novel. These "paradoxically eerie evocations of a flatly commonplace world" are quite different from Napper's paintings ("Gentle, lovingly painted, poetic landscapes of great charm"). Quotes from Gardner's introductory sheet: SD "is an attempt to bring back the illustrated novel" in a way that will confute Henry James's belief that illustrations are always redundant; "... illustrations are always a visual artist's creative comment on a literary idea.... Thus Dore gave Dante's hell new dimensions, and Tenniel transformed Lewis Carroll's Wonderland."

1098 "The Yearbook of the American Short Story: Distinctive Short Stories, 1971." The Best American Short Stories 1972. Ed. Martha Foley. Boston: Houghton Mifflin, 1972, p. 405.
    Lists "The Song of Grendel."

1973

1099 Bell, Pearl K. "American Fiction: Forgetting the Ordinary Truths." Dissent, Winter 1973, p. 31.
    Gardner's "The Way We Write Now" (New York Times Book Review, 9 July 1972) is quoted approvingly.

1100 Bellamy, Joe David. "The Way We Write Now." Chicago Review, 25, i (1973), 45-49.
    Gardner's positon in his essay, "The Way We Write Now" (New York Times Book Review, 9 July 1972), is "aesthetically retrograde" and occasionally "downright silly and wrong." Gardner tries to reduce the "multifarity" of American literature "to a single spurious unifying principle." In doing so he fails to understand the "radical usefulness" of contemporary fiction--i.e., as a way of reinventing ourselves and our world.

1101 Cochrane, Diane. "John Napper: The Return of the Illustrated Novel." American Artist, 37 (July 1973), 26-31, 65-66.
    Napper, who first met Gardner at Southern Illinois University, initially turned down the offer to illustrate SD (an "extraordinarily visual" and "almost old-fashioned novel"). After reading the novel aloud, Napper accepted. He then visited Batavia and subsequently made thirteen illustrations for the novel and thirteen additional

lithographs. (Together they make up his show at the
Larcada Gallery in New York.) The illustrations are all
in black and white in order to "look like an extension
of the print." They are designed to reflect the novel's
"fear and paranoia," "to create resonances," and to cause
the reader to create "his own dialogues for the characters."
Gardner, who believes that adult fiction need not be
"realistic and self-importantly solemn," thinks of illustrations as "a visual artist's creative comment on a
literary idea." Napper's illustrations are "fictions,"
Gardner claims; they "freeze the moment, yet imply full
events...." The essay includes a brief biography of
Napper and Gardner's description of SD: a "metaphysical
novel about life in America" in which Clumly and the
Sunlight Man "obsessively ... hunt each other until they
catch, in the end, themselves." (Cochrane is quoting
from the introductory sheet Gardner prepared for Napper's
illustrations.)

1102 Hills, Rust. "Fiction." Esquire, 80 (September 1973),
10, 28.
Wary of book-length narrative epics, Hills dipped into
JM "fearfully." He comments on Gardner's immense productivity and mentions having read, in manuscript, Gardner's
"fascinating-in-a-way SD."

1103 John Gardner: First Decade: Collected Works: 1962-1973.
Southfield, Michigan: n.p., October 1973.*
Cited in Howell.

1104 Oates, Joyce Carol. Letter. New York Review of Books,
20 (4 October 1973), 37.
In passing, Oates criticizes Morris Dickstein's "scolding
review" of JM in the New York Times Book Review, 1 July
1973.

1105 Prescott, Peter S. "The Writer's Lot." Newsweek, 82
(24 December 1973), pp. 83-85.
Gardner is one of those authors of whom "writers under
45 would approve.... but not Barthelme; he can't read
Gardner."

1106 Shorris, Earl. "In Defense of Cain." Harper's, 247
(August 1973), 90-92.
Foregoing the apocalyptic "cry of amateurs," Gardner
revises our interpretation of the Cain and Abel story in
order that we may learn to love the children of Cain and

ultimately ourselves. Res and SD deal with this theme, but neither "succeeds as allegory or art." The one is too plodding, and the other clumsy and unfocused. Much more successful is G, a novel which shows that despair can be overcome through defiance. WA is "an argument between Socratic humanism and Platonic transcendent philosophy"; it is concerned with numerous socio-political topics and is open to a variety of interpretive approaches. JM is history "rewritten from a humanistic perspective"; it provides "an exciting tangent to our own lives."

1107 Stevick, Philip. "Scheherazade Runs Out of Plots, Goes on Talking; the King, Puzzled, Listens: An Essay on New Fiction." TriQuarterly, 26 (1973), 350, 354.
Gardner's G, Coover's Universal Baseball Association, and Gass's Omensetter's Luck are all "quite relentlessly mythic" and so confute the view (held by Richard Wasson) that "the import of Barth's The End of the Road and the aesthetic of the end of myth are really at the center of recent fiction." Many of "the most audacious and exciting" American writers today, Gardner for one, teach in the universities.

1108 Wilder, Alec. "Back to the Roots of That Novelist from Batavia." Rochester Democrat & Chronicle/Upstate Magazine, 15 April 1973, pp. 20-24.
A loving description of a number of Gardner's relatives, including his parents ("the kind of honorable, honest, moral, clear-headed human beings I used to think of as the backbone of America") and aunt, Mildred Britt (the prototype for Millie Jewel Hodge).

1109 Wolfe, Tom. "Introduction." The Secret Life of Our Times: New Fiction from Esquire. Ed. Gordon Lish. Garden City: Doubleday & Co., 1973, pp. xxii, xxiv, xxvii.
Gardner is one of the "Neo-Fabulists" who parody old forms and write "moral tales with no moral" in which the prevailing tone is dread. "The Song of Grendel" is a highly stylized work, at once nihilistic and comic.

1974

1110 Daillie, Rene. "Afterword." Grendel. Trans. Rene Daillie. Paris: Denoel, 1974, pp. 191-204.*
Cited in Howell.

1111 Fouchet, Max-Pol. "Preface." _Grendel_. Trans. Rene
     Daillie. Paris: Denoel, 1974, pp. 11-18.*
     Cited in Howell.

1112 Lourie, Dick. Letter. _New York Times Book Review_, 3
     February 1974, pp. 34-35.
     Points out that, contra Gardner (_New York Times Book
     Review_, 23 December 1973), Koch's is _a_, not _the_, method
     for the teaching of poetry.

1113 "Novelist John Gardner To Visit SLU During '74 Steinman
     Festival." _Watertown_ (N.Y.) _Daily News_, 10 April 1974.
     Gardner's lecture will open the Steinman Festival of
     the Arts at St. Lawrence University.

1114 Prakken, Sarah L. _Reader's Adviser: A Layman's Guide to
     Literature_. 12th ed. New York: R. R. Bowker, 1974, pp.
     640-41.
     Brief summary of the novels through 1973.

1115 Ruud, Jay. "Gardner's _Grendel_ and _Beowulf_: Humanizing the
     Monster." _Thoth_, 14 (Spring-Fall 1974), 3-17.
     The Grendel of _Beowulf_ is monster, devil, and exiled
     warrior. Gardner's Grendel is patterned on the third, or
     human, element and in his alienation becomes the absurdist
     hero of contemporary fiction. In _Beowulf_, Grendel is
     alienated from society and its accepted values, but in the
     modern world such values do not exist. In the novel,
     Grendel's initial awareness of the absurd nearly leads him
     to that paralysis Barth calls "cosmopsis" in _The End of
     the Road_. Rather than accept either this paralysis or
     Beowulf's unquestioning (and therefore insane) acceptance
     of traditional values, Grendel decides that "it is at
     least _relatively_ better to adopt a role [the monster whose
     existence improves men] than do nothing."

1116 Sokolski, Carol. Letter. _New York Times Book Review_, 3
     February 1974, p. 34.
     Criticizes Gardner's comment in his 23 December 1973
     review of two books by Kenneth Koch that rhyme inhibits
     imagination and honest feeling.

1117 _Who's Who in America_, 39th ed. (1974-75).
     Gardner has subsequently been included in the 40th and
     41st editions.

237

1975

1118 Bellamy, Joe David. "Introduction." Superfiction, or
the American Story Transformed. Ed. Joe David Bellamy.
New York: Vintage, 1975, pp. 11-12.
Experimenting with myth and parable, Gardner in "Queen
Louisa" employs many of superfiction's most characteristic
aspects: fairy-tale form, anti-illusionist technique,
"the droll tone of the put-on." At the end of the story
Gardner "cleverly saves himself from an ending too
simplistically affirmative."

1119 Ekner, Reidar. "Afterword." Grendel. Trans. Reidar
Ekner. Stockholm: Pan/Norstedts, 1975, pp. 127-30.*
Cited in Howell.

1120 Hutman, Norma L. "Even Monsters Have Mothers: A Study
of Beowulf and John Gardner's Grendel." Mosaic, 9 (Fall
1975), 19-31.
G is not criticism but instead "creative vision ...
commenting imaginatively (and hence more than logically)
upon its archetypal mother," Beowulf. In both works,
"decision makes the hero," "God and the Shaper are kins-
men," and "the monster represents some older form of ourselves" that must be defeated for society and redemption
to be possible. Both works also involve opposing
characters and values that are ultimately reconciled in
visionary knowledge; thus the madness Gardner's monster
associates with both the Shaper and Beowulf.

1121 McCaffery, Larry. "Barthelme's Snow White: The
Aesthetics of Trash." Critique, 16, iii (1975), 32.
Gardner is one of those writers who, like Joyce, uses
myth rather than reality for the "basic framework" of
their fictions.

1122 McCaffery, Larry. "The Magic of Fiction-Making." fiction
international, 4-5 (1975), 150.
Includes this oblique criticism of Gardner: "Like those
who wept at the end of Love Story or when Little Nell l
died, Henry [in Robert Coover's The Universal Baseball
Association] confuses a fictional truth with a factual one."
(See Gardner's letter to the editor concerning William
Gass's "The Concept of Character in Fiction," New
American Review, 9 [1970].)

1123 McConnell, Frank. "The Corpse of the Dragon: Notes on
Postromantic Fiction." TriQuarterly, 33 (1975), 273-303.
Like high romanticism, contemporary fiction, especially
that of Barth, Bellow, Pynchon, and Gardner, "struggle[s]
to assert, in the face of the artificiality and facticity
of all thought, an authentically human voice, a civilizing
idea." Their characters live in an "informationally over-
determined" world where they use language mythically in
their war against chaos. At the heart of Gardner's fiction is "the intimation of mortality" worked out in an
"archetypal plot" in which man asserts his "systems,"
even if they are "lies," against the ultimate fact, death.
G's narrator speaks of, or parodies, "the self-confident
voice" of the epic poet; Gardner's object is to create a
fictional world in which the traditional values can be
articulated. JM, presented "as a translation of itself,"
announces the end of the heroic age yet reaffirms "the
dignity, even if fictive ... of human love."

1124 Mulyarchik, Alexander A. "Neueste Tendenzen in Literatur
und Kultur der USA in den siebziger Jahren des 20.
Jahrunderts." Zeitschrift fur Anglistik und Amerikanistik
(Leipzig, East Germany), 23, iii (1975), 217-24.
At the center of Gardner's SD, Kazan's The Assassins, and
Updike's Rabbit Redux is the conflict between traditional
democracy and the counterculture. In SD it is the Sunlight Man, the nominal son of middle America turned a
modern Mephistopheles or a Byronic Cain, who causes the
representative of authority to change. The tone of
Clumly's final speech is not platitudinous but at once
concrete and obliging; what Clumly says provides his
listeners with a guiding ethical principle. NM is an
even more optimistic work.

1125 Peden, William. The American Short Story: Continuity and
Change, 1940-1975. Boston: Houghton Mifflin, 1975, pp.
27, 185.
Mentions KI.

1126 "36 Prizes Awarded in Arts and Letters; Pynchon Rejects
His." New York Times, 22 May 1975, p. 35.
Gardner is listed as one of the recipients of the Arts
and Letters Awards of the Academy Institute.

1127 Weber, Burton J. "Preface." Wedges and Wings: The
Patterning of Paradise Regained. Literary Structures
series. Carbondale and Edwardsville: Southern Illinois

University Press; London and Amsterdam: Feffer & Simons,
1975, p. xiii.
Thanks Gardner, the series editor, for his "advice ...
faith and interest."

1128 "The Yearbook of the American Short Story: Roll of Honor,
1974." The Best American Short Stories 1975. Ed. Martha
Foley. Boston: Houghton Mifflin, 1975, p. 300.
Lists "The Music Lover."

1976

1129 Alexander, John. "Joseph Baber Takes to the Marketplace
to Premiere His New 'Rumpelstiltskin.'" Lexington
(Kentucky) Herald-Leader, 5 December 1976.
Joseph Baber, who would rather take his chances in the
marketplace than in the arts community, describes his
first meeting with Gardner ("this man who looked like he
was from Marlboro Country") and their work together. Their
first opera, Frankenstein, has been accepted for production
in New York but may prove too costly to stage. Rumpelstiltskin, which will be performed at the Lexington Opera
House, 21-22 January 1977, is "somewhere between an opera
and musical comedy," a work for people to enjoy.

1130 Barron, Neil. Anatomy of Wonder: Science Fiction. New
York: R. R. Bowker, 1976, p. 188.
G is "allegorical social criticism" in which the monster
is a tragic figure and Beowulf "the epitome of insensitivity
and cruelty."

1131 Becker, George J. "Postrealism." In Encyclopedia of World
Literature in the 20th Century. Ed. Frederick Ungar and
Lina Mainiero. New York: Ungar, 1976, IV:297.
John Erskine's Helen of Troy and Gardner's Grendel--two
"tours de force"--are outside the modern tendency to use
"the here and now" as subjects for novels.

1132 Detweiler, Robert. "Games and Play in Modern American
Fiction." Contemporary Literature, 17 (Winter 1976), 49,
54.
G is characteristic of that kind of literary play
Detweiler terms "agon": "fiction in which the author plays
a game with the reader." "Thematic game novels" such as
G, The Sot-Weed Factor, Giles Goat-Boy, and The Adventures
of Mao on the Long March, "pretend, through satire or other
humor, toward epic scope."

1133 Detweiler, Robert. "Theological Trends of Postmodern
Fiction." Journal of the American Academy of Religion,
44 (1976), 225.
  Gardner (SD), Gass, Styron, A.J. Langguth, and Updike
have used sermons in their fiction in order to give the
reader an "as-if possibility of belief even if he will not
accept it as an actual possibility."

1134 Heckard, Margaret. "Robert Coover, Metafiction, and
Freedom." Twentieth-Century Literature, 22 (1976), 220.
  "Much derivative literature could be called 'fractured
fairy-tales,'" e.g., Don Quixote, G, and Chimera.

1135 Joost, Nicholas. "PLL: The First Ten Years: A Memoir."
Issued with an index to vols. 1-10 as a special supplement to Papers on Language and Literature, p. 9.
  Joost discusses Gardner's various contributions to PLL,
his scholarly essays, his advisory editorship, and his
co-editing the special Chaucer supplement.

1136 Kovalev, Y., ed. 20th Century American Literature: A
Soviet View. Trans. Ronald Vroon. Moscow: Progress
Publishers, 1976.*
  The Russians are "critically appreciative" of Gardner
and other American writers. (As noted in the review by
Robert E. Spiller, American Literature, 50 [March 1978],
138-39.)

1137 Lepper, Gary M. "John Gardner." In A Bibliographical
Introduction to Seventy-Five Modern American Authors.
Berkeley: Serendipity Books, 1976, pp. 209-11.
  Lists books by Gardner.

1138 McConnell, Frank D. "Gardner, John (Champlin, Jr.)."
In Contemporary Novelists. Ed. James Vinson, 2nd ed.
New York: St. Martin's Press, 1976, pp. 491-94.
  Prolific yet "consummately graceful," Gardner is equally
adept at realism and fabulism. Unlike many of his contemporaries, he is concerned with the "problems of religious belief, traditional ethics, and philosophical
values." In Res, the protagonist learns to accept
traditional values however "perilous" their validity,
and in WA Gardner creates a new genre, the "protest
fantasy." G and SD are more satisfying in their not having
professional philosophers in the leading roles. His next
two works, JM and KI, intensify the tensions "between

fantasy and realism, culture and chaos, philosophical
calm and panic in the abyss"; the latter book may be
Gardner's "most accomplished, polished work yet...."

1139 Murr, Judy Smith. "John Gardner's Order and Disorder:
Grendel and The Sunlight Dialogues." Critique, 18, ii
(1976), 97-108.
Gardner's fiction involves a recurrent pattern in which
"a representative of order and one of disorder" confront
each other in their respective quests to find whether life
is anything "more than a series of comical, meaningless
exercises." Their confrontation is complicated by the
fact that "it is between an order that longs for disorder
and a disorder in pursuit of order," of opposites which
"need each other for definition." As confrontation gives
way to "fusion," the antagonists learn that "Man is
ridiculous, his actions are absurd; but such perception
and his ability to love regardless grant man his seriousness. "

1140 Perkins, James Ashbrook. "Robert Coover and John Gardner:
What Can We Do with the Poets ?" Notes on Contemporary
Literature, 6 (March 1976), 2-4.
As Grendel understands, the Shaper uses his songs to
lead Hrothgar's people "to a greatness that they otherwise
would not have attained." Although poets would like to
be thought of in this way--as legislators for all man-
kind--in the contemporary world they are more often in
the position of Sandy Shaw in Coover's The Universal Baseball Association: the "effective but unwitting tool of
the establishment."

1141 Reed, Max Robert. "The Emergence of the Grotesque in the
Contemporary American Novel, 1919-1972." MA thesis North
Texas State University 1976.*
"The Grotesque Hero finds a solution to the dilemma, not
by escaping his grotesque victimization, but by accepting
it and making it work for him." SD is one of the novels
discussed. (Masters Abstracts, 1976)

1142 Saporta, Marc. Histoire du roman americain. Rev. ed.
Paris: Gallimard, 1976, pp. 468, 483.
G and SD are cited in the list of annual literary events
for 1971 and 1972 respectively.

1143 Strehle, Susan. "John Gardner's Novels: Affirmation and
the Alien." Critique, 18, ii (1976), 86-96.

Gardner's earliest novels, NM and Res, share a similar
setting, omniscient narrative method, theme ("the affirmation of life in the face of death"), and flaw (sentimental endings). His next three novels avoid sentimentality
by means of "self-consciousness and humor." More experimental than the earlier works, they also include an "alien"
whose nihilism serves to improve the complacent, self-
righteous society from which he is estranged. SD and WA
are less "metaphysical" than the earlier books, more concerned with social matters; both employ prison settings
and "opposed perspectives on the same events." In G,
Gardner's "most experimental" novel, the author rejects
the individual ideas presented in each of the twelve
chapters and affirms instead "the seasonal cycle which
provides the frame of the novel." His blackly humorous
monster gradually inherits the Shaper's craft and vision.

1144 "The Yearbook of the American Short Story: Roll of Honor,
1975." The Best American Short Stories 1976. Ed. Martha
Foley, Boston: Houghton Mifflin, 1976, p. 350.
     Lists "The Music Lover."

1977

1145 Allen, Bruce. "Settling for Ithaca: The Fictions of John
Gardner." Sewanee Review, 85 (July 1977), 520-31.
     "A genuinely eclectic novelist," Gardner "is obsessively
interested in the tension between social order and
individual freedom," between the values found in traditional literature and the contemporary "psychological
uncertainty" which makes those values less viable today.
His questing heroes eventually discover the humbling
fact of human limitation (a common theme in medieval
literature). Res, though "forced and clumsily erudite,"
shows that reason by itself is insufficient. NM is a
"fable of aheroic regeneration," and SD, however prolix
and overrich, succeeds because of the focus on Clumly.
Where the first three novels concern common protagonists,
the next three involve heroes of a very different sort.
WA is a thin book poorly fleshed out; G is his "best novel,
and JM, which satirizes the virtues celebrated in epics,
is boldly conceived. KI sums up Gardner's main theme:
settling for that possible knowledge which is arrived at
very slowly in OL (perhaps an old work recently published).
The mystery in Gardner's career is this: "Are the stories

which show his people growing into knowledge newly published
work in an early mode that he unwisely has now abandoned?
Or is he relaxing his thematic hold on characters, permitting them to be persons as well as ideas and symbols?"

1146 Bennett, Robert B. "Homiletic Design in the Towneley
Abraham." Modern Language Studies, 7, i (1977), 5.
Gardner may be correct in attributing the play to the
Wakefield master, but he misreads Abraham's opening speech
("Idea and Emotion in the Towneley Abraham," 1971).

1147 "Book Critics Circle Announces Prizes in Four Categories."
New York Times, 7 January 1977, p. B2.
OL named as the outstanding work of fiction for 1976.

1148 Boren, James L. "Narrative Design in the Alliterative
Morte Arthure." Philological Quarterly, 56 (1977), 318-19.
Gardner's "topical subtitles ... do little to suggest the
poet's own sense of design." Unlike other critics, Gardner
did see in the Templar episode the ironic hint of Arthur's
later decline.

1149 Contemporary Authors. Ed. Jane A. Bowden. Vols. 65-68.
Detroit: Gale Research, 1977, p. 241.
Gardner notes that living near Bennington, Vermont,
"offers 'isolation' and a sense of balance." "Work In
Progress" lists "Three opera libretti; a 'Book of rant'
regarding modern fiction; tales for children; a novel."

1150 DeMott, Robert. "New Directions in Steinbeck Studies."
Steinbeck Quarterly, 10 (1977), 69.
That a major novelist and respected medievalist has
reviewed The Acts of King Arthur (New York Times Book
Review, 24 October 1976) is a sign of the continued
interest in Steinbeck's work.

1151 Dickey, Christopher. "National Book Critics Circle
Awards Announced." Washington Post, 7 January 1977,
p. B10.
OL chosen as the outstanding work of fiction in 1976.

1152 Diehl, Digby. "West View: National Book Critics Square
Off on 1976 Circle Awards." Los Angeles Times Book
Review, 23 January 1977, p. 3.
The New York critics favored Renata Adler's Speedboat
for the National Book Circle award for fiction, dismis-
sing OL as "too long and too philosophical." The judgment

244

of the non-New York critics prevailed. The citation read:
"'OL' is an ambitious work of extraordinary philosophical,
historical, social and imaginative scope. Without the
somber trappings of High Seriousness, this book explores
many contemporary issues and connects us to the roots of
these issues in the past in daring leaps of perception.
Beginning with a comic squabble between a cantankerous
old New England farmer and his 80-year old sister, Gardner
reaches out boldly to grapple with themes such as community,
forgiveness, family, love, the interaction between art and
life and democracy.
In addition, 'OL' is marvelously entertaining, a happily
readable book which surrounds its moments of profundity
with fun, even zaniness. For all the sprawling breadth of
its themes, the novel has prose that crackles with energy.
It is a virtuoso work of lyric flights, jazzy excitements
and absorbing meditations." (The citation also appears
in the "Transcript of Awards Ceremony," National Book
Critics Circle Journal, 3 [Spring 1977], 2-3.)

1153 Dillon, David A. "John C. Gardner: A Bibliography."
Bulletin of Bibliography, 34 (April-June 1977), 86-89,
104.
This list of primary and secondary items is based upon
"the standard indexes and bibliographies" and is complete
"up to May 1977." ("Standard" here should be construed as
"selective"; as a result, the bibliography is considerably
less complete than its compiler assumes. In addition there
are a number of inaccurate entries.)

1154 Ellis, Helen B., and Warren U. Ober. "Grendel and Blake:
The Contraries of Existence." English Studies in Canada,
3 (Spring 1977), 87-102. Rpt. in John Gardner: Critical
Perspectives. Ed. Robert A. Morace and Kathryn Van
Spanckeren. Carbondale and Edwardsville: Southern Illinois
University Press, 1982, pp. 46-61.
Readers of G are often "seduced" into thinking that the
monster speaks for his author. Gardner's actual aim,
however, is to endorse "'the great heroic ideals'" by
"'setting up alternatives in an ironic set of monster
values.'" This aim becomes clear when G is compared with
those works upon which it is in part based: Beowulf, Milton
Paradise Lost, Shakespeare's The Tempest, Browning's
"Caliban upon Setebos," and, most importantly, "when
Grendel allows himself to be defined by the dragon,"
Blake's "The Marriage of Heaven and Hell." "Grendel's
fundamental error is that half-human, he allows another
monster to advise him how to live and thus ignores his
human capacities."

1155 "Extensive Publicity Follows on Awards." National Book
Critics Circle Journal, 3 (Spring 1977), 6.
Notes Gardner's appearances on The Sally Jesse Raphael
Show (WMCA radio in New York) with Richard Locke and Digby
Diehl, and on Straight Talk (WOR-TV in New York) with
Timothy Foote.

1156 Fitzpatrick, W.P. "'Down and Down I Go': A Note on
Shelley's Prometheus Unbound and Gardner's Grendel."
Notes on Contemporary Literature, 7 (January 1977), 2-5.
The "correspondences" between Prometheus Unbound and
G "extend the novel beyond the pastiche/pardy [sic] of
Beowulf into a satire of Godwinian optimism...." In
place of Anglo-Saxon virtu and Romantic optimism, Grendel
finds an inverted world of absurdity, despair, and
materialism.

1157 Fitzpatrick, W.P. "John Gardner and the Defense of
Fiction." Bulletin of the West Virginia Association of
College English Teachers, 4, i (1977), 19-28.* Rpt. in
The Midwest Quarterly, 20 (Summer 1979), 404-15.
KI and OL are at once postmodernist fictions and
critical responses to Barth's "literature of exhaustion"
concept. Gardner's subject in these two books is human
perspective; "if perspective in some measure determines
form, the ultimate shape of creative vision, then form
itself is inexhaustible." Simply stated, Gardner's
position is that "art can never satisfactorily compete
with life as the subject of fiction."

1158 Fredericks, S. C. "Revivals of Ancient Mythologies in
Current Science Fiction and Fantasy." In Many Futures
Many Worlds: Theme and Form in Science Fiction. Ed.
Thomas D. Clareson. Kent, Ohio: Kent State University
Press, 1977, pp. 58-59, 65.
Gardner is among those writers who base their fictions
on well-known myths "in order to extend their own
creativity and the literary possibilities inherent in
the themes of science fiction and fantasy." The protagonist of the "perversely" titled G is "an existential
antihero" whose quest entails the "humiliation of heroism,
beauty, and religion. The novel's black-humor ending is
ambiguous and ironic; "the topsy-turvy perspective"
leads the reader to the "myth of the 'anti-anti-hero,'"
thus restoring "the world of proper heroism."

1159 Fremont-Smith, Eliot. "Making Book." Village Voice, 17
     January 1977, p. 81. Rpt. in National Book Critics Circle
     Journal, 3 (Spring 1977), 7-8.
         Judges for the National Book Critics Circle award for
     fiction were sharply divided over the merits of the two
     final nominees. Renata Adler's Speedboat was attacked as
     "hermetically 'New York'" and "French," while Gardner's
     OL, the winner by an eight to seven vote, was denigrated
     as overtly popular, filled with caricatures, and "inflated
     with pretentious philosophizing."

1160 "Gardner Book Wins." Binghamton Press, 9 January 1977.
         Associated Press release on OL's having won the National
     Book Critics Circle award for fiction.

1161 Gass, William. "Preface." In the Heart of the Heart of
     the Country. New York: Pocket Books, 1977, p. 19.
         Mentions Gardner's ("Gardiner") publication of Gass's
     "The Pedersen Kid" in MSS.

1162 Hutcheon, Linda. "Modes et Formes du Narcissisme
     Litteraire." Poetique, 29 (1977), 92-93.
         Although his own fiction evidences his ambivalent
     attitude towards contemporary narcissistic literature,
     Gardner does recognize its attractiveness. (Quotes Gard-
     ner's review of Woiwode's Beyond the Bedroom Wall, New
     York Times Book Review, 28 September 1975.)

1163 Lingeman, Richard. "Book Ends." New York Times Book
     Review, 18 September 1977, p. 63.
         Gardner, Irving Howe, and Eudora Welty are serving as
     the three final judges for the Harvard University Press
     short novel publishing program.

1164 Locke, Richard. "From TV to Lionel Trilling." New York
     Times Book Review, 12 June 1977, pp. 3, 40-41.
         Gardner's appealingly energetic essay "Moral Fiction"
     (Hudson Review, Winter 1976-77) is "disquieting in its
     self-certainty and underlying, unacknowledged imprecision.
     In his own novels John Gardner uneasily treads the line
     between slick didacticism and sheer virtuosic horseplay."
     Instead of the "rough-rider exhortation" of Gardner or
     the nostalgic optimism of Bettelheim or the art-for-art's-
     sake of Gass, there is the more balanced view of Lionel
     Trilling, who appreciated literature both for its moral
     value and its "controlled release of animal, pre-social
     forces."

1165 McConnell, Frank D. Four Postwar American Novelists:
     Bellow, Mailer, Barth and Pynchon. Chicago: University
     of Chicago Press. 1977, pp. xix, 198.
       Gardner's writings are linked "to the visionary fiction
     of the romantic revolution" and consolidate "the best
     innovations of the postwar tradition."

1166 Maier, John R. "Mesopotamian Names in The Sunlight
     Dialogues: or MAMA Makes It to Batavia, New York."
     Literary Onomastics Studies, 4 (1977), 33-48.
       The numerous Mesopotamian allusions in SD lead the
     reader to the ancient Babylonian wisdom that is the novel's
     "intellectual core." The dialogues pit Biblical wisdom
     against Babylonian thought (as presented by Taggert in
     highly fragmented form) and serve, as do the choral songs
     in Greek tragedy, not to advance the narrative action but
     to comment on it. The dialogues, to which the reader will
     probably pay little attention, cannot be taken as entirely
     representative of the author's own views.

1167 "New Comic Opera At U. of Kentucky." New York Times, 19
     January 1977, p. C17.
       "'Rumpelstiltskin' is said to follow the traditional
     fairy tale, but with sudden switches in tone, from comic
     to frightening, wacky to solemn." The form of the music
     is traditional. Gardner is in Lexington to assist in the
     production.

1168 Olson, Clarence E. "The Bruising Game of Literary Awards-
     manship." St. Louis Post-Dispatch, 9 January 1977, p. F4.
       In discussing the 1976 National Book Critics Circle
     award for fiction, New York critics favored Renata Adler's
     Speedboat and disparaged Gardner's OL as "pretentious and
     overblown"; the "outlanders" defended the latter as a work
     of "greater vision and greater durability." The final
     vote was eight to seven, in Gardner's favor.

1169 Olsson, Kurt. "Character and Truth in The Owl and the
     Nightingale." Chaucer Review, 11 (1977), 367-68.
       Unlike Gardner (The Owl and the Nightingale: A Burlesque,"
     1966), Olsson sees a serious side to the poem's comedy.

1170 Phillips, Cassandra. Interview with Raymond Carver. Eureka
     (Calif.) Times Standard, 24 July 1977, pp. 1-2.*
       Carver discusses his relationship with Gardner, then his
     teacher, at Chico State University. (Cited in David Boxer
     and Cassandra Phillips, Iowa Review, Summer 1979.)

1171 Taylor, John A. Letter. New York Times Book Review, 11
September 1977, p. 56.
    Gardner's highly critical review of Thomas Williams's
Tsuga's Children "seems more personal than critical."
Gardner "makes writing and reading serious novels sound
like pumping iron...." The kind of "'preaching'"
Williams does in this book is in the best tradition of
children's literature.

1978

1172 Arnold, Marilyn. "Nickel Mountain: John Gardner's Testament of Redemption." Renascence, 30 (Winter 1978), 59-68.
    A believer in the moral function of art, Gardner tries
to make redemption real by writing about it. The "thematic
structure" of NM involves "the juxtaposition of the common
and the mysterious, the real and the unreal, the crass
and the sublime, the human and the divine." This process
leads to an affirmation of "the redemptive power of human
goodness" in the novel's final chapter, "a fictional essay
which harmonizes and reconciles the dualities of the novel
just as redemption harmonizes and reconciles the painful
ambiguities of human experience." Henry Soames symbolizes
"the union of the gross and the godlike." The Goat-Lady
is a Disney witch who leaves her curse on the land, and
George Loomis, by choosing not to share his guilt, becomes its redeemer. The novel's imagery is overtly religious and moves back and forth between "the light and
the dark."

1173 Atchity, Kenneth J. "Acknowledgements." Homer's Iliad:
The Shield of Memory. Literary Structures series.
Carbondale and Edwardsville: Southern Illinois University
Press; London and Amsterdam: Feffer & Simons, 1978, p. xi.
    Thanks Gardner, the series editor, for his help in
revision.

1174 Barth, John. "Lil'l Ole Pussycat" (letter to the editor).
Baltimore Sun, 6 May 1978, p. A14.
    Gardner and Barth did not "debate" the issue of moral
fiction as claimed by an uninvited reporter, Tom Nugent,
in his article, "Two Literary Giants Tangle," Baltimore
Sun, 2 May 1978. Rather, Gardner was invited by Barth
to speak at the Johns Hopkins Writing Seminars. The
argument he presented there deserves "no loftier or
further rebuttal than a note to the morning newspaper."

As for Gardner's book, OMF, it is "an intellectually immoral, self-serving, finally demagogical attack on his
contemporaries, many of whom (in my opinion) are immensely
more talented than himself. And his distinction between
'primary' and 'secondary' fiction is an egregious, almost
dangerous muddle." The writers Gardner considers
"secondary" often tell us more about life "than do Gardner's
own later novels, for example: extravagantly overpraised
by lovers of the slack and the simplistic."

1175 Baxter, Robert. "Favorite Old Tale Gets New Twists."
Cherry Hill (N.J.) Courier-Post, [? December 1978].
   Paulette Haupt-Nolan, conductor for the Opera Company
of Philadelphia performance of Rumpelstiltskin, describes
it as "full of surprises," "a kaleidoscopic opera" that
will appeal to all ages and anyone who enjoys "Broadway
tunes, Mozart's 'Magic Flute' and 'Mary Hartman, Mary
Hartman.'" Gardner's libretto, reports director Peter
Mark Shifter, has "an off-beat sense of humor" and
characters possessing "a psychological depth" rarely
found in children's theater; "We've set 'Rumpelstiltskin'
in the late 19th century ["a Dickensian bookland"] and
given it a 1970s feel."

1176 "Biggest Gnome I ever Saw." Philadelphia Bulletin, [?
December 1978].
   Three photographs of Elwood Thornton (Rumpelstiltskin)
during a visit to a local school.

1177 Blair, Walter, and Hamlin Hill. America's Humor: From
Poor Richard to Doonesbury. New York: Oxford University
Press, 1978, p. 470.
   To the twenty-five post-World War II American novelists
cited by James M. Miller, Jr., in Quests Surd and Absurd
(1967) whose work deals with "the nightmare world, alienation and nausea, the quest for identity, and the comic
doomsday vision," Blair and Hill add seven more, including Gardner.

1178 Bush, Douglas. "Literature, the Academy, and the Public."
Daedalus, 107, iv (1978), 173-74.
   Although some critics claim contemporary literature
no longer has any special "moral or spiritual power,"
others--Gardner, Bellow, and F. R. Leavis in particular--
hold to the more traditional humanistic position.

1179 Cacavas, Elena. "Gardner Accused of Foul Play."
Spectrum (SUNY-Buffalo), 28 (14 April 1978), 3.
　　Gardner, who is being considered for the English Department's James McNulty Chair, has been accused of undocumented
paraphrasing in his LTC. (See Peter S. Prescott, "Theft
or Paraphrase," Newsweek, 10 April 1978.)

1180 Chastain, Sue. "'Rumpelstiltskin': Pupils' Grimm Turns
to Giggles." Philadelphia Inquirer, [? December 1978].
　　This report on a visit by the Philadelphia cast to a
local elementary school includes descriptions of several
characters' roles.

1181 Cowart, David. "John Champlin Gardner, Jr. " In
American Novelists Since World War II. Ed. Jeffrey
Helterman and Richard Layman. Dictionary of Literary
Biography, vol. 2. Detroit: Gale Research, 1978, pp.
175-85.
　　The question which Gardner asks in all his work is "how
can existential man . . . live in such a way as to foster
life-affirming values, regardless of how ultimately pro-
visional they may prove?" Toward this end he attempts "to
confute or reshape the fiction of exhaustion and despair
now fashionable." G, for example, involves a "dynamic
tension" between the nihilistic monster and the faith
implied in the book's structure. SD, a dialectical novel
and perhaps his best work, suggests an entropic universe
in which "the horrors of chance [are] harder to gainsay"
than in G. JM is "a vast archaeological restoration
project" the merit of which is as yet uncertain. A major
achievement of Gardner's next published work, NM, is his
"rendering of the verbal inadequacies of people painfully
inarticulate...." And in OL Gardner shows how the kind
of despair found in The Smugglers is also present in
rural Vermont, where it can lead to a far different, affirmative conclusion. (Includes facsimile manuscript
page from an early draft of G.)

1182 DeSchauensee, Max. "A Sophisticated Musical Fairy Tale."
Philadelphia Bulletin, 27 December 1978, p. B38.
　　As Baber has said, Rumpelstiltskin is not a work written
for children; rather it is "a sophisticated comic opera."
The abundance of characters and action (especially the
ballet) tends to obscure the story; nonetheless, the opera
is entertaining.

1183 Dean, Audrey. "It's Not a Children's Opera." Philadelphia Bulletin, [? December 1978].
Gardner and Baber hope Rumpelstiltskin will establish their operatic reputation. Each of their operas has "an explicit message." Frankenstein, "not yet produced in its entirety," concerns the difference between technological progress and love. Rumpelstiltskin, Baber notes, advises adults "'not to forget the ideals you had as children.'" Margaret Everitt, planning director of the Opera Company of Philadelphia, first became interested in Rumpelstiltskin after listening to a National Public Radio tape recording. It is, contends Baber, an opera "for our century," one meant to reach people not ordinarily reached by classical opera.

1184 DeLeon, Clark. "The Scene." Philadelphia Inquirer, 20 December 1978.
Captioned photograph for the Opera Company of Philadelphia production of Rumpelstiltskin.

1185 Fisher, John H. "The Revision of the Prologue to the Legend of Good Women: An Occasional Explanation." South Atlantic Bulletin, 43 (November 1978), 78, 83.
Although he does not dismiss Gardner's explanation of Chaucer's revision (PC), Fisher does disagree with it.

1186 Forman, Nessa. "For Kids: A Season of Delights." Philadelphia Bulletin, 8 December 1978, pp. 29, 32.
Rumpelstiltskin is listed as one of the holiday activities for children.

1187 Fremont-Smith, Eliot. "Making Book." Village Voice, 1 May 1978, p. 77.
Notes the plagiarism charge recently brought against Gardner. In passing, calls LTC "delightful" and OMF "unctuous."

1188 "Gardner, John (Champlin, Jr.)." Current Biography, 39 (October 1978), 13-16. Rpt. in Current Biography Yearbook 1978. Ed. Charles Moritz. New York: The H. W. Wilson Co., 1978, pp. 145-48.
All of Gardner's work evidences the search "for meaning and stability in an alien and indifferent universe." In his fiction he presents himself "as a shaper of conduct" and in his criticism "as a knowledgeable and enthusiastic guide." (The survey of Gardner's life and works is drawn

from the appended list of references, one of which—
Washington Post, 24 January 1977, p. 25—is incorrect.)

1189 "Gardner Reviews Book of Tolstoi's Letters." Binghamton
Press, 31 October 1978.
      Gardner will review Tolstoi's Letters, ed. R.F. Christian,
on 1 November at the Binghamton Public Library

1190 Gibson, Gail McMurray. "'Port haec clausa erit': Comedy,
Conception, and Ezekiel's Closed Door in the Ludus
Coventriae Play of 'Joseph's Return.'" Journal of
Medieval and Renaissance Studies, 8 (1978), 139, 153.
      Gardner (Wakefield) is the only critic who has attempted
to explain Mak's persistent knocking in the Second
Shepherds' Play.

1191 Grumbach, Doris. "Fine Print." Rev. of The World
According to Garp, by John Irving. Saturday Review, 13
May 1978, p. 42.
      In OL, the connection between the main story and the
"Gothic novel within ... is clever rather than symbiotic,"
as in Garp.

1192 Hall, C. Ray. "UK's Baber Revitalized." Lexington
(Kentucky) Herald-Leader, 15 October 1978, pp. E1, E6.
      Joseph Baber discusses his personal life and professional
career, especially his work with Gardner. Their first
opera, Frankenstein, is too costly to produce. Their
second, Rumpelstiltskin, involves a story "so familiar
that we didn't have to use the music to tell it." It
was performed in Lexington in 1977 and will be staged by
the Opera Company of Philadelphia in late December 1978.
Both PBS and CBS are interested in a possible television
showing.

1193 Harris, Harry. "In One Corner, NBC; in the Other, CBS."
Philadelphia Inquirer, 25 December 1978, p. E9.
      There will be a live airing of Rumpelstiltskin Thursday,
28 December 1978, on WUHY-FM and an intermission interview
with Gardner and Baber.

1194 Henderson, Bill. "Introduction." The Pushcart Prize,
III: Best of the Small Presses. Ed. Bill Henderson,
Yonkers, N.Y.: Pushcart Press, 1978, pp. 12-13.
      Gardner has received a Lamport Foundation award for his
essay, "Moral Fiction."

1195 Hendin, Josephine. *Vulnerable People: A View of American Fiction Since 1945*. New York: Oxford University Press, 1978, pp. 24-25, 133-40, 142, 218, 221.

The man of action "who wills one thing intensely enough to get it" fascinates Gardner. His heroes do not "stand for what is right, but simply ... stand in a condition of obsession, fully accepting one's own outrageous wrath." Throughout Gardner's work there are Oedipal conflicts "in which the sons are never up to the fight" and male-female power struggles (NM, for example, parodies the chivalric code: "the helpless princess" turns businesswoman and defeats "the knight of charity"). Pitting one obsession against another, Gardner's novels are fast-paced and complex, but because he is so cynical about the heroic ideal, his novels lack "a sense of masculine purposiveness" and as a result end in "moral paralysis." (Hendin briefly discusses Gardner's children's story, "The Shape Shifters of Shorm," as it conveys the same message found in contemporary adult fiction: "people can endure by self-transformation, by instability, by playing parts, but ... the dream of order and stability kills.")

1196 Howell, John M. "John Gardner." In *First Printings of American Authors, Contributions Toward Descriptive Checklists*. Ed. Matthew Bruccoli et al. Detroit: Gale Research, 1978, III:117-23.

An illustrated (title-pages and dust-jackets), enumerative checklist of first printings (American and English) of Gardner's separate publications (books, pamphlets, journals edited, and broadside) and contributions to books by other authors.

1197 "John Gardner at SUNY." *Binghamton Press*, c. 1 April 1978.

Gardner will read from his works on 4 April.

1198 Keisler, George R. "In Defense of the Bradshaw Shift." *Chaucer Review*, 12 (1978), 195, 197, 200, 201.

Arguments such as Gardner's in "The Case Against the 'Bradshaw Shift'" (1967) and PC are ingenious but cannot be factually supported.

1199 Laskin, Daniel. "Challenging the Literary Naysayers." *Horizon*, 21 (July 1978), 32-36.

As critic, Gardner "is bound to enrich the climate in which fiction is written and read." OMF "is a muscular

book filled with almost embarrassingly traditional asser-
tions about what literature should and should not be."
In it, Gardner "insists that fiction writers must do more
than pose questions." While versatility may seem the keynote of Gardner's own career, what actually unifies his
work--both scholarly and imaginative--is his consistent
"love of fable" and interest in moral literature. In his
novels, settings are usually rural and spiritualized;
despite the abundant literary allusions and philosophizing, they are truly storybooks, often involving "spirirual
quests." His "heroes typically slide into a crisis of
faith, their old values begin to crumble under mysterious,
menacing pressures of the stress of human conflict. But
they grope and stumble toward a new, modified sense of
order in life." Gardner has in-progress one more major
novel and another critical work, "The Art of Fiction";
otherwise, Gardner, recently separated from his wife and
operated on for cancer, seems ready "to scale down his
expectations."

1200 Le Vot, Andre. "New Modes of Story-Telling in Recent
American Writings: The Dismantling of Contemporary Fiction."
In Les Americanistes: New French Criticism on Modern
American Fiction. Ed. Ira D. Johnson and Christiane
Johnson. Port Washington, N.Y.: Kennikat, 1978, pp. 126-27.
   G is a novel in the "conjunctive" mode, "significant in
that its android narrator is first a victim before turning
into an aggressor, and that he remains a victim so far as
he partly identifies with the society he wants to
annihilate."

1201 Levine, George. "Notes Toward a Humanist Anti-Curriculum."
Humanities in Society, 1 (1978), 228.
   OMF is "a cantankerous, even silly book"; Gardner's
demanding moral relevance in the arts is naive and at odds
with his own fine modernist novels.

1202 Lingeman, Richard R. "Book Ends." New York Times Book
Review, 19 March 1978, p. 55.
   Gardner is one of the seven authors included in the
Public Broadcasting System series, The Originals: The
Writer in America, to begin 20 March 1978.

1203 Lunden, Rolf. "American Fiction Today." American Studies
in Scandinavia, 10 (1978), 65-72.*
   Mentions Gardner's review of Beyond the Bedroom Wall, by

Larry Woiwode, New York Times Book Review, 28 September 1975. Cited in Arts and Humanities Citation Index, 1978.

1204 Mack, Maynard. "The Second Shepherds' Play: A Reconsideration." PMLA, 93 (January 1978), 85.
Mack distinguishes his reading from Gardner's in Wakefield.

1205 Main Line (Penn.) Times, 28 December 1978, p. 9.
Captioned photograph of puppets used in Opera Company of Philadelphia production of Rumpelstiltskin.

1206 Milosh, Joseph. "John Gardner's Grendel: Sources and Analogues." Contemporary Literature, 19 (Winter 1978), 48-57.
Gardner has taken liberties "with his most obvious source," Beowulf. His Grendel is not "the static character" of the epic; instead, he is humanized. In the novel, war is "antiheroic" and absurd, and the Shaper is a liar, a basely motivated entertainer. The form of Gardner's novel resembles that of a medieval exemplum and, even more, in its tonal emphasis on human limitations, its "self-conscious parody of rhetoric," and its humor, Chaucer's "Nun's Priest's Tale." As for Grendel's final words in the novel, these may be not a curse but "a Boethian observation meant to remind man that he is not in control."

1207 Minugh, David. "John Gardner Constructs Grendel's Universe." Studies in English Philology, Linguistics, and Literature: Presented to Alarik Rynell 7 March 1978. Ed. Mats Ryden and Lennart A. Bjork. Stockholm Studies in English, 46. Stockholm: Almqvist & Wiksell, 1978, pp. 125-41.*
The structure of G is based on the twelve astrological signs, each of which contributes to Grendel's "understanding of the self in the universe, particularly the role of man as Shaper." (Annotation is drawn from American Literary Scholarship: An Annual/1978, p. 486.)

1208 Morace, Robert A. "John Gardner's The Sunlight Dialogues: A Giant (Paperback) Leap Backwards." Notes on Contemporary Literature, 8 (September 1978), 5-6.
On p. 621 of the first edition (Knopf) of Gardner's self-reflexive novel SD, the Sunlight Man says, "'There's always the future, p. 622.'" This passage appears on p. 655 of

256

the reset "Book Club Edition" where the quoted page is appropriately altered to "656." No similar change was made for the third American edition (the Ballantine paperback) where the passage, unrevised, appears on p. 686. Readers of the paperback edition will, as a result, be confused about and perhaps misled concerning Gardner's intention.

1209 Myers, Robin, ed. Dictionary of Literature in the English Language: From 1940 to 1970. New York and London: Pergamon Press, 1978, p. 114.
Briefly noted.

1210 Nardo, Anna K. "Fantasy Literature and Play: An Approach to Reader Response Criticism." Centennial Review, 22 (1978), 210-13.
G shows the consequence of not being able to play. Though once a playful child and later still tempted by man's play-beliefs, Grendel is for the most part like the modern reader, too "sophisticated" and "self-critical" to participate in play activities. As a result he fails to perceive his world freshly and finds no imaginative escape from the fact of his mortality.

1211 Peck, Russell A. "Chaucer and the Nominalist Question." Speculum, 53 (1978), 753.
Gardner's equation of nominalism with skepticism in PC needs rethinking.

1212 Peck, Russell A. "Preface." Kingship and Common Profit in Gower's Confessio Amantis. Literary Structures series. Carbondale and Edwardsville: Southern Illinois University Press; London and Amsterdam: Feffer & Simons, 1978, p. xviii.
Thanks Gardner, the series editor, for his encouragement.

1213 Philadelphia Inquirer, [? December 1978].
Captioned photograph of a duet from Rumpelstiltskin performed at the Philadelphia Museum of Art.

1214 Philadelphia Inquirer, 29 December 1978.
Captioned photograph of the Opera Company of Philadelphia production.

1215 Rovit, Earl. "The American Novelist: A Semi-Seismological View." Wilson Quarterly, 2 (Winter 1978), 121.
Rovit includes Gardner in his "elite group of 30 of our more successful novelists."

1216 "Rumpelstiltskin Coloring Contest." Jewish Exponent
(Philadelphia), 15 December 1978, p. 98.
Winners receive two tickets each to the Opera Company
of Philadelphia production.

1217 "'Rumpelstiltskin' to Open Tuesday." Wilmington (Del.)
Morning News, 22 December 1978, p. 18.
Cites cast, director, conductor, et al. connected with
the Philadelphia production.

1218 Sale, Roger. "The Golden Age of the American Novel."
Ploughshares, 4, iii (1978), 145.
Gardner is mentioned as one of the writers who have
made this the golden age of the American novel.

1219 Sale, Roger. "Picking Up the Pieces." Rev. of Refiner's
Fire, by Mark Helprin. New York Review of Books, 25 (23
February 1978), 42.
Refiner's Fire does not merit the praise Gardner gave
it (New Republic, 3 December 1977).

1220 Schlobin, Roger C. "An Annotated Bibliography of
Fantasy Fiction." CEA Critic, 40, ii (1978), 38.
G is the story of Beowulf told from the monster's point
of view."

1221 Solomon, Eric. "Stephen Crane: An Autobibliography."
Studies in the Novel, 10 (Spring 1978), 101.
While working on Stephen Crane: From Parody to Realism
(1966) at San Francisco State University, Solomon discussed his "conceptualizations" with his colleague Gardner
"who was then contemplating his own parodic-realistic
novel G."

1222 Stall, Marilyn Hubbart. "Structural Techniques in
Grendel." South Central Bulletin, 38 (Fall 1978), 119.
(Abstract of paper.)
Although Gardner's retelling of Beowulf from the monster's
point of view suggests "a philosophic view of moral relativity," Grendel is not a trustworthy narrator and "in
fact lives in a world of moral absolutes not much different
from those accepted by the Beowulf poet."

1223 Stevick, Philip. "Other People: Social Texture in the
Post-War Novel." Missouri Review, 1 (Spring 1978), 76-78.
Rpt. in revised form in Alternative Pleasures: Postrealist
Fiction and the Tradition (Urbana: Univ. of Illinois

Press, 1981).
Unlike many post-war fictions, NM evidences a recent
interest in characterization and human relationships.
Gardner neither condescends to nor distances himself from
his characters; rather, he deals with them "tenderly" and
asserts "the truth of certain truisms."

1224 Stromme, Craig John. "Barth, Gardner, Coover, and Myth."
D.A. diss. SUNY-Albany 1978, pp. 1-20, 110-93, and
passim.
The general direction of Gardner's fiction, like that
of Barth and Coover, is away from realism and towards a
non-referential fiction of "mythic forms." Believing
that the world is no longer "univocal," each chooses to
create his own "world of discourse, a shared bond built
of words." Despite similarities in Gardner's early works
(especially the theme of social engagement), SD is more
self-conscious and more concerned with myth and philosophical ideas than Res or NM. WA, though badly flawed, is
an important transitional work, especially interesting in
that Gardner here sides with Agathon, his most complete
embodiment of existential freedom in the first four books.
In G and JM the freedom of the mythic characters is cir-
cumscribed by the literary sources from which they are
drawn; in both works, Gardner indicts the universe, not
his characters, as the guilty party. [Stromme's discussion of G has been published separately; see the annotation for "The Twelve Chapters of Grendel," Critique, 1978.]
Only when Gardner creates a world of his own in KI does
he actually overcome his pessimism concerning the warfare
between faith and despair, order and chaos, and achieve
that affirmation about which he so often speaks. The
title novella, which at one level is an allegory of
Gardner's progress from realist to innovative writer, has
as its hero an artist, Upchurch, Gardner's most existen-
tially free character.

1225 Stromme, Craig J. "The Twelve Chapters of Grendel."
Critique, 20, i (1978), 83-92.
The correct basis for interpreting Grendel is not
Beowulf; it is the system of astrological signs and
philosophical ideas which informs the novel. Instead
of developing character, this philosophical book presents
ideas: the Orphic theory of "the world as repetition and
endless cycles"; solipsism; sophism; Old Testament
theology; Whitehead's metaphysics (which "prevents

Grendel from accepting the simplified theological world-
view offered by the Shaper); existential skepticism;
New Testament ideals; Machiavellian statecraft; religious
hypocrisy; Nietzchean nihilism; Sartrean existentialism
(which enables Grendel to move "beyond a received definition of himself" and to define "the world in his own
terms"); and finally Beowulf's empiricism, which
returns Grendel to reality and to poetry, which springs
from contact with reality. Like the astrological year,
Grendel and Hrothgar's village follow a circular course:
their rise and decline and the implied birth of a new age
constitutes "a complete history of man's progress."

1226 Trimmer, Joseph F. The National Book Awards: An Index
to the First Twenty-Five Years. Boston: G.K. Hall, 1978,
pp. xi, xxiv, 241, 255, 272, 281, 282.
    NM was nominated for the 1974 National Book Award. The
failure of the fiction committee (Erskine Caldwell, George
P. Elliott, and Orville Prescott) to consider OL for the
1977 award recalls the "timidity" associated with the
selection of the Pulitzer Prizes.

1227 "UB Withdraws Offer to Novelist." Buffalo Courier-Express.
30 April 1978, p. B3.
    The allegation of undocumented paraphrasing in LTC and
Gardner's failing to submit a budget proposal for a
literary magazine were two reasons given by George R.
Levine, Provost of Arts and Letters at SUNY-Buffalo, for
the University's withdrawing its offer of a creative
writing position.

1228 Webster, Daniel. "It's Rumpelstiltskin and It's a
Miracle." Philadelphia Inquirer, 24 December 1978.
    Joseph Baber explains how planning director Margaret
Everitt's interest in Rumpelstiltskin resulted in the
Opera Company of Philadelphia production at the Walnut
Street Theatre, 26-30 December 1978--a production now
largely out of the hands of composer and librettist.
Baber also describes his relationship with Gardner and
their Samson and Delilah (to be performed at the
University of Iowa) and The Pied Piper (in the planning
stage). "John and I believe that opera should be based
on legends and myths. We like gnomes and dragons....
We don't worry about writing the masterpiece."

1229 Webster, Daniel. "An Opera Witty and Wonderful."
Philadelphia Inquirer, 28 December 1978, p. 5B.
    Baber's score is "workable" but not vivid. The

260

libretto evidences "Gardner's zest for language." Both
are satiric. Setting and characters (only the gnome is
"lovable"), done in caricature, are overtly literary and
successful. The opera's message is that "the point of
life is to do the best you can."

1979

1230 Bahn, Sonja. "The Existential Monster: the Use of Mythic
Pattern in John Gardner's Grendel." In Forms of the
American Imagination: Beitrage zur neuren amerikanischen
Literatur. Ed. Sonja Bahn et al. Innsbrucker Beitrage
Zur Kulturwissenschaft, special issue 44. Innsbruck:
Institut fur Sprachwissenschaft, 1979, pp. 157-64.
Although G is perhaps neither as profound nor as narra-
tively ambitious as Res or WA, it is a more successfully
realized work. In G Gardner measures the modern age "by
subjecting it to the patterns of the past and then, in
typical twentieth-century fashion, debunks his own efforts
with a sweeping gesture of irony" by calling his story a
sand castle. The novel's structure is twofold. The
astrological structure creates "an ascending-descending-
ascending movement" that reflects Grendel's innocence,
knowledge through negative experience, and resignation.
The second structural device corresponds to the idea of
the tripartite soul which Gardner discussed in his
"Fulgentius's Expositio Vergiliana Continentia and the
Plan of Beowulf" (1970).

1231 Baxter, Robert. "A Reason To Exist: Serving the Public,
Young and Old, Is the Goal of the Opera Company of
Philadelphia." Opera News, 44 (November 1979), 25-28.
Among OCP's educational programs are workshops for
students in grades 4-6 dealing with the revival of the
"children's opera Rumpelstiltskin."

1232 Besserman, Lawrence L. "The Wakefield Noah, Lines 55-56,"
Papers on Language and Literature, 15 (1979), 83.
Cites Gardner's "Imagery and Illusion in the Wakefield
Noah Play" (1968) approvingly.

1233 Boxer, David, and Cassandra Phillips. "Will You Please
Be Quiet, Please?: Voyeurism, Dissociation, and the Art
of Raymond Carver." Iowa Review, 10 (Summer 1979), 75,
90.
While a student at Chico State College, Carver would
rummage through his teacher John Gardner's manuscripts,
borrowing titles for use in his own stories.

1234 Brady, Frank. "Move Over, TV--Radio Is Booming." Parade,
7 October 1979, pp. 4-5.
Gardner's The Temptation Game is mentioned as one of the
plays in National Public Radio's Earplay series which
"have captured a new audience of radio followers."

1235 Braudy, Leo. "Realists, Naturalists, and Novelists of
Manners." In Harvard Guide to Contemporary American
Writing. Ed. Daniel Hoffman. Cambridge, Mass.: The
Belknap Press of Harvard University Press, 1979, pp. 118-20.
Gardner's career clearly reflects "the uncertain situa-
tion of the traditional naturalist novel" in contemporary
American literature. Like other American writers, Gardner
identifies with the alien-figure. He locates truth not in
history but in myth and ritual. His moral concerns are
blunted, however, by an intrusive "literary self-consciousness" and this "uncertainty" of purpose is implicit in
OMF.

1236 Butts, Leonard Culver. "Nature in the Selected Works of
Four Contemporary American Novelists." Diss. University
of Tennessee at Knoxville 1979.
Unlike many contemporary American writers, who are pre-
occupied with the bleakness of today's mechanized society,
Gardner, Dickey, Brautigan, and Updike offer an alternative: the return to nature as a way to recover "wholeness
of being." Res, NM, SD, and OL are all concerned with the
discovery of the "universal morality of life" by means of
the human imagination and its corollaries, sympathy, compassion, and understanding. Gardner's nature is an inter-
connected whole, at once chaotic and orderly and therefore a reflection of human life. His characters journey
from self-pity, self-righteousness, and society's
restrictive systems of order to "aesthetic wholeness."
As artists they affirm "the totality of existence" and in
this way erect "a moral center toward which each human
being may aim."

1237 Clark, Jerold. Letter. New York Times Magazine, 12
August 1979, p. 62.
Response to Stephen Singular's "The Sound and Fury
Over Fiction," New York Times Magazine, 8 July 1979;
Gardner unmasks contemporary fiction as the "con" it
really is.

1238 Clute, John. "Gardner, John (Champlin)." In The Science
     Fiction Encyclopedia. Ed. Peter Nicholls. Garden City,
     N.Y.: Doubleday, 1979, pp. 243-44.
        In G Gardner "renders Anglo-Saxon man's triumphs as
     allegorical of the rise of the cruel, modern, industrial
     world."

1239 Cochran, Carol M. "Flyting in the Mystery Plays."
     Theatre Journal, 31 (1979), 187.
        In viewing flyting as a sign of disorder, Gardner
     (Wakefield) subverts the comic intention of the plays.

1240 Corwin, Norman. "Corwin on Media: Hero." Westways, 71
     (October 1979), 68-71.
        The interview published in the July 1979 issue of
     Horizon betrays Gardner's ignorance of radio production,
     his facile approach to the differences between high and
     low art (including his citing incomprehensibility as a
     characteristic of the former), and, as in OMF, his
     tendency to make sweeping and poorly considered judgments.

1241 Cummins, Walter. "Inventing Memories: Apocalyptics and
     Domestics." Literary Review, 23 (Fall 1979), 127-33.
        "Domestics" such as Gardner, have supplanted
     "Apocalyptics," such as Pynchon, and now form the main-
     stream of contemporary American fiction. Although both
     groups are often self-consciously inventive, the
     Domestics are chiefly concerned with personal memories,
     family life, fiction as a means of authenticating reality,
     and love as a way to transcend adversity and death; unlike
     the Apocalyptics, who focus on alientation, the Domestics
     emphasize the themes of hope and continuity. (Discusses
     NM and OL.)

1242 "Curtain rises Friday." Binghamton Press [or Sun-
     Bulletin?], 25 November 1979, p. C14.
        Days of Vengeance, by Gardner, and Eden's Rock, by Jan
     Quackenbush (co-directed by Liz Rosenberg), will premiere
     Friday and Saturday at the Laurel Street Theater in
     Susquehanna, Penn.

1243 Estes, Bruce. "Plays Draw 'Preacher's Crowd.'"
     Binghamton Sun-Bulletin, 1 December 1979.
        Gardner's Days of Vengeance and Jan Quackenbush's Eden's
     Rock "will be the highlight of Susquehanna's drama season."
     Priscilla Gardner's performance as Alice Honeywell is
     "remarkable." (Each play is briefly summarized.)

1243a Fisher, John H. Rev. of LTC. Studies in the Age of Chaucer, 1 (1979), 170-77.

LTC is a pleasure to read, but Gardner's Chaucer is "implausible," his history "unreliable," and his literary interpretations "quixotic." Gardner's views of late Fourteenth-Century England and the roles of John of Gaunt, Alice Perrers, and Richard II in Chaucer's life are unfounded and at times absurd. Instead of using the biography to elucidate the poems, Gardner uses the poems to support his biographical conjectures. The theory that in his late poems Chaucer was "creating intentionally bad art" is chronologically untenable.

1244 Forsman, Theresa. "The Novelist as Actor, Playright, Teacher." Binghamton Press [or Sun-Bulletin?], 25 November 1979, pp. Cl, C?.

Gardner is tired of the uproar that followed publication of OMF, adding that in part the response was "deserved, because I got impatient." The image of Gardner as hatchet man does not square with the Gardner who is co-starring in one play for the Laurel Street Theater in Susquehanna, Penn. (Eden's Rock by Jan Quackenbush) and who has written another (Days of Vengeance, to be performed by his mother). Friends and colleagues agree that there is more to Gardner than just the author of OMF. Edmund Epstein believes Gardner's positive ideas have been distorted. John Howell comments on Gardner's sense of mission and his forthrightness. Robert P. Griffin discusses the way Gardner "fictionalizes real life" and lives in a world he imagines. The dedication to teaching noted by Barry Targan has led Gardner to leave teaching for the next semester in order to devote himself to writing. Gardner also comments on the pleasure he takes in having Days of Vengeance produced by an amateur group, whose spontaneity he prizes. Gardner's mother, Priscilla, describes the work as "a beautiful play" about "the problem of what to do with older people."

1245 Gordon, William M. "Exemplum and Thoma More's History of King Richard III." Clio, 9 (1979), 86.

Quotes Wakefield approvingly.

1246 Griffin, Bryan F. "III. Literary Vogues: Getting Cheever While He's Hot." Harper's, 258 (June 1979), 90-93.

Belittles Gardner's praise of Falconer (Saturday Review, 2 April 1977).

1247 Groth, Janet. "Fiction vs. Anti-Fiction Revisited."
     Commonweal, 106 (11 May 1979), 269-71.
     Discusses the Fiction Festival held at the University
     of Cincinnati in October 1978. Gardner's position is
     that of the traditional realist; the fiction he calls
     moral assumes a moral structure or belief which the anti-
     fiction of Barth, Hawkes, Gass, and Elkin does not. Their
     work is unsettling not simply because it is linguistically
     complex but, more significantly, because it concerns the
     reality of there being no such governing structure, no
     final meanings or messages. In this respect, their work
     is less perverse than Gardner claims--more powerful, even
     moral. (See also the interview conducted by Thomas Le-
     Clair, *New Republic*, 10 March 1979.)

1248 Hari. *Variety*, 24 January 1979, p. 98.
     "Most familiar stories tend to become tedious, but
     novelist John Gardner has introduced many sly surprises
     that continually sustain interest. Also repeatedly
     serendipitous is Joseph Baber's eclectic, sometimes
     Gilbert-and-Sullivan score." There is fantasy for the
     children and satire for the adults. (Characters and
     setting of *Rumpelstiltskin* are described in detail.)

1249 Henderson, Bill, ed. *Pushcart Prize, IV: Best of the
     Small Presses.* Yonkers, N.Y.: Pushcart Press, 1979, p.
     15.
     Gardner is listed among the contributing editors; also
     listed in vols. V and VI.

1250 Hendin, Josephine. "Experimental Fiction." *Harvard Guide
     to Contemporary American Writing*. Ed. Daniel Hoffman.
     Cambridge, Mass.: The Belknap Press of Harvard University
     Press, 1979, 253-54.
     Although "traditional in form," Gardner's fictions are
     thematically "innovative in their concern with the dislo-
     cation of men who attempt to be heroic in the old sense
     in current times." Henry Soames and Taggert Hodge are
     chivalrous knights "done in" by predatory women. *G*,
     Gardner's "most experimental novel," is "a meditation,
     written in spectacular prose"; it "calls into question
     the unlovability of the hero as killer, negator, and
     scourge."

1251 Hoopes, James. "Modernist Criticism and Transcendentalist
     Literature." *New England Quarterly*, 52 (1979), 452.
     Gardner's dismissal (*OMF*) of the early criticism of
     I. A. Richards is "in a sense divorced from life" in that

Gardner fails to connect Richards the critic with Richards the man.

1252 Hubby, Nicholas. Letter. New York Times Book Review, 22 July 1979, p. 23.
      In response to Gardner's 27 May 1979 review of Styron's Sophie's Choice, Hubby calls Gardner's remarks on Polish collaboration with the Nazis glib and entirely unfounded. (Gardner's apologetic reply appears on the same page.)

1253 Hunt, George W. "Between the Groves and the Best-Sellers." Commonweal, 106 (11 May 1979), 267.
      Between the escapism of most best-sellers and the hermetic, "parochial," and ironic academic fiction of Barth et al., is "a middle avenue" comprising, at the first level, Bellow, Updike, Cheever, and Malamud and, a notch below, such writers as Walker Percy, Toni Morrison, and Gardner.

1254 Irving, John. "The Aesthetics of Accessibility: Kurt Vonnegut and His Critics." New Republic, 181 (22 September 1979), 44-45.
      Gardner's criticism of Vonnegut in OMF derives from his failure to understand that Vonnegut is not merely playing literary games or shirking responsibility to mankind. In fact, Vonnegut shares Gardner's desire to use literature to improve the world. Moreover, as Gardner himself points out, the cynicism associated with Vonnegut's work largely derives from readers, not the author.

1255 Ivasheva, Valentine. "How the Mind of Man Is Treated By Modern Writers." Soviet Literature, 5 (1979), 156-57.
      NM, a novel frequently discussed by Soviet critics, is "a good example of the new style of psychological analysis in current American literature," analysis which is subtle and indirect; the reader "must divine what is left unsaid and grasp the full importance of incidents which seem unimportant."

1256 Jacobson, Robert. "Reports: U.S." Opera News, 43 (24 February 1979), 50.
      Rumpelstiltskin is witty, sophisticated, and satirical. "Gardner's language is a joy, constantly animated." "Baber's music cannot be called greatly original, but it is full of lovely craft, clever ideas and an abundance of tunes." The staging--"a kid's world"--is imaginatively done.

1257 Jaeger, Ernest. "John Gardner." Rev. of the PBS series
The Originals. Film News, 36 (March-April 1979), 21.
Chiefly a description of the program; Jaeger notes that
Gardner's "comments are deep and provocative."

1258 Justus, James H. "Fiction: The 1950s to the Present."
In American Literary Scholarship: An Annual/1977. Ed.
James Woodress. Durham: Duke University Press, 1979, p.
337.
Briefly and objectively discusses Gardner's essays,
"Moral Fiction" and "The Idea of Moral Criticism."

1259 Kaes, Anton, and John Carlos Rowe. "Das Ende der
Avantgarde?" Lili, 9 (1979), 284.
Dissatisfied with the formal experimentation of post-
modernist writing, a number of younger writers, including
Gardner, John Irving, and Robert Pirsig, have committed
themselves to a new morality in literature.

1260 Klinkowitz, Jerome, and Loreee Rackstraw. "The American
1970's: Recent Intellectual Trends." Revue Francaise
d'Etudes Americaines (Sorbonnes), 8 (October 1979), pp.
243-54.
Like Gerald Graff in Literature Against Itself, Gardner
believes that art "imitates or translates reality." Con-
demning all innovative fiction as mere texture, he fails
to understand the innovative writer's point of view: that
fiction creates reality. The fiction Gardner endorses
is "escapist" in that (as Mas'ud Zavarzadeh argues in
The Mythopoeic Reality) it presents "'false assurances
about a nonexistent order.'"

1261 Kroll, Jack. "Culture Goes Pop." Newsweek, 94 (19
November 1979), 118.
Quotes approvingly from OMF.

1262 Ladensack, Carl. "Grendel." In "A Novel (Poem, Essay,
Story) To Teach," ed. Susan Koch Judy. English Journal,
68 (February 1979), 42-43.
G is an appropriate novel to teach to adolescents.
Students identify with Grendel, "the pathetic monster
that seeks acceptance, love and beauty" but only finds
"disillusionment" and "rejection" in the course of his
existential search. Thematically the novel is similar
to Salinger's Catcher in the Rye, though Gardner's
resonant tone is quite unlike Salinger's colloquialism.

1263 Laurenzi, L. In Il Ragguaglio Librario, 1979, pp. 4-5.*
     Cited in Dizionario della litteratura mondiale del 900
     (Rome: Edizone Paoline, 1980), p. 1145.

1264 LeClair, Thomas. "The Novelists: John Hawkes." New
     Republic, 181 (10 November 1979), p. 26.
     Although "the novelist's first allegiance is to his
     art," Hawkes adds that fiction must have "a moral center."
     "I haven't read John Gardner's book [OMF], but I would be
     disappointed if he didn't see my work as having the dark-
     est yet most luminous moral center of almost anyone else's."

1265 Lundkvist, Artur. Fantasi med Realism [The Realistic
     Imagination]. Stockholm: Liber Forlag, 1979, pp. 157-
     72. In Swedish.
     In his realistic fantasies (a combination of myth and
     history), Gardner develops a powerful and graphic realism
     that moves from the detailed narration of established
     myths towards the nearly metaphysical interpretation of
     myths and themes. His characters are typically American
     in that they exist on two noninterrelated levels: the
     real and the imaginative. (The works summarized and
     discussed are Res, WA, G, JM, SD, NM (Nickelberget), OL,
     and KI.) In order to continue writing, Gardner may have
     to force himself away from the despair and pessimism of
     his stylistically brilliant later works.

1266 McConnell, Frank. Storytelling and Mythmaking: Images
     from Film and Literature. New York: Oxford University
     Press, 1979, p. 56.
     "Even John Gardner, in his brilliant novel on the
     Beowulf theme, G, acknowledges that accident of memory
     [that usually only the first part of the Beowulf epic is
     remembered], though he manages to compress the whole
     mythic range of the epic into that first struggle."

1267 McDermott, John. "Mrs. Armstid: Faulkner's Moral
     Snag." Studies in Short Fiction, 16 (1979), 181, 182.
     Disagrees slightly with Gardner and Lennis Dunlap's
     interpretation (The Forms of Fiction, 1962) of the
     central conflict in Faulkner's "The Spotted Horses"
     and with their citing luck as the reason Mrs. Armstid
     escapes harm.

1268 Monroe, W.F. "Diagnosing Literary Autism." Rev. of
     Literature Against Itself, by Gerald Graff. Chicago
     Review, 31 (Summer 1979), 43-49.

Gardner and Graff share a number of views, but where
the anti-realists can safely ignore OMF ("uninformed and
unfocused") and its author ("pompously vocal but unconvincing"), Graff should be given serious attention. Unfortunately Gardner's book may have made it impossible
for Literature Against Itself to receive a fair hearing.

1269 Morace, Robert. Rev. of Literature Against Itself, by
Gerald Graff. Literary Review, 23 (Fall 1979), 145, 150.
Briefly discusses Graff's review of OMF (Chronicle of
Higher Education).

1270 Moyle, Natalie K. "Folktale Patterns in Gogol's Vij."
Russian Literature, 7 (1979), 679.
Vij, in which Gogol shifts the usual focus of folk tales
to the middle brother, is like G, which is told from the
monster's point of view.

1271 Nicholls, Peter. "Mythology." In The Science Fiction
Encyclopedia. Ed. Peter Nicholls. Garden City, N.Y.:
Doubleday, 1979, p. 417.
Retelling myths from the point of view of a contempor-
aneous "observer protagonist" is a widely used strategy,
as in three recent versions of Beowulf: G, Henry Treece's
The Green Man (1966), and Michael Crichton's Eaters of
the Dead (1976).

1272 "Novelist Gardner to Speak." Binghamton Press, 31
January 1979.
Gardner will speak about OMF at Temple Concord in
Binghamton.

1273 Pincus, Arthur. Letter. New York Times Magazine, 12
August 1979, p. 62.
Response to Stephen Singular's "The Sound and Fury
Over Fiction," New York Times Magazine, 8 July 1979;
Gardner deserves neither a cover story nor comparison
with Tolstoi.

1274 "Play by Gardner on FM Saturday." Binghamton Press, 28
May 1979.
The Temptation Game, produced by Minnesota Public Radio
in cooperation with the University of Wisconsin, will air
Saturday on Earplay.

1275 Priestley, Michael. "An Interview with John Irving."
New England Review, 1 (Summer 1979), 498.

269

OMF "is the kind of thing critics would write," Irving says, but he adds that Gardner is correct on many points and "a lot closer to the base of literature than William Gass will be for all his articulateness." The "strange polarization" between humanist story-telling and writing "exquisitely" is entirely artificial.

1276 "Publishable but Perishable." Binghamton Sun-Bulletin, 24 April 1979.
Gardner's opinion that most contemporary fiction is "terribly bad" rings true. (See interview with Beth Adelman, Binghamton Press, 23 April 1979.)

1277 Rabkin, Eric S. Fantastic Worlds: Myths, Tales, and Stories. New York: Oxford University Press, 1979, p. 468.
G is "a modern version of Beowulf touchingly retold from the monster's point of view."

1278 Reginald, R. Science Fiction and Fantasy Literature. Detroit: Gale Research, 1979, I:201.
Lists G.

1279 Rochester, Rosemary G. Letter. New York Times Book Review, 22 July 1979, p. 23.
Criticizes Gardner's "disregard for the reader" in giving away the plot of Styron's Sophie's Choice in his 27 May 1979 review. (Gardner's apologetic reply appears on the same page.)

1280 Schneider, Richard J. Rev. of The World Within the Word, by William Gass. Modern Fiction Studies, 25 (Winter 1979-80), 757-58.
Gass's collection of essays can be considered a counter-attack against OMF. Neither Gass nor Gardner is entirely correct; Gardner's fiction reveals his considerable interest in linguistic texture, just as Gass's prose evidences his moral concern.

1281 Scholes, Robert. Fabulation and Metafiction. Urbana: University of Illinois, 1979, p. 4.
Refers to Gardner as a fabulist.

1282 Singular, Stephen. "The Sound and Fury Over Fiction." New York Times Magazine, 8 July 1979, pp. 12-15, 34-36, 38-39.
Gardner is a man alternately friendly and ferocious. In OMF (begun in 1965 and "toned down" in 1975 for

publication) and the forthcoming "The Art of Fiction,"
Gardner "reveals a near-Messianic complex" about art,
one of his several similarities to Tolstoy. Responses
to OMF by Barth, Hugh Kenner, Updike, Bellow, and Mailer
(all of whom are quoted) do not trouble Gardner, whose
"debate" with William Gass continues the controversy over
fiction begun earlier in this century. (Gass, who sees
Gardner as an entertainer, objects to his "glibness and
preachiness" and recommends he "should revise more." In
Singular's judgment, Gardner's novels do not always meet
his own requirements for moral fiction. In G the reader
sides with the monster; SD is not an "'efficient'" use of
"'artistic energy,'" and OL fails to sustain "'a vivid
and continuous dream' in the reader's mind." (Singular
also comments on Gardner's "idyllic childhood" and early
writing.) See also the annotation for this entry listed
under "Interviews," and the "Letters to the Editor" by
Gardner, Singular, Arthur Pincus, Steven Scott Smith,
Ann Snitow, and Jerold Clark, New York Times Magazine,
12 August 1979. A review by Diane J. Cole quoted by
Singular has not been located.

1283 Singular, Stephen. Letter. New York Times Magazine, 12
August 1979, p. 62.
      Denies Gardner's charges (letter published on p. 62)
concerning distortion in Singular's "The Sound and Fury
Over Fiction," New York Times Magazine, 8 July 1979.

1284 Smith, Steven Scott. Letter. New York Times Magazine,
12 August 1979, p. 62.
      Response to Stephen Singular's "The Sound and Fury Over
Fiction," New York Times Magazine, 8 July 1979; Smith,
one of Gardner's former creative writing students, disliked
Gardner's class and assignments but acknowledges that the
"insistence on revision" has improved his writing considerably.

1285 Snitow, Ann. Letter. New York Times Magazine, 12 August
1979, p. 62.
      Response to Stephen Singular's "The Sound and Fury Over
Fiction," New York Times Magazine, 8 July 1979; the kind
of fiction Gardner is calling for is being written by
blacks, women, and the young--Toni Morrison, for one.
Why has Gardner overlooked them?

1286 Stanley, E. G. "Geoweorpa: 'Once Held in High Esteem.'"
In J. R. R. Tolkien, Scholar and Storyteller: Essays in

Memoriam. Ed. Mary Salu and Robert T. Farrell. Ithaca:
Cornell University Press, 1979, p. 117.
  Quotes a passage from chap. 8 of G, saying it "brings
out well Wealtheow's fears for her own sons" in Beowulf.

1287 Stern, Milton R. "Towards 'Bartleby the Scrivener.'"
In The Stoic Strain in American Literature. Ed. Duane J.
MacMillan. Toronto: University of Toronto Press, 1979,
pp. 21, 22, 201, 202.
  Gardner's "Bartleby: Art and Social Commitment" (1964)
is one of the many articles that deal with Melville's
story as a parable of the artist; the parallels Gardner
draws between characters and Bible are, Stern contends,
"rigid and silly."

1288 Stevens, Martin. "The Royal Stanza in Early English
Literature." PMLA, 94 (January 1979), 66, 75, 76.
  Cites LTC approvingly.

1289 Toman, Philip A. "Mostly Music." Newark (Del.) Weekly
Post, 3 January 1979, p. A13.
  Rumpelstiltskin is excellent family entertainment; only
the ballet is weak.

1290 Waldeland, Lynne. John Cheever. TUSAS 335. Boston:
Twayne, 1979, pp. 105-6, 110, 114, 115.
  Quotes extensively and approvingly from Gardner's
"Witchcraft in Bullet Park" (New York Times Book Review,
24 October 1971), which for the first time clearly
established the novel's place in Cheever's oeuvre and in
modern American fiction.

1291 Ward, Martha E., and Dorothy A. Marquardt. Authors of
Books for Young People. 2nd ed. supp. Metuchen, N.J.:
Scarecrow Press, 1979, p. 96.
  Brief sketch; mentions OL, Dragon, and Gudgekin.

1292 Webster, Daniel. "Opera Company of Philadelphia."
Opera Canada, 20 (Spring 1979), 27-28.
  Gardner's libretto for Rumpelstiltskin successfully mixes
narrative, satire, word play and elegant language and
slang. Baber's score is much less interesting. The opera,
which also includes visual puns, has as its themes "greed
... immaturity, self-seeking and the fragility of human
relations."

1293 Webster, Grant. The Republic of Letters: A History of
Postwar American Literary Opinion. Baltimore: Johns

Hopkins University Press, 1979, p. 123.
Bellow, Oates, and Gardner are three of the "eminent figures" who have published articles in the Aristotelian journal, Critical Inquiry.

1294 Wood, Irene. "Films." Rev. of "John Gardner" in the series The Originals: The Writer in America. Booklist, 75 (1 March 1979), 1098.
Describes the film's content, adding that "although Gardner's life appears to have changed considerably since this 1975 interview," his remarks and the relationship between writer and environment evoked in the film make it of lasting interest.

1295 Zanderer, Leo. "Roger Sale's Fairy Tales and After: Looking for Awe." Lion & the Unicorn, 3, i (1979), 113.
Gardner in OMF and Sale in Fairy Tales and After fail to take sufficiently into account the temporal aspect of human values.

1296 Zverev, A.M. "SSHA: Itogi goda--'moralnoe porazhenie'?" [USA. Results of the Year--Moral Defeat?]. Inostrannaya Literatura, 5 (1979), 209-14.*
Zverev takes exception to Gardner's negative view of recent American literature. (Annotation drawn from American Literary Scholarship: An Annual/1979, p. 461.)

1980

1297 Bailey, Peter. "Moral Fiction and Metafiction." fiction international, 12 (1980), 221-31. Also issued as Moral Fiction: An Anthology, ed. Joe David Bellamy. Canton, N.Y.: fiction international, 1980, pp. 221-31.
Gardner's views about the new fiction have changed radically. In 1973 he embraced metafiction; in 1978 he attacked it. His fictional practice, however, belies his recent "moral stance." Moreover, writers such as Barth, Barthelme, and Coover do heed Gardner's injunction that art must create socially useful myths, but they also extend it, maintaining that the critical examination of such myths is also socially useful. (Bailey specifically discusses Gardner's remarks on "Lost in the Funhouse," "Paraguay," and Coover's fiction.)

1298 Barth, John. "The Literature of Replenishment: Post-modernist Fiction." Atlantic, 245 (January 1980), 65-71.

Gardner's "first two published novels" are "distinctly
modernist works; his short stories dabble in postmodernism;
his polemical nonfiction is aggressively reactionary."

1299 Barth, John. In "How Is Fiction Doing?" New York Times
Book Review, 14 December 1980, p. 3.
The "literary convention-busting" which flourished in
the 1960s has given way to the conservativism of the 70s
and 80s. "The decade of the Moral Majority will doubtless
be the decade of Moral Fiction."

1300 Billy, Ted. "The King's Indian: Gardner's Imp of the
Poeverse." Notes on Modern American Literature, 5 (1980),
item 2.
Points to specific borrowings from Poe's Narrative of
Arthur Gordon Pym.

1301 Bjork, Robert E. "Oppressed Hebrews and the Song of
Azarias in the Old English Daniel." Studies in Philology,
77 (1980), 214, 222.
Gardner (CCP) misinterprets Daniel as an exemplum on
pride and obedience.

1302 Brans, Jo. "Stories to Comprehend Life: An Interview with
John Cheever." Southwest Review, 65 (1980), 340-41.
Coming from a New England background, Cheever would never
link fiction and morality, which to him connotes inflex-
ibility. However, because fiction is life-affirming,
Gardner's position in OMF (which Cheever has not read)
is accurate, though Gardner is mistaken in not seeing
Bellow as the most moral of today's writers.

1303 Brown, Rosellen. Rev. of The Bleeding Heart by Marilyn
French. New York Times Book Review, 16 March 1980, p. 29.
"They [the author's "huge audience"] want to know, in
John Gardner's words, how to live the next part of their
lives...."

1304 Butts, Leonard C. "Locking and Unlocking: Nature as
Moral Center in John Gardner's October Light." Critique,
22, ii (1980), 47-60.
In OL, as in other Gardner novels, the return to nature
represents a return to the past and a more satisfying
moral order. When the individual imposes a rigid order
on life, the results are "stasis, a limited vision, and
a lack of wholeness of being." Against these Gardner
posits "imagination, and its corollaries, sympathy,

compassion, and understanding." Both Sally and James cut
themselves off from human community and love and succumb
to the pernicious influence of irresponsible art. In key
scenes, each sees the world "in the light of a new day"
and learns the value of compromise and affirmation.

1305 Butts, Leonard C. "Gathering in John Gardner's Novels."
Tennessee Philological Bulletin, 17, i (July 1980), 54.
(Abstract of a paper read at the Tennessee Philological
Association meeting, February 1980.) In Res, NM, SD, and
OL, the "gathering of family, friends, and neighbors acts
as a catalyst for the release of human feelings and
emotions needed by the protagonist to complete his journey
toward reintegration and recovery of the whole self."
Chandler, Soames, Clumly, and James Page learn from these
encounters "not what life means" but "what life is, 'the
world, the buzzing, blooming confusion itself.'"

1306 Cohen, Andy. "Sunlight Dialogues: The Play Is Tedium
Unleashed." Binghamton Sun-Bulletin, 9 October 1980.
As might be expected of a three and one-half hour play
based on Gardner's "incredibly boring novel," Bielenberg's
work is tedious, despite the excellent sets, some fine
acting, and appropriate (if at times distracting and
atonal) music.

1307 Costa, Richard Hauer. "Notes from a Dark Heller: Bob
Slocum and the Underground Man." Texas Studies in
Literature and Language, 23 (Summer 1980), 164, 178-79,
181-82.
Takes issue with Gardner's criticism of Something
Happened in OMF.

1308 Costanzo, Angelo. "Letters." New York Times Book Review,
23 November 1980, p. 46.
Comments on Gardner's 12 October 1980 review of Calvino's
Italian Folktales.

1309 Cote, Margaret. "Establishing Reading Groups; or,
Selling Your Product on the Open Market." College
English, 42 (1980), 250.
Mentions the teaching of G as comparison/contrast with
Beowulf.

1310 Domini, John. "Letters and Ethics: The Moral Fiction of
John Barth." fiction international, 12 (1980), 248, 258.
Also issued as Moral Fiction: An Anthology, ed. Joe David

Bellamy. Canton, N.Y.: fiction international, 1980, pp. 248-258.
Briefly mentions Gardner's criticism of Barth in OMF.

1311 Duffy, Regis. A. "Unreasonable Expectations." Proceedings of the 34th Annual Convention of the Catholic Theological Society of America. Ed. L. S. Salm. Bronx: Catholic Theological Society of America, 1980, pp. 1-3. Gardner's critique of the reasonable religion of the uncommitted in chapters 9 and 11 of G is justified.

1312 Fish, Stephanie Pace. "Expanding Horizons: Character in the Contemporary Novel." Diss. University of Utah 1980. NM, along with Fowles's Daniel Martin and Patrick White's The Eye of the Storm, offers the reader "a model of human courage for the particular exigencies" of modern life. Having "the courage to be vulnerable" and the ability to accept human failings, Henry learns to live with shame and love. Unlike George and Willard, who evade responsibility and thus fail to become human, Henry embodies the heroism of everyday life, which is ultimately "more real ... than George's justified cynicism." Gardner's characterization of Henry makes this otherwise unexceptionable novel "a major achievement."

1313 Fisher, Benjamin Franklin, IV. "Fugitive Poe References: A Bibliography." Poe Studies, 13, i (1980), 35. In OMF Gardner perceptively notes that Poe's theory of beauty has nothing to do with truth or morality.

1314 Foeller, Elzbieta. "The Mythical Heroes of John Barth and John Gardner." Kwartalnik Neofilologiczny, 27, ii (1980), 183-97. Barth and Gardner emphasize the artist's role as the creator of meanings. They transform and expand mythic stories "to include the mythic hero's (or heroine's) middle age"; they focus attention on seemingly insignificant incidents in the original myths and emphasize the hero's "human aspects." Instead of "follow[ing] their destiny with a firm conviction of their worth," their heroes stumble through life, finding meaning in the act of searching for ultimate values no longer available to modern man. G provides an outsider's perspective of, rather than an ironic commentary on, the Beowulf story. In Gardner's retelling, Beowulf plays a minor part; Unferth is given greater prominence as he self-consciously and vainly attempts to become a genuine hero. And JM

is less an epic than a multi-layered dream vision; the form
supports Gardner's view that reality is ultimately unknowable.

1315 Foust, R. E. "Monstrous Image: Theory of Fantasy Antagonists." Genre, 13 (1980), 449-50.
    Gardner's tour-de-force G illustrates a theme common to
much of fantastic literature: "human society is built upon
the suppression of the organic relationship between civilization and nature, but that relationship establishes itself as a necessary madness taking the imagistic form of
a visual oxymoron, the chthonic doppelganger whose 'lack'
is the mirror image of human substance."

1316 French, Marilyn. "Spouses and Lovers." Rev. of Life
Before Man, by Margaret Atwood. New York Times Book
Review, 3 February 1980, p. 1.
    "Like the 'cheap' novel in John Gardner's 'OL,' these
segments [the Gothic romances imagined by the heroine in
Atwood's Lady Oracle] are more compelling than the novel
proper (which may be intentional, in both cases)."

1317 "Gardner, John (Champlin)." World Authors: 1970-1975.
Ed. John Wakeman. New York: The H. W. Wilson Co.,
1980, pp. 294-97.
    An overview of Gardner's works based upon selected (and
liberally quoted) reviews and the Bellamy-Ensworth interview (1974). The opening paragraph and appended bibliography are not entirely reliable.

1318 Grey, Gene. "Sunlight Man's Message Is Lost in Long
Dialogue." Binghamton Press, 12 October 1980.
    The acting of the two lead actors, the source material
(SD), and the stage design save Fred Bielenberg's play
from being merely an academic exercise on the part of the
SUNY-Binghamton Theater Department. Unfortunately, the
play is too diffuse; too much of the action takes place
offstage (thus the need for awkward narrative bridges),
and the musical score is intrusive. The philosophical
elements and the sentimental melodrama are not successfully combined.

1319 Harris, Richard C. "Ecclesiastical Wisdom and Nickel
Mountain." Twentieth Century Literature, 26 (Winter 1980),
424-31.
    There is a strong relation between NM and Ecclesiastes,
which emphasizes experiential wisdom and man's inability

to explain life in a strictly orthodox way. Both deal
with the accidental nature of life and the inevitability
of death. Henry Soames's despair, which is especially
acute in the "Nimrod's Tower" section, ends when George
Loomis's unspoken confession enables Henry to understand
the universality of suffering and guilt. By accepting the
possibility of human love that Ecclesiastes advises, Henry
attains the dignity his father never had. George, on the
other hand, denies both love and dignity. Willard Freund
attempts to avoid experience and responsibility by remaining "innocent." And Simon Bale retreats into religious
fanaticism. Doc Cathey's wisdom is finally not useful to
Henry because it does not derive from Henry's own
experiences.

1320 Hassan, Ihab. "The Question of Postmodernism." Bucknell
Review, 25, ii (1980), 121.
A number of today's young writers--including Styron,
Updike, and Gardner--are not postmodernists.

1321 Howell, John M. John Gardner: A Bibliographical Profile
Carbondale and Edwardsville: Southern Illinois University
Press; London and Amsterdam: Feffer & Simons, 1980.
Contents: "Preface," "Acknowledgements," "Chronology,"
"Separate Publications," "First-Appearance Contributions
to Books, Pamphlets, Portfolios," "Fiction in Magazines
and Newspapers," "Poetry in Magazines," "Articles and
Essays in Magazines and Newspapers," "Reviews in Maga-
zines and Newspapers," "Letters in Magazines and News-
papers," "Interviews and Speeches," "Miscellaneous:
Blurbs, Cartoons, Journals Edited, Libretti, Playbills,
Radio Plays, Transcriptions," "Articles and Essays on
John Gardner and His Works," "Reviews of John Gardner's
Works," "Afterword by John Gardner," reproduced manuscript
and typescript pages, dust jackets, title and copyright
pages, broadsides, playbills, cartoon, illustration from
KI.

1322 Kellman, Stephen G. "Ut Coitus Lectio: The Poet as Love-
maker." Georgia Review, 34 (1980), 305-6.
Cites Gardner's notion of the reader as a lover of
literature who identifies with characters he comes to
love.

1323 Kessler, Milton, and John Logan, eds. "Statement." Choice
(SUNY-Binghamton), 11/12 (1980), 4-5.
Mentions Gardner's serving as guest fiction editor for
this issue of Choice.

278

1324 Kleinfield, N.R. "The Literary Agent." <u>New York Times</u>
<u>Book Review</u>, 7 December 1980, p. 32.
Gardner is one of the "recherche clientele" of agent
Georges Borchardt; others are Elkin, Coover, and le Carre.

1325 Klinkowitz, Jerome. <u>The American 1960s: Imaginative Acts</u>
<u>in a Decade of Change</u>. Ames: The Iowa State University
Press, 1980, p. 18.
The resistance of conservative critics such as Gardner
and Gerald Graff to innovative fiction and deconstruction-
ist criticism evidences their misunderstanding of the
texture of contemporary life.

1326 Klinkowitz, Jerome. "The Effacement of Contemporary
American Literature." Rev. of <u>The Harvard Guide to</u>
<u>Contemporary American Literature</u>, ed. Daniel Hoffman.
<u>College English</u>, 42 (December 1980), 69-76 (70).
Briefly mentions <u>OMF</u>.

1327 Klinkowitz, Jerome. <u>Literary Disruptions: The Making of</u>
<u>a Post-Contemporary American Fiction</u>. 2nd ed. Urbana:
University of Illinois Press, 1980, p. iv.
Conservative critics such as Gardner and Gerald Graff
have attacked innovative fiction because they uphold
"the standards of an earlier day."

1328 Klinkowitz, Jerome. <u>The Practice of Fiction in America:</u>
<u>Writers from Hawthorne to the Present</u>. Ames: The Iowa
State University Press, 1980, pp. 114, 123, 128.
Conservative critics such as Gardner have refused to
accept the deconceptualization of language and the self-
reflectiveness of contemporary fiction.

1329 Krementz, Jill. <u>The Writer's Image</u>. Boston: David R.
Godine, 1980, p. 77.
Portrait, "John Gardner, London, 1971."

1330 Leonard, John. "More Fact Than Fiction." <u>New York Times</u>
<u>Book Review</u>, 28 December 1980, p. 18.
Gardner is cited as one of the "established American
writers" who, in publishing the novels they did in 1980,
"continue to bask on the warm rock of their reputations."

1331 Logan, William. Letter. <u>Chicago Tribune Book World</u>, 13
April 1980, p. 10.
Reply to Gardner's letter (published on the same page)
critical of Logan's 16 March 1980 review of <u>FB</u>. Logan

repeats his charge that Gardner's unacknowledged borrowings constitute "literary dishonesty" and adds that FB
does not evidence "'the dazzling texture and astonishing
intellectual compression'" which Gardner claims his
"'collage technique'" creates.

1332 Lynch, Dennis. "The Poetry of Lucien Stryk." American
Poetry Review 9 (September-October 1980), 46.
   Quotes from OMF to support his view that Stryk's later
poetry is "morally moving and aesthetically pleasing."

1333 Lyons, Gene. "The Famous Bread Loaf Writer's School."
Harper's, 260 (February 1980), pp. 75-78, 80.
   That much contemporary literature is "derivative,"
"mediocre," and overpraised is partly a result of
corporate publishing and partly of "camp meetings like
Bread Loaf." Gardner is a frequent participant at these
writers' conferences and has set the Aristotelian tone
for the past two years at Bread Loaf, where he maintains
"a vatic air."

1334 Mallon, Thomas. "The Novel on Elba." Shenandoah, 31
(1980), 97-99.
   In Ideas and the Novel, Mary McCarthy proves herself a
better champion of the classical novel than either C. P.
Snow or Gardner, whose "wild swinging" mars OMF.

1335 May, John R. "The Visual Story and the Religious Interpretation of Film." Horizons: Journal of the College
Theological Society, 7 (1980), 250.
   Calls Gardner's position in OMF one of "'ethical'
heteronymy."

1336 Milosh, Joseph E., Jr. "Reason and Mysticism in Fantasy
and Science Fiction." In Young Adult Literature: Background and Criticism. Ed. Millicent Lenz and Ramona M.
Mahood. Chicago: American Library Association, 1980,
pp. 437, 439-40.
   The tension between "reasoned knowledge and felt
knowledge" in G parallels a theme often found in adolescent
literature: "the pains of growth." Gardner uses fantasy
to pose old questions in new ways.

1337 Monroe, W. F. "Jabbing the Sore Spot: 'Alienism' and Its
Cultural Role." Georgia Review, 34 (1980), 19.
   Whether Twentieth-Century literature should be culturally
relevant remains an unanswered question. In OMF, "Gardner's

table-pounding polemics only weaken the 'humanist'
position and make it more susceptible to Alienist attacks."

1338 Morace, Robert A. "New Fiction, Popular Fiction, and the
Middle/Moral Way." fiction international, 12 (1980), 232-
46. Also issued as Moral Fiction: An Anthology, ed. Joe
David Bellamy (Canton, N.Y.: fiction international, 1980),
pp. 232-46; rpt. in revised form as "New Fiction, Popular
Fiction, and John Gardner's Middle/Moral Way" in John
Gardner: Critical Perspectives, Ed. Robert A. Morace and
Kathryn VanSpanckeren (Carbondale and Edwardsville: Southern
Illinois University Press, 1982), pp. 130-45.
   A major thrust in OMF is "the writer's dual obligation
to his art and to his society." Unlike the "elitist
egalitarianism" implicit in much of today's experimental
new fiction, Gardner's moral fiction bridges the gap between the serious and the popular and is clearly in the
tradition of democratic American literature. What Gardner
propounds in OMF he dramatizes in OL, where "the reader
reads Sally reading and as a result learns the difference
between fiction that is 'moral' and fiction that is not,
and learns too what influence fiction can exert and what
effects it can have."

1339 Morace, Robert A. "John Gardner: The King's Indian,
October Light, and the Dear Reader." NYCEA [New York
College English Association] Newsletter, 4 (Summer 1980),
2.
   (Abstract of a paper read at the Fall 1979 NYCEA Conference held at St. Bonaventure University.) Gardner is
less an innovative new fictionist than a writer of fiction
which, in the cases of KI and OL, seeks to instruct its
audience as to "the dangers of literature that is not
morally responsible."

1340 Morace, Robert A. "The Religious Experience and the
'Mystery of Imprisonment' in John Cheever's Falconer."
Cithara, 20 (November 1980), 44.
   Contemporary writers such as Gardner, Bellow, and
Cheever explore "the most insidious of our modern sins:
the retreat into one's self and away from the possibili-
ties and responsibilities of living in the world."

1341 Morace, Robert A. Rev. of Fabulation and Metafiction, by
Robert Scholes. Studies in the Novel, 12 (Winter 1980),
372-73.
   Scholes's criticism of self-reflexive fiction and his

comments on the writer's responsibilities to the audience
are similar to Gardner's views in OMF.

1342 Natov, Roni, and Geraldine DeLuca. "Current Trends in
Children's Books: Fantasy and Realism." USA Today, 109
(1980), 43.
    In Dragon and Gudgekin, Gardner uses novelistic tech-
niques "to root the ... fairy tale in the modern world";
his characters are complex, "their destinies fashionably
uncertain."

1343 Nitzsche, Jane C. "The Structural Unity of Beowulf: The
Problem of Grendel's Mother." Texas Studies in Literature
and Language, 22 (1980), 300.
    Gardner is among those critics who advanced the
"increasingly popular view" that Beowulf has a tripartite
structure.

1344 Prampolini, Gaetano. "Gardner, John." In Dizionario
della Letteratura Mondiale del 900. Rome: Edizioni
Paoline, 1980, pp. 1144-45. In Italian.
    Gardner is prolific and prodigiously talented. He is
both an innovative writer (like Barth) and a firm believer in literature's moral purpose (a view he persuasively argues in OMF). G is his most poetic work.

1345 Reed, A. K. "'A Thing Like a Love-Affair': A Study of
the Passion of Obedience in the York Play of Abraham
and Isaac." Christianity & Literature, 29, ii (1980),
36-37, 44-45.
    In his "Idea and Emotion in the Towneley Abraham"
(1971), Gardner overlooks the play's emotional aspect.

1346 Rubey, Daniel. "Identity and Alterity in the Criticism
of J. R. R. Tolkien and D. W. Robertson, Jr." Literary
Review, 23 (1980), 579-80.
    Gardner's view that Tolkien was unexceptional as
either a man or a critic (New York Times Book Review, 23
October 1977) may be correct.

1347 Shapiro, Lillian L. Fiction for Youth: A Guide to
Recommended Books. New York: Neal-Schurman Publishers,
1980, p. 59.
    Gardner's Grendel is "an emotionally moving hero" in
this beautifully and authentically told saga "about
monsters as people's inventions and about the futility
of war."

282

1348 Shuval, Michael H. "The Experience of Disorder in Three
Works by John Gardner. Diss. University of California-
Santa Cruz 1980.
The major characters in Gardner's fiction occupy, often
uncritically, a social, religious, or philosophical "place"
which is threatened by the outbreak of chaos or disorder
in their lives. Chandler and Clumly respond "by moving
through crisis to greater insight" and to the formation
of "tentative, fresh philosophical and social contexts."
In "The Temptation of St. Ivo," Ivo learns that the form-
lessness of the outside world is preferable to monastic
order; this discovery leads, however, to Ivo's becoming
mad.

1349 Spanos, W. V. "The De-struction of Form in Postmodern
American Poetry: The Examples of Charles Olson and Robert
Creeley." Amerikastudien, 25 (1980), 379.
Robert Pinsky, Gerald Graff, and Gardner (OMF) reach
the "nostalgic conclusion" that the contemporary avant-
garde is a continuation of modernism rather than a
questioning of it.

1350 Stonehill, Brian. "A Trestle of Letters." fiction international, 12 (1980), 260-61, 266. Also issued as Moral
Fiction: An Anthology, ed. Joe David Bellamy (Canton,
N.Y.: fiction international, 1980), pp. 260-61, 266.
Gardner's call for overtly moral fiction "ignores,
overlooks, or deprecates" literature's indirect resources:
"irony, obliquity, and ... metaphor." He mistakenly believes "fiction must be either mimetic or self-referential";
Barth's Letters proves him wrong.

1351 Walters, Ray. "Paperback Talk." New York Times Book
Review, 20 April 1980, p. 40.
The "volunteer committee" who helped editor Bill
Henderson select material for The Pushcart Prize IV
anthology included Gardner, Jerzy Kosinski, Malcolm
Cowley, and John Irving.

1352 Wetherbee, Winthrop. "The Descent from Bliss: Troilus,
III.1310-1582." In Chaucer's Troilus: Essays in
Criticism. Ed. Stephen A. Barney. Hamden, Conn.:
Archon Books, 1980, p. 317.
In discussing these lines in PC, Gardner "does not seem
... to allow for the extent to which forgiveness serves
as a way of easing Pandarus and the lovers over the moral
hurdles."

1353 Wilbers, Stephen. The Iowa Writers Workshop: Origins, Emergence, & Growth. Iowa City: University of Iowa Press, 1980, p. 94.
Incorrectly attributes an unidentified story to Gardner.

1354 Wilde, Alan. "Irony in the Postmodern Age: Toward a Map of Suspensiveness." Boundary 2, 8 (Fall 1980), 27.
Gass's aestheticism and Gardner's "equally restrictive morality of life affirmation" both look backwards to a more orderly age and "the comforts of the extraordinary."

1355 Wilde, Alan. "Surfacings: Reflections on the Epistemology of Late Modernism." Boundary 2, 8 (Winter 1980), 226.
"Resistance to high stylistic finish persists even today," as in OMF.

1356 "A Writers' Forum on Moral Fiction." fiction international, 12 (1980), [51]-25. Also issued as Moral Fiction: An Anthology, ed. Joe David Bellamy (Canton, N.Y.: fiction international, 1980).
Contributors to fiction international were asked to respond to OMF and/or the idea of moral fiction. Max Apple: Although in discussing the specifics of his aesthetic theory Gardner "is solemnly tedious," his "honest and wholesome" anger is a useful corrective to much of today's fiction and criticism. Russell Banks: Gardner's notion of moral fiction is reactionary. Fiction, in order to be truly moral, must measure, rather than merely accept, "the known limits of language." John Barth: Great writers transcend their "aesthetic principles," and great art "pull[s] critical theory behind it like an ocean liner trailing seagulls." Jonathan Baumbach: OMF is a media event; Gardner's criticism is conservative whereas his fiction is "radical." True moral fiction should "make large demands on the readers." Clark Blaise: Although morality is a myth worth cultivating, Gardner's problem is that he asks too much of morality and fiction by insisting they improve mankind. Jerry Bumpus: Despite his call for moral fiction, Gardner has judged Bumpus's story, "A Morning in Arcadia," "terrific" as well as "immoral." Kelly Cherry: The best fiction resists "easy moralistic summation; the moral writer is deeply concerned about characters and structure and attempts to "sustain within an aesthetic framework the contradictions which threaten to divide us" in our lives. Annie Dillard: "Surface dazzle" is not the equivalent of

literary "significance"; nor is careless structure an adequate metaphor for a troubled time. Frederick Exley: Gardner's books are eminently forgettable (rpt. in Critique, 22, ii [1980], 4). Raymond Federman: "Aesthetic value is opposed to the narrow, censorious view of moral fiction characteristic of "totalitarian systems" in which "the ruling class" joins with the "mob" to shout down whatever does not "conform to its idea of morality." Malcolm Glass: A fiction that makes us "less uncertain and afraid in a world of ambiguities" is preferable to one which, contrary to experience, provides simple "answers and absolutes." Harold Jaffe: OMF is "literary McCarthyism." Gardner's insensitivity to the "freaks" he dismisses is especially troublesome. Today's writers should be socially responsible and need not eschew stylistic complexity in their attempts to remind readers of "social 'truths.'" Jerome Klinkowitz: Gardner mistakes the artifice of myth for the will of God. Norman Lavers: True art provides pleasure, not, as in Gardner's "middlebrow" view, moral edification. Gordon Lish: "Heaven Itself had a hand in" writing several of Gardner's books. When the inspiration stopped, Gardner wrote OMF, "some stunt to propitiate the gods." David Long: Gardner's views may have needed saying. "Second wave metafiction" and insignificant stories are prevalent, but there is also a great deal of first-rate fiction being published (far more than Gardner admits)--fiction that does not instruct but instead examines and reveals. David Madden: Although "moral implications" are important, it is their aesthetic expression that makes a literary work significant. Moreover, the creative act is itself moral. James Ashbrook Perkins: Gardner's idea of moral fiction is narrowly prescriptive, false to experience, and dull. Jayne Anne Phillips: Fiction does not define; it invokes the "mystery served by language." James Park Sloan: "The crux of the moral fiction issue is not morality, but content." The preoccupation of critics with structuralism and writers with style indicates a retreat from the idea that fiction should be about life, as it is in Fowles's novel Daniel Martin. "The aesthetics of content, as Gardner correctly argues, is not style but emptiness." Anon.: Quotes Susan Sontag's essay, "On Style"--the pleasure of art "consists in the intelligent gratification of consciousness." Gilbert Sorrentino: As Rimbaud pointed out, morality is the effect of a weak mind. Ronald Sukenick: The "public reception" of Gardner's self-advertisement, OMF, "is related to conglomerate publishing's effort to

bolster its waning literary prestige." In today's culture,
it is realistic fiction that is immoral. John Updike:
The morality of fiction derives from accuracy of detail,
form and style and from the author's intuition. Thus,
moral fiction can never be prescribed. Gordon Weaver:
Gardner neither advocates didacticism nor condemns formal
experimentation (except by those imitators who have debased
literature and made it unappealing to the public). Fiction
is, as Gardner says, essentially conservative. His views
are reinforced in Wayne Booth's Rhetoric of Fiction and
Gerald Graff's Literature Against Itself. Thomas
Williams: The conservative aesthetic Gardner propounds
in his ego-filled book is curiously at odds with his
modernist fiction. Hilma Wolitzer: "The "moral demands"
of living and writing are inseparable. Lee Zacharias:
Fiction is a matter of integrity, not morality; its purpose is not the providing of role-models. Gardner's
prescriptions make him a "traitor" to art, which is essentially free and amoral.

1357 "The Yearbook of the American Short Story: Other Dis-
tinguished Short Stories of the Year 1979." The Best
American Short Stories 1980. Ed. Stanley Elkin and Shannon
Ravenel. Boston: Houghton Mifflin, 1980, p. 466.
     Lists "Nimram."

1981

1358 Ackland, Michael. "Blakean Sources in John Gardner's
Grendel," Critique, 23, i (1981), 57-66.
     Although the plot of Grendel derives from the Anglo-
Saxon epic Beowulf, much of the imagery and the impetus
for its pessimistic vision are drawn from the poetry of
Blake. The determinism implied in the twelve-chapter
structure parallels the cyclical movement of "The Mental
Traveller." Both works employ semi-human narrators, but
whereas Blake's narrator, one of the Immortals, provides
a hopeful perspective and an eternal world beyond "the
vegetative flux," Grendel, because he is trapped in this
flux, represents the denial of eternity and divinity.
This "annulling of Blake's eternal perspective" is most
clearly evident in the way Gardner adapts the scene from
The Marriage of Heaven and Hell in which the narrator,
suspended above the void in the roots of an oak tree,
is given a glimpse of hell. Unlike Blake, who offers a
counterforce in the figure of the harper, Gardner provides

"no redeeming vision," least of all in the "mechanical, even mad" Beowulf. Similarly, Gardner ironically transforms Blake's Orc and Los into the novel's "mad rationalistic priest" Ork and the monster-narrator who embodies the alternate voices of innocence and experience in Blake's poetry. Gardner also borrows a number of Blake's pictorial images, as in chapter 8 where the description of Hrothgar and Wealtheow closely parallels the frontispiece to Visions of the Daughters of Albion.

1359 Barnum, Carol. "John Fowles's Daniel Martin: A Vision of Whole Sight." Literary Review, 25 (1981), 68, 78.
    Twice quotes Gardner's review of Daniel Martin approvingly and concludes that in Daniel Martin Fowles has done what Gardner did in NM: moved from the waste land to the garden.

1360 Barth, John. "Tales Within Tales Within Tales." Antaeus, 43 (Autumn 1981), 45-63.
    In distinguishing between what he calls "primary fiction," which is about life, and "secondary fiction," which is about fiction, and in asserting the moral superiority of the former, Gardner makes two fundamental errors. One is that, as Borges has shown, fiction about fiction, frame tales in particular, is ultimately fiction about life in that it serves to remind the reader of the fictiveness of his own existence. Two, as Tzvetan Todorov has demonstrated all literature is about language and to narrate is in effect to live. Moreover, the digression and return that characterizes frame tales mirrors the pattern of our everyday experience.

1361 Booth, Wayne. C. "Criticulture: Or, Why We Need at Least Three Criticisms at the Present Time. In What Is Criticism. Ed. P. Hernadi. Bloomington: University of Indiana Press, 1981, pp. 168-70.
    The fact that OMF is "a slovenly, slapdash work" only accounts in part for its controversial reception" which resulted chiefly from Gardner's "unfashionable" belief in "ethical criticism." Ethical criticism is not only important but difficult as well; Gardner labels works as moral or immoral without bothering to explain why they are so.

1362 Bhatnagar, O.P. "Nickel Mountain: An Anti-Pastoral Pastoral Novel." Mahanadi Review (India), 8 (April-June 1981), 20-29.

The world of NM provides neither "an ideal retreat" nor
a vision of human innocence nor a substitute for man's
perplexities. Gardner shows that the natural world is
insufficient; it must be supplemented by human community.
In NM, love is not Arcadian but human; emotional changes
are realized in time rather than through "pastoral
miracle." Thus, Gardner's pastoral is secular and open,
and his emphasis is on experience rather than pastoral
design.

1363 Brady, Karen. "Amherst Kitchen Is Home Office for First-
Time Novelist." Buffalo Evening News, 7 August 1981, p.
C7.
   Marian Schwartz, author of the novel Realities, studied
with Gardner at the Bread Loaf Writers Conference.

1364 Chamberlain, David. "Musical Signs and Symbols in
Chaucer: Convention and Originality." In Signs and
Symbols in Chaucer's Poetry. Ed. John P. Hermann and
John J. Burke, Jr. University: University of Alabama
Press, 1981, pp. 43, 52.
   Twice mentions approvingly Gardner's view of musical
signs in Chaucer's poetry (LTC, PC).

1365 Chenetier, Marc. "'Even Posthumanists Get the Blues':
Contemporary American Fiction and Its Critics; A Lament
and a Plea." In The American Identity: Fusion and Fragmentation. Ed. Rob Kroes. European Contributions to
American Studies, 3 (1981), 346.
   Contemporary American criticism is unnecessarily
polemical; critics feel compelled to be either for or
against, for example, Gardner or Gass.

1366 Childs, B. "Poetic and Musical Rhythm: One More Time."
In Music Theory Special Topics. Ed. R. Browne. New York:
Academic Press, 1981, pp. 33-57.*
   Cited in Arts and Humanities Citation Index, 1981.

1367 DeMott, Benjamin. "2,000 Years After the Berstyn Fyr."
Rev. of Riddley Walker, by Russell Hoban. New York Times
Book Review, 28 June 1981, p. 25.
   Riddley Walker is vaguely similar to such contemporary
novels as G.

1368 Federman, Raymond. "Fiction Today or the Pursuit of Non-
Knowledge." Humanities in Society, 1 (Spring 1978), 115-

31. Rpt in Surfiction: Fiction Now and Tomorrow, 2nd
ed. (Athens: Swallow/Ohio University Press, 1981), 291-
311.
Gardner's aesthetic and his morality are anachronistic;
he fails to understand that today's fiction of language
is a fiction of man.

1369 Fiedler, Leslie A. "Literature as an Institution." New
Republic, 30 May 1981, pp. 24-26, 28.
The point made by anti-academic critics--"either piously
moralistic defenders of the 'eternal verities,' like John
Gardner, or snide exponents of high camp, like Gore Vidal"
--is valid, for academics have created a division between
serious literature and that literature which appeals to
the general reader.

1370 Foeller, Elzbieta. "John Gardner's Tale 'The King's
Indian' as a Fabulation based on the 19th-Century Litera-
ture Tradition." In Traditions in the Twentieth Century
American Literature. Ed. Marta Sienicka. Poznan, Poland:
Adam Mickiewicz Univ., 1981, pp. 81-89.
Borrowing freely from Poe (Pym and "Ligeia"), Melville
(Moby-Dick, Billy Budd, "Benito Cereno," and Confidence
Man), Conrad (Heart of Darkness), Coleridge ("Ancient
Mariner"), and Shakespeare (Tempest), Gardner has fash-
ioned "a craftily wrought whole," "a tale by a bookish
author, for bookish readers." Although a parody-novel,
"KI" is not merely a literary exercise; rather, it re-
flects modern man's "confusion about reality and illusion,
his search for absolutes, and his discovery of the redeeming qualities of human love." Thus, it conforms to
Scholes's definition of fabulation: "ethically controlled
fantasy."

1371 Fowler, Doreen A. "Answers and Ambiguity in Percy's The
Second Coming." Critique, 23, ii (1981-82), 13, 23.
Gardner is one of the critics who have complained of
Percy's "equivocation" and "indecisive" endings.

1372 Griffin, Bryan F. "Panic Among the Philistines: The
Collapse of the Literary Establishment." Harper's, 263
(August 1981), 44, 47.
The tendency on the part of book reviewers to herald
each new publication as significant is shared by Gardner,
who has "decided that everything he's ever read is
'immensely important.'"

1373 Hart, Thomas Elwood. "Calculated Casualties in Beowulf:
Geometrical Scaffolding and Verbal Symbol." Studia
Neophilologica, 53 (1981), 28.
Agrees with Gardner's contention in CCP that the Anglo-
Saxon poets "worked with formal poetic principles in mind"
despite the fact that no handbook of their poetics is
extant.

1374 Hazard, Mary E. "A Literary Tale of Two Passages." New
York Times, 13 December 1981, sec. IV, p. 28.
In her letter to the editor, Hazard points out that the
excerpt from Gardner's "Shadows" published in the New
York Times, 29 November 1981, is taken from A.S. Edding-
ton's Gifford Lecture, The Nature of the Physical World
(1928).

1375 Hermann, John P., and John J. Burke. "Introduction."
Signs and Symbols in Chaucer's Poetry. Ed. Hermann and
Burke. University: University of Alabama Press, 1981,
pp. 9-10.
Gardner's contribution, "Signs, Symbols, and Cancella-
tions," is summarized and briefly discussed.

1376 Horowitz, Sylvia Huntley. "The Ravens in Beowulf."
Journal of English and Germanic Philology, 80 (1981),
504, 509.
In his study of Beowulf Gardner shows himself to be
especially sensitive to the brutality of the Geats. In
a letter to Horowitz, Gardner claimed Beowulf was an
antediluvian work.

1377 Johnson, Charles. "Philosophy and Black Fiction."
Obsidian: Black Literature in Review, 6, ii (1981), 55,
61.
In OMF Gardner correctly defines fiction as "a form
of philosophical method." Black writers, of whom only
five are cited in Gardner's "manifesto," should enter the
debate set off by his "angry yet important essay."

1378 Klinkowitz, Jerome. "Critifiction, American Style."
New Mexico Humanities Review, 4 (Spring 1981), 81-84.
Gardner's argument in OMF is in part reactionary; he
fails to acknowledge that the texture of modern life
necessitates modification of the form of the novel. Where
Gardner, one of the "last-stand-traditionalists," argues
for a fiction of character, the innovative contemporary

290

writers call for a fiction of language which is itself
moral in that the writer's "intelligence is used to put
human imagination back into the lifeless forms we've
come to ignore (and thus let rule us) ...."

1379 Klinkowitz, Jerome. "Fiction: The 1950s to the Present."
In American Literary Scholarship: An Annual/1979. Ed.
James Woodress. Durham, N.C.: Duke University Press,
1981, pp. 278-79, 296-97, 300.
 Discusses Gardner's realist position and various published responses to it. Gardner's "posturing" in the
New York Times Magazine, 6 July 1979, suggests that "OMF
may have been more publicity stunt than reasoned
criticism."

1380 Kolve, V. A. "From Cleopatra to Alceste: An Iconographic
Study of The Legend of Good Women." In Signs and Symbols
in Chaucer's Poetry. Ed. John P. Hermann and John J.
Burke, Jr. University: University of Alabama Press, 1981,
p. 241.
 Mentions Gardner's acceptance of the plausible con-
jecture that Thomas Chaucer was John of Gaunt's illegitimate son (LTC).

1381 Kort, Wesley A. Rev. of The Story of Identity: American
Fiction of the Sixties, by Manfred Puetz. American
Literature, 52 (January 1981), 664.
 Writers such as Gardner do not share the characteristic
of 60s American fiction noted by Puetz: the use of
fantasy to transcend experience and to create identity.

1382 LeClair, Thomas. "William Gaddis, Jr. & The Art of
Excess." Modern Fiction Studies, 27 (Winter 1981-82),
589, 597.
 Denies Gardner's charge (New York Review of Books, 10
June 1976) that Gaddis's outrage in The Recognitions is
private and uncontrolled and maintains that works such
as JR are concerned with finding new modes of communication, not, as Gardner charges in OMF, with denying communication.

1383 McDowell, Edwin. "Behind the Best Sellers: John Gardner."
New York Times Book Review, 7 June 1981, p. 30.
 American readers may confuse this John Gardner, the
British mystery writer, with the American novelist of
the same name.

1384 McHale, Brian. "On Moral Fiction: One Use of Gravity's
     Rainbow." Pynchon Notes, 6 (June 1981), 34-38.
     Gardner is wrong in believing that Gravity's Rainbow
     cannot be read as a "sober analysis" of certain aspects
     of World War II.

1385 Morace, Robert A. "Gardner, John Champlin, Jr." In
     Critical Survey of Short Fiction. Ed. Frank N. Magill.
     Englewood Cliffs, N.J.: Salem Press, 1981, pp. 1458-64.
     Far more important than either his "pyrotechnic style"
     or his "literariness" is Gardner's emphasis on his
     characters who, overcoming romantic agóny and existential
     despair, choose "to perform those 'trivial heroic acts of
     everyday life'" that Gardner endorses. "The Song of
     Grendel" involves the conflict between rational existen-
     tialism and poetic intuition. Grendel's "fatal mistake"
     is his failure to accept the life-affirmations implicit
     in the Shaper's songs; he is defeated by literature--or
     more specifically, by the hero of the literary epic,
     Beowulf, Gardner parodies. "KI" suggests that all be-
     liefs are fictions--hoaxes--but some are useful and bene-
     ficial while others are destructive. Betrayal of their
     beliefs leads some of the characters to despair and others
     to comic affirmation. "Pastoral Care" parodies the fiction
     of John Updike; specifically it concerns the need to act
     compassionately despite human limitations and uncertainty.
     The semi-autobiographical story "Redemption" makes plain
     that the life of the individual is redeemed by social
     commitment. Gardner's stories are often parodic; however,
     his parodies differ from those of most contemporary
     writers in that their purpose is to test values. His
     fiction is stylistically protean but thematically con-
     sistent.

1386 Morace, Robert A. "Invention in Guy Davenport's Da
     Vinci's Bicycle." Critique, 22, iii (1981), 71-72.
     Gardner's praise of Davenport's fiction is justified,
     despite its resemblance to "linguistic sculpture," be-
     cause Davenport takes both as his method and his subject
     that process which Gardner associates with moral fiction:
     the search for affirmative human values.

1387 Morris, Gregory L. "A World of Order and Light: A
     Critical Introduction to the Fiction of John Gardner."
     Diss. University of Nebraska 1981.
     Gardner's traditionalist aesthetic involves a return to
     a sense of the world's orderliness and the artist's

responsibility to seeking this order and affirming the
moral values it implies. His fiction derives from an
"emotional metaphysic" that declares the primacy of intuition over reason. Characters who act in accordance with
the promptings of their heart overcome their existential
doubts and serve as Gardner's heroes. As a neo-humanist,
Gardner eschews the self-consciousness of metafiction and
posits instead a fiction of beliefs. (Annotation is drawn
from an abstract supplied by the author.)

1388 Motylyova, Tamara. Quoted in Soviet Literary Critics'
Forum on "Fyodor Dostoevsky and World Literature."
Soviet Literature, 12 (1981), 174.
In OMF Gardner cites Dostoievski and Tolstoi to support
his view that the purpose of great art is to humanize man.

1389 Peterson, Dale E. "Nabokov's Invitation: Literature as
Execution." PMLA, 96 (October 1981), 834, 835.
OMF is a "remarkably intemperate tract against
'aesthetic game-players,'" whom Gardner considers mere
exhibitionists.

1390 Post, Robert C. "A Theory of Genre: Romance, Realism,
and Moral Reality." American Quarterly, 33 (1981), 369.
Gardner correctly defines the novel as "an affirmation
of what ought to be and what, in the artist's devout
opinion, is...." The novel as a genre can thus best be
approached in terms of "moral reality" rather than "an
ingenuous philosophical realism."

1391 Rev. of Klytaimnestra Who Stayed at Home, by Nancy
Bogen. Choice, 18 (February 1981), 792.
Bogen's novel is written in a manner similar to the
"contemporary Gothic" of Gardner and Percy in which
action and characterization are domesticated and humanized but also trivialized.

1392 Roth, Mary Kay. "John Gardner's 'Helen' Misses the Boat."
Binghamton Press, 2 November 1981.
Helen at Home, written and directed by Gardner and
performed at the Laurel Street Theater in Susquehanna,
Penn., is a "confusing and inane" philosophical comedy.
The play begins with an interesting enough idea (following
the Trojan War, Helen becomes bored), but the play suffers
from Gardner's silliness and sermonizing.

1393 Safer, Elaine B. "The Allusive Mode and Black Humor in Barth's Sot-Weed Factor." Studies in the Novel, 13 (1981), 436.
    Black humorists like Barth are not morbidly fascinated by ugliness as Gardner (OMF) claims; rather they use black humor to make the reader vulnerable to and troubled by the absurdity of the human situation.

1394 Sandler, Florence, and Darrell Reeck. "The Masks of Joseph Campbell." Religion, 11 (1981), 1.
    Gardner's appreciative review of The Mythic Image (New York Times Book Review, 28 December 1975) is characteristic of the way writers of imaginative literature have responded to Campbell.

1395 Schell, Edgar. "The Distinctions of the Towneley Abraham." Modern Language Quarterly, 41 (1981), 315.
    Gardner is one of the many critics who have wrongly treated all of the plays as imitations of a single action.

1396 Sheppard, R. Z. "Life into Art: Garp Creator John Irving Strikes Again." Time, 31 August 1981, p. 46.
    Irving teaches at Bread Loaf "with such admired colleagues" as Gardner and Elkin.

1397 Simon, Jeff. "A Writer's Town." The Magazine of the Buffalo News, 22 February 1981, p. 10.
    Three brief paragraphs on Gardner as a controversial writer from western New York; quotes interview with Herman Trotter published in Buffalo Evening News, 25 December 1977.

1398 Slights, William W. E. "The Incarnations of Comedy." University of Toronto Quarterly, 51 (Fall 1981), 25.
    Gardner's discussion of tripartite design in "Structure and Tone in the Second Shepherds' Play" (1967) may be more mechanical than necessary.

1399 Stern, R. A. M. "The Doubles of Post-Modern Architecture." Architectural Design, September 1981, pp. 63-68.*
    Cited in Arts and Humanities Citation Index, 1981.

1400 Sugnet, Charles. "Introduction." The Imagination on Trial: British and American Writers Discuss Their Working Methods. Ed. Alan Burns and Charles Sugnet. London and New York: Allison and Busby, 1981, pp. 11-13.

Discusses Burns's interview with Gardner (pp. 40-50) and Gardner's theory of moral fiction, which is ahistorical and shows Gardner to be much more certain about what is true than other contemporary writers. Given the diminished importance of the novel today, his view will probably prove ineffective.

1401 Tanner, Stephen L. "The Moral Measure of Literature." Brigham Young University Studies, 21 (1981), 279-89.
      Gardner's position in OMF is radical because the moral approach to literature is unfashionable today. True moral criticism is difficult; it must never be "practiced narrowly or incompletely."

1402 Whatley, Gordon. "The Figure of Constantine the Great in Cynewulf's 'Elene.'" Traditio, 37 (1981), 162.
      Gardner ("Cynewulf's Elene," 1970) is cited among those critics who, in following Stanley B. Greenfield's approach to the poem, have produced "a substantial body of criticism."

1403 Winn, David. Rev. of Shame the Devil, by Philip Appleman. American Book Review, 3 (November-December 1981), 15.
      Appleman's annoyingly symbolic novel reminds the reviewer of the fiction of Walker Percy and Gardner.

1404 Zverev, A. "Puteshestvia s Gardnerom." Literaturnoe Obozrenie: Organ Soiuza Pisatelet SSSR, 10 (1980), 71-75.*
      Discusses NM and KI. (Cited in MLA Bibliography, 1981.)

1982

1405 Abbey, Harlan C. "Collectibles." Buffalo Courier-Express, 30 August 1982, p. B3.
      Quotes a book dealer who claims a mint-condition copy of Res is worth $500; whether Gardner is worth collecting, however, will depend on his future reputation.

1406 "About the Author." In Contemporary Sources: Readings from "Writer's Workshop." Intro. William Price Fox. New York: Holt, Rinehart and Winston, 1982, p. 70.
      Biographical sketch drawn from several published interviews. "About the Author" is followed by "Gardner on Writing: (p. 71) and excerpts from NM (pp. 72-90).

1407 "Award-Winning Writer Was University Prof." Batavia (N.Y.) Daily News, 15 September 1982, p. 1.

Briefly discusses Gardner's career, quotes Carl Dennis on the "brilliance" of "Shadows" and Clifford Clark (President of SUNY-Binghamton) and Bernard Rosenthal (Gardner's department chairman) on Gardner's dedication to teaching. His mother points out that Gardner, who was to have married Susan Thornton on 18 September, spent much of his summer working on his parents' farm and helping his father recover from a stroke.

1408 Baber, Joseph. "John Gardner, Librettist: A Composer's Notes." In John Gardner: Critical Perspectives. Ed. Robert A. Morace and Kathryn VanSpanckeren. Carbondale and Edwardsville: Southern Illinois University Press, 1982, pp. 97-105.
  Although Baber was reluctant to write operas, Gardner's enthusiasm and, more importantly, his willingness to make the composer an equal partner finally persuaded Baber. Their truly collaborative method begins with a "skeleton" of the libretto, aimed by Gardner at "the particular strengths" of the composer. Then the music is added and the two gradually patched together in such a way that the "discoveries" of both the librettist and the composer are utilized and "the needs of the music" and "the philosophical purpose" are not sacrificed. Specific examples of the Gardner-Baber collaboration on Frankenstein and Rumpelstiltskin are discussed.

1409 Barth, John. In "Symposium: Books that Gave Me Pleasure." New York Times Book Review, 5 December 1982, p. 64.
  "Good new books" by Gardner and others have made 1982 "a bountiful year for fiction."

1410 Basler, George. "John Gardner: Author-Teacher Dies in Motorcycle Crash." Binghamton Press, 15 September 1982, pp. Al, A7.
  Summarizes Gardner's career, notes colleagues' remarks on his dedication to teaching, and quotes Malamud who "today called Gardner 'a born writer.'"

1411 Basler, George. "SUNY Plans Gardner Fund." Binghamton Press, 16 September 1982, p. Bl.
  The university plans to continue Gardner's efforts to establish a creative writing endowment of one-half million dollars. The English Department has scheduled a memorial service for 22 September that will feature readings by Gardner's students. The Laurel Street Theater in

Susquehanna, Penn., plans to stage the two projects on
which Gardner was recently working: an original musical
and a Christmas play. Owners of bookstores in the Binghamton area report an increase in the sales of Gardner's
works.

1412 Basler, George. "Author's Wit, Vitality Recalled at
University Memorial Service." Binghamton Press, 23
September 1982.
The memorial service held at SUNY-Binghamton was at-
tended by 600 people and included 27 speakers. William
Spanos, Susan Strehle, Gayle Whittier, Joanna Higgins,
Priscilla Gardner, Liz Rosenberg, and Anthony Miceli are
either quoted or paraphrased. Most noted Gardner's dedica-
tion to teaching and to his work and his having lived as
if he knew his life would be short.

1413 Beye, Charles Rowan. "Preface." Epic and Romance in the
Argonautica of Apollonius. Literary Structures series.
Carbondale and Edwardsville: Southern Illinois Univ. Press,
1982, p. xiv.
Thanks Gardner, the series editor, for his many valuable
editorial suggestions.

1414 Bingham, Sallie. "John Gardner: An Appreciation."
Louisville Courier-Journal, 19 September 1982, p. D5.
Gardner leaves behind "an impressive legacy": his books,
the creative writing program at SUNY-Binghamton, and his
commitment to young writers. In an age of specialization,
he was a man of varied interests. As he grew older and
became interested in the themes of life and death, he lost
the playfulness that characterized his earlier work. OMF
"fell victim to its own lofty purposes." But throughout
his career he remained dedicated to survival, affirmation, and the art of writing.

1415 Bonnazza, Blaze O., Emil Roy, and Sandra Roy. Studies in
Fiction. 3rd ed. New York: Harper & Row, 1982, p. 369.
Briefly discusses Gardner's use of Graustarkian romance
in "Queen Louisa" as a means of liberating the child inside the reader, thus permitting escape from logic and
everyday reality. Instructor's Manual, pp. 66-67, provides a 12-item quiz and answers to discussion questions.

1416 Boyd, Robert. "Assaying the Legacy of John Gardner." St.
Louis Post-Dispatch, 5 December 1982, pp. 2, 8.
Traces the publishing history and critical reception of

the "almost pathologically prolific" Gardner, emphasizing the tendency of reviewers to "pounce": first after the early successes of G and SD (a novel "so rich and so broad in scope as to tax the reader's credibility"), then with the plagiarism charge leveled against LTC, and finally after the publication of OMF (which may have been "a deliberate act of braggadocio, a romantic hero's defiant gesture"). Just how Gardner will ultimately be judged is hard to say: perhaps as an experimentalist (one of his friends has said Gardner's impatience with ideas he had used and his gift for mimicry prevented him from formulating his own distinctive style); perhaps as the author who made his books into something more than mass-produced objects; or perhaps, as Gardner probably would have preferred, as the heroic defender of his artistic vision against the compromises and conformism of his age.

1417 Raymond Carver. "Fires." Antaeus, 47 (Autumn 1982), 156-67.

Carver, who was Gardner's student at Chico State College in the fall of 1959, acknowledges Gardner as one of the most important influences on his career. Carver recalls Gardner's arrogance, distaste for large-circulation magazines, patience, emphasis on using the right words and common language, and his many kindnesses, including allowing Carver to use his office for writing. Although Gardner recently said that his advice then was probably wrong--"I've changed my mind about so many things"-- Carver says he was "a wonderful teacher."

1418 Cheuse, Alan. Rev. of Different Seasons, by Stephen King. New York Times Book Review, 29 August 1982, p. 17.

In "The Body" (one of four works included in Different Seasons) King takes "some swipes at writers such as John Gardner," one of King's "biggest fans."

1419 Churcher, Sharon. "Gardner's Latest: Not So Novel." New York Magazine, 28 December 1981-4 January 1982, p. 15.

In response to Mary Hazard's letter (New York Times, 13 December 1981) concerning "Shadows," Gardner's agent, Anne Borchardt, has pointed out that the novel's protagonist is an alcoholic who, like many of Gardner's characters, cannot adequately distinguish "between reality and what he's read." Gardner's borrowings will be acknowledged when the novel is published.

1420 "Clinging to Dreams in an Exploding World." Rochester
Democrat and Chronicle, 16 September 1982, editorial page.
The deaths of Gardner, Princess Grace, and Bashir
Gemayel attack "our sensibilities" at various levels.
Gardner wrote "about people and their often vain efforts
to become human"; "he forged words into powerful dreams
for his readers," providing the alternative of sensitivity
in a world of explosive violence.

1421 Coale, Samuel. "'Into the Farther Darkness': The
Manichean Pastoralism of John Gardner." In John Gardner:
Critical Perspectives. Ed. Robert A. Morace and Kathryn
VanSpanckeren. Carbondale and Edwardsville: Southern
Illinois University Press, 1982, pp. 15-27.
Gardner's fiction is in the mainstream "tradition of
the American fable," the subject of which Faulkner
described "as the human heart in conflict with itself."
American literature is characterized by a tension between
the "pastoral impulse" ("restoration, escape, regeneration")
and the melodramatic confrontation which derives from
Calvinist Manicheanism. Gardner's postmodernist techniques and sympathy for his anarchist characters evidence
his contemporaneity. But in the conflict between order
and chaos, love and hate, Gardner is always hopeful that
man can achieve an "armed reconciliation." (Gardner's
comments concerning the writing of NM as a tribute to his
father and fiction as a "dream unfolding in the mind" are
quoted by Coale and were made by Gardner 31 March 1979 in
Hartford, Conn.)

1422 Cohen, Andy. "Gardner Sped Headlong into Life, and to
Death." Binghamton Sun-Bulletin, 15 September 1982, p. Bl.
Chiefly made up of discussion of Gardner's dedication
to teaching, remarks culled from several interviews, and
reactions of colleagues Elizabeth T. Tucker, John E.
Vernon, and Susan Strehle, and David Kalish, editor of
the student newspaper, Pipe Dream, who will issue a special
edition in Gardner's memory.

1423 Cohen, Andy. "Gardner's Talent Grew from a N.Y. Farm."
Binghamton Sun-Bulletin, 15 September 1982, p. Bl.
Surveys Gardner's life, emphasizing OMF and the death
of his brother Gilbert.

1424 Collins, R. G., ed. Critical Essays on John Cheever.
Boston: G. K. Hall, 1982, pp. 1, 6, 17-18, 80-84, 208, 257-
61, 262, 266, 269-70.

Gardner's criticism of Cheever is briefly discussed by
Collins and Lynne Waldeland; Samuel Coale calls Cheever
and Gardner romancers; and Gardner's reviews of Bullet
Park (New York Times Book Review, 24 October 1971) and
Falconer (Saturday Review, 2 April 1977) are reprinted.

1425 Collins, Robert G. "From Subject to Object and Back
Again: Individual Identity in John Cheever's Fiction."
Twentieth Century Literature, 28, i (1982), 7, 12.
  In "Witchcraft in Bullet Park," Gardner corrects some
misreadings of Cheever's novel but mistakenly confirms
the commonly held view that Cheever is the defender of
suburban values.

1426 Cowart, David. "Et in Arcadia Ego: Gardner's Early
Pastoral Novels." In John Gardner: Critical Perspectives.
Ed. Robert A. Morace and Kathryn VanSpanckeren. Carbondale and Edwardsville: Southern Illinois University
Press, 1982, pp. 1-14.
  In Res, WA, and NM, Gardner employs pastoral conventions
and a flexible approach to point of view in order to deal
"creatively with the artistic problem of treating in a
positive manner the morbid subject of a protagonist's
death." Gardner's pastoral world is "simplified" but not
"idealized"; it is one in which death "may be recognized
and accepted as part of a natural process" and the author
sides with human choice rather than entropic chance.
(Parallels to Sidney's Arcadia and Gay's The Beggar's
Opera are noted.)

1427 Cryer, Dan. "John Gardner: The Enigmatic Moralist."
Newsday, 15 September 1982, sec. 2, p. 2.
  "Gardner was a contradictory and controversial figure
in American literature." Although a successful author,
he chose to war with the literary powers. In his books,
which were conventional rather than experimental, he
tried to make the world more understandable for his Main-
Street readers. Preachiness and philosophizing at the
expense of plot (as in MG) may have been his faults; however his prose was "enthralling" and deeply moving.

1428 Cummins, Walter. "The Real Monster in Freddy's Book."
In John Gardner: Critical Perspectives. Ed. Robert A.
Morace and Kathryn VanSpanckeren. Carbondale and Edwardsville: Southern Illinois University Press, 1982, pp.
106-13.

Gardner is more a "moral realist" than a fabulist.
Like his other fiction, which concerns human values and
behavior and affirms connections rather than alienation,
FB is a "compassionate probing of the stigmatized outsider." The novel's main subject is history, "in particular the causes of events that lead to change."
Winesap, Agaard, and Freddy each represents a way of
explaining these changes. "Freddy posits a pre-psych-
ological world" in which the causes of human error are
external. His story ends with the death of the devil
and "the birth of modern consciousness" and "the rise of
Protestantism and individualism." Man subsequently becomes "the center of the universe"--a rather hollow center,
as the portraits in part one suggest. The novel's chief
flaw is not structural, as some reviewers have thought,
but "a hammering obviousness of message that ignores a
great potential for moral subtlety and complexity."

1429 DeLuca, Geraldine, and Roni Natov. "Modern Moralities for
Children: John Gardner's Children's Books." In John
Gardner: Critical Perspectives. Ed. Robert A. Morace
and Kathryn VanSpanckeren. Carbondale and Edwardsville:
Southern Illinois University Press, 1982, pp. 89-96.
Gardner's five children's books evidence his interest
in moral fiction and formal literary experimentation.
Each, however, seems "contrived" and written for an older,
more sophisticated audience than Gardner intended. The
three collections of tales explore "the extraordinariness
of the ordinary" and question "what is traditionally de-
picted as goodness." Relativity and uncertainty abound
in these modernized tales, and the middle-class virtues
of "cunning and necessity" replace "classist assumptions"
about morality. ISM is "a sympathetic portrait of the
'misfit,'" but the "intrusive" tales told by the abbot
make it "a trying work." CB is written in the Belloc-
Nash tradition, but because it scans so poorly children
will probably find it unappealing.

1430 Dillard, Annie. Living by Fiction. New York: Harper &
Row, 1982, p. 37.
As in G, the narrators of many contemporary fictions are
nonhuman.

1431 Dowd, Joe. "He Played French Horn Well, But a Boy Called
'Bud' Became a Writer." Rochester Democrat and Chronicle,
16 September 1982, pp. B1-B2.
Gardner's guidance counselor at Batavia High School,

where the class of 1951 voted him the "most studious,"
recalls Gardner as shy but likeable and possessing a fine
sense of humor. Pauline Gehring, his speech teacher, says
he was modest about his considerable potential; as the lead
actor in The Valiants, he held the audience spellbound.
Gardner transferred from Alexander High School to Batavia
because of the latter's superior music program. Although
his music teacher, Robert Cook, encouraged him to attend
the Eastman School of Music, where he was offered a $300
scholarship, he accepted an $1800 scholarship from DePauw
University instead. (Includes yearbook photograph and
Gardner's senior grades.)

1432 Dunlap, David W. "John Gardner, 48; Novelist and Poet."
New York Times, 15 September 1982, p. D27. Additional
photo on p. Al.
    Notes details of Gardner's death; recounts literary
career, emphasizing OMF; and briefly sketches biography.

1433 Foy, Nick, and James M. Odato. "Police Rule Gardner Lost
Cycle Control." Binghamton Press, 15 September 1982, p.
A7.
    A detailed account of the accident and the cause of
death (severe abdominal injuries).

1434 "Funeral Services Today for Novelist Gardner." Rochester
Democrat and Chronicle, 19 September 1982, p. B1.
    Brief notice.

1435 "Gardner: A 'Thinker and Philosopher.'" Rochester Times-
Union, 15 September 1982, pp. C1, C3.
    In a telephone interview Joe David Bellamy eulogizes
Gardner as "a literary lion" who influenced such contemporary writers as Clark Blaise and Joyce Carol Oates. He
was a "mover and shaker," firmly committed to a humanistic
fiction. Article also briefly discusses G, quotes from
OMF, and quotes Bernard Rosenthal on Gardner's generosity
to young writers.

1436 "Gardner Memorial Today." Binghamton Sun-Bulletin, 22
September 1982.
    Brief announcement of the details of the memorial
service and the John Gardner Creative Writing Endowment.

1437 Gass, William. "Adventures in the Writing Life." Interview with Stanley Elkin. Washington Post Book World,
10 October 1982, pp. 1, 10.

Elkin says Gardner "worried death the way a kid might worry a loose tooth"--a point that should have been obvious to everyone at the Bread Loaf Writers' conference this past summer. Gass agrees that Gardner seemed to move progressively from the accident which killed his brother Gilbert to his own death.

1438 Greiner, Donald J. "Sailing Through The King's Indian with John Gardner and His Friends." In John Gardner: Critical Perspectives. Ed. Robert A. Morace and Kathryn VanSpanckeren. Carbondale and Edwardsville: Southern Illinois University Press, 1982, pp. 76-88.

"Sailing through the tricks and masks is part of the fun. The other part is trying to determine Gardner's attitude toward this kind of writing." The collection "is at once Gardner's parody of gimmickry, his illustration of literature reassessing traditional values, and his homage to art as entertainment." Not what is said in these stories but how it is said is the chief concern; Gardner's heroes are in fact his narrators, and readers are invited to become active participants in the stories.

1439 Harkness, James. "In Memoriam: John Champlin Gardner: 1933-1982." The News (State University of New York), October-November 1982, Forum sec., p. 2.

In person Gardner was prosaic. In 1970 he was prone to philosophizing and making "impromptu manifestoes," but by 1979 he had learned the consequences of saying things to see if they were true. Oft-rejected and revised, his early works evidence greater "technical facility" than the later, more hurriedly composed writings. Essentially Gardner is a romantic pastoralist emphasizing setting, character, moment, and soul. In an age whose hold on the present is at best tenuous, Gardner's reworkings of old forms in new voices (as in his "inexplicably neglected masterpiece" JM) is especially important. (A notice concerning the John Gardner Creative Writing Endowment appears on the same page.)

1440 Hart, Richard E. Letter to the editor. Newsday, 22 September 1982, p. 55.

Gardner may have deserved some of the criticism he received during the past few years. However, "at bottom, he was an extraordinarily decent and caring human being, an eloquent voice for tradition and the possibilities of human nobility and greatness." Dan Cryer's tribute to Gardner (15 September 1982) was "sensitive and balanced."

1440a Harvey, John. "Dealing with Death." Rev. of Mickelsson's
    Ghosts. Times (London), 14 November 1982, p. 44.
    The imagination is given room to breathe in this comfort-
    ably long book. Like Gravity's Rainbow, it is "another
    American epic of political superstition." Although its
    fears are more localized than in Pynchon, Gardner still
    manages to find "the right uncanniness for a ghost story
    of our times." Mickelsson is chiefly frightened by "the
    large-scale human agencies he encounters."

1441 Harwood, John T. Critics, Values, and Restoration Comedy.
    Carbondale and Edwardsville: Southern Illinois University
    Press, 1982, p. 115.
    Quote from OMF is used as an epigraph for chapter 6.

1442 Hassan, Ihab. "Wars of Desire, Politics of the Word."
    Salmagundi, 55 (Winter 1982), 121.
    Cites Gardner's criticism of Gass as a writer concerned
    solely with language.

1443 Hokenson, Jan. "Gardner, John (Champlin, Jr.)." In
    Contemporary Novelists. Ed. James Vinson. 3rd. ed. New
    York: St. Martin's Press, 1982, pp. 238-41.
    Gardner's heroes are "flawed samaritans doing their
    best to act responsibly in an incomprehensible world.
    Learning the inadequacy of their dualistic vision (good/
    evil; morality/immorality; sanity/madness), they come to
    accept their mortality and common humanity.

1444 Holliday, Barbara. "John Gardner Left a Legacy of
    Quality." Detroit Free Press, 19 September 1982, p. D5.
    Summarizes Gardner's career, agrees with Benjamin
    DeMott that "hospitality to ideas" is the strongpoint of
    his fiction, and quotes John Aldridge (University of
    Michigan) on Gardner's having made "a decisive difference
    in the quality of our literary culture" and Janice Lauer
    (Purdue University) on his having been wise, shrewd,
    brilliant, "at times gentle," and quick to detect folly,
    especially in himself. His death, Lauer says, means the
    loss of his unique perspective, his espousal of "a
    hierarchy of values."

1445 "John Gardner." Times (London), 18 September 1982, p. 8.
    Surveys Gardner's career, emphasizing Gardner's erudite
    style. G concerns "the difficulty of living graciously
    in the face of the contemporary materialistic mentality."

1446 "John C. Gardner Jr." [editorial]. Batavia (N.Y.) Daily
      News, 16 September 1982, p. 2.
          Although a genius, Gardner "never lost the common touch"
      and in the face of criticism stood as firm as a farmer.
      He spent much of his past summer helping in the rehabil-
      itation of his father, who had suffered a stroke.

1447 "John Gardner, Author, Dies." Washington Post, 15
      September 1982, p. Al.
          Two-sentence notice; photograph.

1448 Kalish, David. "The Continuing Dream." Pipe Dream (SUNY-
      Binghamton), 15 September 1982, p. 2. Special issue.
          Gardner was a "workaholic" and "a visionary." He strove
      to understand his characters' moral and emotional natures.
      In the six hours he met with his fall 1982 fiction work-
      shop, he told students to dream, to become children again,
      to undergo the process of self-discovery in order to
      cultivate the dream-state necessary for the creation of
      any work of art.

1449 Kakutani, Michiko. "John Barth, in Search of Simplicity."
      New York Times, 28 June 1982, sec. III, p. 1.
          Notes Gardner's criticism of Barth's literary games-
      playing.

1450 King, Stephen. "Afterword." Different Seasons. New
      York: Viking Press, 1982, p. 521.
          King prefers to be a writer of horror fiction than
      either an "important" writer like Heller or a "brilliant"
      writer, like Gardner, "of obscure books for politically
      liberal academics.

1451 Klinkowitz, Jerome. "John Gardner's Grendel." In John
      Gardner: Critical Perspectives. Ed. Robert A. Morace
      and Kathryn VanSpanckeren. Carbondale and Edwardsville:
      Southern Illinois University Press, 1982, pp. 62-67.
          Gardner's concept of moral fiction, with its emphasis
      on the heroic deal, is his response to the "presumed
      decadence" of the 1960s. The technique of G also derives
      from that same period--specifically, the emphasis on in-
      novation and experimentation at the Iowa Writers Workshop.
      Though a "clever exercise," G, like most Iowa experiments,
      is not entirely successful as a published work. His
      "anti-myth" seems a rather "private affair" written by
      and for John Gardner. Moreover, his sympathetic portrayal

of the monster puts the work at odds with the author's
idea of moral fiction and thus makes the novel "self-
contradictory."

1452 LeClair, Thomas. "Avant-Garde Mastery." TriQuarterly,
53 (1982), 259, 262.
"Critical conservatives" like Gardner and avant-garde
writers are both wrong; works such as Barth's Letters,
which are at once experimental and referential, "large,
ambitious, syncretistic systems," will serve as the moral
standard of the decade.

1453 LeClair, Thomas. "Robert Coover, The Public Burning, and
the Art of Excess." Critique, 23, iii (1982), 5.
The "conscience and communication" Gardner calls for
in his "noisy attack," OMF, are present in works such as
The Public Burning.

1454 Littlejohn, Beth, Rebecca Parke, and Charles Israel.
"Writer's Workshop" Study Guide. New York: Holt, Rinehart
and Winston, 1982, pp. 27-30. Also published in Overview:
Writer's Workshop (Columbia: University of South Carolina
and the South Carolina Educational Television Network,
1982, pp. 22-24.
Contents: biographical sketch, overview of telecourse
(Gardner's discussion with students in William Price
Fox's and James Dickey's writing courses), "Reading
Assignment," "Learning Activities," "Journal Entry and
Writing Suggestions," and checklist of major works.

1455 "Loving Gardner." Southern Illinoisan (Carbondale), 16
September 1982, p. 4.
Gardner was both engaging and energetic; he loved
southern Illinois and was in turn loved by its people, who
recall him as "a country boy riding his horse." The
peacefulness of the area "helped him to explore the meaning of life, death and human purpose" in novels that are
at once philosophical and entertaining. His former student,
Stephen Falcone, said Gardner was "shy" and "sweet"; "in
the finest way, he was mad."

1456 McCaffery, Larry. The Metafictional Muse: The Works of
Robert Coover, Donald Barthelme, and William H. Gass.
Pittsburgh: University of Pittsburgh Press, 1982, pp.
261-62.
OMF ("stimulating but carelessly conceived") created
"illusory polarities" that obscured and simplified key

issues in the debate over contemporary fiction. In FB
Gardner uses postmodernist techniques in a seemingly
traditional novel.

1457 McDowell, Edwin. "The Paperback Evolution." New York
Times Book Review, 10 January 1982, p. 27.
"In the works [at Ballantine Books] are new mass-
market paperbacks by John Gardner" and others.

1458 Martin, Richard. Rev. of The Comfort of Strangers, by
Ian McEwan. American Book Review, 5 (November-December
1982), 23.
Gardner is cited among the innovative writers of the
1960s and 1970s.

1459 "Milestones." Time, 27 September 1982, p. 49.
Death notice; briefly discusses Gardner as teacher,
"philosophical fabulist," and critic of contemporary
fiction.

1460 Miller, Ivy, and Barbara Jorgensen. "The Philosopher
Warrior Battled With a Pen." Pipe Dream (SUNY-Binghamton),
15 September 1982, p. 2. Special issue.
Summarizes Gardner's career and his view of contemporary
literature; concludes that Gardner advocated moral discovery not moral didacticism. He "wished to channel new
literary talent, not teach it." (An excerpt from OMF is
reprinted alongside this article.)

1461 Mitgang, Herbert. "About Books and Authors: Fiction as
Meditation." New York Times Book Review, 12 December
1982, p. 34.
Gardner recommended Kikuo Itaya's Tengu Child to
Southern Illinois University Press, which will publish
the translation by Nobuko Tsukui and Gardner (who put
Tsuki's work into idiomatic English) in January. Article
quotes from Gardner's introduction, which the book's
editor, James Simmons, calls "the most original analysis
of the Buddhist literary method available in the West."
Another Gardner book, "On Becoming a Novelist," will be
published by Harper & Row in May.

1462 Morace, Robert A. "Introduction." John Gardner:
Critical Perspectives. Ed. Robert A. Morace and Kathryn
VanSpanckeren. Carbondale and Edwardsville: Southern
Illinois University Press, 1982, pp. xiii-xxii.
The "Introduction" briefly surveys the critical recep-

tion of Gardner's fiction, adding that "In sum, his is a fiction which mediates between innovation and tradition in terms of both literary techniques and human values." Gardner's characters are often idealists who find themselves betrayed; they find it difficult to act in a world that is ambiguous or, worse, unstable. Some embrace the existentialist position; others become Gardner's characteristically "peculiar heroes" who attain a limited sense of dignity by choosing to act for others. The "fundamental choice" in all of Gardner's fiction is "whether to affirm life or to deny it" (this theme is discussed at some length in relation to "two lesser known works," "The Old Men" and Vlemk.

1463 Morace, Robert A., and Kathryn VanSpanckeren, eds. John Gardner: Critical Perspectives. Carbondale and Edwardsville: Southern Illinois University Press, 1982.
Contents: "Preface," by [Kathryn VanSpanckeren]; "Introduction," by [Robert A. Morace]; "Et in Arcadia Ego: Gardner's Early Pastoral Novels," by David Cowart; "'Into the Farther Darkness': The Manichaean Pastoralism of John Gardner," by Samuel Coale; "A Babylonian in Batavia: Mesopotamian Literature and Lore in SD," by Greg Morris; "G and Blake: The Contraries of Existence," by Helen B. Ellis and Warren U. Ober; "John Gardner's G," by Jerome Klinkowitz; "Survival and Redemptive Vision in JM," by John Trimbur; "Sailing Through KI with John Gardner and His Friends," by Donald J. Greiner; "Modern Moralities for Children: John Gardner's Children's Books," by Geraldine DeLuca and Roni Natov; "John Gardner, Librettist: A Composer's Notes," by Joseph Baber; "The Real Monster in FB," by Walter Cummins; "Magical Prisons: Embedded Structure in the Work of John Gardner," by Kathryn VanSpanckeren; "New Fiction, Popular Fiction, and John Gardner's Middle/Moral Way," by Robert A. Morace; "Afterword," by John Gardner; "Checklist of Principal Works." (For annotations see the entry listed by individual author.)

1464 Morris, Greg. "A Babylonian in Batavia: Mesopotamian Literature and Lore in The Sunlight Dialogues." In John Gardner: Critical Perspectives. Ed. Robert A. Morace and Kathryn VanSpanckeren. Carbondale and Edwardsville: Southern Illinois University Press, 1982, pp. 28-45.
For SD Gardner has borrowed extensively from the Epic of Gilgamesh and A. Leo Oppenheim's Ancient Mesopotamia:

308

Portrait of a Dead Civilization (1964) in order to create
"a vast cross-cutting of Time and Space, moving with ease
between antique Mesopotamia and 20th-century western New
York." Gardner's borrowings range from specific chapter
titles and the general attributes of his characters to
the overall themes of his novel. In Gilgamesh, the
thwarting of man's desire for immortality leads to pessimism; it is against this pessimism that Gardner holds
up "the value of human action." The tragic friendship of
Gilgamesh and Enkidu is mirrored in Clumly and the Sunlight Man. The former is the Babylonian king, while the
latter is the magician-priest-diviner whose purpose "is
to bring Clumly closer to the proper state of divine
kingship and to illuminate the dark spots in Clumly's
world." Gardner's borrowings--what he calls his "'collage
technique'"--add emotional and intellectual richness to
his novel; they suggest that "the proper ethical and
political stance most appropriate for the 20th-century
world" is neither Babylonian nor Hebraic but instead in
"the proper mix of anarchy and conservatism, of foresight
and immediacy, of devotion to culture and to destiny."

1465 Morrow, Lance. "We Need More Writers We'd Miss." Time,
120 (26 July 1982), 64.
Morrow includes Gardner among those contemporary writers
whose silence would not be a great loss to American
literature.

1466 Ness, Jean. "Novelist Gardner Left His Mark on Southern
Illinois." Southern Illinoisan (Carbondale), 15
September 1982, p. 1.
Gardner, who was to appear in Carbondale next week, is
recalled by local friends: Judy Carter claims his accident
was "inevitable" given the intensity with which he lived;
John Howell recalls Gardner's "passionate" involvement
in life, concern for students and writers, and obsession
with his brother Gilbert's death. Article briefly surveys
Gardner's career and mentions his unsuccessful campaign
for election to the local school board and his basing a
character in SD on Robert Faner, former chairman of the
English Department at SIU-Carbondale.

1467 Norris, Tim. "Another Life of Legendary Scope."
Rochester Times-Union, 15 September 1982, pp. C1, C3.
Includes a biographical sketch emphasizing the OMF
controversy and a reading at St. Lawrence University where

Gardner, dressed like a magician, remained aloof from faculty but was "patient and kind" with students. His mother comments on the outpouring of sympathy from around the world, on Gardner's weekly visits home following his father's return from a nursing facility in May, and on his marriage to Susan Thornton that that was to have taken place on 18 September in Rochester. Warren Benson discusses his collaboration with Gardner on the song-cycle "Songs for the End of the World"; Gardner's poems concern "an elderly woman looking back on her life and her children" and eventually realizing "she's done her best."

1468 "Novelist John Gardner Dies at 49." Newsday, 15 September 1982.

This article, drawn from "Combined News Services," provides details of Gardner's death, overview of career (emphasizing SD and OL), quotes from July interview in Washington Post, and quotes Bernard Rosenthal on Gardner's dedication to teaching.

1469 "Novelist John Gardner Killed in Motorcycle Accident." Buffalo Courier-Express, 15 September 1982, pp. Al, A8.

Notes details of Gardner's death and career; quotes Bernard Rosenthal on Gardner's dedication to teaching, Gardner from July Washington Post interview, and Gardner's close friend Carl Dennis on Gardner's seriousness as a writer and the brilliance of his unfinished novel "Shadows." Also recounts the circumstances of Gardner's not having been appointed at SUNY-Buffalo in 1978. (The Associated Press release from which this article derives, also forms the basis for obituaries in the following newspapers published 15 September 1982: Albany Knickerbocker News, p. B12; Atlanta Constitution, p. Al; Boston Globe, p. 42; Denver Post, p. All; Des Moines Register, p. A6; Syracuse Herald-Journal, p. A9; Syracuse Post Standard, pp. Al, A8 [annotated above]; Watertown [N.Y.] Daily Times, p. 2.)

1470 "Novelist Killed." London Times, 15 September 1982, p. 1.
Brief notice.

1471 Odato, James M. "Gardner Talent Called 'Important.'" Binghamton Press, 15 September 1982, p. A7.

Malamud regrets the loss of Gardner, whom he calls "a born writer" who did not always realize his imagination's potential. Gass says Gardner was indisputably an important writer who appealed to readers of traditional fiction.

Anatole Broyard claims Gardner was "crowding the heels of
the best novelists of the age." Christopher Lehmann-
Haupt notes that as a writer Gardner was as reckless as
he was gifted. His work is "overwritten, over-ripe, having
that quality of searching"; he was at his best when writing
of the people and country of upstate New York.

1472 Odato, James M. Binghamton Sun-Bulletin, 20 September
1982.
Detailed description of the ceremony devised by the
family and emphasizing music ("family favorites" and a
song composed by Gardner's friend Walter Benson). During
the ceremony the Rev. John T. Dunham said, "The words of
comfort he often gave his loved ones, 'Come on, now, we're
going to be all right,'" will long be remembered. Dorothy
Moynihan, of Batavia, identifies herself as the girl in
NM.

1473 Odato, James M. "Memories Flow at Gardner Rite."
Binghamton Press, 20 September 1982, p. A7. Additional
photograph on p. Al.
Describes service arranged by daughter Lucy and composed
chiefly of music. Notes Gardner's trouble with Internal
Revenue Service. Quotes comments of friends and colleagues.
Neighbor John Rodriquez said Gardner always "wanted to do
so much"; the Laurel Street Theater in Susquehanna will
be renamed in Gardner's honor. Novelist Ron Hansen spoke
of the John C. Gardner Fellowship in Writing to be
established at Bread Loaf. Ted Solotaroff briefly described Gardner's "Becoming a Novelist," to be published
in the spring. Susan Strehle said the service "was so
like John." According to Lucy Gardner, her father "over-
booked himself."

1474 Orsini, Joe. "John Gardner, Literary Master, Dead at 49."
Pipe Dream (SUNY-Binghamton), 15 September 1982, p. 1.
Special issue.
Details of the accident; quotes various members of the
SUNY-Binghamton community. Bernard Rosenthal (English
Department chairman) and Clifford Clark (university pres-
ident) on Gardner's devotion to students, Susan Billert-
Duffy (a student in his fiction workshop), John Bielenberg
(who adapted SD for the stage) on his generous nature, and
Christian Graber (of the English Department) who said
Gardner gave the writing program a focus, was well-liked
and virtually "irreplaceable."

1475 Owen, Charles A., Jr. "The Alternative Reading of The Canterbury Tales: Chaucer's Text and the Early Manuscripts." PMLA, 97 (March 1982), 237, 247.
  Gardner ("The Case Against the 'Bradshaw Shift,'" 1966; PC) is among the many contemporary scholars who have erroneously accepted the Ellesmere order as Chaucer's own.

1476 Palmer, R. Barton. "The Problem with Gardner's On Moral Fiction." Renascence, 34 (Spring 1982), 161-72.
  Although more a cri de coeur than a reasoned argument, OMF deserves serious attention. Unfortunately Gardner's views are muddled. On the one hand he says literature must be free of conscious intention while on the other he claims it must be consciously moral. He is vague about what is wrong with didactic literature and "about the process of unconscious moral writing." Without conscious intent, the imagination can produce immoral works just as easily as moral. It is possible to read G as a denial of all moral values and of the power of literature to transform reality. Although Gardner probably intended readers to reject Grendel's views, he fails to provide the reader with the means to do so because Gardner mistakenly accepts "the aestheticist bias against didacticism."

1477 Pearson, Richard. "John C. Gardner, Novelist, Dies." Washington Post, 15 September 1982, p. C11.
  Briefly surveys Gardner's life and career, emphasizing OL.

1478 Pfalzer, Marilyn. "Abdominal Hemorrhage Blamed for Author's Death." Batavia (N.Y.) Daily News, 16 September 1982, p. 1.
  Brief summary of accident and autopsy reports; notes calling hours at the Turner funeral home and plans for memorial service at SUNY-Binghamton. (The funeral home's "In Memoriam" appears on p. 4.)

1479 Pfalzer, Marilyn. "Mourners Crowd Church for Gardner Funeral." Batavia (N.Y.) Daily News, 20 September 1982, pp. 1, 4.
  Attended by more than 400 mourners, the service at Batavia's First United Presbyterian Church was "a musical celebration" of Gardner's life. During the service, the Rev. John T. Dunham read from Gardner's inscription in his parents' copy of Res (not "Redemption" as the article

reports); a special French horn solo written for the service by Warren Benson was also played. Burial will be on 20 September at Grand View Cemetary. On Wednesday, there will be a memorial service at SUNY-Binghamton. Contributions for the creative writing endowment begun by Gardner and Anthony Miceli are being accepted.

1480 "A Poet: Motorcycle Crash Kills Author, SUNY Professor John Gardner." Syracuse Post Standard, 15 September 1982, pp. A1, A8.

To Associated Press release (see "Novelist John Gardner Killed in Motorcycle Accident," Buffalo Courier-Express) adds Mordecai Richler's praise of Gardner's talent, originality, and distinctive style and comments from an unlocated UPI interview in which Gardner said that writing is both "exhilarating" and "tiring." The kind of factual reportage Tom Wolfe writes is not really literature. In his own writing, Gardner likes to enter "a trance state"; he prefers writing novels rather than short stories, which "seem all overweighted. I'm one of those persons who stands back ... and slings paint at the canvas. And they look good if you stand far enough away." Gardner also considers his fiction autobiographical: "I'm always living the novels I write."

1481 Prampolini, Gaetano. "Italian Contributions." In American Literary Scholarship: An Annual/1980. Ed. J. Albert Robbins. Durham, N.C.: Duke University Press, 1982, p. 572.

Gardner's "A Writer's View of Contemporary American Fiction" (Dismisura, 1980) is "a spirited, provocative, and at times amusing survey" which "reads like a preliminary draft" of OMF.

1482 Ragovin, Helene, and Steve Spero. "Campus Flecked with Dismay." Binghamton Press, 15 September 1982, p. A7.

Notes students' reactions to Gardner's death. Gregory E. Donovan, a Ph.D. candidate in creative writing, describes Gardner as having been honest, dedicated, concerned, and "completely unpretentious."

1483 Rapkin, Angela. "John Gardner: The Technique of Moral Fiction." Diss. University of South Florida 1982.

In OMF Gardner criticizes postmodern writers for emphasizing language and foregoing the search for understanding and affirmation which characterizes moral fiction.

Yet in WA, G, OL, ISM, and FB, Gardner utilizes postmodern techniques. Gardner ha's learned not only to ac-
commodate these techniques in his work but, in FB, that
postmodernism and moral fiction need not be incompatible.

1484 Ravenel, Shannon. "100 Other Distinguished Short Stories
     of the Year 1981." The Best American Short Stories 1982.
     Ed. John Gardner and Shannon Ravenel. Boston: Houghton
     Mifflin, 1982, p. 366.
         Lists "Come on Back."

1485 "Revelation in Death." [editorial]. Southern Illinoisan
     (Carbondale), 20 September 1982, p. 4.
         The media's response to the deaths of Gardner and
     Princess Grace is worth pondering. Whereas Princess Grace,
     who reflected our fantasies, received front-page attention,
     Gardner, "one of his generation's best writers," "a
     creator of our culture" whose work serves as "a measure
     of our civilization," was relegated to the back pages.

1486 Rout, Kay Kinsella. "The Ghoul-Haunted Woodland of
     Southern Illinois: John Gardner's 'The Ravages of Spring.'"
     Studies in Short Fiction, 19 (Winter 1982), 27-33.
         The story's narrator is schizophrenic and unreliable;
     his experience with John Hunter may be nothing more than
     a "psychotic episode ... triggered by anniversary mourning,"
     or so the references to Poe and MacBeth suggest. Like
     "Young Goodman Brown" and The Turn of the Screw, Gardner's
     story deals with "the borderline between dream and reality."

1487 Rubins, Josh. "Variety Shows." Rev. of George Mills, by
     Stanley Elkin, and The Names, by Don DeLillo. New York
     Review of Books, 29 (16 December 1982), 46.
         Recent novels by Barth, DeLillo, Elkin, Malamud,
     Vonnegut, and Gardner (MG) "suggest the fatigue (or
     uneasinesss) that dogs recent attempts to reach beyond
     life-sized storytelling" to the epical and the fantastic.

1488 Schmidt, Josephine. "The Man, His Life and His Work."
     Pipe Dream (SUNY-Binghamton), 15 September 1982, pp. 1,
     2. Special issue.
         Biographical sketch; dates acceptance of Res by New
     American Library 9 October 1964.

1489 Simon, Jeff. "Novelist Gardner Was Table Banger."
     Buffalo News, 19 September 1982, p. F5.

Gardner's polemics in OMF forced his opponents to
clarify their positions, identified a major failing in
much of contemporary fiction, which is too academic, and
made American fiction healthier than it had been. As
Jayne Anne Phillips recently said, "I, for one, am kind
of grateful to him." Gardner was not immune to the charge
of literary gamesplaying, as MG makes clear. All his
works are hybrids: half upstate conservative and half
literary showmanship designed to impress the sophisticated
downstaters who read Barthelme.

1490 Sinkler, Rebecca. "Novelist John Gardner Remained
'Promising.'" Toledo Blade, 26 September 1982, p. E2.
Knight News Service.
   Robert Gottlieb, Gardner's editor at Knopf, says that
even Gardner's early fiction seemed the work of a mature
writer. Gardner, who may have been "indiscriminately
praised" at the beginning of his career, was deeply hurt
by the harsh criticism of MG. He was "wonderful to work
with," Gottlieb reports; so "clever and ingenious" he
could transform an idea into a book quickly and effectively.
Joel Conarroe, President of the Modern Language Association, says LTC damaged Gardner's reputation; except for
the "magical" G, his works have not been accepted into
the canon of American literature. Deidre Bair, of the
University of Pennsylvania, says her students liked to
discuss G, though always on ethical rather than literary
grounds; the promise of that early novel was never realized, she claims; instead Gardner became repetitive.
And William Gass doubts Gardner's work will continue to
be read unless, like Kerouac, he becomes a mythic figure.
Gardner expressed the discontent of the average reader
of contemporary fiction far better in late night talks
with Gass than he did in OMF.

1491 Sullivan, Jerry. "Author John Gardner Is Killed in Crash."
Binghamton Sun-Bulletin, 15 September 1982, p. A3.
Additional photograph on p. A1.
   Notes details of accident and cause of death; brief sum-
mary of Gardner's career.

1492 "SUNY Mourns Gardner." Binghamton Sun-Bulletin, 23
September 1982.
   Brief description of the memorial service held 22
September at SUNY-Binghamton.

1493 "SUNY Plans Gardner Endowment." Binghamton Sun-Bulletin,
17 September 1982.
Based on Basler article, 16 September 1982.

1494 Suplee, Curt. "John Gardner." Washington Post, 25 July
1982, pp. H1, H8-H9.
Gardner is a contradictory figure, energetic and generous
but also debauched and self-destructive. As Gail Godwin
has said, Gardner has the ability "to revise himself almost instantly." MG, "a highbrow potboiler" and one of
Gardner's best novels, is partly autobiographical. See
also the annotation for this item listed under Interviews.

1495 Suplee, Curt. "John Gardner's Driven Life." Washington
Post, 15 September 1982, pp. B1, B15.
Drawn chiefly from Suplee's 25 July 1982 interview with
Gardner.

1496 Taylor, Robert. "The Voices of John Gardner." Boston
Globe, 16 September 1982, p. 38.
In OMF, Gardner proved himself a "formidable polemicist."
Setting for himself and others the standard of the major
novelists of the 19th Century, he combined a yearning for
the certitudes they enjoyed with his own modern sensibility.
He viewed life as a quest for awareness; he gave expression to the many and varied voices within him and provided not answers but participation "in the mystery and
awe of existence." Gardner was erudite but never didactic;
SD and OL (which is "a contemporary religious novel" as
well as fiction about fiction, are his best works. In a
taped interview aired 15 September 1982 on National Public
Radio, Gardner compared himself to an action painter
slinging paint onto a large canvas and claimed that the
purpose of fiction is to take the reader out of the real
world and "into the eternal sunlit world where novels
take place" (a transformation which illustrations in
books facilitate).

1497 "Three Suns Eclipsed" [editorial]. Binghamton Press, 16
September 1982, p. A6.
Gardner, Princess Grace, and Bashir Gemayel are the
three "suns" that have been eclipsed by sudden death.
Gardner, who quickly became "community property" in
Binghamton, was a man of boundless energy," candor, and
devotion to young writers.

316

1497a Torrens, James. "John C. Gardner: 1933-1982." America, 147 (25 December 1982), 414-15.

Gardner's accomplishments are both varied and many, but his reputation remains uncertain. Although his scholarship has been attacked by medievalists and his fiction and literary theory have been scorned by the avant-garde, Gardner has left his imprint on his age. He had a "vigorous mind and roving imagination." His criticism of Saul Bellow seems especially odd in light of his own penchant for abstract thought in G, SD, JM, FB, and MG.

1498 "Transition." Newsweek, 27 September 1982, p. 63.

Death notice; describes Gardner's fiction as "richly textured, idea-studded," and stylistically varied.

1499 Travin, Tom. "Writer John Gardner Dies in Accident." Daily Egyptian (Southern Illinois University-Carbondale), 15 September 1982, pp. 1-2.

Provides details of accident and death, mentions the reading Gardner was to give at SIU-C on 22 September, surveys Gardner's career, and quotes members of the SIU-C faculty: John Howell (on Gardner as a major writer), William Simeone (on Gardner as a successful teacher and novelist), Richard Lawson (on his helpfulness and reputation as a medievalist), and Manuel Schonhorn (on his "roots" in Carbondale).

1500 Travin, Tom. "'Celebration of Life' Was Gardner Goal." Daily Egyptian (Southern Illinois University-Carbondale), 16 September 1982, p. 1.

Surveys Gardner's career; mentions details of accident and funeral arrangements; quotes John Howell on the "workaholic" Gardner's passionate involvement in the life he celebrated in his fiction, his "playing around with old themes," his literary preferences, and his novel-in-progress, "Shadows."

1501 "Tribute to Gardner Planned Tomorrow by Local Station." Binghamton Press, 18 September 1982.

WSKG-FM will present a Gardner "Retrospective" which will include a previously recorded interview, a performance of his "Songs for the End of the World," and readings from SD.

1502 Trimbur, John. "Survival and Redemptive Vision in Jason and Medeia." In John Gardner: Critical Perspectives. Ed.

Robert A. Morace and Kathryn VanSpanckeren. Carbondale
and Edwardsville: Southern Illinois University Press,
1982, pp. 68-75.
Gardner, like his source, Apollonios Rhodios, parodies
the epic in order "to play its form against the values of
the heroic tradition." Their Jason is "passive" and
"introspective." In Gardner's story, Jason has "no redeeming vision"; morally impotent and intent solely on
his own survival, he is unconcerned with "matters of
principle" and even his tale-telling is self-serving.
Gardner's concern is with "the imperfections of human
nature and the limits of heroism," yet he ironically
exposes the contemporary "cultural malaise that identifies all too readily with the moral weakness of Jason as
victim, that draws an easy equation between Jason's crimes
and his helplessness in a world he did not make." Gardner
ends up affirming "not simple survival but the pursuit
of life" and "its sacred indivisibility."

1503 VanSpanckeren, Kathryn. "Magical Prisons: Embedded
Structures in the Work of John Gardner." In John Gardner:
Critical Perspectives. Ed. Robert A. Morace and Kathryn
VanSpanckeren. Carbondale and Edwardsville: Southern
Illinois University Press, 1982, pp. 114-29.
A recurrent figure in Gardner's work is the shaper, the
manipulator of reality who, by means of tales and magic
tricks, either enhances or violates reality. Often the
shaper is an outlaw or prisoner, and appropriately there
are numerous "metaphoric prisons" which serve both to
restrict individual freedom and to give man a needed sense
of place and being. Gardner's language serves a similar
purpose. In G, for example, he indicts existential language
as privatistic and imprisoning and defends the truly liberating "language of relatedness and obligations." The
solipsism implicit in the former Gardner overcomes by
means of embedding. His embedding, which ranges from
individual phrases to entire narratives, creates suspense,
delaying the narrative and thus serving as a temporal
equivalent of imprisonment. Given that embedding depends
on subordination, Gardner's embedded flashbacks, imagery,
and delays in plot also deepen the moral dilemma from which
character and reader are liberated at the story's end.
This technique enables Gardner "to create arenas in which
alternate realities clamour for our allegiance." His
"true magician" not only manipulates the various "frames"
of reality; he "passes through them to gain a greater
perspective...."

1504 VanSpanckeren. "Preface." In <u>John Gardner: Critical</u>
<u>Perspectives</u>. Ed. Robert A. Morace and Kathryn Van
Spanckeren. Carbondale and Edwardsville: Southern
Illinois University Press, 1982, pp. ix-xii.
Discusses the book's genesis (the 1979 convention of
the Northeast Modern Language Association, in which Gardner
participated) and provides an overview of the twelve
essays.

1505 Vernon, John. "John Gardner's Loss Was Our Loss."
<u>Binghamton Press</u>, 19 September 1982, pp. E1, E2.
Vernon, Gardner's friend and colleague, surveys the
major works (dividing them into two classes: realistic
novels and extended fables) and comments on Gardner's
compassionate treatment of his characters and admirable
preoccupation with upstate New York. <u>OMF</u>, which Gardner
never thought would be taken as seriously as it was, had
the unfortunate result of causing reviewers to judge <u>FB</u>,
<u>AL</u>, and <u>MG</u> on the basis of the author rather than the
writing. <u>MG</u> is a powerful novel, reminiscent of Mann's
<u>The Magic Mountain</u>.

1506 Vrazo, Fawn. "Motorcycle Crash Kills Novelist Gardner, a
Native of Batavia." <u>Buffalo Evening News</u>, 15 September
1982, p. A4. Knight News Service. Additional photograph
on p. A4.
In addition to biography and details of accident and
funeral arrangements, article notes that Gardner was to
marry Susan Thornton on 18 September, paraphrases Bernard
Rosenthal's view that <u>MG</u> is autobiographical, and quotes
from Gardner's July <u>Washington Post</u> interview.

1507 Westcott, Holly Sims. "Joyce Carol Oates." In <u>Dictionary</u>
<u>of Literary Biography Yearbook 1981</u>. Ed. Karen Rood et
al. Detroit: Gale Research, 1982, p. 123.
Quotes approvingly from Gardner's review of <u>Bellefleur</u>
(<u>New York Times Book Review</u>, 20 July 1980).

1508 Wigler, Stephen. "Literati, Hometowners Say Goodbye to
John Gardner." <u>Rochester Democrat and Chronicle</u>, 20
September 1982, pp. B1, B4. (Title appears as "Literati,
Hometowners Say Their Farewells to Novelist John Gardner"
in edition received in Syracuse, N.Y.)
Gardner would have enjoyed the service attended by 600
mourners spanning Gardner's several worlds (academic,
rural, etc.). Since Gardner was suspicious of organized

religion, the service, planned by his daughter Lucy,
emphasized the music he loved instead of religious talk.
It was his love of hymns that led his family to call him
"Bard," shortened to "Bud," Patricia Benson explained.
After the service, Ted Solotaroff spoke of Gardner's "Becoming a Novelist" (to be published by Harper & Row); it
is the kind of book Gardner wished he had had as a young
writer. Novelists Ron Hansen and John Gillespie mentioned
Gardner's willingness to work with them at Bread Loaf.
Lucy Gardner said her father's death did not surpise her;
he was always overextending himself and having to rush to
keep all his appointments and obligations.

1509 Wolcott, James. "Straw Dogs." Rev. of Virginie: Her Two
Lives, by John Hawkes and Sabbatical, by John Barth. New
York Review of Books, 29 (10 June 1982), 17.
The problem with these two novels is not that they violate Gardner's notion of moral fiction but that they are
so characteristic of their authors' already familiar
concerns.

1510 Wood, Leonard Green. "Writer John Gardner Dies in Crash:
Classicist Noted for Innovative Stories Killed on Motorcycle." Los Angeles Times, 15 September 1982, sec. 2,
p. 5.
Briefly surveys Gardner's life, emphasizing Gardner's
divided personality (conservative and bohemian) and his
books OMF, SD, and OL.

1511 Ziegler, Heide, and Chris Bigsby. The Radical Imagination and the Liberal Tradition. London: Junction Books,
1982, pp. vii-viii, 1-13, 69.
The starting point for this collection of interviews
is OMF, which, in effect, is a criticism of the way the
radical imagination has supplanted the liberal tradition.
Although OMF is a self-serving and inconsistent book, it
must be taken seriously because Gardner, like Gerald
Graff, speaks for the many readers interested in or
troubled by the relationship between literature and life,
imagination and reality. The British novelist and critic
Malcolm Bradbury is sympathetic towards Gardner's theory
of moral fiction but questions Gardner's "bid to possess
the moral void of fiction in a way to which he is not
entirely entitled."

1512 Bradbury, Malcolm. <u>The Modern American Novel</u>. New York:
Oxford University Press, 1983, pp. 164, 185-86.
Works such as <u>OMF</u> have increased in number as literary
experimentation has become "simple convention and mannerism."
<u>G</u> is cited in an appended list of "major" American novels
published since 1890.

1513 Budd, John. "Gardner vs. Barth." <u>Notes on Contemporary</u>
<u>Literature</u>, 13 (January 1983), 6-7.
Gardner's distaste for the fiction of Barth and other
contemporary writers is implicit in <u>MG</u>, a novel that lends
support to Barth's view of Gardner as a literary reactionary.
"Like Mickelsson, though, Gardner worries little about the
criticism of his contemporaries"; he feels secure enough
to write according to his own standards only.

1514 Carver, Raymond. "Foreword." In <u>On Becoming a Novelist</u>,
by John Gardner. New York: Harper & Row, 1983, pp. ix-
xix. Also published as "John Gardner: Writer and Teacher,"
<u>Georgia Review</u>, 37 (Summer 1983), 413-19.
Carver recalls the semester he spent in 1958 as a
student in Gardner's Creative Writing 101 course at Chico
State College. At the time, Gardner was new to the school
and, as a fiction writer, unpublished. Although he
dressed conservatively, he liked to break rules. In
class, he emphasized endless revision and the honest
development of a story and introduced his students to the
best writers, both new (e.g., Gass) and old. He advised
Carver to read all of Faulkner and then to read Hemingway
to get the Faulkner out of his system. Gardner taught
and represented the "writer's values and craft." He gave
freely of his advice, time, encouragement, and (to Carver)
office space. He was a gifted teacher and writer, as his
"wonderful Book," <u>OBN</u>, plainly shows.

1515 Cascio, Chuck. "Great Writing." <u>Washington Post</u>, 1
March 1983, p. B7.
At the August 1982 Bread Loaf Writers' Conference,
Gardner was, despite his overt pugnacity, sympathetic
towards his audience of would-be writers. In his first
lecture (which lasted sixteen minutes instead of sixty),
he chastised his listeners for wanting to be "great
writers" and for forgetting that their real purpose is to
save mankind. When charged with "cheating" and laughing
at his audience, Gardner advised them to believe that
their work can make a difference. As he explained to

Cascio, the writer has to believe in himself and write honestly; "the hell with everything else." But at one point Gardner also claimed he was no longer interested in writing. His message was, in poet Carolyn Forche's words, "disturbing in many ways."

1516 Cheuse, Alan. "Revenge and Fraud." Rev. of Mean Time, by Christopher T. Leland, and The Brenda Maneuver, by Stephen N. Rosenberg. New York Times Book Review, 16 January 1983, p. 12.
According to Gardner, there are only two good plots: the story of the stranger coming into town and the story of the hero setting forth.

1517 Cowart, David. "The Dying Fall: October Light." Twentieth Century Literature, forthcoming 1983.*

1518 Cowart, David. Arches and Light: The Fiction of John Gardner. Carbondale and Edwardsville: Southern Illinois University Press, forthcoming 1983.*
Chapter 2 appeared in slightly different form in John Gardner: Critical Perspectives, ed. Robert A. Morace and Kathryn VanSpanckeren, 1982. Chapter 6, "The Dying Fall: October Light," will appear in Twentieth Century Literature in 1983.

1518a Daly, Robert. "John Gardner and the Emancipation of Genres." Georgia Review, 37 (Summer 1983), 420-28.
Gardner's early novels are "hybrids, philosophical fictions about what epistemology and point of view have to do with more basic concerns such as staying alive." In them, Gardner provides the reader with characters that make clear the protagonist's limitations. Gardner uses point of view and different genres to free his characters from the limitation of a single point of view in order to widen their perspective, not to propound relativism or absolute freedom. This is what makes his fiction moral. As he wrote to his son Joel, "all tragedy is a limited point of view." In MG Gardner extends his technique to the point that some reviewers have called the novel incoherent. Because Mickelsson's is the only center of consciousness, the limitations of his point of view "become evident not through the minds of other characters but through subsequent narrative action." His fixing up his farmhouse--analogous to the medieval quest--draws Mickelsson out of his solipsism. Lawler and the Spragues

322

are images of isolation. Jessica Stark is "a combination
of genres." Gardner rejects the humanist position, believing that the community is greater than the individual.
The variousness of his own career and his concern for all
aspects of his books, from typeface to illustrations, is
indicative of his belief in the necessity of the larger
view, which is also the theme of his best works, G, OL,
and MG and was to have been the subject of his unfinished
novel, "Shadows."

1519 DeMott, Benjamin. "Domestic Stories." Rev. of The Moons
of Jupiter, by Alice Munro. New York Times Book Review,
20 March 1983, p. 1.
Mentions Gardner's having admired Munro's The Beggar
Maid (1979).

1520 Fredrickson, Robert S. "Losing Battles against Entropy:
The Sunlight Dialogues." Modern Language Studies, 13
(Winter 1983), 47-56.
SD and G are self-deconstructing fictions in which order
is "illustory" and language "both reveals and conceals."
Similarly, the plot of SD is at once familiar (because
mythlike) and enigmatic. Instead of a single omniscient
narrator, Gardner creates numerous plotmakers. In this
way he calls art and language into question. "Anti-
intellectual and anti-art," Gardner prefers life to
artifice and believes that the only true alternative to
entropy is human relationships.

1521 Goodman, Walter. "Giving Business the Business." New
York Times Book Review, 17 April 1983, p. 39.
Quotes approvingly from a paper Gardner wrote for a
seminar at the American Enterprise Institute shortly
before his death. Gardner observes that the image of the
businessman in recent literature is negative.

1522 Howell, John M. "John Gardner." First Printings of
American Authors: Contributions Toward Descriptive
Checklists. Ed. Matthew Bruccoli et al. Detroit:
Gale Research, forthcoming.*
Supplement to Howell's 1978 checklist.

1523 Howell, John M. John Gardner. Twayne's United States
Authors series. Boston: Twayne, forthcoming.*

1524 John Gardner. Living Author Series, no. 5. Edinburg,
Texas: School of Humanities, Pan American University,

323

forthcoming 1983.*
A collection of essays.

1525 Klinkowitz, Jerome. "Fiction: The 1950s to the Present."
In American Literary Scholarship: An Annual/1981. Ed.
James L. Woodress. Durham, N.C.: Duke University Press,
1983, pp. 278, 279, 290, 304.
Sums up Gardner's "serious view" of literature as ex-
pressed in his interview with Ziegler and Bigsby (1981);
notes his "fancy dodging" on KI in the interview with Per
Winther (1981); and identifies the two "hot" topics in
Gardner studies: OMF and the plagiarism charge.

1526 LeClair, Tom, and Larry McCaffery. Anything Can Happen:
Interviews with Contemporary American Novelists. Urbana:
University of Illinois Press, 1983, pp. 1, 3, 5-7, 20-31,
49, 51, 68, 83, 111, 138, 187, 246, 288.
LeClair and McCaffery discuss Gardner's literary gamesplaying (FB) and conservative stance (OMF) and quiz several
of their subjects on the idea of "moral fiction." Rosellen
Brown says writers are not "moral guidance counsellors";
self-reflexive writers are not immoral but neither are
they interested in the lives of the common man. Robert
Coover denies that fiction must be any one thing. Stanley
Elkin calls Gardner a "bore" who propounds second-hand
ideas; genuine works of art, Elkin says, are necessarily
moral. Raymond Federman rejects Gardner's view that
writers should furnish readers with a better world. John
Irving prefers Gardner's view to that of William Gass.
Diane Johnson believes great art does not advocate; it
represents. Joseph McElroy says recent fiction is not
immoral; it is merely different from the fiction of
earlier periods; the greatness of any literary work is
in its process, not its moral message. Ronald Sukenick
claims that great art always becomes moral; Gardner cannot
deal with a great yet immoral writer like Celine, nor can
he understand that the narcissism of self-reflexive fiction
can actually be good for the reader. LeClair's "William
Gass and John Gardner: A Debate on Fiction" (New Republic,
10 March 1979), is reprinted on pp. 20-31.

1527 Morace, Robert A. "Freddy's Book, Moral Fiction, and
Writing as a Mode of Thought." Modern Fiction Studies,
29, ii (1983).
FB exemplifies Gardner's belief that moral fiction is
not didactic but instead a mode of thought in which the

act of writing leads to the discovery of truth. Winesap
and Freddy are writers whose individual narratives reflect significant changes in their ways of understanding
the world and themselves. Neither Winesap's journal nor
Freddy's tale can be called great art; they do, however,
evidence that "groping" after truth that Gardner associates with the initial stages of moral fiction. Winesap
moves from a breezy relativism to a darker (and to the
reader, comic) vision and style (gothicism). Freddy
gradually abandons his history-textbook approach as both
his art and his understanding begin to deepen. Significantly, Gardner went through a similar process; "at some
point during its composition, the story Gardner had designed as an aesthetic joke was transformed into a fairly
complicated parable on the aesthetics of narrative and
the relationship between literature and life."

1528 Morace, Robert A. "John Gardner." In Critical Survey
of Long Fiction. Ed. Frank N. Magill. Englewood Cliffs,
N.J.: Salem Press, forthcoming 1983.
General overview including sections on other literary
forms, achievements, biography, and analysis of all the
novels through MG. The analysis focuses on Gardner's
"common heroes ... who intuitively understand that whatever the odds against them, they must act as if they
could protect those whom they love." Although Gardner
sympathizes with his existential realists, "who show
the world as it is," ultimately he sides with his common
heroes and their affirmative vision of what "should be."

1529 Morace, Robert A. "Mickelsson's Ghosts." In Literary
Annual 1982. Ed. Frank N. Magill. Englewood Cliffs, N.J.:
Salem Press, forthcoming 1983.
Although MG is not Gardner's best novel, it is far better
than many reviewers (e.g., Gilder and Wolcott) have been
willing to admit. As in SD, Gardner weaves together his
numerous characters and multiple plots into a unified
vision that contrasts with and serves as an alternative
to the protagonist's sense of social fragmentation and
spiritual discontinuity. Based in part on Gardner's own
life, Mickelsson is chiefly representative of the contemporary man who finds himself in the midst of a personal
and cultural crisis of faith, Mickelsson is a heroic,
nearly tragic figure as well as a gothic split personality.
His plan to restore his farmhouse--and thereby himself as
well--only partly succeeds. What finally saves Mickelsson

is his reaching out to others for help, first by admitting
his individual helplessness and then by confessing his sins.

1529a Morace, Robert A. "The Moral Structure of John Gardner's
'The King's Indian.'" Midwest Quarterly, 24 (Summer
1983), 388-99.
"KI" is neither an example nor a mere parody of the
funhouse fiction Gardner attacks in OMF. Rather, as in
OL and FB, "Gardner adapts the self-conscious techniques
associated with the new fiction to his moral-fiction
purposes" as he dramatizes the writer-reader relationship.
Stories and storytellers, as well as tricksters and their
victims, abound in Upchurch's tale and the larger story
of which it is a part. Just as Upchurch and the other
characters are deceived by appearances and their own un-
tested ideals, so too is Upchurch's listener and Gardner's
reader tricked by Gardner's "crafty" fabulations.
Gardner's theme is betrayal and its consequences; his
purpose is to remind the reader that while all beliefs
may be fictions, some are useful, even necessary. The
reader is advised to adopt the same "healthy doubleness
of vision "that enables Upchurch to steer a course between
the real and the ideal. Whereas the immoral artist (Flint)
destroys and enslaves, the moral artist "creates and
liberates."

1530 Pieiller, E. Rev. of FB. La Quinzaine Litteraire, no. 390
(16 March 1983), 11.*
Cited in Current Contents: Arts and Humanities, 1983.

1531 Schreiber, Le Anne. "Strange Fish." New York Times
Book Review, 3 July 1983, p. 23.
Quotes extensively from OBN to support the view that
writers do not really understand what they are doing
while they are writing.

Part V
Addendum to Works by John Gardner
Listed in
John Gardner: A Bibliographical Profile (1980)
by John Howell

Separate Publications

1532 Grendel. Hammondsworth, England: Penguin, 1980. Paper-
      bound.* (British National Bibliography)

1533 Bennington College Dedicates Its Arts Complex. Ed. John
      Gardner and Tyler Resch. Bennington Banner, 21 May 1976.
      Special supplement.

1534 In the Suicide Mountains. Illustrated by Joe Servello.
      Boston: Houghton Mifflin, 1980. Paperbound.

1535 Vlemk the Box-Painter. Illustrated by Catherine Kanner.
      Northridge, Calif.: Lord John Press, 1979. Three issues:
      400 signed copies*; signed copies of the "trade edition"*;
      unsigned copies of the "trade edition." (Letter from
      the publisher)

1536 Freddy's Book. Illustrated by Daniel Biamonte. New
      York: Knopf, 1980.

1537 Freddy's Book. New York: Ballantine, 1980. Paperbound.

1538 Freddy's Book. London: Secker and Warburg, 1981.*
      (Times Literary Supplement, 23 October 1981, p. 1231)

1539 The Temptation Game. Dallas: New London Press, 1980.
      Issued in a "limited edition" only, 326 signed copies.

1540 The Art of Living and Other Stories. Illustrated by Mary
      Azarian. New York: Knopf, 1981. Contents: "Nimram,"
      "Redemption," "Stillness," "The Music Lover," "Trumpeter,"
      "The Library Horror," "The Joy of the Just," "Vlemk the
      Box-Painter," "Come on Back," "The Art of Living."

1541 Death and the Maiden. Dallas: New London Press, 1981.*
      (Cited in Books in Print and the publisher's catalogue.)

1542 MSS: A Retrospective. Ed. John Gardner and L. M. Rosenberg.
      Dallas: New London Press, 1981.* Three issues: limited
      signed "edition," cloth, and paperbound. (Booklist, 15
      May 1980, p. 1338; reviewed but never distributed)

1543 **The Thistle.** [Binghamton, N.Y., 1981].* Broadside offered
to patrons of MSS. Cited in MSS.

1544 **The Best American Short Stories 1982.** Ed. John Gardner and
Shannon Ravenel. Boston: Houghton Mifflin, 1982. "Introduction" by John Gardner, pp. ix-xix.

1545 **Mickelsson's Ghosts.** Photographs by Joel Gardner. New
York: Knopf, 1982. Also issued by the Book-of-the-Month
Club.

1546 **Mickelsson's Ghosts.** London: Secker and Warburg, 1982.*
Cited in London Review of Books, 4-17 November 1982, p. 22.

1547 **On Becoming a Novelist.** "Foreword" by Raymond Carver.
New York: Harper & Row, 1983.

1548 **Tengu Child,** by Kikuo Itaya. Trans. John Gardner and
Nobuko Tsukui. Carbondale and Edwardsville: Southern
Illinois University Press, 1983. "Preface" by Gardner
and Tsukui, pp. vi-ix; "Meditational Fiction: An Introduction to the Stories of Kikuo Itaya" by Gardner, pp.
xi-xxv. An excerpt, entitled "Tengu-Child," appeared in
StoryQuarterly, 11 (1980), 1-9.

Contributions to Books

1549 "Moral Fiction." The Pushcart Prize, III: Best of the
Small Presses. Ed. Bill Henderson. New York: Avon, 1979,
pp. 52-68. Paperbound printing of the original edition
published by the Pushcart Press in 1978.

1550 "Afterword." John Gardner: A Bibliographical Profile,
by John Howell. Carbondale and Edwardsville: Southern
Illinois Univ. Press; London and Amsterdam: Feffer and
Simons, 1980, pp. 143-47.

1551 "Foreword." Becoming a Writer, by Dorothea Brande. Los
Angeles: J. P. Tarcher, 1981, pp. 11-18.

1552 "Foreword." Herbert L. Fink, Graphic Artist, by Judith
Quevreaux and Richard D. Carter. Carbondale and Edwardsville: Southern Illinois Univ. Press, 1981, pp. xi-xvi.

1553 "Signs, Symbols, and Cancellations." In Signs and Symbols
in Chaucer's Poetry. Ed. John P. Hermann and John J.

Burke, Jr. University, Ala.: Univ. of Alabama Press,
1981, pp. 195-207, 248.

1554 "Afterword." John Gardner: Critical Perspectives. Ed.
Robert A. Morace and Kathryn VanSpanckeren. Carbondale
and Edwardsville: Southern Illinois Univ. Press, 1982,
pp. 149-52.

1555 "Foreword." In Epic and Romance in the Argonautica of
Apollonius, by Charles Rowan Beye. Literary Structures
series, ed. John Gardner. Carbondale and Edwardsville:
Southern Illinois University Press, 1982, pp. ix-xi.

1556 "A Novel of Evil." Rev. of Sophie's Choice, by William
Styron. In Critical Essays on William Styron. Ed.
James L. W. West III and Arthur D. Casciato. Boston:
G. K. Hall, 1982, pp. 245-52. Rpt. from New York Times
Book Review, 27 May 1979. Includes a headnote, dated
3 July 1981, written expressly for this collection.

1557 "On Miracle Row" and "Witchcraft in Bullet Park."
Reviews of Falconer and Bullet Park, by John Cheever.
In Critical Essays on John Cheever. Ed. R. G. Collins.
Boston: G. K. Hall, 1982, pp. 80-84, 257-61. Rpt. from
Saturday Review, 2 April 1977, and New York Times Book
Review, 24 October 1971.

1558 "Queen Louisa." In Studies in Fiction. Ed. Blaze O.
Bonazza, Emil Roy, and Sandra Roy. 3rd ed. New York:
Harper & Row, 1982, pp. 362-69. Rpt. from KI.

1559 "The Warden." In The Best of TriQuarterly. Ed. Jonathan
Brent. New York: Washington Square Press, 1982, pp. 77-
105. Rpt. from TriQuarterly, 29 (Winter 1974).

1560 "The Wedding" and "The Edge of the Woods" (excerpts
from Nickel Mountain). In Contemporary Sources:
Readings from Writer's Workshop. Intro. William Price
Fox. New York: Holt, Rinehart and Winston, 1982, pp.
72-90 ("About the Author," p. 70; "Gardner on Writing,"
p. 71). Contemporary Sources, a textbook, is part of an
educational package that also includes a study guide by
Beth Littlejohn et al., and a telecourse produced by
the University of South Carolina.

1561 "Redemption." In Matters of Life and Death. Ed. Tobias
Wolff. Green Harbor, Mass.: Wampeter Press, 1983, pp.
62-74. Rpt. from AL.

1562 "Cartoons." In In Praise of What Persists. Ed. Stephen
Berg. New York: Harper & Row, 1983, pp. 125-34.

Fiction in Magazines and Newspapers

1563 "The Grave." Rpt. in Quarterly Review of Literature,
special "Retrospective" issue, 19, iii-iv (1975), 487-
504.

1564 "Come on Back." Atlantic, 247 (March 1981), 52-60. Rpt.
in AL.

1565 Excerpt from "Shadows" (novel-in-progress). In "Of
Literature Science and Shared Mysteries." New York Times,
29 November 1981, p. E20.

Poetry in Magazines

1566 "The Ruptured Goat." Rpt. in SD, VII, 2.

Articles and Essays

1567 "The Old Men." Dissertation Abstracts, 19 (1959), 1757.

1568 Excerpt from Gardner's remarks prepared for the publisher's
notice that accompanied review copies of SD. "Briefly
Noted." New Yorker, 48 (13 January 1973), 92.

1569 "We Teach and Study and Raise All the Hell We Can."
Illustrated by Herbert L. Fink. Change, 5 (June 1973),
42-48.

1570 "Amber (Get) Waves (Your) of (Plastic) Grain (Uncle Sam)."
New York Times, 29 October 1975, p. 41. Rpt. in condensed
form as "A Thing Worth Celebrating," Reader's Digest,
April 1976, pp. 136-38.

1571 "Thomas P. Brockway." Bennington College Dedicates Its
Arts Complex. Bennington Banner, 21 May 1976, Special
Supplement, p. 8. "A brief profile by John McCullough,
joined by John Gardner."

1572 "What Johnny Can't Read." Saturday Review, 7 (1 March 1980), 35-37.

1573 "Statement." Choice, 11/12 (1980), 6-7.

1574 "A Writer's View of Contemporary American Fiction."
Dismisura (Altari, Italy), 39-50 (1980), 11-31.

1575 "What Writers Do--Techniques of Fiction." Antaeus, 40/41
(Winter/Spring 1981), 416-26.

1576 "Fiction in MSS." MSS, ns 1, i (Spring 1981), [vi-vii].
Rpt. Dallas: Press Works, 1981, in a limited edition of
276 signed copies.

1577 Excerpt from "The Art of Fiction" [On Becoming a Novelist].
New York Times Book Review, 10 October 1982, p. 10.
Advertisement for the John Gardner Creative Writing Endow-
ment at SUNY-Binghamton.

1578 "Learning from Disney and Dickens" ["Cartoons"]. New
York Times Book Review, 30 January 1983, pp. 3, 22-23.
Rpt. in In Praise of What Persists, ed. Stephen Berg.

1579 "Notes on Gilgamesh, Tablet XII." MSS, ns 2, ii (Spring
1983), 159-63.

1580 "Gilgamesh: XII." Trans. by Gardner and John Maier.
MSS, ns 2, ii (Spring 1983), 165-70.

1581 "Do You Have What It Takes to Become a Novelist?"
Esquire, 99 (April 1983), 77-80. Excerpt from On
Becoming a Novelist.

1582 Excerpts from a paper prepared for an American Enterprise
Institute seminar (read in absentia). Quoted in Walter
Goodman, "Giving Business the Business," New York Times
Book Review, 17 April 1983, p. 39.

Reviews

1583 "Alice Through the Looking Glass." Rev. of Aspects of
Alice, ed. Robert Phillips, and Alice in Wonderland, ed.
Donald J. Gray. New York Times Book Review, 30 January
1972, pp. 3, 22.

1584 "Change Was the Church's Dirty Little Secret." Rev. of
Bare Ruined Choirs, by Garry Wills. New York Times Book
Review, 29 October 1972, pp. 1, 10.

1585 "Children's Books Fall 1972." Rev. of Snow White and the
Seven Dwarfs, trans. Randall Jarrell. New York Times
Book Review, 5 November 1972, part II, pp. 1, 18, 20.

1586 "They Clapped When He Entered the Classroom." Rev. of
Wishes, Lies, and Dreams and Rose, Where Did You Get That
Red?, by Kenneth Koch. New York Times Book Review, 23
December 1973, pp. 1, 14-15.

1587 "Where Have All the Heroes Gone?" Rev. of The Adventurer,
by Paul Zweig. New York Times Book Review, 22 December
1974, p. 7.

1588 "Optimistic Prophet of Doom." Rev. of There Must Be More
to Love Than Death, by Charles Newman. Washington Post
Book World, 31 October 1976, p. 3.

1589 "On Miracle Row." Rev. of Falconer, by John Cheever.
Saturday Review, 4 (2 April 1977), 20-23.

1590 "The Strange Real World." Rev. of Bellefleur, by Joyce
Carol Oates. New York Times Book Review, 20 July 1980,
pp. 1, 21.

1591 "For All Who Like Stories." Rev. of Italian Folktales,
by Italo Calvino. New York Times Book Review, 12
October 1980, pp. 1, 40-41.

1592 "Fun and Games and Dark Imaginings." Rev. of Jumanji, by
Chris Van Allsburg, and Outside Over There, by Maurice
Sendak. New York Times Book Review, 26 April 1981, pp.
49, 64-65.

1593 "Critic of the Month: John Gardner." Rev. of Minotaur, by
Benjamin Tammuz. Book-of-the-Month Club News, August
1981, pp. 6-7.

1594 Rev. of Dance of the Tiger, by Bjorn Kurten. Scandinavian
Review, 69 (December 1981), 98-99, 101.

Letters

1595 Land, Irene Stokvis. "First Novelists--Spring 1966: Introducing 61 New Writers." <u>Library Journal</u>, 91 (1 February 1966), 725. Comments on career and <u>Res</u>.

1596 "Front Matter: Contributors." <u>Kenyon Review</u>, 31 (1969), 436. Excerpt.

1597 <u>New American Review</u>, #9. New York: New American Library, 1970, pp. 232-35. Reply to William Gass's "The Concept of Character in Fiction."

1598 "John Gardner: On 'Borrowed' Fiction and 'Freddy's Book.'" <u>Chicago Tribune Book World</u>, 13 April 1980, p. 10. Reply to William Logan's 16 March 1980 review of <u>FB</u>.

1599 Horowitz, Sylvia Huntley. "The Ravens in <u>Beowulf</u>." <u>Journal of English and Germanic Philology</u>, 80 (1981), 504, 509. Paraphrases portions of Gardner's letter to Horowitz on <u>Beowulf</u>.

1600 <u>Choice</u>, 19 (September 1981), 42. Reply to review of Nancy Bogen's <u>Klytaimnestra Who Stayed at Home</u>, <u>Choice</u>, 18 (February 1981), 792.

1601 <u>New York Review of Books</u>, 28 (22 October 1981), 15. Letter to Nancy Bogen, quoted in an advertisement for her <u>Klytaimnestra Who Stayed at Home</u>.

1602 Daly, Robert. "John Gardner and the Emancipation of Genres," <u>Georgia Review</u>, 37 (Summer 1983), 420-28. Quotes from Gardner's letter to his son Joel, dated 23 November 1981.

Blurbs

1603 <u>Faith and the Good Thing</u>, by Charles Johnson. <u>New York Times Book Review</u>, 27 October 1974, p. 32.

1604 <u>A Dove of the East and Other Stories</u>, by Mark Helprin. <u>New York Times Book Review</u>, 23 November 1975, p. 42.

1605 In the Flesh, by Hilma Wolitzer. New York Times Book
      Review, 11 September 1977, p. 28.

1606 Airships, by Barry Hannah. New York Review of Books, 25
      (29 June 1978), 8.

1607 Sherbrookes, by Nicholas Delbanco. New York Review of
      Books, 25 (25 January 1979), 44.

1608 Hearts, by Hilma Wolitzer. New York: Farrar, Straus &
      Giroux, 1980. Dust-jacket.

1609 Searches & Seizures, by Stanley Elkin. Boston: Godine,
      1980. Back cover.

1610 Fly Away Home, by Mary Hedin. New York Review of Books,
      27 (7 February 1980), 24; PMLA, 95 (November 1980), 1182;
      New York Review of Books, 27 (20 November 1980), 41.
      (Three different blurbs.)

1611 Dance of the Tiger, by Bjorn Kurten. New York Times Book
      Review, 28 September 1980, p. 31. (Blurb does not derive
      from Gardner's review of Dance of the Tiger.)

1612 The New Life Hotel, by Edward Hower. New York Times Book
      Review, 19 October 1980, p. 60.

1613 Nathanial Hawthorne in His Times, by James R. Mellow.
      New York Times Book Review, 30 November 1980, p. 29.

1614 Ellis Island and Other Stories, by Mark Helprin. New
      York Times Book Review, 25 January 1981, p. 30.

1615 The White Hotel, by D. M. Thomas. New York Times Book
      Review, 22 March 1981, p. 19.

1616 Shame the Devil, by Philip Appleman. New York Times Book
      Review, 5 April 1981, p. 29.

1617 Contraries: Essays, by Joyce Carol Oates. New York Times
      Book Review, 3 May 1981, p. 28.

1618 Onliness, by Dave Smith. Baton Rouge: Louisiana State
      Univ. Press, 1981. Dust-jacket.

1619 An Exile from God. by Patricia Wilcox. American Poetry
      Review, 11 (January-February 1982), 21.

1620 On the Way Home, by Robert Bausch. New York Times Book
      Review, 25 April 1982, p. 21.

1621 Jericho, by Anthony Costello. New York Review of Books, 29 (27 May 1982), 48.

1622 The Story of the Stories, by Dan Jacobson. Griffin (The Readers' Subscription), 32 (June 1982), 8.

1623 The Twofold Vibration, by Raymond Federman. Bloomington: Indiana Univ. Press; Brighton, England: Harvester, 1982. Dust-jacket.

1624 Oxherding Tale, by Charles Johnson. Bloomington: Indiana Univ. Press, 1982. Advertising circular, Fall 1982.

Drawings

1625 Britton, Burt, ed. "Seventeen Self-Portraits." Harper's, 253 (October 1976), 66-67. Rpt. in Self-Portraits: Book People Picture Themselves, ed. Burt Britton (New York: Random House, 1976), p. 32.

Journals Edited

1626 Boulder [DePauw], 15 (1952). Member of editorial staff.

1627 Reflections: Washington University Student Review, Nos. 3-4 (1954-55). Member of editorial staff.

1628 Western Review (State University of Iowa). Assistant Editor, 21, 3 (Spring 1957)-22, 4 (Summer 1958).

1629 Papers on Language & Literature. Advisory Editor, 3-- (1967--).

1630 Choice (SUNY-Binghamton), 11/12 (1980). "Special Editor for Fiction."

1631 MSS (SUNY-Binghamton), new series (1981--).

Index